W0010291

MORNING & EVENING
D E V O T I O N A L

For
I Know
the
Plans

BroadStreet
P U B L I S H I N G

BroadStreet Publishing
Savage, Minnesota, USA
Broadstreetpublishing.com

For I Know the Plans: MORNING AND EVENING DEVOTIONAL

Devotional entries composed by Dan Boal, John Brandon, Robert Campbell, Kathy Castor, Ken Castor, Troy Mapes, Tony Myles, Kelly Nelson, Rachel Riebe, Luke Trouten, Tony Roos, and Jared Van Voorst. Compiled by Ken Castor.

978-1-4245-5844-5 (faux leather)
978-1-4245-5845-2 (ebook)

Design by Chris Garborg | garborgdesign.com

Printed in China.

19 20 21 22 23 24 25   7 6 5 4 3 2 1

*The Lord's plans
stand firm forever;
his intentions
can never be shaken.*

Psalm 33:11 NLT

Introduction

God has prepared the way for you each day,
from morning to evening! The year ahead may
be full of unexpected twists and turns, but God
knows you and has set a path for you to follow.

This unique devotional encourages you
to pursue God's blueprint for your life all day
long, between waking and sleeping. Take this
challenge to frame every day walking in step
with God's plans for you.

Order from Chaos

The earth was formless and empty,
and darkness covered the deep waters.
And the Spirit of God was hovering
over the surface of the waters.

GENESIS 1:2 NLT

Typically, when we think about God in the creation narrative, we picture nothingness and then something takes its place—light, animals, humanity, etc. It's perhaps more complex than that. The text says that the earth was formless and empty. It had no function or order to it, but it had incredible potential. God begins to assign functions, purpose, and order to each element of creation.

When you think about your day, it's not necessarily stepping into plans of nothingness, but instead, starting to make sense of the day that lies before you. It's a new opportunity to bring purpose and order to what might seem like chaos. Ask the Holy Spirit to hover over the surface of your day.

God, thank you for making each day an opportunity to live out my purpose. Help me to be someone who can bring order to chaos.

The earth was without form and void,
and darkness was over the face of the deep.
And the Spirit of God was hovering
over the face of the waters.

GENESIS 1:2 ESV

Reflecting back on a day, there are all kinds of moments that can bring joy or pain. You may have made plans that failed or succeeded. It's easy to dwell on those times where perhaps it felt more formless or dark. Maybe you even go to sleep feeling out of sorts or a sense of chaos.

What's inspiring when reading about creation is the anticipation of God's creative act in the universe. God is constantly bringing order to chaos, but you get the sense that the chaos will always provide some level of resistance. We see that the resurrection of Jesus doesn't come without resistance—death. Don't be discouraged because of darkness or resistance. God will bring order out of chaos even when you can't.

God, thank you that even in the midst of my plans, you still bring hope and purpose for each new day. Help me to trust your plans and that you'll bring order to chaos.

How is God bringing order or hope in your life right now?

In this Place

When Jacob awoke from his sleep, he thought, "Surely the LORD is in this place, and I was not aware of it."

GENESIS 28:16 NLT

Sometimes, when we talk about God's "plans for our lives," we usually think about that in the future tense. What college will I go to? What job will I have? How much money will I make? Those are good thoughts, but it is also important to remember that God's presence is just that—the present tense. God is in the business of the here and now and if we're caught up in the future we might miss him in the present.

Know that as you go throughout your day, no matter how mundane the task, God is with you—in every "place" you are. Jacob found himself running from place to place and it wasn't until he stopped and rested that he became aware of God in that very moment.

God, thank you that even in this moment of this day, you are right beside me. Thank you that you concern yourself with the details in this present time, not just for the future.

Jacob awoke from his sleep and said, "Surely the LORD is in this place, and I did not know it."

When we get to the end of the day, sometimes it feels like it went by at a million miles an hour. We can often wonder, "What actually happened today?" Can you remember? Do you remember what you ate? Do you remember the moments you felt tired, excited, sad, happy, or nothing at all? Do you remember God's presence was with you in every one of those moments?

As you reflect on your day and think back, can you pinpoint moments where you not only knew that God's presence was with you, but were consciously aware of it to where it caused you gratitude, peace, joy, or hope?

God, thank you for your presence today even when I didn't realize it. Thank you for sustaining me and broadening my view of you and the world.

How can you become more aware of God's presence?

Change of Plans

Moses sought the favor of the LORD his God. "LORD," he said, "why should your anger burn against your people, whom you brought out of Egypt with great power and a mighty hand?"

EXODUS 32:11 NIV

The word "but" here shows a major turning point in this story. It would seem that God had become fed up with his people constantly turning away from him and putting their hope and trust in other things. God reveals his plan to Moses to remove this chosen nation, "but Moses…"

It's almost as if Moses is the one reminding God of his own faithfulness and love toward his people. The story continues that God listens to the cry of Moses and indeed continues with his covenant people. Appeal to God in prayer even when it feels like God has given up on you. His faithfulness remains.

God, thank you for your faithfulness. Help me to see it even when it feels like you're not there.

Moses tried to pacify the LORD his God. "O LORD!" he said. "Why are you so angry with your own people whom you brought from the land of Egypt with such great power and such a strong hand?

EXODUS 32:11 NLT

Does God really change his mind? Or is this one of those moments where God is actually testing the faith of Moses? Often when we feel like God isn't present or concerned with something in our lives or in our circumstances, it may be in that moment when our faith is most refined. God is looking to elevate our trust in him as we affirm his power and appeal to his love.

Take a moment to think about a challenge you faced today. Pray with boldness, if it seems right according to the will of God, to intervene and bring about hope and change in that situation. But even more, pray that whatever the plan is, God would form your heart regardless of the outcome.

God, form my heart to understand your ways. Help me to see how you're moving in my life no matter how I feel.

In what areas of your life do you wish you could change God's mind? Why?

God Is Pleased

The internal organs and the legs must first be washed with water.
Then the priest will burn the entire sacrifice on the altar as a burnt
offering. It is a special gift, a pleasing aroma to the LORD.

LEVITICUS 1:9 NLT

These verses are weird, let's be honest. We are modern people who don't understand animal sacrifice and so when we come across Leviticus, we'd prefer to not deal with it. And yet, what is highly significant is that within an ancient culture that lived in fear and anxiety of not knowing how the gods felt about the people and their sacrifices, this God—YHWH—is pleased.

This is a major turning point in what seems to be an ancient and barbaric society. The truth is, sometimes in our modern world, we still live in fear and anxiety wondering if God is pleased or upset with us for any number of reasons. Know today that this God was pleased with you before you even got up this morning.

God, thank you that no matter what I do or leave undone, you are pleased with me. Help me understand this in my heart.

*You are to wash the internal organs and the legs with water,
and the priest is to burn all of it on the altar. It is a burnt offering,
a food offering, an aroma pleasing to the Lord.*

LEVITICUS 1:9 ESV

God makes a covenant—or promise—with his new people in
the book of Leviticus and gives them a new way of being and
living. Sure, it involves some strange activity that we're not
used to. But they come out of centuries of slavery where they
were dehumanized and treated horribly. When that is woven
into your very being, it can be hard to adjust to a God who
takes pleasure in you. When Pharaoh calls you a slave, God
calls you "chosen." God wants to be very specific with this
new way to be.

We no longer participate in animal sacrifice, but we do offer
our lives as a sacrificial act of worship toward God. God is
pleased with you and calls you his own. He will faithfully
rescue you and set your life on a track toward hope. Live every
day sacrificially.

*God, thank for your pleasure in me today and that my identity
isn't as a slave to this world, but a chosen child in your family.*

How do you see yourself through God's eyes?

In a Pit

You have thrown me into the lowest pit,
into the darkest depths.
Your anger weighs me down;
with wave after wave you have engulfed me.

PSALM 88:6-7 NLT

It would seem the author is writing to God, which can confuse
things a bit. Does God really put us in suffering, while anger
weighs down on us? It certainly can feel like that when our
plans don't go the way we want them to go. One thing we
know for certain is that this Psalm gives a foretaste of what
Jesus endured when he was imprisoned, and the weight of
our sin and brokenness crushed him.

When you're tempted to think that God has placed you within
a plan of hardship, first ask if God is responsible for it, or if
he's allowing it. Either way, know that Jesus identifies with
you as one who has endured the darkest depths.

God, whatever difficulty comes my way today, I trust that you are
with me and that ultimately you will pull me out of the pit.

You have put me in the lowest pit,
in the darkest depths.
Your wrath lies heavily on me;
you have overwhelmed me with all your waves.

PSALM 88:6-7 NIV

Perhaps you experienced something that was hard today. How did you feel God's Spirit guiding and comforting you in the midst of it? Did it feel as though you were stuck? If so, did you feel as though you had a taste of what Jesus experienced?

Part of living the Christian faith, or God's plan for your life, may include suffering. It may not necessarily be to the extent that some of the early church followers endured, but it's important to prepare your heart and character in such a way that makes room for embracing difficulty and plans that aren't favorable.

God, help me to be the kind of person that can handle and embrace the difficult things of life. Refine me in the midst of struggle.

How do you typically deal with difficulty?

15

It's All Free

"Come, all you who are thirsty,
come to the waters;
and you who have no money,
come, buy and eat!
Come, buy wine and milk
without money and without cost."

ISAIAH 55:1 NIV

Sometimes in our culture, we are running all around trying to make plans, trying to figure out what we're going to eat or how to entertain ourselves. Very rarely do we stop our planning and labor. Yet all throughout the Bible, God is reminding his people to rest and receive.

Isaiah provides this future image of when all is renewed in Christ. All of humanity will be able to come, rest, and receive everything they could ever need—and it's all free. Rushing, working, and striving will cease and everything that God has for us will simply be available. How could you live today with that mentality?

God, thank you for providing everything I need before I even know I need it. Help me to live with a grateful heart.

> *"Is anyone thirsty?*
> *Come and drink—*
> *even if you have no money!*
> *Come, take your choice of wine or milk—*
> *it's all free!"*

How did today go? Did you find moments where you were tired, exhausted, thirsty, hungry, or even hangry? Perhaps you felt those things physically, but what about spiritually or emotionally? Isaiah seems to be appealing to a need that goes beyond a biological desire. A few hundred years later, Jesus says something similar when he asks if anyone is weary or heavy burdened. They should go to him for rest.

You can't control everything. Maybe that's the first time you've ever read that. Your plans may be great or ambitious or exciting, but at the end of the day, Christ will give you everything you need. Allow him to give you rest from striving.

God, help me to put my trust in you. I want so badly to do things my way and it might work for a while, but I truly want to follow your way.

What are the plans in your life that are the hardest to hand over to God?

Seventy Years

This is what the LORD says: "You will be in Babylon for seventy years. But then I will come and do for you all the good things I have promised, and I will bring you home again."

JEREMIAH 29:10 NLT

The verse that immediately comes after this one talks about God knowing the plans for his people. But this verse rarely gets talked about. Is it because we want to jump right ahead to the good parts? We like things as fast as we can get them. We usually want to be the first to get things. When it comes to a relationship with God or the plans for our lives, however, it's not something we can click on, microwave, or experience with any immediacy.

As you think about your day today, are you wishing you could jump right to the end of it? Or is today a day that can be lived with all of the joy, struggle, and even mundane parts. Yes, God knows the plans for you; and God is calling you to live out those plans.

God, help me to slow down and not expect immediacy; but to be present in each and every moment.

"When seventy years are completed for Babylon,
I will visit you, and I will fulfill to you my promise
and bring you back to this place."

JEREMIAH 29:10 ESV

It would seem after reading this verse that God was somehow not present in order for him to come and visit. And perhaps the people who were in exile for seventy years felt like God was no longer with them. Seventy years is a long time and certainly would cause anyone to get a little stir crazy. This is why the following verses that talk about God's plans for his people are so powerful.

God is faithful to restore his people no matter what, no matter the amount of time. God has all of eternity to bring about restoration and renewal, and he has shown up consistently in the lives of those who follow him, so we can trust that he will do as he says he will.

God, thank you for showing up today and for always extending your grace when I lose hope.

At what point in the day is it hardest to know that God is with you? Why?

Anger at God

He prayed to the LORD and said, "O LORD, is not this what I said when I was yet in my country? That is why I made haste to flee to Tarshish; for I knew that you are a gracious God and merciful, slow to anger and abounding in steadfast love, and relenting from disaster."

JONAH 4:2 ESV

Sometimes life is hard. Sometimes the plans that God has for us are plans we don't want to carry out. Jonah is given a plan to tell a foreign people that God will show mercy on them and Jonah doesn't want to be part of it. He gets really angry at God.

Is it okay to be angry with God? What about when God's plan includes someone with whom you disagree? God can handle your emotions—good, bad, and ugly. But also know that it's an opportunity to reflect on why you're angry in the first place. It will require some humility and self-awareness to recognize that God's plan isn't just about individuals, but whole people groups.

God, thank you for allowing me to express my frustration at times. Help me to move toward joy.

*He prayed to the L*ORD*, "Isn't this what I said, L*ORD*, when I was still at home? That is what I tried to forestall by fleeing to Tarshish. I knew that you are a gracious and compassionate God, slow to anger and abounding in love, a God who relents from sending calamity."*

JONAH 4:2 NIV

This morning, we talked mostly about our anger and a little about God's inclusion of others into the plans. Now, let's focus even more on God's radical mercy. Jonah isn't the first person to be frustrated about God's plan of inclusion for outsiders, and he certainly won't be the last. But God is always moving his people toward a greater extending of his love, grace, and mercy.

Maybe you've dealt with someone recently that you've given up on and you're wondering how that person fits into God's plan. It's okay to be frustrated or confused about that, but it's also important to be formed to look more like Jesus. Instead of being angry with our enemies, we are called to love.

God, help me to have new eyes and a new heart for people that I feel are on the outside.

Why do you think it's okay to express anger toward God?

Didn't See It

Salmon was the father of Boaz (whose mother was Rahab).
Boaz was the father of Obed (whose mother was Ruth).
Obed was the father of Jesse.

MATTHEW 1:5 NLT

These verses seem extremely odd for a devotional. They're probably not changing your life right now. But think about one of the names in this list—Rahab. If you know anything about Rahab, you know she was a prostitute. Somehow, she gets involved with helping out the people of God. It's a long and complex story, but ultimately, it highlights the character of God and his plans for his people. As the grand story continues, Matthew points out that Rahab is actually in the lineage of Jesus.

Can God actually use a prostitute to carry out his plans? There's a very emphatic "yes!" In fact, that's exactly what God is all about. He uses the unlikeliest people and situations to show how great, how merciful, and perhaps how creative he is. How might God use you today in unexpected ways?

God, thank you that the whole story includes those people and situations that are the least likely.

Salmon was the father of Boaz by Rahab, Boaz was the father of Obed by Ruth, and Obed the father of Jesse.

MATTHEW 1:5 NASB

What's interesting about the Bible is that it continues to highlight a people group that is often the underdog. They are almost always outmatched and yet every single time, God shows his faithfulness. It proves a greater point that no matter how weak we feel to carry out the plans God has for us, he will always show his power in our weakness.

Jesus didn't come as a powerful ruler riding on a white horse but as a poor peasant refugee. And through Jesus, all evil is and will be vanquished. When you're frustrated that things don't seem to be working out, wait and watch. See how God shows up.

God, help me to trust you in the moments where it seems like all is lost.

How has God moved in unexpected ways in your life?

Running Away

Because Joseph her husband was faithful to the law, and yet did not want to expose her to public disgrace, he had in mind to divorce her quietly.

MATTHEW 1:19 NIV

Sometimes, when plans don't go the way we want them to, it's really tempting to take the easy way out, give up, or run away. When Joseph finds out that Mary is pregnant, he immediately assumes the worst. In that culture, he had every right to feel that way. It was confusing and was probably going to make his life really difficult. He wants to run away, but God intervenes and asks him to bear with the difficult situation for a greater good.

You may enter into moments today that are challenging, and it might be easier to just avoid the confrontation. What would happen if you didn't run away, though? What if God wants to use that situation to cause your faith to grow and to enhance the plans he has for you? Don't run away. Ask God for help.

God, at some point, I'm going to run into situations that are challenging. Help me not to run away.

Joseph, to whom she was engaged, was a righteous man and did not want to disgrace her publicly, so he decided to break the engagement quietly.

MATTHEW 1:19 NLT

When Joseph ultimately decided to not break off the engagement with Mary, what must have been going through his mind? Sure, the Son of God was going to be born to his fiancée, but what would it look like to his family or his village to see that Mary was pregnant before they were married? That would have brought about extreme shame in that culture. It couldn't have been easy.

Perhaps you didn't run away from a tough situation, but actually engaged the challenge. What went through your mind as you chose the tougher path? Did people think differently of you? Every day we're going to encounter situations that are challenging and the answer isn't always going to be clear. It's important to continue to seek the wisdom of God through the Holy Spirit.

God, fill me with your Holy Spirit and help me to understand your leading when I encounter hard things.

How have you felt God lead you in tough situations in the past?

A Different Way

Being warned in a dream not to return to Herod,
they departed to their own country by another way.

MATTHEW 2:12 ESV

There are moments in our lives where we're called to face hardship; and then there are other moments where God actually wants to take us in another direction. In this passage, Herod has a clear motive to find out where Jesus is so that he can get rid of him. He tries to use the wise men to get closer, but God reveals his plans to the wise men, instructing them to stay far from Herod after visiting the King of kings. They know that danger is looming, but Jesus needs to be alive to carry out a greater plan.

Sometimes God wants to take a different direction and that might look like avoiding destruction for your life. It's important that you are prepared to hear his voice and his leading. For the wise men, that message came through a dream. God can and will use any means to get your attention, so be prepared to listen.

God, help me to hear you when you are leading me in a different direction.

Having been warned in a dream not to go back to Herod,
they returned to their country by another route.

MATTHEW 2:12 NIV

We don't know a lot about the wise men that visit Jesus after he is born. Did they believe in a different god or gods? They definitely paid attention to the stars and came from the east; but did they know why it was so important to travel such a long and dangerous journey to visit this baby? Either way, somehow they were able to receive a message from God about their travel plans.

Sometimes it's easy to talk about being in tune with God and the Bible in order to follow God's leading. We think that we need to have a solid faith. And while much of that is true, it's important to remember that God will get his message across to whomever he pleases in whatever way or ways he chooses. You might not feel all that strong in your faith from time to time, but he will still reveal himself to you no matter what.

God, thank you for using whatever means possible to get my attention.

What are some areas in your life where you need to go a different way?

Turn Around

*"Repent of your sins and turn to God,
for the Kingdom of Heaven is near."*

MATTHEW 3:2 NLT

Early on in the ministry of Jesus, we see talk about repentance and the Kingdom of Heaven a lot. Typically, when we talk about repentance, it ends up being a discussion about saying sorry for some sin we may have committed. There is some truth to that. But there is also a greater and deeper turning that's happening here. Turning to God and toward his Kingdom is not just a behavior change, but also an entire mindset shift.

It's one thing to make an individual decision to avoid a destructive choice in one isolated moment. It's another thing to ask the greater question, "Why do I make these choices to being with?" Repentance, or turning around, is looking at your whole life differently. When you turn around and turn toward God, it has a dramatic impact on the plans for your life.

God, help me to turn to you; not just in isolated moments, but my entire being.

"Repent, for the kingdom of heaven has come near."

MATTHEW 3:2 NIV

Turning around and recognizing the Kingdom of Heaven in the New Testament was a big deal for those first followers of Jesus. They had been engulfed in different kinds of kingdoms that were oppressive, dehumanizing, and lifeless. These kingdoms had been around for so long that it was easy to lose hope and just feel like, "Well, this is the way it's always going to be."

When Jesus calls those people to repent, it's almost as if he is saying, "Don't buy into these kingdoms and what they stand for anymore; it doesn't always have to be like this." Jesus is calling us to wake up to something more. It's easy to look at our situation or our world and lose hope. But don't buy into that system or that kingdom; repent, turn around, and turn to the way of God's Kingdom.

God, I repent of my ways where I've lost hope in you. Help me to trust that your Kingdom has and will continue to come.

What ways have you turned around and turned toward God in your life?

Get Yours

Again, the devil took Him to a very high mountain and showed Him all the kingdoms of the world and their glory; and he said to Him, "All these things I will give You, if You fall down and worship me."

MATTHEW 4:8-9 NASB

In our culture, there are lot of messages coming at us every second and from every angle all saying basically the same thing: "Get yours!" In other words, do whatever you can to consume more and get what you want. When Jesus is in the wilderness, the devil tempts him with the same message. But how do you tempt someone with anything when they already possess all things? God, in Christ, has everything he needs and from him all good things flow. It would seem the devil is wasting his time.

There's an obvious difference between us and Jesus in that he is God and we are not. But we are tempted in the same ways and it can often disrupt the plans God has for us when we give in to those temptations. The Bible also reminds us, however, that in Christ we have everything we need.

God, thank you for your provision and lead me not into temptation to want more than what I need.

Next the devil took him to the peak of a very high mountain and showed him all the kingdoms of the world and their glory. "I will give it all to you," he said, "if you will kneel down and worship me."

MATTHEW 4:8-9 NLT

Our culture makes a lot of false promises, much like the devil. When the devil says, "I will give it all to you," that's a lie. It was never his to begin with. In the same way, every magazine cover, every commercial, and every social media advertisement are all promising to give love, acceptance, and fulfillment when it was never theirs to begin with.

Only God will fill you with true love, acceptance, and joy that our culture could never give you eternally. When this is God's plan for our life, it can help us walk away from temptation. It's not always easy, but that compels us to be in constant communion with the one who holds all things in his hands.

God, help me to not believe the lie when the world promises me happiness and fulfillment. Fill me with your good things.

What are the tempting things in your life?

Two Masters

"No one can serve two masters. For you will hate one and love the other; you will be devoted to one and despise the other. You cannot serve God and be enslaved to money."

MATTHEW 6:24 NLT

Many of the plans in our lives tend to revolve around money. How much do I want? How much will I make? How much will make me happy? We go to colleges that help us to learn what our career path will be and oftentimes that path is determined by how much that career will pay us in the long run. We spend a lot of time thinking about such things. It dominates our thoughts because our culture tells us this is what matters.

Jesus says this is equal to enslavement. What's interesting, however, is that he's talking to poor people. What this means is no matter how much money you have—rich or poor—it has the potential to enslave you. Money is important, but it is not the object of our worship.

God, thank you for money, but help me not to worship it.

"No one can serve two masters. Either you will hate the one and love the other, or you will be devoted to the one and despise the other. You cannot serve both God and money."

MATTHEW 6:24 NIV

Have you ever had two very different friends? You hang out with one or the other, but never together because they are complete opposites. Perhaps they don't even like each other. Do you find yourself being one way with one friend and another way with the other friend? It can be exhausting.

Jesus appeals to this exhaustion and complexity of serving two masters. It's almost like having two different jobs with two different bosses that have very different expectations. It can be utterly tiring. It's not good for you. In the same way, when we try to put our trust in money, it feels very different than putting our trust in God and it makes life very tiring, very confusing. Learn to manage your money but put your trust in God.

God, help me to direct my attention and energy to serving you.

How often do you think about money?

Don't Worry

"Do not worry about tomorrow, for tomorrow will worry about itself. Each day has enough trouble of its own."

MATTHEW 6:34 NIV

When Jesus speaks about God's plans for the Jewish people two thousand years ago, he's talking to very poor and oppressed people. They had every reason to worry and feel dejected given their sad state. Yet he tells them not to worry. It seems like an arrogant statement, but when we consider Jesus and the lifestyle he lived to identify with us as well as his work on the cross, it becomes more palatable.

Thinking about our plans, it could be easy to feel worry or anxiety because of the unknown. But Jesus says it doesn't add anything to our lives. When you think about your day, what are you worried about the most? Is it adding any value to your life right now?

God, help me to trust you with the things I am worried about.

> *"Don't worry about tomorrow, for tomorrow will bring its own worries. Today's trouble is enough for today."*
>
> MATTHEW 6:34 NLT

Remember what you prayed about this morning? Did the worry go away, increase or stay the same? If you worried, did it feel like more trouble for the day as Jesus talked about? Did it add any value to the day? In some ways, it's better to live knowing that things are going to be hard, easy, and somewhere in between, but worrying about them won't change that fact.

It's a hard truth to recognize that worry is something that stands in the way of our spiritual formation. Trusting God with your plans will cause your faith to grow. It's not easy by any means, but it's preparing you for the rest of your life and how you'll deal with adversity in the future.

God, I'm sorry that I worry, but I will choose to trust that you are in control.

In what ways is God healing your worry?

Keep Asking

*"Ask and it will be given to you;
seek and you will find;
knock and the door will be opened to you."*

MATTHEW 7:7 NIV

Oftentimes when we see these verses, we tend to think material things. It makes Jesus out to be like Santa Claus or some kind of vending machine. But as the verse goes on, Jesus is encouraging his followers to ask for the Holy Spirit to fill them and guide them in their lives. It's really about asking for and seeking God; and then out of that, God provides.

When you think about your plans for the day or for your distant future, what kinds of things are you asking and seeking? Is God's presence part of that request? It's okay to be bold in asking for specific things; and know that the aim of whatever you ask is to be in deeper communion and connection with God.

God, help my plans to be aligned with yours. Amen.

> *"Ask, and it will be given to you;*
> *seek, and you will find;*
> *knock, and it will be opened to you."*

MATTHEW 7:7 ESV

There's an element of persistence here when approaching God. It seems strange, though. Why wouldn't you just appeal to God one time? Does he not hear right away or answer right away? Perhaps the persistence is less about the outcome of how God responds and more about the formation of your heart in the asking and seeking.

A great writer once said that to pray is not so much to influence God but to change the nature of the one who is praying. The same is true of your plans. They are not just about the outcomes of those plans; the persistence of seeking God and knocking on the door is impacting the journey toward those plans.

God, help me to not only think about the end, but form my heart as I persistently seek you.

How is God impacting you on the journey and not just the destination?

Narrow Gates

"The gateway to life is very narrow and the road is difficult, and only a few ever find it."

MATTHEW 7:14 NLT

All throughout the ministry of Jesus, he keeps telling his followers that the way of the Kingdom is not like the way of the world. They wanted to be out from under Roman oppression and they expected Jesus to do that. But the way he goes about it is the opposite of what they were expecting. Instead of being powerful, fighting back, and overcoming, Jesus says things like, "To gain your life, you must first lose it." He ultimately ends up on a cross.

When we think about our plans, we want to try to control every little detail and be in charge; but the narrow way actually looks like giving up control and trusting that God is leading and guiding you through. Few find that way because it's counterintuitive to our culture. Ask God to help you find the narrow way.

God, help me to trust you when even when it seems backwards.

*"The gate is small and the way is narrow that leads to life,
and there are few who find it."*

MATTHEW 7:14, NASB

Think about your day and moments where you went against
the crowd or against what our culture typically does. How was
that? The goal isn't necessarily to do everything opposite of
what everybody else does all the time; but oftentimes when
following Jesus, it certainly doesn't always look like cultural
norms. It can be hard to remain firm in Christ.

As you think about the plans or goals for your life (college,
career, relationships, etc.), do they look like what everybody
else expects, or do they reflect the heart of God in you?
Sometimes they can be one in the same if you are surrounded
by faithful people who genuinely love you and support you.
Keep evaluating your plans in the light of God's narrow way.

God, show me the narrow way of the plans you have for me.

Make a list of goals you have for yourself. Are they centered
on Jesus?

Solid Rock

"Everyone who hears these words of mine and puts them into practice is like a wise man who built his house on the rock."

MATTHEW 7:24 NIV

When we think about a house being built, there are plans that have been set in motion; and as long as the plans are followed, the house is built properly. When we think about the plans for our lives, it's usually in such a way where we make the plans and our lives are the house. But what if there's a different way of thinking about it? What if we are actually the house and God not only provides the plans but is the plan. The rock is Jesus who provides the foundation of our house.

It'll be easy to take control of your own plans for your life; and there's something to being proactive and setting goals. But before you do, first ask God what his plans are so that you can come into alignment with them.

God, thank you that you are the plan for my life. There are a lot of details that go along with that, but ultimately your Son Jesus provides the foundation.

"Everyone then who hears these words of mine and does them will be like a wise man who built his house on the rock."

MATTHEW 7:24 ESV

As you went throughout your day, did it feel like you were standing on solid rock or sinking sand? Perhaps it felt at times like you were just surviving and trying to get by. Maybe storms came and battered your "house" a little bit. That's normal, but it's not the end of your story.

May you have the wisdom to realign your heart with the heart of God so that your house can be relocated back on solid rock. Look to Jesus, to his life, to his ways; and begin (or continue) to be filled with his Spirit so that as you rest, you wake up tomorrow on solid ground once more.

God, help me to reestablish my footing on solid ground and fill me with your Spirit.

What are some of the storms that come up against your house?

Willing

Suddenly, a man with leprosy approached him and knelt before him. "Lord," the man said, "if you are willing, you can heal me and make me clean."

MATTHEW 8:2 NLT

There's probably a lot in this devotional about setting aside your plans or laying down your wants and yet every once in a while, it seems that Jesus actually appeals to our desires. A man who is upset about the cards he's been dealt—the plan for his life—wants a change in plans. He simply asks, "Jesus, are you willing?"

Ultimately, we want to be in alignment with God's heart and we want to trust his grand plan for our lives, and there may be some things that you want changed. Will you have the boldness to ask God if he is willing? God wants love, healing, and justice to play out in your life, whether it's this side of eternity or the other side. What do you need? Ask him.

God, if you are willing, you can heal me and make me clean.

*A leper came to Him and bowed down before Him, and said,
"Lord, if You are willing, You can make me clean."*

MATTHEW 8:2 NASB

Asking to be made clean may seem like an odd request. But in ancient culture, a person with a skin disease was considered unclean, and there was an entire stigma that went along with that in the Jewish world. You were ostracized by everyone in your community. You had to shout out, "Leper!" so that those in your path knew to step aside.

Do you ever feel like a complete outcast, unwanted and unclean? Jesus makes no distinction. To him, there are no insiders and outsiders, clean and unclean. Jesus brings love and compassion to anyone and everyone who desires it. Jesus confidently answers this man, "I am willing." Jesus is willing to bring about the right kinds of things in your life.

God, thank for your willingness to show me love and compassion no matter what's going on in my life.

What kinds of things are you asking God if he is willing to do?

Even Him

Then Jesus said to the centurion, "Go! Let it be done just as you believed it would." And his servant was healed at that moment.

MATTHEW 8:13 NIV

These verses can easily be ones that we pass right by. Great! Another person put their faith in Jesus; that's how it's supposed to happen. What we might notice is the word "centurion." This is the enemy—a soldier from the Romans. The Romans, particularly the soldiers, were infamous for terrorizing the Jewish people. And now, Jesus has the audacity to not only have a conversation with this man, not only heal the man's servant, but he also later praises the man's faith.

Do you ever have those moments where you see the people that seem least deserving of something, somehow get something good? It causes you to wonder, "Even them?" with great surprise. This is what Jesus does when he shows up. He messes with our plans and starts throwing curve balls.

God, help me to see everyone like you see them and not be surprised that you would include everyone in your plans.

Then Jesus said to the Roman officer, "Go back home.
Because you believed, it has happened."
And the young servant was healed that same hour.

MATTHEW 8:13 NLT

As you reflect on your day, were there interactions with people with whom you don't normally interact? Are there people in your life that you would rather just write off? When Jesus interacts with this Roman officer and heals his servant, he's acting out his own principle to love one's enemies. This is hard to do because it messes with our plans.

As you continue to grow in your faith, God may continue to shift your plans in such a way that calls you to include others that seem least deserving. It's helpful when you reflect on just how undeserving we all were of God's love and yet he extended it to us in Jesus. We are called to the same kind of action, no matter where your plans take you.

God, help me to understand that no matter what my plans are,
I am still called to love my enemies.

Who would you normally consider an enemy?

Nature Obeys

The disciples were amazed. "Who is this man?" they asked.
"Even the winds and waves obey him!"

MATTHEW 8:27 NLT

There's an incredible story where Jesus is out on the Sea of Galilee and at a moment's notice, a storm just takes over and threatens to bring harm against Jesus and his disciples. This was common for this particular body of water, so they shouldn't have been surprised by it. However, it doesn't change the fact that they were still afraid. Jesus simply spoke to the storm and calmed it.

We believe something unique about God in that even nature obeys his very commands. That might not necessarily mean that you ask God to make it sunny and seventy-two degrees every time you step outside; however, it tells a greater story. Even though you know storms may come and disrupt your plans, your response to them might still be fear or confusion. Call on Jesus to bring about some level of calm to it.

God, thank you that you are present in the midst of storms and disruptions in my life.

The men were amazed and asked, "What kind of man is this?
Even the winds and the waves obey him!"

MATTHEW 8:27 NIV

The question these men ask, "What kind of man is this?" is such a loaded one. They have so much intrigue and wonder; perhaps they are even excited or confused altogether. If you are a follower of Jesus, go back to some of those early moments in your life where you started to turn toward him. Was there intrigue, wonder, excitement, and confusion about what kind of man Jesus is?

In our very nature, we are prone to do our own thing, but something supernaturally changes within us when we turn toward Jesus. We might say that it's his presence or the Holy Spirit that brings about a new kind of nature with a new kind of obedient lifestyle. Take a moment to reflect on those moments and thank God for them.

God, thank you for the days, weeks, and months of turning toward you. Continue to fill me with a new nature led by your Spirit.

What were those first moments like when you turned to Jesus?

Second Chances

As Jesus went on from there, He saw a man called Matthew, sitting
in the tax collector's booth; and He said to him, "Follow Me!"
And he got up and followed Him.

MATTHEW 9:9 NASB

You may have heard that tax collectors were not exactly highly
respected people in Jesus' day. They were mostly Jewish
people who had one foot in with the Jews simply because of
their background and one foot in with Romans because they
were willing to work for them. Today, we would call them
traitors; some of the worst kind of people. Jesus asked one of
them to be his disciple.

We don't get to see a lot of interaction between Jesus and
Matthew, but this story alone says enough about the character
of God that he is absolutely not willing to give up on anyone—
even a tax collector. No matter what kind of person you think
you are because of what you do, think, or say, God will always
give you another chance to be restored and renewed.

God, thank you for never giving up on me.

*As Jesus passed on from there, he saw a man called Matthew
sitting at the tax booth, and he said to him, "Follow me."
And he rose and followed him.*

MATTHEW 9:9 ESV

As you reflect back on your day, did you make mistakes?
Did you turn away from God or disregard his presence? It's
very possible. Some church traditions have a regular rhythm
of confession or liturgy where people are reminded of the
simple fact that they have sinned against God or others by
things done or undone. But it always follows with a line that
pleads with God, "For the sake of your son, Jesus Christ,
forgive us, renew us, and lead us, so that we may delight in
your will and walk in your ways."

These words can become empty if they're said out of
obligation or with a religious heart, but they also hold great
power. Consider taking these words and rewriting them in
your own way with your own understanding as you recommit
your life, heart, soul, and mind to God.

*God, please forgive me for the things I did that were dishonoring to
you, myself, others, and the world around me.*

What has been your experience with a regular rhythm of
confession?

New Family

"Whoever does the will of my Father in heaven is my brother and sister and mother."

MATTHEW 12:50 NIV

Sometimes faith can take us down a path that we were expecting. It may even cause stress in our friendships and maybe even our own families. When Jesus' ministry really starts to take off, the relationship with his family seems to change. He warns the crowd around him that true family looks different in the Kingdom of God. By our faith, we are somehow uniquely joined together as brothers and sisters.

As you consider your own faith and the path you're on, how has that affected your relationship with your family? Do you feel that you have a good sense of "family" with other people of faith? If you do, seek out those people today and express your gratitude to them.

God, thank you for making me part of greater family in the kingdom of God.

"Anyone who does the will of my Father in heaven is my brother and sister and mother!"

MATTHEW 12:50 NLT

When Jesus says these words, doing the "will of my Father," it is high calling. Have you considered what the will of the Father is in your life? Could it be as simple as loving God and loving others? It's simple in words, but in practice can be much more difficult. Love requires sacrifice and humility beyond what we are, in ourselves, capable of providing. But when we seek God's will, we become like family and he fills us with his Spirit.

Ask God to fill you with the Holy Spirit even more as you rest tonight. Then, when you awake tomorrow, you'll be refreshed and refilled to do the will of the Father, continuing to be part of a greater family that is connected to Jesus.

God, as part of your family, help me represent you and your name well.

What does it mean to you to be part of a family?

For All People

He said to them: "You are well aware that it is against our law for a Jew to associate with or visit a Gentile. But God has shown me that I should not call anyone impure or unclean."

ACTS 10:28 NIV

These verses may not seem like a big deal, or they may even sound harsh; but the context provides probably one of the greatest turning points in the early church. For centuries, Jews had not even associated with non-Jews (Gentiles). Now, God was instructing them to invite the Gentiles to be part of a new movement that was centered on Jesus. It becomes a pretty challenging journey for some.

Sometimes we do this in our modern world where we create our own separations. We may even begin to determine who's in and who's out when it comes to the church. But because of what Jesus has done, there are no more barriers anymore. He is for all people. When you consider the plan for your life, it's not an individualistic thing, but for something much bigger than just you.

God, give me a vision for all people.

> Peter told them, *"You know it is against our laws for a Jewish man to enter a Gentile home like this or to associate with you. But God has shown me that I should no longer think of anyone as impure or unclean."*

ACTS 10:28 NLT

When you reflect back on your day, was there anyone with whom you felt disconnected or as though you'd rather not be around them? What is it about them that causes you to think and feel that way? Have you considered praying for that person or at least asking God to help you change your mind about them?

Something happens when God fills us with his Spirit and begins to transform us. He gives us his eyes to see that all people are deserving of God's love, no matter how ridiculous it might seem to us. It can be really hard, but when God is absolutely unfailing in love, he can do no other thing. He will continue to love you, so why wouldn't he also extend love to others?

God, help me to grow in my love for the people that are harder to get along with in my life.

Consider setting a goal to make friends with someone you wouldn't normally be friends with.

It Seemed Good

"It seemed good to the Holy Spirit and to us to lay no greater burden on you than these few requirements."

ACTS 15:28 NLT

This phrase doesn't seem like it should be in the Bible—"it seemed good to us." When talking about God's plans for us, we usually tend to think in more black and white terms. Going with what seems right almost gives the impression that you get some level of control in the plans. But instead of thinking about control, consider it more of a partnership. The presence of the Holy Spirit is crucial.

Following the leading of the Holy Spirit isn't always going to be crystal clear. It's important to remember that God has wired us with a mind to use in partnership with the Holy Spirit. When living out the plans for your life, you're going to encounter moments where you're going to have to go with what "seems good" to you and the Holy Spirit.

God, help me to be in constant alignment with you so I discern what seems good.

"It seemed good to the Holy Spirit and to us to lay upon you no greater burden than these essentials:

ACTS 15:28 NASB

The context of this verse is that the apostles who were Jewish found that non-Jewish Gentiles were coming to faith in Jesus Christ. There was a question of whether or not these new Christian Gentiles should follow all 613 of the Jewish laws. It seemed good to a few of the apostles to remove as many burdens as possible so that their faith could thrive.

Do you find that you put any unnecessary burden or expectations on yourself or on others when it comes to living out your faith and God's plan for your life? As you grow to understand the Holy Spirit's presence in your life as well as engage in healthy community, you'll be able to discern what's essential and what's a burden.

God, thank you for the freedom I have in Christ. Help me to live for what is essential.

What has seemed burdensome as you've lived out your faith?

Others Are Listening

About midnight Paul and Silas were praying and singing hymns to God, and the other prisoners were listening to them.

Acts 16:25 NIV

Paul and Silas were in prison during this event. Prison in the first century wasn't exactly a cake walk. And the only illegal thing they did was tell people that the risen Jesus was Lord. It doesn't seem to faze them one bit, because they continue to sing out their hymns. Even the jailor turns to Jesus toward the end of the story.

When you think about the plans God has for your life, they're not just for you. Others are watching and listening. How you respond to adversity with your faith matters. When plans don't go the way you think they should, it may be challenging, but respond with prayer and worship and others will notice.

God, help me to live my life so that others see you and come to know Jesus.

Around midnight Paul and Silas were praying and singing hymns to God, and the other prisoners were listening.

ACTS 16:25 NLT

It's important that the author Luke points out the time of day when this event happens. It's midnight and yet they still hold true to their faith. Perhaps it's midnight as you're reading this. It's late, you're tired, and it probably feels like faith goes to sleep just like you do. The reality is that someone is always watching or listening.

What do you think people notice while you live out your faith? What would people say about you and how you follow Jesus? It's important to not base your whole life on others' perceptions or expectations of you, and yet it's also realistic to expect that others will sometimes look to you as long as you look to Jesus.

God, I know that my life serves as a witness to you; help me shine your light.

What do think people's perceptions of you are?

Some Will Laugh

When they heard Paul speak about the resurrection of the dead, some laughed in contempt, but others said, "We want to hear more about this later."

ACTS 17:32 NLT

In these verses, the greater story shows us that Paul talks about God to a group of highly educated people who know nothing about Jesus. That doesn't seem to stop Paul from sharing about this God that has become present in Jesus and experienced death and resurrection. This seems ridiculous to some, but others show interest.

You may have come across people along your path where you talked about Jesus and some thought you were joking. Why would you stake your life on some guy that lived two thousand years ago? It can be a little deflating to be laughed at because of your faith. Part of God's plan for your life is that you be filled with the Holy Spirit, so you are not afraid to share the hope you have in Jesus when an opportunity presents itself.

God, give me the boldness to talk about you and share the love of Christ with others.

When they heard of the resurrection of the dead, some mocked.
But others said, "We will hear you again about this."

ACTS 17:32 ESV

Sharing your faith comes in all shapes in sizes. What's interesting about this story is that Paul appeals to their culture and even their poetry to show them that some of their beliefs are really great—they just need clarity. He's patient with them and doesn't use any "Christianese" that might confuse them.

Sometimes, when we think about God's plan for our life, we may mention the idea of sharing our faith. What that looks like may depend on who the audience is. It doesn't mean you change the message, it simply means you change the language in a way that makes sense to them. No matter what you do, however, sometimes people will laugh or write you off. That's to be expected, but don't be discouraged.

God, thank you for the hope I have in your Son Jesus. Help me articulate my faith to many different kinds of people.

What has been your experience with sharing your faith so far?

You Are New

This means that anyone who belongs to Christ has become a new person. The old life is gone; a new life has begun!

2 CORINTHIANS 5:17 NLT

The plans God has for your life could take you a million different directions. The ultimate plan is summed up nicely here when the author of this letter says that everything is now different—brand new—because of Jesus. Where you go and what you do will now look more and more like the life of Jesus.

When you think about newness of life, what has changed in you up to this point because of your faith in Jesus? Some things may have taken a long time, some things change in an instant, but when you go throughout your day today, remember God will do new things in and through you.

God, thank you for making me new.

Therefore, if anyone is in Christ, the new creation has come:
The old has gone, the new is here!

2 CORINTHIANS 5:17 NIV

You may look back at your day and think, "that's all in the past now." How can you begin to think about newness as you close out the day? Most likely, you're about to go to sleep and rest up for another new day. That requires you to lay down, close your eyes, and give up control. You probably won't even think about the fact that God will sustain you through the night to prepare you for more newness.

God will work in any and every situation to bring about new life—even your sleep. So when you wake up tomorrow, it will be another new day. It will be a day full of new opportunities to live out the plan that God has for you.

God, thank your faithfulness even to care for me as I sleep through the night. Prepare me for another new day tomorrow.

What's your favorite thing about something that's new?

Stop Striving

Now that no one is justified by the Law before God is evident;
for, "The righteous man shall live by faith."

GALATIANS 3:11 NASB

If we are completely honest, most of us struggle with control.
We are raised to become independent to make our choices
in life. The problem with that is, when we talk about giving
up control and trusting God, it's counter to everything we've
learned about how to live. But what the author of this letter
is trying to say is that when it comes to honoring the Law of
God, something given to ancient Hebrew people thousands
years ago, no one can do it perfectly.

Only Jesus lived a life perfectly fulfilling all of God's
expectations. So now when it comes to your plans, as a
person of faith, you no longer need to strive to meet God
expectations other than trusting in God through Jesus.

God, help me to put aside my control issues and trust you for
today.

*Clearly no one who relies on the law is justified before God,
because "the righteous will live by faith."*

Living by faith can seem like this blind activity walking out
in the unknown. But what makes this possible is the fact that
God first set example by coming to be with us in the humanity
of Jesus. Something we don't often talk about is Jesus living
by faith. Jesus gave up control when he gave up his divine
privileges as God. He had to experience all of the challenges
that come with simply being human.

Because of this, we look to Jesus as our example of perfect
faith. Blind faith is like feeling around in the air without
having a clue where we are or where we're going but moving
forward because God tells you to. Fortunately, God gave us
the Scriptures, the presence of the Holy Spirit, and faithful
community to point us toward Jesus.

*God, surround me with everything I need to put my faith in you for
every part of your plan.*

What are the areas of your life where you tend to strive the
most?

A Process

Being confident of this, that he who began a good work in you will carry it on to completion until the day of Christ Jesus.

PHILIPPIANS 1:6 NIV

Life is a process. That's hard to believe when everything is available with the touch of a button or the activation of a voice command. Our culture tells us everything should happen or be available to us instantly, and yet God's plan for your life is going to be a process.

Even this very day that lies before you takes twenty-four hours to unfold completely. When something challenging happens, it's not the end. When something great happens, give God thanks. Either way, know that with each second, minute, hour, day, week, month, and year that goes by, God is slowly working on you as you continue to be made complete.

God, help me to trust in the process and not be tempted to want everything to be complete right away.

Maybe the focus can be more on the process and not so much the outcome.

I am certain that God, who began the good work within you, will continue his work until it is finally finished on the day when Christ Jesus returns.

PHILIPPIANS 1:6 NLT

As you reflect on your day, you might take comfort in the fact that things took time. Not all of your big questions were answered perfectly. Things are still unfolding. Sometimes life goes really fast; other times, it's like you can't get it to go fast enough. The key is recognize that it will come to completion.

The interesting piece about this verse is that none of it is fully complete until Jesus returns. That's a promise he gave us and it could seem really daunting, overwhelming, and even far away. Who knows when? Not even Jesus knows that date. But it should come as a comfort to know that you don't have it all figured out when you're sixteen or when you're sixty.

God, thank you for the promise of Jesus' return. Help me to live in this moment.

What's the hardest thing about waiting? 1-30-2022

The end result! Not the patience or impatience in between, but the end result. The finished work. We never focus on the inbetween but what'll happen at the end. The end/finish is what we anxiously wait for. I could care less about the process at times. The trying not to figure it all out is very daunting. Ugh! Nevertheless there'll be an end.

Routing System

Your word is a lamp for my feet,
a light on my path.

PSALM 119:105 NIV

If someone wanted to drive from one location to another, it's likely that they'd type the destination address into a mapping app on their phone and hit the prompt for "Directions." The app would then likely generate three different routes, provide estimated driving times, and reveal potential traffic or construction hazards.

God's Word is kind of like that for our lives. In a way, it's an app to map out the way we could go, the truth we could live by, and the life we could have. The Bible routes the destination, suggests routes to take, and tells us what obstacles to avoid along the way. Its pages are filled with real-life examples that give us insight into paths that lead safely home and other roads that create horrific collisions.

Lord, let me seek your directions for my activities today.

Your word is like a lamp for my feet and a light for my path.

PSALM 119:105 NCV

This day was filled with a few important decisions and many mini-decisions. Each choice, big or small, led you somewhere. Because of your choices, you ended up interacting at certain times with certain people, thinking certain thoughts at certain moments, feeling certain emotions in certain circumstances. You probably experienced unexpected detours that caused you to reroute your steps. You may have been stuck in a dead end, or perhaps you felt like you got caught in a rush-hour traffic jam. Or, at some moments, you may have hit your stride and felt like nothing could stop your momentum.

All of the directions of your day will find their greatest fulfillment if they are illuminated by the light of God's Word. Spending time at the beginning and end of each day in the Bible is essential to discovering how our many choices during the day are to be a part of God's overall direction for your life.

Lord, thank you for guiding me today. Forgive me for those moments I went my own way, without your input. Help me wake up tomorrow ready to live by your Word and to follow your plans for my life.

In what ways did you follow God's steps for your life today? 1-31-22
Doing this devotional before the rest of my day unfolds. Don't look at how things are or stem but what they can become.

Thinking of You

How precious to me are your thoughts, O God!
How vast is the sum of them!
If I would count them, they are more than the sand.
I awake, and I am still with you.

PSALM 139:17-18 ESV

God values you. In fact, he thinks so much of you that he made this world for you. Yes, you could honestly say that God thinks the world of you. He has considered you and has been convinced that you are worth his time, worth his attention, and worth his presence.

You are made by a loving God who wants to be with you so that you can be with him. He never stops thinking about you. He never forgets you. He is always constantly thinking about you. Innumerable thoughts. You couldn't count all the thoughts God has about you. More than the grains of the sand of this earth (that he created for you) is how many times God thinks about you. And every single day is like that. From day to day, every time you wake up, God loves you and is already thinking about you.

Lord, let me catch you in the act of thinking about me today.
Awaken me to how much you think of me. And then, let me think
more of you.

God, your thoughts are precious to me.
They are so many! If I could count them,
they would be more than all the grains of sand.
When I wake up, I am still with you.

PSALM 139:17-18 NCV

Only God can completely understand the day you have had.
After all, he has known your every pulse since the day you
were conceived. He mapped out and then recorded every day
of your life. His mind springs for you. His heart gushes over
you. His thoughts about you are more focused and attentive to
your true needs than your best thoughts could ever fathom.

God sees you. He knows you. He knows the day you have had.
He has thought about you all day, he is thinking about you
right now, and he will be thinking of you as you sleep. May
you live refreshed and secure in the knowledge that God
knows you.

Lord, thank you for being more aware of the activity of my day
than I was myself. You paid more attention to what happened to
me than I did. Thank you for caring for me so much. Please watch
over me tonight and shelter me in your thoughts tomorrow.

If God thinks this much of you, do you think he might think
this much of others? If so, how does that change the way you
could think of others? Absolutely. Intention thinking of
others. Be intentional.

Examined Thoughts

Search me, O God, and know my heart;
test me and know my anxious thoughts.
Point out anything in me that offends you,
and lead me along the path of everlasting life.

PSALM 139:23-24 NLT

God's presence is so wonderful that we are presented with
a real-life choice today: We can press into his presence and
be directed by him, and potentially overwhelmed by him. Or
we can settle for casual irregular acquaintance with God and
miss the deep life he has for us.

Ultimately, there is only one right choice to make because our
identity is found in him only. But it's not easy to press into
God. It means you might have to deal with some stuff that
wasn't made by him and has invaded your life. That's why the
writer of Psalm 139 is overwhelmed with his own thoughts.
When he explores his thoughts and feelings, he's surprised
by what wells up within him. He finds things in his mind and
heart that he knows don't belong with God.

Lord, search me and know my heart. Test me and know my
anxious thoughts. Point out anything in me that offends you, and
lead me along the path of everlasting life.

God, I invite your searching gaze into my heart.
Examine me through and through;
find out everything that may be hidden within me.
Put me to the test and sift through all my anxious cares.
See if there is any path of pain I'm walking on,
and lead me back to your glorious, everlasting ways—
the path that brings me back to you.

PSALM 139:23-24 TPT

There are some things we pursue in life that just don't fit with how amazing God is. It just doesn't make a lot of sense to settle for having inferior thoughts or actions in our lives when we could have God's Spirit living within us. The gaze of God's searching eyes might feel uncomfortable at times, but getting aligned with God's creative goals enables us to become fully alive.

Like a car in the mechanic's shop, or a person in the doctor's office, sometimes the repair work needs to be pointed out. God invites us to spend time with him so that he can continue to shape us and make us into the person he created us to be.

Lord, I invite you to gaze into my heart tonight. Examine me and then do any repair work necessary. Let my soul find itself on the path you have set out for me.

2-2-22

How do you feel when people point out your flaws? Mixed feelings! I'm up for it usually unless it's not a valid flaw. Constructive criticism is always good.

71

Weaving Hope

*Joseph said to them, "Don't be afraid. Am I in the place of
God? You intended to harm me, but God intended it for good to
accomplish what is now being done, the saving of many lives. So
then, don't be afraid. I will provide for you and your children."
And he reassured them and spoke kindly to them.*

GENESIS 50:19-21 NIV

As Joseph looked out at his brothers, he had every right to
be angry. After all, his brothers had beat him, stripped him
bare, and sold him into slavery. It turns out that they had
also lied about the whole thing, telling their father Jacob that
Joseph was dead.

The ensuing years were hard on Joseph. He was mistreated
and accused, imprisoned and neglected. But because of his
consistent character and faithful service, Joseph eventually
rose to a position of power in the government. That's when
he found himself staring at his brothers, who had come to the
governor in need of help. They had become poor and were
starving. And Joseph was the one who could either turn them
away or offer them help.

*Lord, when I face trouble today, give me a deep resolve to do what
is right.*

Joseph said to them, "Do not fear, for am I in the place of God? As for you, you meant evil against me, but God meant it for good, to bring it about that many people should be kept alive, as they are today. So do not fear; I will provide for you and your little ones." Thus he comforted them and spoke kindly to them.

GENESIS 50:2 ESV

Joseph's brothers didn't know if they would receive retribution for their cruelty or redemption from their brother. They knew that what they had done all those years ago was terrible and deserved consequence. But they also cared for their family and begged Joseph for mercy. The reply they heard was like salvation for their souls: "Do not fear," Joseph said, "I will provide for you and your little ones."

We don't always know God's long-range plan. He often brings beautiful stories out of miserable circumstances. God wanted to weave hope into middle of Joseph's desperate story. Perhaps God has a similar long-range goal in mind for our stories too.

Lord, thank you for working your plans for good. While I cannot always see what you are doing, please give me the trust to know that you are weaving a beautiful story through all of my circumstances.

What is one difficult thing you have experienced in your life that you want God to weave into a hopeful story? 2-3-22 He has continued to do just that, as I sit here healed today. Nothing less from God.

Rest and Restoration

He makes me lie down in green pastures,
he leads me beside quiet waters.

PSALM 23:2 NIV

A shepherd intentionally leads his sheep to green meadows so that they can find rest. A shepherd does not push the sheep into barren fields filled with snarling thorns and dangerous ambushes. A shepherd does not steer the sheep into dark parking lots filled with broken glass and debris. The Good Shepherd leads his sheep into a field with wide open vistas under the warmth of the sun and the protection of his gaze. He provides rest. He provides peace. He provides safety and protection.

A shepherd also intentionally leads his sheep to a peaceful brook so that they can find restoration. A shepherd does not lead the sheep to dried up streams, nor raging currents, but calm streams with safe drinking spots, clean water, and refreshing coolness away from the heat and dangers of the day.

Lord, lead me today. Let me hear your voice and follow your commands. Protect me from anything that could entrap me. And let me find moments to notice the peace that you place in my life.

He lets me rest in green meadows;
he leads me beside peaceful streams.

PSALM 23:2 NLT

Life is filled with thorns and thickets, rocks and barrenness. Every day brings potential dangers that could ensnare us or deplete us. We need to be on our guard, ready to respond against any trouble that comes our way. But even more so, we need to be looking for the staff of our shepherd, listening to his confident voice, following his guidance and instructions throughout the day. Psalm 100:5 says that "we are his people, the sheep of his pasture." In John 11, Jesus tells us that he is the Good Shepherd and that his sheep listen to his voice.

That's why we pray each day that God will lead us away from temptation or harm. That's why we seek the Lord for protection. That's why we ask God to watch over us, to heal us, to refresh us. We look for the arm of God because he is our Good Shepherd who leads us to rest and restoration.

Lord, I love your guidance in my life. Thank you for watching over me throughout the day and throughout the night. Let me entrust myself to your leadership in my actions, thoughts, and plans.

How did the Lord shepherd you today? Where do you want him to lead you tomorrow?

Wait Actively

Wait for the Lord;
be strong and take heart
and wait for the Lord.

PSALM 27:14 NIV

One of the worst words a person can hear at any given point of the day is "wait." To "wait" means growing stressed when someone is late picking you up. To "wait" means standing for a really long time, in a really long line, at the Department of Motor Vehicles. To "wait" means to agonize in the emergency room of a hospital with a broken arm while others with more serious injuries are ushered ahead of you. To "wait" means you don't get your dinner right away, you don't get the answer you want right now, and you don't get to binge-watch the next episode of your favorite show because it hasn't been released yet. This word, "wait," seems like it is against you.

So, then, how could you ever "be strong and take heart" in those intervals of soul-crushing second-passing? Well, what if God might just have something to say to you in those in-between times today? Instead of filling your soul with clutter all day long, what might happen if you saw those halted moments as opportunities to turn your heart bravely toward God?

Lord, I am so impatient sometimes. Give me the courage to wait for your plans… to wait for your prompting… to wait for you today.

Wait for the LORD's help.
Be strong and brave,
and wait for the LORD's help.

PSALM 27:14 NCV

God doesn't want your heart filled with hurried worry today. He doesn't plan for you to squirm in frustration if something doesn't happen in your timing. God actually wants you to do something if you find your plans halted in time. God wants you to wait—actively. He doesn't want you to be passive and spoiled. He wants you to seek him. In those downtimes, he wants you to pursue his answer, to listen for his voice, to learn his will, to take advantage of the moment to lean more and more into him.

God wants you to stay with him. Sometimes what he does in the middle of the waiting-time is even more significant than what he does in the get-up-and-go moments. Throughout the Bible he urges you to "be still and know" that he is your God.

Lord, thank you for waiting for me to come around to you. Your patience for me is comforting. Let me be strong and take heart in you tonight.

What unresolved things from today will you still be waiting upon tomorrow? Take a moment to trust that to God's faithful hands.

Forever Plans

The LORD nullifies the counsel of the nations;
He frustrates the plans of the peoples.
The counsel of the LORD stands forever,
The plans of His heart from generation to generation.

PSALM 33:11 NASB

One way to guarantee that your plans in life will fail is to make them yours and not God's. If your plans are yours and yours alone, then God is not in them. And if God is not in your plans, then why are you even trying to pursue them? Without God, your goals, your dreams, your desires, are all in vain.

God will frustrate people who try to accomplish things that go against his will. It may seem for a time that their schemes are working, but the Lord will disrupt those plans. He is a great agitator of people who run counter to his purposes.

So seek to live today in the plans of the Lord. Seek to live in the steps of his already-established paths. His plans for you are wise. His goals for you are long-lasting. His advice for you is eternal. And his goals for you leave a legacy for generations.

Lord, let me walk faithfully in your plans for my life, rather than asking you to walk in my plans for my life.

> *The LORD frustrates the plans of the nations*
> *and thwarts all their schemes.*
> *But the LORD's plans stand firm forever;*
> *his intentions can never be shaken.*

PSALM 33:10-11 NLT

One way to guarantee that your plans in life will succeed is to make sure that you are following God's plans for your life. After all, God's plans stand firm. God's intentions last well beyond the scope of your life.

Walking in God's plans is the key to a good life. The idea is to measure your goals and ideals up against what you know about God's goals and ideals. Place your desires up against God's desires. Where there is a match, take confident steps in that direction. Where there is a mismatch, redirect your feet to align with God's steps.

Lord, show me where I got out of step with you today and keep me on track tomorrow. And let me walk confidently in your will for my life.

Where do you see yourself in ten years? What would you like to be doing?

Good Advice

*If you are truly wise, you'll learn from what I've told you.
It's time for you to consider these profound lessons
of God's great love and mercy!*

PSALM 107:43 TPT

If you want to fall apart today, if you want everything to go poorly, then ignore good advice. If someone offers you a good suggestion, just do the opposite. If you know someone who has been through a difficult situation that is similar to one that you are facing, don't ever ask them about how they got through it—you might actually learn some things that could help you.

Deflecting good advice is the best way to ruin your life. Closing your mind to possibilities feels so much easier than actually being open to ideas. Getting stuck in habits that hurt you is just so much more comfortable than pondering what steps you could take to develop healthier patterns.

If you want to wreck your life, ignore wisdom from those around you.

Lord, don't let me be an idiot today. Hit me with good advice and wise counsel. It's time to really consider what you have been trying to tell me about what I should do with my life.

Let the one who is wise heed these things
and ponder the loving deeds of the LORD.

PSALM 107:43 NIV

If you want to live confidently, if you want to pursue all that God has for you, then seek good advice. If someone offers you a good suggestion, do it. If someone you know has experienced a situation that is a lot like the one you are experiencing, ask them for wisdom on how to navigate the difficult circumstance. If someone surprises you with truth that could only come from the Lord, let it sink in to your soul. If someone admonishes you with wisdom, cast away your pride and accept it with humility.

If you want to build your life, heed wisdom from the Lord. He loves you more than you will ever know. His plans for you are the best practices for your life. Seek his guidance in all your ways.

Lord, I acknowledge your truth in my life. Let me always follow your best advice, your most loving instructions, your eternal knowledge. May I reflect your profound lessons in the days ahead.

What aspect of this devotional do you need to most ponder and put into practice?

God Is Here

If I rise on the wings of the dawn,
if I settle on the far side of the sea,
even there your hand will guide me,
your right hand will hold me fast.

PSALM 139:9-10 NIV

The disconnected, lonely life that many people feel presents an incredible opportunity for the gospel of Jesus Christ. The good news is that there is, in reality, no one who is actually alone. God is here. No place can someone go to escape God's Spirit. No emotion can someone have that God doesn't understand. No thought can someone spring to mind that God doesn't already know. A person could travel to the farthest reaches of the earth and still never extend past the reach of God.

This is the most present of truths. God is here with you right now, wherever you are, in whatever experience you are having. God is here.

Lord, I need to recognize your presence with me throughout this day. Don't let me wander away from you, since you are right there beside me.

*If I take the wings of the morning
and dwell in the uttermost parts of the sea,
even there your hand shall lead me, and your right hand shall
hold me.*

PSALM 139:9–10 ESV

The other aspect of God's everlasting reach is that he also has a never-ending desire to guide a person and to uphold a person. God isn't just present. He's engaged with people. He isn't just a thought or an entity with whom we might have some alien contact. He is brimming with life and overflowing with love toward his people. He is actively at work directing people wherever they are to wherever he wants them to go.

When you go to sleep at night, God is here with you and for you. When you rise in the morning, God is here with you and for you.

Lord, uphold me in your magnificent hand. Let me quit flailing about in fear and allow me to rest a while in you.

At what times in life do you feel most alone? How could the truth of God's presence direct your thoughts in those moments?

Wonderfully Complex

*You made all the delicate, inner parts of my body
and knit me together in my mother's womb.
Thank you for making me so wonderfully complex!
Your workmanship is marvelous—how well I know it.*

PSALM 139:13-14 NLT

God is convinced that you are an amazing person. Do you think God is wrong? He made you. Every delicate little fiber of your body was put together by him. You are a miraculous quilt of blood and skin and muscle and tendons and tissues and hair. He knit you together in your mother's womb. He could see what he was doing in you.

God has made you wonderfully complex. People are writing books about you and your youthful life, wondering about you, mesmerized by the complexities of who you are. But only God truly knows all of your intricate soul. If someone says to you, "I can't figure you out sometimes," you can say back to them, "That's because I'm wonderfully complex."

Lord, I'm more complicated than I want to be sometimes. Today, would you help me realize that the intricate fabric of who I am is incredibly wonderful in your sight?

You formed my inward parts;
you knitted me together in my mother's womb.
I praise you, for I am fearfully and wonderfully made.
Wonderful are your works;
my soul knows it very well.

PSALM 139:13-14 ESV

God is the only one who knows you fully. Only God can completely understand your deepest passions. Only God. Be encouraged tonight. May you understand that you are understood. May you never feel like a lesser person ever again. May you always feel so important, so special, so loved.

When God made you, he put his heart and soul into you. God mapped out a plan that is uniquely suited for just you. May you live refreshed and re-powered in the knowledge that God created you and that he loves who he has made you to be.

Lord, let me lavish in your love for me. Let it sink in. I don't always feel like I deserve your love. But the truth is, you made me. You care for me. You love all the intricate details of who I am. Thank you for making me so wonderfully.

What aspects of yourself do you struggle to love? Take a moment to listen to what God has to say to you about who you are and how much love he has for you.

Working Out

The LORD will work out his plans for my life—
for your faithful love, O LORD, endures forever.
Don't abandon me, for you made me.

PSALM 138:8 NLT

Ten years from today, what do you think you might be doing? What can you see yourself doing? If you had no obstacles in the way, no concerns about money, no problems with people or potentials, what would you choose to be doing in ten years?

Do you think God has goals for what you will be doing in ten years? Are there any obstacles that God might be able to overcome? Any problems or people or potentials that God could work out in your favor? Do you think, to get you where he wants you to be in ten years, that God might want to see certain things happen in your life along the way?

Lord, starting today, I agree to work out with you. The plans you have for me—make them mine too. And set me on a course to fulfill them in my life.

You keep every promise you've ever made to me!
Since your love for me is constant and endless,
I ask you, Lord, to finish every good thing that you've begun in me!

PSALM 138:8 TPT

Here's some good news for those plans God has for you:
He will work them out. Every good thing that God starts in
your life will be brought to completion. What God wants to
do, he does. And since God loves you, his plans for you are
loving. And since God is eternal, his love for you is endless.
His promises are true. His work in your life is faithful and
enduring. He will not leave you to work out the plans for your
life on your own. He made you and has committed himself to
working out with you.

But working out requires daily attention. Pursuing God's
long-range plans means participating with his active work in
your heart, mind, and soul. Don't give up. Don't grow lazy. Be
prepared to get up again tomorrow focused on tending to the
work he has set before you.

*Lord, give me an ounce of your endurance, so that I may pursue
your plans for me again and again, each day.*

At what moments today did you work out with God? What
happens within you when you partner with God to accomplish
the plans he has for you?

Be Real

You draw near to those who call out to you,
listening closely, especially when their hearts are true.

PSALM 145:18 TPT

Have you ever had that feeling that someone is keeping something from you? Or that a friend is not sharing the whole story? Maybe you've done that yourself? Have you ever kept back some information that would have been embarrassing or gotten you into trouble?

Not being fully truthful is tough on a relationship. It erodes trust. It puts up walls. It creates a distance between the one sharing and the one listening. It says to the listener, "I don't want you too close to my real self, so I'll just reveal part of me." Have a true, honest heart that shares openly with God.

Lord, I'm not holding back today. You know what's in my heart and on my mind. You know what I've been doing and what I'm going to be doing today. I'm not going to put up any walls or false faces with you today. Please let me call out to you with a true heart.

> *The LORD is close to all who call on him,*
> *yes, to all who call on him in truth.*
>
> PSALM 145:18 NLT

God never expects your heart to be perfect when you call out to him, but he does expect you to call on him. And when you do, he wants you to be honest.

You can't fool God, so there's no use lying or pretending. God just wants you to be real. So be authentically yourself whenever you pray, or worship, or talk about God. There is no need to puff yourself up to look good to God. There is no need to spin stories nor wander around your actions. There is no need to avoid telling the truth and there is absolutely no need to tell little lies. When you call out to God, just be truthful. Let your heart be honest. Say, "Lord, this is what's going on...."

Lord, you know what kind of a day I've had. You know what's been on my mind. You know what I've done and what I could have done. I give the day I've just had to you. Please direct me tomorrow to be nothing but real in all of my interactions with you.

If you know when someone isn't being fully truthful with you, how much more can God see through you?

Team Up

Without consultation, plans are frustrated,
But with many counselors they succeed.

PROVERBS 15:22 NASB

Our world teaches us to become independent creatures who make our own decisions. We are supposed to become self-reliant and self-supporting. We're told that we should "grow-up" to depend on ourselves.

That sounds like an incredibly lonely and disappointing way to live. By ourselves, we are fools who make fool-hardy choices. But with others who want to see us excel, we are enriched and supported, launched and blessed. Why lurch along alone in life when we could move powerfully and joyfully with others?

Lord, give me the courage to seek out advice from those you've put into my life.

Plans fail for lack of counsel,
but with many advisers they succeed.

PROVERBS 15:22 NIV

God created us to live in community with others, not alone in a self-sustained bubble. God designed each person with different talents, interests, strengths and, yes, weaknesses. He blueprinted each person to contribute their unique experiences and wisdom to the table.

Our plans will naturally work better if we seek input from wise people. If we're honest, we'd admit that many of our own best plans could be improved or tweaked here and there. Furthermore, if we try to accomplish our plans with a team of people supporting us, believing in our cause, then we will be much more successful in the long-run.

Lord, your counsel is the most important of all. I ask for your wisdom in my decisions and choices in the days ahead.

What decisions are facing you tomorrow? Who could you consult for some additional insight into the best choices to make?

Under Control

In their hearts humans plan their course,
but the LORD establishes their steps.

PROVERBS 16:9 NIV

Oh, we human beings think we are so smart. We assume that the plans we have are all set. We strut our confidence in our schemes. At times, we actually believe that we have things under control. Whose control? Our control? Do we actually, honestly, think that is true?

Perhaps we need to be put into our place a little today. Perhaps we could ask, "What role does God play in the events of my day?" Do we really believe that God is distant? Is he unconcerned with the mundane moments of the course of our lives? Do we really think that we are the masters of our universe? Are we the ones who control the outcomes of our lives?

Lord, make me aware of something big today: you. Let me recognize how you direct my steps. And when I notice your work, give me a renewed sense of awe.

Within your heart you can make plans for your future,
but the Lord chooses the steps you take to get there.

PROVERBS 16:9 TPT

Be humble. Recognize God's role and God's oversight and God's power in the ordinary steps of our days. See the hand of the Almighty in the big events of the world. Be attentive to the heart of the Savior in the small happenings of each day. Notice the activity of God.

Is there a chance that the Lord might be much more involved in the moments of our lives than we could ever imagine? What if God is actually all-powerful? And what if he also actually cares about you? What would an all-powerful God who cares for you with an un-diminishable love do for you? Do you think there's a chance he might actually be interested in what happens to you?

Lord, I've either been too self-centered to notice or too unaware to care. But tonight, I admit you are in charge.

If God directs the steps, wouldn't it be worthwhile to ask where he is leading you?

Love

Love is patient; love is kind; love is not envious or boastful or arrogant or rude. It does not insist on its own way; it is not irritable or resentful; it does not rejoice in wrongdoing, but rejoices in the truth. It bears all things, believes all things, hopes all things, endures all things.

1 CORINTHIANS 13:4-7 NRSV

Valentine's Day is upon us. Is this a day you get excited about or absolutely dread? Do you hope for the perfect gift from a special someone or purposely avoid the greeting card aisle at your favorite all-purpose store? Whether you are in a relationship or not, this is a great day to review what love should really look like.

Read over the description of love in 1 Corinthians above. What stands out to you? Which words make you excited about love? Which make love seem like a lot of work? It is sometimes hard to imagine a love that fits all of those attributes, yet that is the kind of love to look for in others and to have for others. As you walk through today, remember this kind of love above all else.

Heavenly Father, Valentine's Day makes me feel _____ because _____. Will you remind me today what true love can really look like? Help me to love the way you want me to and be loved that way too.

Love is patient, love is kind. It does not envy, it does not boast, it is not proud. It does not dishonor others, it is not self-seeking, it is not easily angered, it keeps no record of wrongs. Love does not delight in evil but rejoices with the truth. It always protects, always trusts, always hopes, always perseveres.

1 CORINTHIANS 13:4-7 NIV

This may sound cheesy, but here goes: God wants to be the number one love of your life. All those descriptions in 1 Corinthians about love… they fit Jesus perfectly. Think about all the ways that Jesus loved people in the Bible. He cared for people that others ignored (is not proud). He healed people from physical and spiritual ailments (always protects). He listened to people share their hard stories (patient and kind). He went to the cross for all (always hopes and perseveres).

That is how he loves and how he wants us to love. Of course this is not the "romantic love" that we think of on Valentine's Day, but this kind of love is the foundation of all other types of love. Spend time thinking about how much God loves you and how that shapes the way you can love others.

Jesus, thank you for loving me more than I will ever understand. Help me to love like you do.

Which part of the love description in 1 Corinthians do you want to work on?

For I Know

"For I know the plans I have for you," says the LORD.
"They are plans for good and not for disaster,
to give you a future and a hope."

JEREMIAH 29:11 NLT

God's people had ignored him, rejected him, and followed
other gods. They had taken advantage of their workers,
mistreated widows and orphans, and distorted their court
systems with bribes and loopholes for the rich. Then, God's
people were invaded by a powerful enemy. This enemy
destroyed their nation and then scattered their families,
exiling many of their best and brightest to Babylon.

Jeremiah, a powerful, but sad, messenger of God, offered
some hope. He informed them that God would come and
accomplish all of the good things he had promised. He would,
Jeremiah assured God's people, bring them home again.

In the midst of troubling times, it can be difficult to see how
God is mapping things out for you. Romans 8:28 teaches us
that God works in all things for the good of those who love
him. He doesn't promise everything will work out the way you
want it to. But he does promise he will work out what he has
planned for you. And what he has planned is good.

Lord, throughout this day, please help me see your long-range
plans—how you intend to prosper me and shape me for the future.

"I say this because I know what I am planning for you," says the LORD. "I have good plans for you, not plans to hurt you. I will give you hope and a good future."

JEREMIAH 29:11 NCV

All day long today, God knew what he had planned for you. Looking back, ask yourself some questions about what he had planned:

Did things work out like you expected? What moments surprised you or caught you off guard? Where were you right in line with what God had in store for you? Where did you go astray from God's good plans? Was there a difficult moment today where God might have had some good intention for your life? How did God shape your future through the events of today?

Lord, I don't always understand how you are working out your plans, but I trust you. Help me see where you are taking me. And help me trust your good plans for my life.

Of all the questions asked in this devotional, which one do you most need to ponder some more tomorrow?

God Promised

The LORD of Heaven's Armies has sworn this oath:
"It will all happen as I have planned.
It will be as I have decided."

ISAIAH 14:24 NLT

Don't go against God's plans for your life. (Ever heard of Jonah? Don't be that guy.) You can't avoid dealing with God's intentions for your life. You could try to run counter to the determination of the Lord of Heaven's Armies, but it's probably not your best career move. It may be better to learn now, at this point in life, that participation with the Almighty's direction would be a wise course of action.

The prophet Isaiah, a man who spoke the truth of God, tried to help people see that the Lord's plans were set. It could be said, after all, that God is a person of his Word. What he has said will happen, will happen. What he declares will take place, will take place.

Lord, I want to run in your plans today. Don't let me fall away or step out of line. I know your plans are good. I don't want to go against them. So give me eyes to see your purpose and ears to hear your Word.

> *The Lord Almighty has sworn,*
> *"Surely, as I have planned, so it will be,*
> *and as I have purposed, so it will happen."*

Isaiah 14:24 NIV

Remember, just because you don't see something doesn't mean that God isn't doing something. It is possible that God hasn't shared all the details with you, right? Hard to believe, huh?

When the Bible expounds on God's name, it's time to listen. And when the Bible emphasizes that the Lord has sworn an oath, it's really time to listen. Here, in Isaiah 14:24, we are taught that the "Lord Almighty" (or the Lord of Heaven's Armies), has sworn a promise. It's clearly not worth trying to take matters into your own hands. Assuming that God is dropping the ball or failing to finish the work he promised is a wrong assumption.

Lord, let me be a person who keeps my word, just as you are a God who keeps his. I was made in your image. Help me trust you and help me be a trustworthy person.

What promises have you made that you still need to keep? And what promises have you taken into your own hands that you never should have, because God actually has it under control?

The Good Plan

It was the LORD's will to crush him and cause him to suffer,
and though the LORD makes his life an offering for sin,
he will see his offspring and prolong his days,
and the will of the LORD will prosper in his hand.

ISAIAH 53:10 NIV

One of the most startling lines in the Bible is found in this verse, Isaiah 53:10. If you read the whole chapter, you can't help but to realize that verse 10 is an alarming statement.

It says that everything that happened to God's "suffering servant"—all the crushing and grieving, the accusations and execution, the carrying of humanity's sin and disdain—was all a part of the Lord's "good plan." How is someone—someone innocent—being betrayed, arrested, falsely accused, tortured, and executed a "good plan"? That doesn't sound fair. That doesn't sound right. And that certainly doesn't sound "good."

Lord, your idea of "good" is so much different and, I know, so much better than mine. Thank you for being so good.

It was the LORD's good plan to crush him
and cause him grief.
Yet when his life is made an offering for sin,
he will have many descendants.
He will enjoy a long life,
and the LORD's good plan will prosper in his hands.

ISAIAH 53:10 NLT

The good in God's plan is the key. God created everything good, but because death was brought to creation through sin, Jesus took it all upon himself through the cross so that he could offer forgiveness and new life. That "suffering servant" in Isaiah 53 is God's one and only Son, Jesus.

In other words, God's rescue blueprint called for the terrible things that happened to Jesus in order to restore "good" to this earth. As a result of what Jesus did, the day of crucifixion became known as "Good Friday," and the day of resurrection would prove victory over death.

Lord, without your good plan there would be no good news. Thank you for sending your Son, Jesus, to die for me.

How many good things that may have first seemed bad can you discover in God's plan of salvation?

God's Thoughts

"My thoughts are not your thoughts,
Nor are your ways My ways," declares the LORD.

ISAIAH 55:8 NASB

Sometimes we try to recreate God in our own image. We assume that if we think a certain way about something, then God must think that way too. We conclude that our opinion about a controversy or our arguments about a topic must be the way God thinks about that issue as well. If we have an idea, we assume God must be so impressed with our brilliance.

But God created us in his image, not the other way around. Any legitimately good idea we have is a reflection of his brilliance. Any right opinion we hold is a glimpse of God's righteousness. But it would be wrong to conclude that God would agree with any of our bad ideas, any of our limited foresights, or any of our distorted arguments.

Lord, I'm working on being less self-centered and more aware that just because I have thoughts about something doesn't mean you have that same thought. Let me seek alignment with your ways, instead of trying to make you align with mine.

> *"My thoughts are not like your thoughts.*
> *Your ways are not like my ways."*
>
> ISAIAH 55:8 NCV

We don't even have the same thoughts as our friends, parents, or teachers. How many times in a day do we run into disagreements with others or see situations from different perspectives? How often do we run into the limits of our brain power?

Proverbs 3:5 says that we shouldn't lean on our own understanding, but in all of our ways, acknowledge the Lord. Instead of trying to figure out everything on our own, and then assuming that God agrees, we should begin by trusting God with all of our heart, seeking his will, and then working to make ourselves agree with his opinions. If the world would start seeking agreement with God's thoughts and start working alongside the way that God works, it would be a better place.

Lord, it's so simple that I can't believe how much I struggle with it. I want to follow your ways, instead of trying to make you follow mine. I surrender my plans to you and ask you to lead me in your paths for my life.

Tomorrow when you wake up, how would your thoughts be changed if you started by asking God what he planned on doing that day?

Surpassed

"As the heavens are higher than the earth,
So are My ways higher than your ways
And My thoughts than your thoughts."

Isaiah 55:9 NASB

At its farthest distance from the earth, the moon is 252,088 miles away. Mars is 33.9 million miles away. The Sun is 93 million miles away. The nearest galaxy to the Milky Way, the Andromeda Galaxy, is 2.5 billion light years away. So how much higher would you say are the heavens than the earth? Answer: mind-bogglingly higher. Our ways and our thoughts cannot fathom the reaches of the universe. We are, by necessity, tethered to this third rock from the sun.

God, however, is not tied to anything. He created the air; he doesn't need to breathe it. He made the sun, the moon, and the stars. He separated the seas from the land and the night from the day. His ways are beyond our imagination and his thoughts are beyond our scope of comprehension.

Lord, I am amazed by you. I am overwhelmed that you care for me. With you as my God, what do I have to fear?

*"Just as the heavens are higher than the earth,
So are my ways higher than your ways
and my thoughts higher than your thoughts."*

ISAIAH 55:9 NCV

It's rather remarkable that mankind would ever boast about being great. We are but specks on a speck of a planet among millions of galaxies spread across the heavens. Our playgrounds have slides and swings; God's playgrounds have black holes, giant stars, nebulas, and comets.

And then, one day God decided to make mankind in his own image. He decided to endow man and woman with a glimmer of his glory. Remarkably, he chose to care for the well-being of human beings. And when they disobeyed him, he chose to harness himself to the surface, confined as a human, ready to suffer and die on behalf of those he had made.

Lord, I praise you. I praise the works of your hands. I praise you for lavishing us with your attention. I praise you for not giving up on us. I praise you for your thoughts about us and for the ways you work to draw us close to you. I praise you.

Why would the Creator of the universe suffer for such small creatures?

Continued Guidance

The LORD will guide you continually,
giving you water when you are dry
and restoring your strength.
You will be like a well-watered garden,
like an ever-flowing spring.

ISAIAH 58:11 NLT

Life can be harsh. There are days that sap of us our energy. There are moments that destroy our joy. There are seasons that deplete us of optimism. Life, at times, can feel like a long drought, where our enthusiasm is dried up and our hope is weak.

We need the Lord. When life scorches our soul, he will be there for us. When life runs us dry, he will refresh our soul. But we must seek his guidance. We must follow his ways. We must listen to his instructions and follow his advice. If we go astray, we will wither. If we follow him, we will overflow with life.

Lord, guide me in your ways today. Fill me to overflow with life so that I can nourish others.

The LORD will guide you always;
he will satisfy your needs in a sun-scorched land
and will strengthen your frame.
You will be like a well-watered garden,
like a spring whose waters never fail.

ISAIAH 58:11 NIV

This refreshing verse in Isaiah 58 comes near the end of some powerful truths. God points out to his people that they've become dried up in their souls because they have not followed his ways. Instead, they've tried to take advantage of the weak, to steal their joy, to rob their hope, to gain energy off the backs of others. And their actions have left them dry.

God declares that he will save those who have been depleted. He wants those who have been wrongly imprisoned to be set free. He wants people to humble themselves before him. He wants his followers to give their clothes to the needy, shelter to the homeless, food to hungry. Their needs will be satisfied, their sins forgiven, their souls refreshed. They will then be like a well-watered garden, never failing to produce all that God has for them.

Lord, water my soul, strengthen my resolve. Let me follow you in all of my ways.

What part of your life needs a renewal of hope?

Unchanging God

> *"I the LORD do not change. So you, the descendants of Jacob, are not destroyed. Ever since the time of your ancestors you have turned away from my decrees and have not kept them. Return to me, and I will return to you," says the LORD Almighty.*
>
> MALACHI 3:6–7 ESV

This is not the most cheery devotional verse, right? It's a sobering thought to be reminded that humanity stands judged because of sin. People have gone against God. Romans 3:3 reveals that everyone has sinned. Romans 6:23 adds that the wages of sin is death. In other words, even good people, even God's people, have missed the mark and have fallen short of God's glory.

So why hasn't God given up? Why hasn't he just thrown in the towel and judged mankind with a final sweep of his arm? Why does he give people the opportunity to receive his forgiveness? Well, it's simple really. The Lord does not change. And ever since humanity needed his mercy, the Lord has always offered it. God longs for people to return to him. Since the advent of sin, this has always been God's preferred method of operation.

Lord, thank you for always being faithful. I am sorry for my own sin. Please forgive me. Thank you for always wanting me to turn back to you.

> *"I the LORD do not change. So you descendants of Jacob have not been destroyed. Since the time of your ancestors, you have disobeyed my rules and have not kept them. Return to me, and I will return to you," says the LORD All-Powerful.*

MALACHI 3:6-7 NCV

The book of Malachi is the last book in the Old Testament. It is concerned with God's people returning to a faithful relationship with the Lord. It also points to God being faithful to his promises to redeem and restore his people to a holy status. Through Malachi, positioned just before the Gospel of Mathew, it's almost as if God is reminding his people that he has always prioritized mercy and he has always invited people into a close relationship with him, and that he will continue to do so.

Jesus is the fullest evidence of God's unchanging desire that people would return to him. Even though he is the God of the armies of heaven, he is patient with sin and longs for people to turn to him. That's why Jesus came to earth. God wants humanity to receive his invitation to return to him.

Lord, draw me close to you. In every way that I've wandered away, turn me back to you so that we can walk closely together.

Have you received the Lord's invitation to have a personal relationship with him? In what ways could you accept an even closer friendship?

Compassion

Jesus saw the huge crowd as he stepped from the boat, and he had compassion on them because they were like sheep without a shepherd. So he began teaching them many things.

MARK 6:34 NLT

So Jesus began to teach them. So. What an intriguing word. Jesus saw that the people were like sheep without a shepherd, so he did something about it. He noticed they were wandering, so he stepped up and began to lead the people.

Sheep without a shepherd are a pitiful bunch. They don't have a prayer of thriving in life without a shepherd. They are natural wanderers. Their curious and oblivious strolls can entrap and endanger them. So, when Jesus sees God's people stumbling in life and getting lost in their souls, his heart breaks. He has compassion for them. Compassion means to "suffer with." In other words, he takes their fear and pain upon his own heart, and then steps in to address the problem.

Lord, I need you to guide me today. Do not let me wander away from your direction for my life.

*By the time Jesus came ashore, a massive crowd was waiting. At
the sight of them, his heart was filled with compassion, because
they seemed like wandering sheep who had no shepherd. So he
taught them many things.*

MARK 6:34 TPT

In the New Testament, Jesus refers to himself as the Good
Shepherd who lays down his life for his sheep. He calls his
followers his sheep. He says that his sheep know his voice.
He teaches that he would do anything to find one of his sheep
that gets lost. The Old Testament refers to God's people as
sheep who are shepherded by their God. One of the most
familiar passages of the Bible, Psalm 23, declares that "the
Lord is my shepherd."

So, when Jesus sees people wandering, lost, in danger, the
Good Shepherd begins to teach them. He teaches them about
a shepherd who is willing to lay down his life for his sheep.
And he teaches them about a shepherd who became the Lamb
of God to take away the sins of the world.

*Lord, thank you for loving me and guiding me so compassionately
today.*

What does it mean to you that Jesus, the Good Shepherd, is
also the Lamb of God who takes away the sins of the world?

Preach to Everyone

He said to them, "As you go into all the world, preach openly the
wonderful news of the gospel to the entire human race!"
MARK 16:15 TPT

At some point in your life you will need to "own" your faith.
That means your faith is not something that can be inherited
or bought. Just because your parents or peers are faithful
people doesn't mean you are automatically full of faith.

However, as soon as you take serious ownership of your faith
you realize it is not yours, but yours to give away. This is why
faith, true faith, can never be a private matter. God gave you
your faith. He offered it to you. He made it possible. If faith
was yours and yours alone to own, then it would be your
prerogative whether to keep your faith private, but faith was
given to you so you could give it to others.

Lord, help me share my faith in you today.

He said to them, "Go into all the world
and preach the gospel to all creation."

MARK 16:15 NASB

If others interacted with you today, would they have known
that you have a living relationship with Jesus? You don't have
to be a wonderful preacher to share God's Word with others.
You don't have to have a biblical studies degree. You don't need
to know how to say the word "propitiation" without laughing.
You just need to let Jesus live in you and through you.

Invite his Holy Spirit to transform your heart, your focus,
your character, and your soul. You are undeservedly blessed
to have faith in Jesus. You are remarkably blessed to have
received forgiveness and to have begun walking with God. So,
share it. Faith is not to be kept.

Lord, let me be ready to share your good news with everyone
I encounter.

What does preaching look like if it doesn't use words?

Active Dispenser

The disciples went everywhere and preached,
and the Lord worked through them,
confirming what they said by many miraculous signs.

MARK 16:20 NLT

Shifting into an intentional gear is an important aspect of being a follower of Jesus. You are not merely to be a passive receiver of God's blessing. You are called to be an active dispenser of his love as well. How does God want us to participate in this? Do we need to become missionaries to faraway lands? Do we need to leave our homes and families and familiar communities in order to share the message of Christ?

You could do those things if you want. But really, it's much simpler than that. Just ask yourself where you are going today. Look ahead to the next several hours and wonder where you will be. Where will you be eating? Where will you be waiting? Where will you be driving or walking? Even more importantly, where will you be seeing people? That's where you have an opportunity to share the good news of Jesus.

Lord, keep me focused on the opportunities I have to share your message today.

The apostles went out announcing the good news everywhere, as the Lord himself consistently worked with them, validating the message they preached with miracle-signs that accompanied them!

MARK 16:20 TPT

As you go intentionally throughout your day, preaching everywhere you go, God will do extraordinary things in you. God will act through you so that people can see the truth of your message. The Lord himself will confirm what you say through his power. He will validate the beautiful news with his healing and restorative work for this world.

In God's plan, Jesus wants you to join his purpose to save people from their sin, to let the world know his good news, and to let them know what he has done. Jesus himself will support you. His Spirit will go before you and after you. Jesus' own miracles evidenced the authority of his preaching. Signs and wonders affirmed the authority of the preaching of the early church in the book of Acts. Jesus promised his followers that they would preach in that same power.

Lord, don't let me preach in my own power, but let me see how your Holy Spirit works through your message. In the days ahead, give me boldness to share with people wherever I go.

Where will you be tomorrow? How could you use that opportunity to share the good news of Jesus with others?

Pray with Jesus

About eight days after Jesus said this, he took Peter, John and James with him and went up onto a mountain to pray.

LUKE 9:28 NLT

It's such a good thing you have this devotional. After all, Jesus invited his disciples to pray with him. It was a major aspect of how he spent time with them. So it is fitting that you are choosing to start and end each day in prayer with him too. In this case, in Luke 9, Jesus had just spent time with his disciples in the northern part of Israel. Around a week or so after that, Jesus invited three of his followers to pray with him up on a mountain.

What did he want to pray about? We don't really know. Why did he ask these three young men? We don't really know that either. We just know that Jesus invited them to pray. Each morning and each night, for a whole year, you are invited to pray. You won't always know exactly what you are supposed to pray about, but the most important thing is that you accept the invitation to pray.

Lord, I accept the challenge to pray each morning and each night through this devotional. You know the plans you have for me. I want to be an active part in those plans.

About eight days after Jesus said these things, he took Peer, John, and James and went up on a mountain to pray.

LUKE 9:28-29 NCV

Is there some significance to the fact that the disciples had to climb to the top of a mountain to pray with Jesus? They certainly could have prayed in the valley. They most certainly could have prayed in someone's house over a meal. They could have prayed on a hillside, or by a lake, or as they traveled along the road.

It takes effort to pray sometimes. This circumstance, on top of the mountain, would have been one of those times. Prayer is supposed to be a simple process, but it is good to strive for it on occasion. It is a remarkable thing that we are invited to pray with the Almighty God of Heaven. If we always want it to be on our own terms, in our own comfort, then our time of prayer won't be challenged to grow closer to Jesus.

Lord, forgive me for those times that I treat prayer like an add-on or a lazy moment. Thank you for challenging me to put forth effort and take prayer more seriously.

What do you think Jesus would like you to be praying about this evening?

Love and Listen

"If you love me, keep my commands. And I will ask the Father, and he will give you another advocate to help you and be with you forever— the Spirit of truth. The world cannot accept him, because it neither sees him nor knows him. But you know him, for he lives with you and will be in you."

JOHN 14:15-17 NIV

If you follow Jesus, then you won't have only the Son of God defending your back, you'll also have God the Father and the Holy Spirit. You're covered. In a world where abandonment is such a big problem, this is indeed good news. Be sure that you don't miss a key concept embedded here. It is true that God won't ditch you, but he also longs for you to not give up on him either. He asks you to love him and, in your love, to obey what he has asked you to do.

To obey simply means to listen. Jesus states the obvious: if you love him, then you'll listen to him. If you listen to him, then you might just hear him asking the Father to give you his Spirit, who will come to your aid, comfort you, empower you, and stand up for you in every circumstance at any given moment.

Lord, thank you for your attention and care. I love you and will listen to you today.

"If you love me, obey my commandments. And I will ask the Father, and he will give you another Advocate, who will never leave you. He is the Holy Spirit, who leads into all truth. The world cannot receive him, because it isn't looking for him and doesn't recognize him. But you know him, because he lives with you now and later will be in you."

JOHN 14:15-17 NLT

Look back at your day. How did you do with the "obey" part of these verses? Did you follow God's commands? Were there moments where you ignored any of God's directions? Would God have been pleased in your big events and in the normal activities?

Did you notice God's Spirit alive within you today? Did he steer you toward helping anyone? Did you recognize a moment where he led you or gave you the right words to say? If you love God, it's simple to understand that you would naturally want to live in agreement with his ways. But he doesn't require you to do all the work. He gives you his Spirit so that you can live wholly for him.

Lord, fill me with your Spirit. Be alive within me.

Of all the questions in the evening portion of this devotional, which one is God's Spirit highlighting in your heart?

Chosen

Even before he made the world, God loved us and chose us in Christ to be holy and without fault in his eyes.

EPHESIANS 1:4, NLT

Even sin didn't mess up God's plans for you. His idea of drawing you close to himself has withstood every test. His goal of sharing his life with you has never been derailed. It was his plan before the world began. It was his plan after sin tried to break it apart. God won't let something as unholy as sin disrupt his plan.

God has had you on his mind for a long-time. He's not one to lose his focus. Before the world was made, God had already decided that you, and many others, would be made holy through his Son. When God looks at you, he doesn't see a messed up, sinful person. God sees someone that he made, and that he made blameless, without fault, through Jesus Christ.

Lord, your long-range plan is beyond my understanding. Let your love for me sink deeply into the core of my identity... and change the way I live each day.

Chose us to be his very own, joining us to himself even before he laid the foundation of the universe! Because of his great love, he ordained us, so that we would be seen as holy in his eyes with an unstained innocence.

EPHESIANS 1:4 TPT

God chose you to be holy. So be holy. God chose you to be blameless. So be without blame. Sin has tried its best to blemish you. It even succeeded for a while. But then Jesus redeemed you. He paid your penalty. He has freed you. Jesus has recreated you. Jesus has cleansed you and made you holy.

You are holy. You probably don't feel like it. You are still, after all, working it all out. God has declared you holy in his sight, but he's also bringing you along in the process. His Holy Spirit is sanctifying you, making you holy. He is wrestling every day against those things that stain your soul. As a result, you are being made holy. God appreciates good work when he sees it. He likes the work he is doing in you.

Lord, make me holy as you are holy. Thank you for seeing me through your eyes. Let me see myself and others that way too.

What areas of your life would you like God's Spirit to work on next?

Infinitely More

Now all glory to God, who is able, through his mighty power at work within us, to accomplish infinitely more than we might ask or think.

EPHESIANS 3:20 NLT

Infinity is impossible to measure. We know infinity is huge, but its never-ending limitlessness is beyond our scope. It leaves us in awe. We can capture enough of the concept to comprehend the idea of "boundless," but never enough to fully grasp it. The greatest imaginations of our mind could never control infinity.

This is what God wants to do in us today. He is able, after all, to do anything he desires, and he desires to do a lot within us. He could absolutely revolutionize the world through us, if he so desired. And he does so desire. Will you notice that his power is at work within you? Will you then be willing to allow God to do more than what you could imagine?

Lord, may your glory be seen through your work in my life today.

2/2022

You can do more than we ask, say or do. Thank you Jesus.

Never doubt God's mighty power to work in you and accomplish all this. He will achieve infinitely more than your greatest request, your most unbelievable dream, and exceed your wildest imagination! He will outdo them all, for his miraculous power constantly energizes you.

EPHESIANS 3:20 TPT

Perhaps our thoughts about our regular days are pretty small. We follow the Living God. What could he do in us?

This is the pondering of the apostle Paul as he describes just how much God can accomplish when he works through us. Take the greatest thoughts, the greatest dreams, the most inventive requests that any of us could conjure up, lift them up to God, and even that wouldn't scratch the depths of what God is able to do. This reveals God's glory. The beauty, wonder, and power of his action is absolutely boundless. It is why creatures like us fall to his feet in awe. So why would we not expand our understanding of what is possible with God?

Lord, expand my horizon. Knock down my boundaries. Be at work in my soul.

What's the biggest thing you think God could do through his people, if they would allow him? Save, heal, lead, teach, deliver, raise, and love all as He loves all. Forgive too.

Calling

I, a prisoner for serving the Lord, beg you to lead a life worthy of your calling, for you have been called by God. Always be humble and gentle. Be patient with each other, making allowance for each other's faults because of your love.

EPHESIANS 4:1-2 NLT

There comes a point where we need to recognize defeat. Our constant pursuit of flailing-failings teaches us, if we are wise that is, to give up the race of independence from God and give in to complete reliance upon his mercy and grace. The crescendo of crisis in our sapped soul propels us to a complete surrender to Christ. Voluntarily, we become prisoners for serving the Lord.

As a result, even if we have acknowledged what Jesus has done for us, even if we have accepted the benevolent invitation of his outstretched arms, we must take the steps, daily, to willingly embrace his surrendered body on the cross. Would it be right to receive Jesus as Savior only to refuse him in the daily routines of our lives? Would it be appropriate to receive the outpoured breath of his life only to continue in the practices that led us to drown?

Lord, I surrender all to you. I want to follow you with all I have, holding nothing back.

As a prisoner for the Lord, then, I urge you to live a life worthy of the calling you have received. Be completely humble and gentle; be patient, bearing with one another in love.

EPHESIANS 4:1-2 NIV

A defeated life, in Jesus, becomes a victorious one. By serving the Lord, we are free to live generously on the behalf of others. In other words, because Jesus lives within us, we can be freed from the tyranny of ourselves and have the audacity to treat others with the same dignity and honor that Christ treats them with.

Jesus died for your family. He laid down his life for your friends. He weeps for your classmates and coworkers. He cherishes your neighbors. So can you. Because Jesus teaches you how to be humble and gentle, how to be patient with others, and how to make allowance for people's faults. Yes, it's true. Jesus teaches you how to love. That's the kind of life you have surrendered yourself to: one that is worthy of the name of Jesus and calls you out of self-centered entrapments into a glorious love.

Lord, let me live freely for others because you have lived so freely for me.

What humble and thoughtful action could you do for a friend tomorrow?

Imitate Christ

You are God's children whom he loves, so try to be like him. Live a life of love just as Christ loved us and gave himself for us as a sweet-smelling offering and sacrifice to God.

EPHESIANS 5:1-2 NCV

As a kid, did you ever play that fun but annoying game where you repeated everything someone said and did? Of course, you thought this was hilarious. If they moved an arm, then you would move your arm in the same way. If they spoke, you would repeat them verbatim. If they said, "Hey, stop it!" then you would say "Hey, stop it!" too. And it was funny (for a while, or unless you were the one being copied), until it eventually got on everyone's nerves.

When we imitate God, we aren't playing a game where we merely repeat him like a robot responding to a command. When people copy God like that it can become really annoying really quickly. Instead, as we watch God, we learn to do what he does. When we follow his actions, his words, and his heart, we tend to put his movements into practice. In this way, when we mimic God, a smile spreads across his face, for we are becoming more and more like him. Do what pleases Him.

Lord, so much of my life doesn't imitate you. Align my thoughts, my words, and my actions with yours

It's doing what you know is right in your heart!

> *Imitate God, therefore, in everything you do, because you are his dear children. Live a life filled with love, following the example of Christ. He loved us and offered himself as a sacrifice for us, a pleasing aroma to God.*

EPHESIANS 5:1-2 NLT

Imitating God is a lot different than that childish mimicking game. It's more like the moment when a little boy, after watching his dad shaving in the mirror, puts shaving cream on his face, picks up a razor (with the cap still on, of course), and begins to practice the strokes up and down his face. Every father who has experienced this moment can't help but smile.

Our goal is to watch God and see what he does. We should soak in his presence, learning what he says in situations and what stirs him to action. We should learn who he cares about and what he wants from this world. And then we should try to be like him.

Lord, I want to be more like you. I pray that you would shape me into a person who reflects your character and your concerns.

If you were to watch God tomorrow, what do you think you would see? *Same as yesterday and today— Loving, gracious, merciful, willing, helpful, doing Himself, good, great, awesome, making all things work together for OUR good always and forever. Amen.*

Run for God

> *Therefore, since we are surrounded by such a huge crowd of witnesses to the life of faith, let us strip off every weight that slows us down, especially the sin that so easily trips us up. And let us run with endurance the race God has set before us.*
>
> HEBREWS 12:1 NLT

Would you like to be a hero of faith? Would you like to be the type of person who can run for God every day of your life? The type of person that motivates others to keep pace? Would you like to inspire a marathon of speed and agility for the Almighty God? Would you like to share with others that it is possible to live a life of faith even through circumstances that make it difficult? This world needs people like that. People like you.

Back one chapter, in Hebrews 11, there is a "crowd of witnesses" who endured tremendous pressures and still were able to run the race of faith in God with courage and freedom. Their faith in God was proven victorious. There's Noah, Abraham, Joseph, Moses, Rahab, Gideon, David, Samuel, and so many others. Throughout history and down to this very day countless believers have run for God through fire and trial, stress, suffering and persecution, unhindered and free. Wouldn't you like to be like that?

Lord, thank you that I am surrounded by many others who have run this race of faith. Let me join that marathon list of faithful runners.

We are surrounded by a great cloud of people whose lives tell us what faith means. So let us run the race that is before us and never give up. We should remove from our lives anything that would get in the way and the sin that so easily holds us back.

HEBREWS 12:1 NCV

Today you might have found that you have a problem. Like many others, you carried things that hindered your speed and strength, that weighed down your ability to run faithfully. You may have attached yourself to some baggage, things that God did not place in your arms, which burdened and slowed down your faith. When God asked you to do something, to go somewhere, to help someone or to spend faithful time alone with him, you wanted to respond well, but you couldn't. You were entangled.

The race of faith is a daily endurance run. It demands freedom, not baggage. So, the writer of Hebrews says, get rid of the stuff that distracts you.

Lord, let me run unhindered. Free me from those things that have entangled me.

What baggage do you keep holding that weighed down your faith in God?

God Perfects

We do this by keeping our eyes on Jesus, the champion who initiates and perfects our faith. Because of the joy awaiting him, he endured the cross, disregarding its shame. Now he is seated in the place of honor beside God's throne.

HEBREWS 12:2 NIV

On this marathon journey of faith, Jesus understands where you are beginning from. Jesus has been there. He has run the race to perfection. He knows the conditioning of your faith. He knows what you're carrying around in your soul. He knows if you're holding on to jealousy or weighed down by bitterness or unforgiveness. He knows if you're holding on to somebody else too tightly. He knows if you're slowed down by lies or a hidden sin, or a temptation that you can't seem to ignore.

The cool thing is that Jesus also knows what steps you should take to break free in a sprint and to get to the finish line. He knows the layout of the path. He is the author and perfecter of your faith.

Lord, thank you for making it possible for me to run for you today. Keep pressing into my soul.

*Let us look only to Jesus, the One who began our faith and who
makes it perfect. He suffered death on the cross. But he accepted
the shame as if it were nothing because of the joy that God put
before him. And now he is sitting at the right side of God's throne.*

HEBREWS 12:2 NCV

Jesus wants to inspire you to run, free and alive—all because
you no longer are carrying around all that extra weight. He
is. It's a remarkable thing that God should carry all of your
baggage. When he endured the cross, scorning its shame, he
carried your iniquities. Jesus lifted up your burdens, your
sins, and your infirmities and carried them to the cross.
Don't pick up that baggage again. Run free for God.

You can be a hero of faith. You can go on a baggage diet. You
can cast away all of those things that would hinder you from
following Jesus, running the race of faith with endurance.

*Lord, let me run in such a way that I can look back and see your
endurance giving me strength.*

What's the hardest part about running a long race of faith?
When the obstacles seem so big and distract
and the temptations that can derail me
from the path He lays out and knows.
Thank you that i can run this race.

Accept Discipline

No discipline is enjoyable while it is happening—it's painful! But afterward there will be a peaceful harvest of right living for those who are trained in this way.

HEBREWS 12:11 NLT

If God didn't love you, he would never let you suffer the consequences of your sin or your wrong actions. If he didn't love you, he wouldn't take time to tell you were harming yourself. If God didn't love you, he wouldn't bother instructing you to replace your bad habits with healthy ones.

Part of what it means to follow Jesus is to accept your need for complete surrender to the life Jesus has for you. It makes no sense to say you follow Christ only to keep parts of yourself dedicated to old patterns of living or compromising habits. If you say you follow Jesus, the challenge is this: follow him. Every day, keep surrendering yourself to his work in your life. Let God produce his will in you.

Lord, I have given my life to you. Now help me to keep doing so.

*All discipline seems to be more pain than pleasure at the time,
yet later it will produce a transformation of character, bringing a
harvest of righteousness and peace to those who yield to it.*

HEBREWS 12:11 TPT

Discipline means "to learn." If you are disciplined for your
actions (or inactions), it's not because God doesn't like you,
it's because he loves you and wants you to learn what is best
for you. He loves you so much that he actually expects you
to rise to his challenge. He raises the bar for you because he
believes you can meet the bar.

You are worth his time, his effort, and, yes, even his trouble.
He would do anything to transform you into the person he
created you to be. Like a sculptor or gardener, his disciplined
focus may seem painful in the moment. But in the long run,
he produces a masterpiece in you.

*Lord, chisel away. Cut out those aspects of my heart that don't
belong. Make me into the person you designed me to be.*

For you, what's the hardest part about receiving discipline?

God Is Patient

The Lord isn't really being slow about his promise, as some people think. No, he is being patient for your sake. He does not want anyone to be destroyed, but wants everyone to repent.

2 PETER 3:9 NLT

God doesn't want anyone to perish. It is God's intention that people would not die. He created people to dwell with him forever. And when they fell away from him, he launched his salvation plan into high gear. Through Jesus, anyone in all of humanity can reconnect with God and the eternal life he intended for people to have with him.

God doesn't want anyone to perish; he wants them to repent. To repent means to turn toward God. It's time for some big, theological words: repentance refers to the process of changing from sinful actions and attitudes with sorrowful determination toward a remission of sins and restoration to relationship with God. The good news of the gospel that must be proclaimed is that Jesus came to seek and to save the lost.

Lord, I need to let this truth sink in deeply: You want to rescue people. Give me even just a portion of your passion for people in this world.

This means that, contrary to man's perspective, the Lord is not late with his promise to return, as some measure lateness. But rather, his "delay" simply reveals his loving patience toward you, because he does not want any to perish but all to come to repentance.

2 PETER 3:9 TPT

To discover and then embrace that Jesus Christ offers you salvation from the consequences of sin and, therefore, the restoration of a relationship with God can be a life-changing awakening in your soul.

Personally, as a follower of Jesus, you are encouraged to be overwhelmed by God's patient plan to save you. You are urged to accept what Jesus accomplished purposefully on your behalf. Your sin is forgiven through the death of Jesus. Your life is restored through his love and power. The salvation that Jesus has given you, and sustained within you, compels you to share with others what Jesus has done through the cross and resurrection.

Lord, thank you for giving me a chance. Thank you for rescuing me. And thank you for patiently loving me even when I don't understand or recognize how you are at work. I love you.

How does God's patience for humanity change the way you approach people in your life who need Jesus?

Work Hard

*Be all the more diligent to make certain about His calling
and choosing you; for as long as you practice these things,
you will never stumble.*

2 PETER 1:10 NASB

Are you one of the growing number of people who need
a swift kick in the backside to get you going today? There
is a mentality in society today known as "benign neglect."
Basically, it means that people feel like they can put the
normal responsibilities of life off until some other time in
the future. They feel like they can extend their adolescence
for years, even into their thirties or forties, and that "real
life" begins later when they feel more ready.

It is benign because it doesn't feel bad (at first), but over
time it can be neglectful of a person's potential and gifts and
calling in life. Now is not the time to put off doing what you
need to do. Don't fall into the pit of this off-putting chronic
illness. Don't give in to benign neglect. Rather, work hard to
prove that God has made you alive by his Spirit.

*Lord, give me the guts to get rid of any laziness in my faith. What
you have called me to do, motivate me to do it.*

Work hard to prove that you really are among those God has called and chosen. Do these things, and you will never fall away.

2 PETER 1:10 NLT

One of the most powerful stealth weapons used against Christianity is laziness. Many people have walked away from faith because they didn't see the vibrancy of life that one would expect to see. After all, if people are really following the Lord Almighty, the living God, then boredom and apathy shouldn't be found within the activities of his people. Lazy faith is an easy, and understandable, reason to walk away.

So Peter's challenge to a young church is this: Work hard. Prove that you belong to carry the name of Christ. Prove that you aren't just freeloading the church. When you put your heart and soul into something, you commit to it. So put your heart and soul into the mission of Jesus.

Lord, challenge me to work hard in my faith. I have said I have committed myself to you. Let me be a person of my word.

What is something that you should strive to accomplish, but have been putting off?

Listen Up

*The LORD came and stood there and called as he had before,
"Samuel! Samuel!" Samuel said, "Speak, LORD. I am your servant
and I am listening."*

1 SAMUEL 3:10 NCV

You'll have to stare at this question a bit before
you understand it: How does God speak to you in
SnIoLiEsNeCsE? It's an odd question, even if you can read
between the lines. God speaks in both the silence and noises
of life. Ironically, we tend to seek him more often in one
versus the other (and are frustrated when he isn't found in
the way we're looking for him).

The key is to remember that we aren't in a cryptic spiritual
journey but in a relationship with a person. Just as you can
talk with or listen to a trusted friend in a crisis, so can you
connect with Jesus no matter what's going on. You are made
for community with him. Don't underestimate the power
of pausing and choosing to "listen up." And for that matter,
don't underestimate the power of inviting God to listen to
you. He already is.

*Lord, I love you. I'm pausing even now to recognize how you and I
are in a relationship together. May we connect today in a way that
reminds me of this.*

The LORD came and stood and called as at other times, "Samuel! Samuel!" And Samuel answered, "Speak, for Your servant hears."

1 SAMUEL 3:10 NKJV

Samuel was a pre-teen who worked for a priest named Eli. Simply being around a spiritual person and doing religious things, though, didn't mean Samuel was mature. He needed to somehow become aware of how God's voice was speaking to him. Did you catch that? God was speaking before Samuel realized it.

Sometimes our circumstances can make us feel like God isn't saying anything to us. It leaves us discouraged and deflated, believing nothing spiritually significant is happening in us. That's not entirely true. In these moments we play a role in slowing down for some peace and clarity. It's all about recognizing God is in that moment with you so that you become open to him beyond the funk you feel. Be honest by holding nothing back from him. Invite him to be honest with you too. God does great things in whispers and whirlwinds alike.

I know that you have something to say to me, God. Maybe it's about my day, or perhaps it's a reminder of something you told me in the past. I'm open, ready to receive.

What might be a fresh, biblical way for you in this season of life to "listen up" to God?

X-Ray Vision

"God sees not as man sees, for man looks at the outward appearance, but the LORD looks at the heart."

1 SAMUEL 16:7 NASB

Ever broken a bone? If so, you probably were x-rayed so someone could see underneath your skin. This tool helps doctors understand what's happening at the source instead of guessing why something is bent in a way shouldn't be. It also enables them to respond with the proper treatment.

Imagine having that ability at home, school, among friends, within your church and more. Instead of reacting to why people or things were bent out of shape, you'd understand what was happening beneath the surface. You could then use the abilities, skills, and attitude God has given you to help others tap into deeper truths.

Jesus, you saw things in people that they'd never see without you. Teach me to pay attention to what you pay attention to.

"The Lord does not look at the things people look at. People look at the outward appearance, but the Lord looks at the heart."

1 Samuel 16:7 NIV

When the prophet Samuel went looking in a large family for the next king of Israel, he assumed that it might be the tallest or strongest looking son. God told him otherwise, in that what mattered most was if that person had a heart for the Lord. It wasn't the kind of thing you might quickly see physically but could take note of spiritually.

Have you ever stopped to look for how God might be at work in someone or something you've overlooked? Movies, television, music, books, and national conversations reveal how everyone is searching for something (despite how so many settle for something less). Popular trends, world events, and politics likewise show how easily we invent human-sized answers for God-sized questions. Celebrate the heart behind this by helping others see how God is at work in both the good and the bad.

Father, this is your world. I don't always catch the opportunities before me, but I'm willing to pay better attention. Give me your perspective so I can share it.

Who has God called you to reach out to and invite into a relationship with him?

Transformation

As far as the east is from the west,
so far has he removed our transgressions from us.

PSALM 103:12 NIV

When you were younger, a grownup probably told you not to be a tattletale. Kids are regularly told things like this: mind your own business, don't stare. Our eventual takeaway is that the lives of other people are somehow separate from our own. Culture underlines this in trying to get us to believe we shouldn't interfere if someone is happy.

But sin does exist. You see this, right? Sometimes sin might appear to make someone happy, even if it's destroying them in the process. You've probably seen this too. What if we make it our business to stare at Jesus and let him tell us the tale of who needs him? What if God's promise of removing sin isn't merely for us to experience, but also for us to share? People may cringe if you look into their lives, expecting you to judge them. Let them know that the plans God has for them include forgiveness and a new kind of freedom.

Holy Spirit, what are you up to in the lives of the people around me? I'd like to join you today.

He has removed our sins as far away from us
as the east is from the west.

PSALM 103:12 TLB

Who is it? Perhaps a person who bullied you. Maybe a
stranger who hurt someone you care about. It could be
someone in your home. It's common to struggle with people
we regard as not deserving God's grace. It happens publicly,
for example, when a serial killer claims they found Jesus
while in prison and the world (and sometimes even the
Christian community) cries "Unfair!" After all, it's easier to
assume that clean people go to heaven and unclean people are
kept out.

But the Bible assures us that we're all unclean people until
God removes our sins—something he is willing to do and
does. None of us are so clean that we are above receiving
God's grace, nor are any of us so dirty that we can't be made
white as snow. We can all be transformed.

Jesus, you are willing to save and transform everyone—me, my
loved ones, and even those I can't stand. Instead of resenting you
for that, I'm going to be grateful.

Be honest—who do you hope one day will be held accountable
for how they've hurt you or others? Are you willing to instead
pray for that person to be forgiven by God?

Sharpened

As iron sharpens iron, so a friend sharpens a friend.

PROVERBS 27:17 NLT

Remember the pinky swear? It happened when you said you would do something, and a friend would ask, "Pinky swear?" You'd lock fingers, as if to say, "I'm all in." Over time, the pinky swear can seem kind of silly. Can you imagine the next President of the United States being sworn in, only at the end of the ceremony someone asks, "Pinky swear?"

Still, the Bible records many people making special covenants with each other where they agreed to follow through on something. A great version of this was committing to be the kind of friend who'd spur others on with God, like iron sharpens iron. It defies making relationships all about feelings. Maybe that's the real reason the Pinky Swear disappears from our lives. We're inclined to let our emotions lead our commitment, instead of letting our commitment lead our emotions. What kind of friend do you want, and which kind of friend are you willing to be?

In all the ways you have been a friend to me, God, may I be a friend to others.

As iron sharpens iron,
so people can improve each other.

PROVERBS 27:17 NCV

In any relationship, we can get on each other's nerves. Wrinkles happen between us and others that need ironing out. At times the only thing holding us together will be the fact that we committed to be friends. This is why church is so important, because through it we can form our friendships on the very foundation of God himself.

If you're a genuine Christian, you have no excuse for not attempting to work on those wrinkles in your relationships. Even if it's one-sided, an iron-like commitment to love that person "no matter what" matters. Don't pretend like things aren't weird. Speak redemptive truth into their lives. Resolve to personally work hard to make that relationship healthier and vibrant.

Lord, show me how to be solid when my relationships feel like they're falling apart. I want to do that through your strength and not my own.

Which old friends do you have some unresolved "stuff" with? What's a possible step to take?

God Is God

In the year that King Uzziah died, I saw the LORD, high and exalted, seated on a throne; and the train of his robe filled the temple.

ISAIAH 6:1 NIV

Isaiah was an ordinary man who had an extraordinary encounter with God. In an unexpected moment, he became aware of the Lord's presence as the realm of heaven spilled over him like a tidal wave crashing over an ant. He gasped spiritually, trying to make sense of it all inwardly, outwardly, and upwardly. Imagine what that must have felt like for Isaiah. No matter what his opinions about God were, he had to face the reality of who God is. It's why after this experience Isaiah stepped into a mission to tell others about the Lord. He couldn't deny who and what he'd seen.

There's a good chance you're reading this book because you've had powerful moments with God or crave something epic with him now. Such moments are great, but are meant to prod us into a mission beyond the moment. How willing are you to really stare at God in all his greatness? What if, like Isaiah, it changes the rest of your life?

Lord, show me your glory. Show me you.

In the year that king Uzziah died I saw also the LORD *sitting upon a throne, high and lifted up, and his train filled the temple.*

ISAIAH 6:1 KJV

Here's a weird truth—all around you, everyone has a philosophy about something. An athlete you know believes in a right way to train. A local teacher thinks students should learn a certain way. An entrepreneur is excited about a way to earn some money. For all their clarity, what they may not remember is how they came to believe in their philosophy.

God is personally knowable, yet impossible to completely define. He's revealed himself in ways that he gave us words for, such as Savior, Lord, Redeemer, Friend, and Counselor. Yet he's also always beyond human words and understanding. Even in heaven, God will be God and never stop surprising us with how amazing he is. Now put all of that together. You have a philosophy about who God is, but you may not be fully aware of how you came to believe that. And yet, somehow, it's still possible to be clear on God.

Father, I may not know how every moment of my life contributed to my understanding of you, but I do know that I have a relationship with you. May it always be growing into truth and not tradition.

What are five defining moments in your faith journey?

Confession

I said: "Woe is me! For I am lost; for I am a man of unclean lips,
and I dwell in the midst of a people of unclean lips; for my eyes
have seen the King, the LORD of hosts!"

ISAIAH 6:5 ESV

"One of these things is not like the others. One of these things just doesn't belong." Ever play that game? It could involve a simple comparison, like two farm animals and a glass of juice. Or it could mean thinking through harder challenges where you couldn't easily see what was unique.

In Isaiah's case, he clearly knew he was out of his league as he stood before God and all of heaven. It's why he confessed out loud that nothing unholy could be in the presence of the Lord's holiness, including him and all of humanity. Think of it this way — if God declared that at midnight tonight nothing "unholy" would be around, who or what would honestly be left after midnight? That is, unless Christ has made you clean. Confession is simply truth-telling. It isn't meant to keep us from God, but to recognize our need for him and his saving.

I can't be in your presence, Lord, without your grace. Thank you
for offering it to me through Jesus.

I said, "Oh, no! I will be destroyed. I am not pure, and I live among people who are not pure, but I have seen the King, the LORD All-Powerful."

ISAIAH 6:5 NCV

Do you see it? As Isaiah was convicted by his own sin, the next thing out of his mouth was recognizing that he lived in a community full of sinful people. Maybe you can identify with this as you've realized your own need for God, noting others in your life who need him too. A key part of your life mission is keeping these two truths together and acting on them.

Do you see it? That you have a life mission? It isn't to fix people, but to love and lead them to Jesus. He regularly let his heart break for the people around him, being passionately mindful of how they were spiritually lost. He didn't just move from town to town and do miracles, but let his heart break, knowing he had what they needed. Do you see it? You and the people around you need Jesus.

Holy King, you remind me of who I am as I gaze at who you are. Even more, you call me into who you created me to be. Thank you.

Do you have a secret temptation or sin no one other than God knows about?

Friendly Friends

As Jesus was having dinner at Matthew's house, many tax collectors and "sinners" came and ate with Jesus and his followers. When the Pharisees saw this, they asked Jesus' followers, "Why does your teacher eat with tax collectors and sinners?"

MATTHEW 9:10–11 NCV

Among those whom Jesus called to be his twelve disciples, Matthew was definitely networked. We see it in how just as he began following Jesus, he decided to get his old friends together with his new friend. Even as some of the more popular and religious people in society came around to give Jesus a hard time for spending time with the rejects and sinners of society, the party went on.

Jesus had a way of turning an "us" and "them" crowd into a "we" thing. He always gave people a choice but worked hard to make sure that they could join into his mission on earth. It's something he still does even today, and as his disciples it's something we can also do. What if all through the next few days you were intentional about introducing the people in your life who don't know Jesus to your friends who do? It could mean not overlooking people you normally overlook, or even being kind and hospitable to a stranger. Who might get to know Jesus better because you decided to be a friendly friend?

Jesus, I want everyone I meet to meet you, and I mean everyone. Show me where to start today.

While Jesus was having dinner at Matthew's house, many tax collectors and sinners came and ate with him and his disciples. When the Pharisees saw this, they asked his disciples, "Why does your teacher eat with tax collectors and sinners?"

MATTHEW 9:10-11 NIV

When you hear the words "us versus them," what do you think or feel? When have felt most like an "us?" When have you felt most like a "them?"

Imagine what would happen if you asked questions like this on a regular basis. It could create the sort of pause that gives you just a few seconds of perspective before you only think of yourself or your current circle of friends. It's the revolutionary impact of simply loving our neighbor all throughout each day, by taking the time to consider them. While we may not always catch every need, we can be committed to giving it our best shot. Being a friendly friend is just that easy, just that human, and just that supernatural.

I probably walked by hundreds of people recently, Lord, who are always on your mind. What would it mean for them to be on my mind too? Teach me.

In what part of your life are you most tempted to treat other people like they're just scenery to whatever you feel is more important?

Fluff or Faith

"All those who stand before others and say they believe in me, I will say before my Father in heaven that they belong to me. But all who stand before others and say they do not believe in me, I will say before my Father in heaven that they do not belong to me."

MATTHEW 10:32-33 NCV

Do you know the difference between dying for your faith and living for your faith? Which one do you think would be more difficult to do? Some people around the world are actually faced with the hard reality of being threatened, or even killed, because they are followers of Jesus Christ. These people have to be ready, at any moment, to trust in the Lord with everything.

Other people around the world are faced with the oddly different and difficult challenge of trying to live a vibrant faith in the midst of an apathetic society. In this situation it can sometimes be easier just to go with the flow of the crowds and avoid getting serious in relationship to Jesus. It takes tremendous courage for a follower of Jesus to break out of this suppressed version of faith.

Lord, be completely honest with me—do I just show up for my faith in dramatic moments, or are we really on a daily journey and mission together?

"Everyone therefore who acknowledges me before others, I also will acknowledge before my Father in heaven; but whoever denies me before others, I also will deny before my Father in heaven."

MATTHEW 10:32-33 NRSV

Here's a fact: Wearing a sports jersey is easy. You can put one on and say, "Oh yeah, I'm totally a fan" yet not be able to name any of the players. Perhaps you support a team out of nostalgia, but that doesn't equal knowledge.

You've seen this in Christianity too. People like the faith they grew up with and want to honor it, assuming that tradition equals conviction. You may see in them a true desire to "go to heaven when they die" yet not see any true moments of transformation. Maybe when you seriously want to talk about God they don't want to. They may not even know why. Jesus called this out so we'd see the difference between Christian fluff and Christian faith. Even if we fool everyone around us, we can't fool him. It might be time to die to a tradition to experience life in Christ.

I have my favorite patterns and habits of living my faith, Lord. Show me which ones truly are a bridge to you, and which ones have become walls against you.

What are all the reasons you take part in church? Be brutally honest—celebrate what is worth celebrating, and address what is worth addressing.

153

The Stranger

Six days later, Jesus took with him Peter and James and his brother John and led them up a high mountain, by themselves. And he was transfigured before them, and his face shone like the sun, and his clothes became dazzling white.

MATTHEW 17:1-2 NRSV

Jesus is Swedish. Or perhaps Italian. Maybe some other random ethnicity. It all depends on which Nativity set you have under your tree at Christmas. Jesus is also muscular. Or perhaps thin. It could be he looks like a cross between your art teacher and your local coffee house barista. Again, it all depends on the artwork you saw of him growing up and presume is correct.

Whether your Jesus wears a blue sash or a red sash, sandals or bare feet, that Jesus isn't Jesus. In fact, one day Jesus showed his disciples who the real Jesus was—and for a brief moment, they were overwhelmed by his true glory. One of your greatest temptations will be to look to Jesus for what he can do for you instead of who he is. Reconsider that. Reconsider this stranger we all know.

Lord, be completely honest with me—do I just show up for my faith in dramatic moments, or are we really on a daily journey and mission together?

Six days later, Jesus took Peter, James, and John, the brother of James, up on a high mountain by themselves. While they watched, Jesus' appearance was changed; his face became bright like the sun, and his clothes became white as light.

MATTHEW 17:1-2 NCV

How many times in your life have you worn a blindfold? Count every random kids or youth ministry game where you tied one on. Remember every birthday party game involving candy-filled piñatas or paper donkeys. Whether you wore a blindfold for fun or for education, it's awkward to walk around wearing a visible symbol that you're not able to see. People really like to mess with you in these moments, don't they? Someone will pop up beside you and say, "Boo!" or randomly tickle you. It's enough to make you reconsider wearing the blindfold altogether.

Maybe this is why we don't know what to do with Jesus revealing himself beyond what we can naturally see. We know how to put on and take off blindfolds but can be awkward in owning our spiritual blindness. Jesus doesn't want to scare us or taunt us. He's trying to show us all of who he is. Ready to see?

Jesus, you are the Christ. You are the one and only Messiah. Can I somehow see you for the first time again?

What is your earliest memory of discovering who Jesus really is?

No Favoritism

"'You must love the LORD your God with all your heart, all your soul, all your mind, and all your strength…Love your neighbor as yourself.' No other commandment is greater than these."

MARK 12:30-31 NLT

Trying to understand or grow with God isn't easy, but it is simple. (You may have to reread that.) You might use one or three of the approaches Jesus mentioned while missing out on the others. Doing so means we end up missing out on a key way that our faith is to meant to be rooted. Even our best efforts can create blind spots.

Someone may have never really learned to love God with their mind because they first encountered him through a hands-on experience. Or someone else may have come to God through deep studying, and yet their faith is so intellectual that they've never truly worshipped Jesus from the depths of their soul. We all have a favorite way to follow the Lord. Jesus calls us to be all-in. Otherwise, something may rock one part of your world and you won't be familiar with knowing God there.

Father, I'd like to know you in every part of my life. Let's start where we know each other well and then work our way into some new areas together.

"'You must love him with all your heart and soul and mind and strength… You must love others as much as yourself.' No other commandments are greater than these."

MARK 12:30-31 TLB

You may be so familiar with this passage that it might be helpful to break some things down. For example, loving God with your heart means enjoying who he is and what he's done for you. It involves your deepest empathy for how he feels about people and things. It ultimately involves giving and receiving the deepest affection possible.

Loving God with your soul means passionately giving him your eternal self—the core you, along with the core direction of your life and any details that includes. Loving God with your mind involves focusing your thoughts on things above and not of this earth, including getting rid of lies and seeking out truth. Like enjoying good food out loud, may the world wholly know the goodness of God through you as you wholly value him.

There is no one else who deserves my attention like you do, Lord. Thank you for investing in me as I invest in you.

How might your preferred way of connecting with God be helpful, and in what ways might it be holding you back?

Heart and Soul

"A time is coming and has now come when the true worshipers will worship the Father in the Spirit and in truth, for they are the kind of worshipers the Father seeks."

JOHN 4:23 NIV

If you've ever tinkered on a piano, you may know the song "Chopsticks" which younger students play to gain some musical basic structure. Another song called "Heart and Soul" kicks this up a notch, involving at least two people who each play parts that help with the overall chord progression. It's a style that many musical hits of the 1950s and 1960s used.

We also need spiritual foundational structures for similar reasons. Worship is such a gift, for through it we discover the essentials of who God is so that we can build our lives on him. When he doesn't make sense to us mentally, our souls can engage him eternally in the here-and-now. When our hearts need to experience a deep emotion, we can do something with those feelings. This is the true duet of worship. If you worship him in spirit and in truth, things really take off and make music in the world around you.

Lord, show me through others the kind of relationship you want to have with me.

"The hour is coming, and now is, when the true worshipers will worship the Father in spirit and truth; for the Father is seeking such to worship Him."

JOHN 4:23 NKJV

One thing to be careful about with musical instruments is that strings are stretchable. Guitars can be wound down or wound up to make certain notes sound completely different. Pianos can get completely out of tune on the inside no matter how clean the keys look on the outside. You may think you're playing a G, when in reality it's an F.

The analogy couldn't be clearer—it's easy to let life stretch you out of tune with the Lord. In fact, you may (sadly) on occasion choose it, hoping that whatever F you strum, the G will sound okay. God is graceful, but he does hold us accountable. Worship is a unique reset, for by choosing to recognize who he is we set ourselves up to respond to him accordingly. Keep taking the time to tune your soul each day. It's essential if you want to hit life's true high notes.

Almighty Lord, may every inspiring song about you that I sing remind me of who you are, what you're capable of, and your hope for my life.

What was the last worship lyric that made you pause and (re) consider God?

War

> "The thief comes only to steal and kill and destroy;
> I came that they may have life, and have it abundantly."
>
> JOHN 10:10 NASB

There is always, always more going on than you realize.
In every experience, relationship, victory, setback,
opportunity... even in this very moment... life is more
than what you can perceive with your natural senses. The
supernatural realm that you can't see is truer to reality than
the earthly realm you can see.

Breaking through that is Jesus Christ, who offers you a full
life. He didn't come to institute religious burdens but to
proclaim life out of his cross and resurrection. While he
offers us transformation, Satan creates temptation. If the
devil can't keep you sinning or busy, know that he'll do
whatever he can to stand against you and others living in
Jesus' presence and power. Don't fail to recognize how many
problems in life are more than everyday issues. You're on the
battlefront of a war for the souls of the world. There is always
more going on than you realize.

*In the name, grace, and power of Jesus Christ, I declare to my
enemy, "Not today, Satan. Not any day."*

*"A thief comes only to steal and kill and destroy.
I have come so they may have life.
I want them to have it in the fullest possible way."*

JOHN 10:10 NASB

How wild would it be to see a football player run onto the field wearing a swimsuit? Or a hockey team to skate onto the ice with cotton candy fastened to their heads instead of helmets? These absurd examples just don't make sense for someone preparing to go all-in on a competition.

So why do so many Christians run into battle naked? Ephesians 6 describes the full armor of God we're called to wear—go on and look it up right now. Because chances are you may not have gone through a checklist today to ensure you were at your best against an enemy giving his worst. Our struggle in the war isn't against flesh and blood, but against Satan and his evil representatives. Our weapon isn't our willpower, but Jesus himself. Call upon him with all the protective assurances and offensive pathways he's given you to claim a victory today.

God of angel armies, suit me up. I don't want to drop my guard in the war, nor streak into battle spiritually naked. Win a soul through me this week as I prepare for it each morning.

Why do you think God hasn't yet given Satan the final punch? What is he waiting for? How might that involve you?

Here, There, Everywhere

"You will receive power when the Holy Spirit has come upon you, and you will be my witnesses in Jerusalem and in all Judea and Samaria, and to the end of the earth."

ACTS 1:8 ESV

Whatever your opinion is of yard sales, they have a way of moving things around town. They also tell a story of someone who isn't hanging onto their stuff anymore, from favorite hobbies, exercise equipment, and clothing that they want to pass on to others. Soon what was in one household can serve another household.

If you think even deeper, though, yard sales remind us how everything we own ultimately goes to someone else—whether on purpose or inadvertently by death. Only one thing you can see lasts forever—people. It's why Jesus told his disciples to get moving around town (and beyond) to tell his story. Just as his story interacts with your story, that story can interact with another person's story. Soon what was in your household can serve another household. What a gift! And we get to be a giver—here, there, and everywhere.

In the name, grace, and power of Jesus Christ, let me change this world for you, Lord.

> *"When the Holy Spirit comes to you, you will receive power. You will be my witnesses—in Jerusalem, in all of Judea, in Samaria, and in every part of the world."*
>
> ACTS 1:8 NCV

It's common for churches to have a missions department or ministry that ensures any relationships with missionaries in foreign countries are healthy. It's also about regional investments happening to bless the under-resourced. This is all great and well-needed. Be aware, though, that this doesn't cancel your own calling to be a missionary. As a follower of Jesus Christ, you're a part of what God is doing globally, starting right where you are.

This is not about guilt, but joy. This is not about religious activity, but spiritual expression. This is not about charity, but compassion, justice, and grace. This is about seeing the story of God get extended out of us as we make a personal investment here, there, and everywhere.

You sent someone into my life with your message, Jesus. Now I will carry your name and message to others.

Where is one place you know God wants you to be a missionary on a mission with him?

History

The church then had peace throughout Judea, Galilee, and Samaria, and it became stronger as the believers lived in the fear of the Lord. And with the encouragement of the Holy Spirit, it also grew in numbers.

ACTS 9:31 NLT

Think back to your earliest experiences with church. If you grew up with your family attending one, it might be hard to remember what it was like in the nursery or preschool classroom. Even if you didn't attend as a kid, though, you had some opinion of church throughout the years. The positive and negative experiences you had (or others in your life had) informed what you thought of it.

Now flip that and consider the potential for your church experience to impact others in a positive way. The words and experiences people have about church could be transformed by the words and experiences you share with them. What God allowed to happen in Acts 9 isn't just church history, it's "his story" of church. If we come together in awe and honor of Jesus, new people can come to know him. Don't just go to church, be the church.

In the name, grace, and power of Jesus Christ, let the church become stronger and grow in numbers.

The church everywhere in Judea, Galilee, and Samaria had a time of peace and became stronger. Respecting the Lord by the way they lived, and being encouraged by the Holy Spirit, the group of believers continued to grow.

ACTS 9:31 NCV

What's on your bedroom shelf now that has been on your shelf for years? Is it a favorite, comfortable stuffed animal you won't ever part with? Maybe a dusty souvenir you haven't thought about in a while? Odd how both can be right next to each other, huh?

The meaningful things in our lives strangely shift in importance, largely because we're always changing. Some things should remain, though, for better or for worse. Church is God's idea for a community meant to draw them all together and reach more in the process. Will you stick with church, for better or for worse? Or will it collect dust in the years to come? Sort this out now so that you're not surprised in the future by letting his story become history.

Jesus, you died for us to not only become Christians but to become your Church. Show me how to sacrifice and invest in it like you do.

The only perfect church is heaven itself, yet the current imperfect one still matters to God. How will it matter to you in the coming years?

Options

As I walked around and looked carefully at your objects of worship, I even found an altar with this inscription: to an unknown god. So you are ignorant of the very thing you worship —and this is what I am going to proclaim to you.

ACTS 17:23 NIV

As the apostle Paul lived as a missionary from one place to the next, he ended up in Athens, Greece. There the people had put up altars to try to "cover" themselves spiritually. By giving a shout out to any random god they may have missed worshipping, they hoped that god would show them favor. It's like when someone today talks about believing in a higher power without taking the time to figure out who the genuine higher power is.

We can pick on people for doing this or take a much different approach. In fact, our response impacts the world's response. If the church ignores the world, the world will ignore the church; if the church doesn't shape culture, culture will shape the church; if the church condemns culture, culture will condemn the church; but if the church redeems the culture, the culture will redeem the church.

God, thank you for making yourself known. How can I help?

As I passed along and observed the objects of your worship, I found also an altar with this inscription: To the unknown god. What therefore you worship as unknown, this I proclaim to you.

ACTS 17:23 ESV

Can you picture the apostle Paul proclaiming who Jesus is to a crowd of people who believe in multiple gods? Keep in mind that this proclamation came from a guy who once found Christianity to be offensive to his Jewish beliefs. Through God's help, Paul realized that Christianity didn't start in the first century from misguided humans, it is a story rooted before time.

It may be a struggle to show different Christian perspectives to the people around you, especially if they're more interested in debates or sound bytes. Take a cue from Paul. Find one thing someone believes in that's a start in the right direction. Honor them for that, and then begin revealing who Jesus is. Perhaps what someone believes is off-base, but their attempt to believe in something beyond themselves isn't.

Holy Lord, thank you for how you brought someone into my life to let me know who you are. Grant me the wisdom to find an opportunity in any conversation I'm in to help others clearly encounter you.

What is one right thing that someone you know doesn't yet believe in Jesus currently believes?

Awkward Awesome

God shows his great love for us in this way:
Christ died for us while we were still sinners.

ROMANS 5:8 NCV

For a moment, remember a time when you were really selfish. You may have thought you deserved something and didn't care if it was right or wrong. Perhaps you crossed a line that you now regret. Even further, consider a temptation you almost gave into. Maybe one you did give into.

Now, own that God saw it. He saw you. He saw what was in your heart. He saw your intentional carelessness. He saw you reject him. And, right then, right there, he loved you at his best. It was while you were a sinner that Christ died for you. Not just to be in your life when you obey, but in your selfish, sinful choices. (If you feel good because you can't think of a time you've ever been bad, Christ died for your pride too.) Stay humble. Embrace his grace.

Jesus, on my worst day you gave me your best day. I am so thankful to you for the cross.

God shows his love for us in that while we were still sinners,
Christ died for us.

ROMANS 5:8 ESV

Try to set aside your calendar for the day. Pretend like you don't have one. And as you do, peel off the expectations or label put on you, be it athlete, artist, alternative, or otherwise. This exercise is so that you can be you—bare and open before God. Are you there yet? If not, go back and do it again. Rinse and repeat.

Once you do, consider what's in your heart. Deep down, what longs to come out of you? What keeps you up at night? What do you have imaginary conversations about? What prompts you to groan because it hasn't completely happened yet? What won't you give up on? This deep dream of yours is a taste of the deep dream Jesus has for you. He pursued you when it wasn't easy. He pushed through the awkward, so you can get to the awesome.

God, today I ask for help claiming the new life you offer me.
Help me not to hold onto anything untrue that keeps me from
what is true.

If Jesus was physically before you right now, what is one thing he would tell you or do? Why?

Unexpected Example

Be imitators of me, as I am of Christ.

1 CORINTHIANS 11:1 NRSV

Some of what you know about porcupines may not be true. Cartoons portray them shooting pointy quills at others, but in truth those sharp needles just pop off easily when touched. As other animals bump into them or attack, they're prodded in another direction. Porcupines also have soft hair. It's not what we think about them first, though, because of how their quills stand up when the animal is threatened.

For all that bad press, porcupines remind us that we can't recklessly do what we want without eventually getting poked for it. Paul learned the art of this. While he was previously known for sharp words against Christians, he became a church leader worth following. If other Christians lived recklessly, he poked them back to Jesus. He also had a soft heart to be a solid example. His life was like an arrow pointing to Jesus.

Lord, you're truly, truly great. May my life receive that and share it. I know I'll never be perfect, but I can be a good example.

Follow my example, as I follow the example of Christ.

1 CORINTHIANS 11:1 NCV

It can feel overwhelming to be an example. People commonly run from the idea for that reason. If no one will step up, it's no wonder the world keeps falling down. What does this practically look like, though? Maybe it means you choose faithfulness where others settle or stop. Or you continually let God reorganize your priorities, so you're involved with things that give life instead of steal life. There's also seemingly natural temptations we face down, like coasting on your skills and charm at the expense of your soul... or letting others do hard work we refuse to do.

We can't be Jesus, but we can become attached to Jesus. And a church of people trying to help one another become faithful to the right things will change the world in all the right ways. Be an unexpected example.

When I'm weak, Lord, you're strong. And when I'm strong in you, others who feel weak find strength. Help me honor you in all my ways.

What is one thing you'd love to discover others do because of your example?

gifted

I want you to understand about spiritual gifts.

1 CORINTHIANS 21:1 NCV

Are you open to some revealing questions? Pay attention to your answer, but also your emotions and thoughts.

What are things you enjoy doing, but don't necessarily do well?

What are things you don't enjoy doing, but tend to do well?

What are things you enjoy doing, and tend to do well?

What are things you have that you don't mind sharing with others?

What are things you don't have, but if you did you'd share with others?

What are things you don't have, and if you did you wouldn't share with others?

What are things you have, but don't want to share with others?

Now go back and answer the questions again. Be intentionally slower this time. Notice how you've been gifted. Pay attention to what you overlook.

Dear Lord, you've wonderfully made me to be full of wonder. Turn every gift in me, on me, or around me into a gift to others.

Concerning spiritual gifts, brothers and sisters,
I do not want you to be uninformed.

1 CORINTHIANS 12:1 NRSV

Sometimes we forget the choice that Jesus made when it came to his life mission. Aren't you glad he didn't say, "I don't do crosses. Got something else?" We may not naturally have that kind of bravery, but supernaturally are gifted by the Holy Spirit to do what we don't think we can do. That's why it's important to submit to his leadership and presence within us as Christians, or else we'll focus on all the excuses of not doing what he's asking us to do instead of claiming how he's empowered us to do it.

As you sort out your life mission with God, it will be important to realize the spiritual gifts he's given you. Galatians 5:22-23 talks about how he gifts us all the same internally, while 1 Corinthians 12 and Romans 12 cite the unique gifts that different Christians have to add to God's mission. He's not calling you to be someone you're not to tell others who he is, but he does want you to be(come) yourself.

How have you gifted me, Lord? And how can I grow in those gifts?
Lead me. Mold me. Use me.

What might be a spiritual gift you have? How do you know?

glocal

God placed all things under his feet and appointed him to be head over everything for the church, 23 which is his body, the fullness of him who fills everything in every way.

EPHESIANS 1:22-23 NIV

The word glocal references how everything that happens globally affects you locally, and everything that affects you locally affects others globally. For example, if your region supplies the world with blueberries but a massive storm destroys the local fields, then stores need to find other suppliers. All that money goes to new places and affects people's lives.

Similarly, there are two types of ways to think about the church: "The uppercase C" Church: All Christians are a part of the Church at large—God's people scattered throughout the globe who advance his kingdom in ways that transcend any personal or local emphasis. "The lowercase c" church: Jesus established the first local church through imperfect people, and so as we regularly gather, we recognize the organic flaws in each other as we do life together, follow Jesus, and make him known. Put all of that together. How is God calling you to be a glocal Christian?

Father, may your kingdom come, your will be done, all over the earth, as it is in heaven.

He has put all things under his feet and has made him the head over all things for the church, which is his body, the fullness of him who fills all in all.

EPHESIANS 1:22-23 NRSV

The first Christians never defined themselves by a building or by a location. While at times in letters written to them their city was referenced, they all understood themselves to be a collective community and movement. Gathering together was a daily priority, but so was spreading the good news under the power of Christ.

You have the means to do this glocally in person, by phone, and online in ways other generations haven't. It all comes down to if you limit yourself to "going to church" instead of seeing yourself as "being the Church." This is something special that crosses all ethnic, cultural, socioeconomic, generational, and political lines. Each local church is made up of believers who worship, pray, learn, encourage, and connect—all so that they can better go out and change the whole world, one step at a time.

Sovereign God, what is life like for believers in other parts of the world? What's it like for the people in front of me? Give me a compassionate heart for them all.

If every Christian had a glocal view of Christianity, what would be different?

Think about It

Whatever is true, whatever is noble, whatever is right, whatever is pure, whatever is lovely, whatever is admirable—if anything is excellent or praiseworthy—think about such things.

PHILIPPIANS 4:8 NIV

All throughout your life, you've had inklings of what other people are thinking. Even if they didn't say a thing, it was obvious what was going through their heads. You intuitively knew they were angry, happy, upset, thankful, and so on based on an inner awareness you couldn't quantify.

If that's the case, then what do you think people have perceived about your thought life over the years? Every personal desire, rant, or joy was spilling out of you somehow. What if that also includes the temptations you struggle with? Philippians 4:8 dares us to think about what we think about. By choosing things that are pure and godly, we better set ourselves up for a purer, godly thought life. If we instead focus on lies, spooky entertainment, sexual images, and more, we set ourselves to keep thinking on those things. What do you want in you? What do you want spilling out of you? Think about it.

Father, may your kingdom come, your will be done, all over the earth, as it is in heaven.

Fix your thoughts on what is true and good and right. Think about things that are pure and lovely, and dwell on the fine, good things in others. Think about all you can praise God for and be glad about.

PHILIPPIANS 4:8 TLB

One of the consequences of sin is the memory of it. God is willing and able to separate us from our sins through Jesus' sacrifice on the cross, but we tend to take a more human approach. Many Christians keep kicking themselves over and over again for things that happened years ago. Others run so quickly away from their past that they never own what happened. Somewhere in between these two approaches, the Lord invites us to be honest and transformed.

God also wants you to be free of accusations you or his enemy put into your head. Philippians 4:8 lets us in on the secret— filling our minds with God's thoughts and truth. We will regularly, unconsciously focus on the worst things life has to offer—unless we intentionally, consciously look for the best things Jesus has to offer. Be innocent of evil and excellent in what is good.

Good, good Father… you are kind, caring, and full of wisdom on what you want for me. I confess my temptation to drift, but also confess my desire to be anchored in you.

When was the last time, if ever, that you deliberately invited God to be the Lord of your thought life?

Backstory

The Son is the image of the invisible God,
the firstborn over all creation.

COLOSSIANS 1:15 NIV

Throughout the centuries, Christians and non-Christians
alike have had half-ideas about Jesus rather than truly getting
to know him. Many commonly view him as a law enforcer,
and so their faith is like being a driver followed by a police
officer—they're nervous of any behavior that may lead to a
ticket, trying to be as steady as possible while being fearful
they're about to get busted.

Search Jesus' backstory for perspective on that. He has always
existed, but he came to earth to live among us for thirty-three
years. The first three decades of that involves being a working
man. Then one day he began his public ministry after being
baptized. Despite temptations and accusations, he did not
stop or hold back. He showed who God is by showing us who
he is, so that we can learn who we really are. His backstory
reveals your future-story. Which raises the question: Is Jesus
out to give tickets, or to protect and serve?

Infinite Savior, your love can't be measured, yet it is somehow
clear. Just as you have no beginning or end, I trust that your love
for me has no limits.

He is the image of the invisible God,
the firstborn of all creation.

COLOSSIANS 1:15 NRSV

Jesus Christ is the more than a historical figure or "great teacher." Jesus is and has always been a Person of the Trinity. He walked the earth as a man but was more than a man. Through his life, death, and resurrection, he offers us a future in heaven and transformation now. Pause to take that in and enjoy it. Seriously, just let yourself enjoy it. Since Jesus showed us who he is, we can set down our masks, our pretending, our shame, and our guilt.

In a world that often feels hypocritical and guarded, this is good news. Jesus created his church to enjoy community as we grow with him. Instead of wasting energy being fake or making up rules the Creator never created, every person can get a clean slate, share their burdens, and find healing for hurts. In doing so, we reveal a glimpse of the Savior and his backstory even today.

How do you do it, God? You're perfect and unchanging yet involved and interacting with me in the mucky moments of my life. Teach me to see you with a larger perspective that is somehow just as personal.

What is one question you'd like to ask Jesus to try to understand his identity better?

Things Above

Set your minds on things that are above,
not on things that are on earth.

COLOSSIANS 3:2 NRSV

Make no mistake about it: you are either a missionary or a mission field. God calls you to follow Christ by responding to him with your entire life. We're together challenged to be the Church—a growing community of people and God who help lost people become disciples of Jesus. This inherently requires that we stop seeing things through a natural point of view. To start connecting the dots for other people to get back into a right relationship with God, we need to see those dots and gaps. This is what can make us missionaries who wake up others to the hope and truth of Jesus Christ.

If you say no to all of this, however, then you become a mission field, meaning someone will have to come after you and nudge you out of your comfort zone. That'll get awkward, by the way. So, are you a missionary or a mission field? What does your thought life reveal?

God, help me to be a missionary and not a mission field. I want to respond to you with my life and share your love with others.

Think only about the things in heaven,
not the things on earth.

COLOSSIANS 3:2 NCV

Life passes by, moment by moment. If you've ever been stuck at a set of train tracks, you've felt this as the train passed by car-by-car. Sometimes it feels like the train will never end. But what if you had a friend in a helicopter who could see the whole thing at once? You could call him (or vice-versa) and he'd tell you what to see and expect. It would give you perspective on what you couldn't see.

When we pray to God or worship him in truth, we enter into his birds-eye perspective on what we're feeling in the trenches. The community we live in is our place to connect with him and how he's active in the lives of others. By dialing into him daily, we become able to reclaim seemingly ordinary moments into extraordinary ones. God dares each of us to "bring it," but first we have to "see it." Attach yourselves to Jesus and the things above, wherever you are.

Father, I know all too well the disconnect between what I feel and what you know. Yet I know that you are with me. Show me what I don't yet see about you, life, myself, others, and my life mission.

How would you describe the plans God has for you?

Opportunities

Be wise in the way you act toward outsiders; make the most of every opportunity. Let your conversation be always full of grace, seasoned with salt, so that you may know how to answer everyone.

COLOSSIANS 4:5-6 NIV

The circles of people and communities in which we live, work, study, play, and grow are more than random places we've ended up in. God has a plan for us there to invest in the individuals we see every day. He's already working in their lives and we get to join him in it. It's like all around us are lives that are like sketches on a canvas. Each person is penciled in, yet without any splashes of Jesus on them just yet. We need insight to know what is the right way to paint, otherwise we're just throwing up random colors and hoping it looks good.

That's where wisdom comes in—specifically, us taking a moment to seek it in every opportunity. What we say and how we say it could be a combination of our preparation and the Holy Spirit's intervention. Consider your day and the ways Jesus might be able to brighten up each life through yours.

Father God, what would it look like for me to make the most of every opportunity today? I choose in advance to do whatever you show me.

Walk in wisdom toward outsiders, making the best use of the time.
Let your speech always be gracious, seasoned with salt, so that
you may know how you ought to answer each person.

COLOSSIANS 4:5-6 NIV

A freshman girl stands at a bus stop. She's with other teenagers on the first day of school and is obviously dressed to impress. Yet she's standing five feet away from the other kids. With her right arm cocked on her hip, her left hand is grabbing a strap on her backpack for security. What does she need to hear from Jesus?

A senior is talking with his date about an upcoming dance. Due to new school standards on inappropriate dancing, several students have organized an alternative dance where they can do what they want without getting in trouble for it. His girlfriend tells him that she doesn't want to go to the new dance, but he's torn because he told his friends that he'd go to support their rebellion against the school. What does he need to hear from Jesus? These are everyday life situations. But aren't they also spiritual opportunities?

Lord, I am sorry for any missed opportunities where I didn't speak up or into someone's life on your behalf. Show me the next conversation you want me to be part of.

What is happening right in front of you? What does that person need to hear from Jesus?

Training

While bodily training is of some value, godliness is of value in every way, as it holds promise for the present life and also for the life to come.

1 TIMOTHY 4:8 ESV

If you walk into any professional weightlifting gym, local school athletic training area, or community center, you'll quickly see their selection of training equipment. Some may have worn out machines that were purchased decades ago, while others use the latest state-of-the-art resources. Despite any difference in quality, they all can help you physically grow in some way.

This same value is at play in any church that is foundationally based on Jesus and the truth of the Bible. Perhaps some churches look older or newer in their approaches than others, but wherever the Scriptures are faithfully opened there is a chance to grow in your faith. Even if they sing songs you aren't into, they're into the Jesus that you're into. Value this. There are already way too many cynics and critics who put down what they don't like. Grab hold of what's before you and start working on your soul. It's training day.

Your blessings for me, God, are there, waiting for me to tap into them. Use them to train me and strengthen me in the deepest places of my soul.

Training your body helps you in some ways, but serving God helps you in every way by bringing you blessings in this life and in the future life, too.

1 TIMOTHY 4:8 NCV

By now someone (if not several people) have tried to teach you the importance of taking care of your physical body. If you don't, over time you'll wear down and end up with a gut full of weight. If you do, you'll likely end up strong and energetic, ready for life. The same principle is true spiritually. When we don't train our faith, it gets weak and weighted down. But if we make the most of the chance to get stronger each day, we're better prepared to face down our enemy.

This is also why we're to take care of the body of believers God has given us. We will at times get on each other's nerves, but because we're committed to Christ, we develop the love and courage with one another to work things out. Urge each other with the intensity of a pro athlete into God's mission. Train well. Train together.

Lord, I know I will be presented with opportunities to be uncertain or quit on the things that matter as life hits me hard. What can I do in this season to prepare for it?

When was a time you felt ready or trained for a challenge presented to you spiritually?

Leader

Let no one despise your youth, but be an example to the believers in
word, in conduct, in love, in spirit, in faith, in purity.

1 TIMOTHY 4:12 NKJV

You are a leader. Yes, you. No matter if you're timid, bold,
lazy or courageous, you're a leader above someone, below
someone, or right next to someone. You influence others in
how they see life and make decisions. Think about how you've
been led in life. You've learned what to say and what not to say
in social situations based on how others informally treated
you for it. You've also told others your opinion, influencing
them back.

Everyone is a leader, whether they realize it or not. What
would happen if you realized it? What if you were a light,
brightening up every situation with intentional words and
actions? What if your example inspired others to live for
Jesus like you are? How could your social media platform,
classroom, or job become mission fields? You are a leader.
Yes, you.

Make me a servant-leader, Jesus. As I step into your footsteps,
may they be that much more noticeable for others to step into.

Let no one despise you for your youth, but set the believers an example in speech, in conduct, in love, in faith, in purity.

1 TIMOTHY 4:12 ESV

School mascots are rallying symbols meant to bring everyone together. In some places you'll see it as a colorful drawing painted on a wall. Other times it's represented in a costume someone wears to pump up a crowd. All of this serves as motivation for athletes and spectators alike, reminding them they're a part of something collective.

Your life is like a mascot for the Lord in this way. You can lead people toward something of worth, like a worthy cause or important decision. Even more important, you can cheer them on to embrace an eternity with Jesus Christ. They'll also watch you if you go backward. It's possible for you to be so discouraging that others follow that example. Even if you think you're being neutral, you can become neutralizing. It's time to lead.

Lord, help me every morning to see you and help others to see you. As that happens, may our faith in you exponentially deepen and widen.

Who are five people you know you influence in some way, even casually?

The Whole Truth

*All Scripture is inspired by God and is useful for teaching, for
showing people what is wrong in their lives, for correcting faults,
and for teaching how to live right.*

2 Timothy 3:16 NCV

A teenage girl walking out of school noticed an art pad on
the ground. She guessed that someone had accidentally
dropped it, but she didn't have time to turn it into the office.
She threw it into her bag and went home, uninterested in
the drawings inside. That night she met some friends for ice
cream. They struck up a chat with a new boy who had recently
moved to town for the great art program at their school. He
was frustrated, though, because he'd lost his art pad after
visiting the school to register. Immediately the girl perked
up, realizing that she had the boy's art pad. She told him she'd
bring it to school the next day.

Something odd happened that night. She found herself more
interested in looking through the art pad than she did before.
Nothing had changed in the drawings, except she now knew
the artist. She thought by looking at his work she might get to
know something about him that she didn't yet know. Where
do you see yourself in this story as an analogy to your time
with the Bible?

*You made it possible for us to read your words every day, Lord.
I pray for those who may overlook this, including me.*

*All Scripture is inspired by God and is useful to teach us what is
true and to make us realize what is wrong in our lives. It corrects
us when we are wrong and teaches us to do what is right.*

2 TIMOTHY 3:16 NLT

The Bible is a key way we get to know who God is, who we
are, and what our life mission is. It is God-breathed, written
through imperfect people to share his perfect message.
Through it we discover a supernatural network of ordinary
people in a relationship with an extraordinary God and one
another. All of this is so that we can each grow into the same
opportunity with the Lord and share it with others. Why do so
many Bibles collect dust? Why do Christians treat them more
like trophies on a shelf than food for the soul?

Instead of feeling nothing but guilt, think about it this way.
What is one thing you wish people really knew about you?
What would you do to help them know this? And how does
that compare to what God has done in creating the Bible? Dig
into the whole truth, and not just the parts you're already into.

*Creator of everything, you make yourself known not only through
creation but through your Bible. I want to know you, more than
ever before.*

What is something from the Bible that is important for you to
personally memorize?

Imperfect

What is causing the quarrels and fights among you? Don't they come from the evil desires at war within you?

JAMES 4:1 NLT

Jesus Christ perfectly created the Church using imperfect people. On its best days, a church reveals the true colors of God's kingdom in an otherwise dim and gray world. We do this by putting God first, letting him guide our relationships and sharing all he's given us to lovingly restore every person, family, and way of life back to him. It eventually impacts the community (and beyond).

On its worst days, a church thinks it looks like that but is actually something uglier. Instead of letting Christ actually change us, we try to look like he has. Rather than working out relational tensions, we try to appear right. Any resources we have are used as a power play, for we hold back on serving or giving until things are how we like them. As outsiders look at us, they say, "That's why I won't ever be a part of a church." Once again, Jesus Christ perfectly created the Church using imperfect people. What do you think of that?

Father, I'm so sorry for the way I might get grumpy or critical about my church family. Please forgive me for my attitude when things don't go my way.

What is the source of quarrels and conflicts among you? Is not the source your pleasures that wage war in your members?

JAMES 4:1 NASB

Every church has good days and bad days, as well as best days and worst days. For some strange reason, God chose us to be his number one plan in this world, knowing we would blow it over and over again. We will have to give each other grace and forgiveness on a regular basis. After all, if you want a church to love you despite your imperfections and sins, shouldn't you love it in the same way?

A warning along these lines: to speak against a church because you don't like what they're doing is dangerous ground. If the Spirit of God is working there even in the slightest bit, you run the risk of critiquing him. Perhaps things are not happening in a way you like, but what if the change is less about the church and more about your attitude? Part of your life's mission involves adding to the church, not subtracting from it. You'll be imperfect at this, just as others will be imperfect toward you. Are you willing to go all in on the church like Jesus did anyway?

Lord, lead me to appreciate your faith in your church. You really are in control and I trust you.

What are several ways that being a part of an imperfect local church has blessed you?

Names

Beloved, I urge you as aliens and exiles to abstain from the desires of the flesh that wage war against the soul. Conduct yourselves honorably among the Gentiles, so that, though they malign you as evildoers, they may see your honorable deeds and glorify God when he comes to judge.

1 PETER 2:11–12 NRSV

It's one thing to know someone's face, and another thing to know their story. Every day in every week in every month, you run into some of the same strangers on a regular basis. It's the person you pay at the gas station, the stranger at the restaurant table next to you, the teenager who walks into his house the same time you walk into yours. Maybe you've never taken the time introduce yourself. Maybe you have.

Who are these people you regularly rub shoulders with in your community? These are the real people where you live, where you work, where you exercise, where you study, where you shop, where you relax, where you drive, and so on. By you getting to know their name, how can they eventually get to know and call on the name of Jesus?

Jesus, who is near me regularly whom I overlook? Give me the courage to get to know them.

Dear friends, you are like foreigners and strangers in this world.
I beg you to avoid the evil things your bodies want to do that fight
against your soul. People who do not believe are living all around
you and might say that you are doing wrong. Live such good lives
that they will see the good things you do and will give glory to God
on the day when Christ comes again.

1 PETER 2:11-12 NCV

If you were going to a new country, you would study up on it,
including its symbols and entertainment. You'd know you were
a stranger yet want to make sure you could fit into the culture
somehow. You'd think about how to navigate everything from
restaurants to entertainment to going to the bathroom.

We don't tend to take this approach as Christians, though.
We treat this world as if it's our home instead of a temporary
home. That's like thinking the hotel you stay at on vacation
is your permanent residence. Imagine the impact of naming
things appropriately. How would that change how you live,
who you live for, and if you'd help others find their way home?

I'm a cultural alien to this world, Lord. I feel like I'll be here so
long that I want to treat it like home. But my citizenship is in
heaven. I'm claiming that address now.

What is the end-all, be-all question that will help you see that
this world isn't the end-all, be-all everything?

Giving and Receiving

"Give, and you will receive. Your gift will return to you in full—pressed down, shaken together to make room for more, running over, and poured into your lap. The amount you give will determine the amount you get back."

LUKE 6:38 NLT

It's easy for us to get this backwards in life. "I'll be kind to them if they're kind to me. I'll forgive and move on if they forgive me first." In other words, we think once we receive, then we will give. We withhold our love waiting to see how others will respond. But the ways of the kingdom of God are opposite to ways of the world.

Jesus implores us to start with giving. To open our hearts with generosity. To avoid condemning and judging others, even those who have condemned or judged us. To be the first to forgive. The way of Jesus is self-sacrificial love with no guarantee of being loved by people in return. Keep your heart open to giving today and be ready for all you will receive from God as a result.

Heavenly Father, help me to start with giving today and lay aside my expectations of receiving. I trust you to take my gift and do something magnificent with it.

> *"Give generously and generous gifts will be given back to you,*
> *shaken down to make room for more. Abundant gifts will pour out*
> *upon you with such an overflowing measure that it will run over*
> *the top! Your measurement of generosity becomes the measurement*
> *of your return."*

LUKE 6:38 TPT

Our God is a lavish and extravagant giver. He doesn't hold
back his love from us requiring a response from us first.
Instead, Jesus gave up his life for us when our hearts were
hardened and rebellious against him. He died for those who
would never love him in return. The way of Jesus is to give,
even if there's no guarantee of receiving.

God's desire is that his people would reflect his heart on this
earth. He longs for us to love with that same extravagance.
The beautiful promise of this passage is that there is great
blessing on the other side of giving. When we love the
world with Jesus' heart, we will be blessed beyond our
comprehension.

Lord Jesus, I want to love the world with your heart. Help me to be
a giver first.

What is God asking you to give today?

Right with God

Since we have been made right in God's sight by faith, we have peace with God because of what Jesus Christ our Lord has done for us.

ROMANS 5:1 NIV

When we compare our own lives to the perfect life of Jesus, it can be easy to get sucked into the shame cycle. How can we ever measure up? How can we ever be good enough? Compared to Jesus, God must be disappointed in us, right?

Wrong. God's will has always been for you to have peace with him. He longs for you to know that when he looks at you, his heart swells with love for you. Hear these words over your life today: God is not disappointed with you. You are right with God, not because of your human effort at being good, but because of the life, death, and resurrection of Jesus Christ.

Jesus, thank you for all you have done to make me right with God. Help me to stand firm in the reality that I have peace with you because of your love and sacrifice.

Since we have been made right with God by our faith, we have peace with God. This happened through our Lord Jesus Christ.

ROMANS 5:1 NCV

How often do we feel like our lives are the farthest thing from together? Even on our best days, we still fail to be all that God has called us to be. We hurt others and ourselves, and we turn our hearts away from God.

But we can rejoice in the incredible truth that in Christ we have it all together. God looks at us through the lens of Christ, which means he sees us as fit for him, clean and pure. Our weaknesses and flaws don't change God's view of us. We simply enter into this reality through faith in what Christ has done for us.

Lord Jesus, I rejoice today knowing that I have it all together in you. I set my heart on trusting I am right with you in Christ.

Do you see yourself in the same way God sees you?

Privileged

Because of our faith, Christ has brought us into this place of undeserved privilege where we now stand, and we confidently and joyfully look forward to sharing God's glory.

ROMANS 5:2 NLT

Privilege is a hot button topic in our culture these days. The socioeconomic status a person is born into can affect their ability to succeed in life. People criticize others for their unawareness of the privilege that helps them get a leg up in life. Privileged people work hard to avoid the stigma of the privilege they were born into.

God's design has always been that you step into your place as one of his privileged children. Because of Christ, we can stand in confident joy knowing our Father, the Creator of heaven and earth, has given us this undeserved privilege. You have access to all the benefits and rewards of children of God. Love, joy, peace, grace, and purpose to name a few. Stand confident in this reality today.

God, thank you that you have made a way for me to stand in the place of undeserved privilege before you. Help me receive all the gifts you want to give me as your child.

Who through our faith has brought us into that blessing of God's grace that we now enjoy. And we are happy because of the hope we have of sharing God's glory.

ROMANS 5:2 NCV

Are there areas of your life where you have closed the door to God and pushed him away? His door always stands wide open, inviting all who would say yes to him to come. Throw open the doors of your heart to Jesus today, inviting him into every dark corner and hidden place.

We don't worship a God of cramped spaces, small living, and restriction. He has designed you to jump for joy and run in vast fields of freedom. This freedom comes through letting him in. A life surrendered to Christ is nothing short of free and glorious.

Lord, help me to fully open the door of my heart to you. I trust that you have good things in store for me.

What gifts does God want to give you as one of his privileged children?

Refined

We can rejoice, too, when we run into problems and trials, for we know that they help us develop endurance. And endurance develops strength of character, and character strengthens our confident hope of salvation.

ROMANS 5:3-4 NLT

When something goes wrong in life, it's so easy to respond with complaints, frustration, or a whole other slew of human emotions. But this passage turns the tables on our perspective of troubles. When we walk with Christ there is another way to approach life's challenges: choosing to rejoice.

It is only through adversity that character is developed in us. In other words, we are formed more and more to be like Christ when we walk through suffering. When your next problem in life surfaces, look to Christ. Trust that he will use this situation to make you more like him. You will come out shining on the other side.

Lord Jesus, thank you that you endured great suffering because of the joy on the other side. Help me to rejoice in my troubles knowing you're refining me.

We also have joy with our troubles, because we know that these troubles produce patience. And patience produces character, and character produces hope.

ROMANS 5:3-4 NCV

Hope is a powerful substance that keeps us going in life. We all have hopes and dreams for our future. Oftentimes our hopes can have names, faces, and specific scenarios attached to them. But when things don't go as planned, it can be easy to lose hope and perspective of what God is doing in it all.

This passage describes hope as keeping alert for whatever God will do next. Even in disappointments, we can trust that God is still working behind the scenes. He is not standing passively by. He is developing patience and character in us. If you're in a trial, keep watch for God to move in your situation. Keep your hopes up.

Lord, I trust that you're using the trials in my life to make me more like Jesus. Help me watch for whatever you will do next.

What is God forming in you during this trial?

Alert Expectancy

Hope does not put us to shame, because God's love has been poured out into our hearts through the Holy Spirit, who has been given to us.

ROMANS 5:5 NIV

If you've ever hoped for something that didn't come to pass, you're not alone. Life can be full disappointments and setbacks. But when our hope is securely in Christ, we are promised that this hope will never leave us shamed, saddened or disappointed. Instead of shame, God gives us the gift of the Holy Spirit. And there is a very real and tangible love available to us in the Spirit.

If you ever struggle with doubting God's love for you, remember that you have the Holy Spirit dwelling inside of you. If you have surrendered your life to Jesus, the Spirit of God lives in you. And through the Spirit, God wants to lavish you with his love in even deeper measure. Ask him to fill you again with his love today.

Heavenly Father, thank you for the gift of the Holy Spirit living in me. Fill me up again and open my heart to receive greater measures of your love for me.

This hope will never disappoint us, because God has poured out his love to fill our hearts. He gave us his love through the Holy Spirit, whom God has given to us.

ROMANS 5:5 NCV

Have you ever felt like everyone around you is living their best life and you're just sitting back missing out on all the fun? Maybe you have fallen victim to FOMO, or the fear of missing out. There is good news knowing that when we place our hope in Christ, this hope isn't going to leave us feeling like we have been shortchanged or like we have missed out.

Placing your hope in Christ is the best thing that could ever happen to you. Your small act of faith opens the door to his enormous generosity that is greater than your heart can receive or your mind can begin to understand. Open your heart today to receive everything he wants to pour into your life.

Heavenly Father, thank you that in you I never have to be disappointed. I place my faith in Christ again today. Help me receive everything you want to give me.

What does God want to pour into your life today through the Holy Spirit?

Hope in the Desert

Even the wilderness and desert will be glad in those days.
The wasteland will rejoice and blossom with spring crocuses.
Yes, there will be an abundance of flowers and singing and joy!

ISAIAH 35:1-2 NLT

If you've spent any time traveling in a desert land, you know that heat can steal life quickly. If you don't come prepared with a water supply on a hike in the desert, you're in trouble. A desert elicits feelings of hopelessness and despair. But even in desert land, Isaiah paints the picture that God is the great restorer.

If you have found yourself in a spiritual desert or wilderness, overwhelmed by a sense of despair, fear, or hopelessness, you can place your trust in Jesus. He is the one who made all things out of nothing. He'll take your brokenness and bring hope and restoration. Embrace the promise of singing and joy on the other side of the desert. Hold onto hope that God will bring beauty out of your wilderness season.

Jesus, thank you that you are the great restorer. I place my trust in your restoration work in my life.

The desert and the parched land will be glad;
the wilderness will rejoice and blossom.
Like the crocus, it will burst into bloom;
it will rejoice greatly and shout for joy.

ISAIAH 35:1-2 NIV

God has always had the desire to restore the broken places in your life and bring new life and new hope. This is work that Jesus loves to do in you. If there are areas of your life that feel like a desert or parched land, you need a touch of God's restoration work.

Are there seeds in your heart lying dormant, just waiting for the Spirit of God to breath on them again? Are there hopes that God has placed in you that you're struggling to hold onto? The time is coming for these hopes to burst forth into full bloom. Ask God to restore hope to your heart and just wait for what he is going to do with your desert.

Lord, I give you permission to search my heart for the areas where I have lost hope of restoration. Take my sadness and turn it into joy.

What area of your life needs God's restoration work?

Take Heart

Say to those with fearful hearts,
"Be strong, and do not fear,
for your God is coming to destroy your enemies.
He is coming to save you."

ISAIAH 35:4 NLT

It can be easy to place our focus on the things that threaten to steal our life and joy. Sickness, death, depression, despair, fear, insecurity—the list goes on. We have a lot of enemies standing against us. But Isaiah foretells the coming of a Messiah that would destroy our enemies. And he has already come.

If you are walking in fear, the good news is that Jesus has come to save you. You can stand strong and firm knowing that Jesus' saving work on the cross has dismantled the weapons the enemy uses against you. Fear does not need to have a grip on you any longer. Your God has come to save you from your enemies. Rejoice today in what Jesus has done to save you.

Thank you, Jesus, that you have come to destroy the work of the enemy in my life. I can stand strong knowing you have come to save me.

Say to people who are frightened,
"Be strong. Don't be afraid.
Look, your God will come,
and he will punish your enemies.
He will make them pay for the wrongs they did,
but he will save you."

ISAIAH 35:4 NCV

When we are left to our own devices, we find a way to make quite a mess of things. There are so many things in our world that are not as they should be. Humanity's rebellion against God at the dawn of time left several key relationships fractured: our relationship with God, others, self, and creation.

God's promise to put things right was accomplished through Jesus, and that means restoration of all these severed relationships. We can be made right with God. Our relationships with others can be restored. We are able to see ourselves as deeply loved children and our relationship with all the things God has made can be put into its proper order. When you survey your own life, which area needs God's restoration work? Invite him into that area of your life today and see the restoration work he will do.

Heavenly Father, thank you for promising to put things right in my life. I trust you to do this work in me.

What enemies is God coming to destroy in your life?

Blind Eyes Opened

Then will the eyes of the blind be opened
and the ears of the deaf unstopped.
Then will the lame leap like a deer,
and the mute tongue shout for joy.
Water will gush forth in the wilderness
and streams in the desert.

ISAIAH 35:5-6 NIV

God's overall mission on this earth has remained the same through all time; to bring about the full restoration of all creation, under God's rule and reign. When Jesus the Messiah comes on the scene, he announces and inaugurates the kingdom of God's arrival on earth. Jesus goes about saying the kingdom of God is here now and proves it through his life, miracles, death, and resurrection.

Isaiah pens these words centuries before the coming of the Messiah and proclaims the work that he will do. Eyes and ears opened, lame walking, mute singing. And this is the work that Jesus continues to do today, in and through his church. Be expectant today that God is giving new vision to those who seek him.

Jesus, thank you for bringing your kingdom to earth with displays of love and power. Open my eyes to see how you're working.

When he comes, he will open the eyes of the blind
and unplug the ears of the deaf.
The lame will leap like a deer,
and those who cannot speak will sing for joy!
Springs will gush forth in the wilderness,
and streams will water the wasteland.

ISAIAH 35:5-6 NLT

When Jesus came, he fulfilled Isaiah's prophecy through mighty displays of God's power. He healed the physically blind, deaf, mute, and lame, and he challenged those walking in spiritual blindness to open their eyes to the coming of the kingdom of God. A sign of the arrival of God's kingdom is this amazing restoration work. He still heals today in both physical and spiritual ways.

Are there areas of your life where you are walking in spiritual blindness, unable to see things clearly? Do you need new vision to see from God's perspective? Are you deaf to the voice of God in your life? Ask God for eyes to see him and ears to hear him. As you seek more of God in your life, you can rest assured he will respond.

Jesus, I ask you today for eyes to see things from your perspective
and ears to hear your voice more clearly in my life.

How might things change if God opened your eyes to see from his perspective?

Light and Darkness

God, all at once you turned on a floodlight for me!
You are the revelation-light in my darkness,
and in your brightness I can see the path ahead.

PSALM 18:28 TPT

Many young people, as they embark on their future, can fall into the fear that they're going to somehow miss God's plan for them. Questions about choosing the right college or career can paralyze many from moving forward.

Perhaps you're afraid you're going to miss out on God's calling. The very nature of God is that he is light, and he brings light into our confusion and darkness. When you fix your focus on Jesus, you are able to see the way forward by his brightness. A heart abiding in Christ and surrendered to Jesus can trust that God's light is more powerful than any uncertainty or fear that lurks in the darkness. You can trust him to shine a floodlight and show you the path ahead.

Jesus, help me to trust that you're guiding me on the right path for my life and that I don't have to walk in fear of the darkness.

You light a lamp for me.
The LORD, my God, lights up my darkness
PSALM 18:28 NLT

Darkness has a way of making us feel scared, lost, or confused. Things get knocked over in the dark. Toes get stubbed in the dark. We get turned around, unsure of the way ahead. But when the light is turned on, everything changes. We suddenly see things clearly.

Light is always going to be more powerful than darkness. It fills every corner of a room. Darkness doesn't stand a chance when light comes on the scene. God is the one taking action in this verse. He is the one turning on a light in darkness. If you're feeling lost or confused in any area of your life, ask God to turn on a light. Trust that God brings light even in our darkest of situations and the way ahead will be clear.

Heavenly Father, I invite you to shine your light in my darkness. Remove my fear and confusion by your powerful light.

How might you see things differently if God turned a light on in your life?

Faithful Community

*All the believers devoted themselves to the apostles' teaching,
and to fellowship, and to sharing in meals (including the Lord's
Supper), and to prayer. A deep sense of awe came over them all,
and the apostles performed many miraculous signs and wonders.*

ACTS 2:42-43 NLT

You were created to be in relationship with others. A
significant part of God's plan for you is to be in community
with other believers who will challenge you to grow. But the
church is also filled with broken people (just like you) who
have the capacity to mess up. The truth is, when you devote
yourself to this kind of community that God created you to be
in, you are formed even more into the image of Christ. The
challenging people, even church people, have a way of being
like sandpaper, that smooth away your rough spots and cause
you to truly love like Jesus loves.

Lean into the Christian community God has put around you.
If you're disconnected from community, ask God to lead you
to people who will challenge you. This is part of God's plan to
help you grow.

*Heavenly Father, help me to devote myself to the Christian
community you have put around me and grow deeper in my faith
as a result.*

Every believer was faithfully devoted to following the teachings of the apostles. Their hearts were mutually linked to one another, sharing communion and coming together regularly for prayer. A deep sense of holy awe swept over everyone, and the apostles performed many miraculous signs and wonders.

ACTS 2:42-43 TPT

As we read further in Acts and the Epistles, things in the early church weren't always sunshine and rainbows. There were challenges, division, and dysfunction. Yet even in the challenges, this passage is a true reflection of what God was still doing in their midst. What made the early church look like this? Faithful devotion to the community with Christ at the center.

Who is God nudging you to enter into deeper community with? Unity with other brothers and sisters in Christ, as broken as they may be, is a necessary part to seeing God's power displayed in our world. Commit to coming together with your community for prayer and fellowship. It's incredible what you will see God do.

God, help me to have a heart open to being mutually linked to other believers. I want to be in true Christ-centered community.

How might your church more fully embody Acts 2:42-43? What is God calling you to do?

Generous Community

All the believers met together in one place and shared everything they had. They sold their property and possessions and shared the money with those in need.

ACTS 2:44-45 NLT

Our individualistic culture has a way of influencing our view of Scripture. This passage can stir up some discomfort for us. Is God asking us to share everything and sell all our stuff to help the poor? Maybe. But the deeper question here is the condition of our hearts. God's desire for the church has always been that we be a reflection of his heart for the world. We are to love the world with a self-sacrificial love that is counter-cultural to our self-centered tendencies.

God is calling us to live with a spirit of generosity marked by open hands and open hearts. And this isn't just monetary generosity. Are we quick to see and respond to the needs of others? When God gives you his heart, it's amazing how generosity begins to flow out.

Heavenly Father, I ask for your heart today to see people's needs. Give me the grace and strength to respond as you would.

*All the believers were in fellowship as one body, and they shared
with one another whatever they had. Out of generosity they even
sold their assets to distribute the proceeds to those who were in
need among them.*

ACTS 2:44-45 TPT

We live with the illusion that all the things we have in our
possession belong to us—that there exists a mine and yours.
But it seems for these early Christians there was no concept
of mine. Instead, they viewed all their possessions as ours.
How did they get there?

The starting point for a shift in our mindset is the
understanding that every good gift we have in our lives comes
from God. Nothing we have is ours to begin with. Let's not
hold on so tightly to our stuff that we miss God's heart for the
surrounding community. God's plan for us is that we might
live as one body, caring for the needs of each part as though
they were indeed part of us, as though they were our very own
flesh and blood.

*Lord Jesus, help me care for the body of Christ is the same way I
would care for my own body, with tender care.*

What would change in your life if God increased generosity
in you?

Growing Community

*They worshiped together at the Temple each day, met in homes
for the Lord's Supper, and shared their meals with great joy and
generosity— all the while praising God and enjoying the goodwill
of all the people. And each day the Lord added to their fellowship
those who were being saved.*

ACTS 2:46-47 NLT

Jesus said that the world will know we are his disciples by
the way we love each other. Do we love each other in such a
way that those far from God want to know him? Would your
city notice if your church wasn't there? The church Jesus is
calling us to be will be attractive to those who are distant and
disconnected from God.

Does your church truly reflect Jesus' heart for those far
from him? Healthy growth happens through individuals
responding to the call to connect in community with great joy
and generosity. Invite some friends over for dinner. Spend
time praising God with other believers. The Lord will bring
growth through your faithfulness to the community.

*Lord Jesus, as I commit to the community of Christ, help us to be
a place where outsiders are welcomed into a saving relationship
with Jesus.*

Daily they met together in the temple courts and in one another's homes to celebrate communion. They shared meals together with joyful hearts and tender humility. They were continually filled with praises to God, enjoying the favor of all the people. And the Lord kept adding to their number daily those who were coming to life.

ACTS 2:46-47 TPT

The early church in Acts was marked by joyful hearts and tender humility. No one likes an arrogant person or group of people. No, instead our attitude should be the same as Christ. The King of kings humbled himself to death on a cross that we might have life in him. When we look to Jesus as our model, and ask him to transform us into his likeness, humility will naturally flow out of us.

Ask God for a joyful heart and tender humility today. When you become more and more like Christ, those who are far from God will be drawn to you, and in turn drawn to Jesus. His plan for you is to be part of a growing community that is coming to life.

Jesus, I want to walk in joy and tender humility. Make me more and more like you, that I may influence those who are distant from you.

What might change in your life if you walked in greater humility?

Open Hearts

Break open your word within me until revelation-light shines out!
Those with open hearts are given insight into your plans.

PSALM 119:130 TPT

Prayer is all about aligning our heart with God's heart. It's not about making our requests known simply so God bends to our will and desires. It's saying, "Here is my heart, God, and I need you to show me your heart for this situation. How do you see things? What am I missing here? How do you want me to see this situation differently?"

Is your heart truly open to hearing what God has to say? He has a much more hopeful perspective on things than you probably do. He has a world full of love and compassion for the people who have deeply hurt you. There may be some wrong motivations driven by fear and insecurity that he wants to point out and deal with. Open your heart to God's revelation-light to shine in you, trusting that God will give you his heart for the world.

Lord God, I open my heart to hear from you today whatever it is you want to say. I ask for revelation-light to shine out.

Learning your words gives wisdom
and understanding for the foolish.

PSALM 119:130 NCV

Are you wandering around life with confusion about what
God is saying or where he is leading you? God wants to speak
to you. The big question is, are you putting yourself in the
position to listen and hear him?

We can easily be distracted by so many other voices. But if you
want to hear from God, open up his Word today. His Word has
the ability to shine light into the dark spots in our lives and
reveal truth and understanding. He wants to show you the way
ahead. He'll reveal all that he is preparing for you in the right
timing. It's not too difficult. Even the simple-minded and
childlike can hear from God.

Lord Jesus, give me a childlike heart that is expectant to hear
from you. I ask you to shine your light into my life and give me
understanding.

What is God saying to you today?

Fastened

Fasten your hearts to the love of God and receive the mercy of our Lord Jesus Christ, who gives us eternal life.

JUDE 1:21 TPT

God's love is there for the taking. He has outstretched arms to you, offering you an undying love that can't be shaken. Anchor yourself deeply in God's love today. Start your day with the confident assurance that whatever this day holds, it has no power to shake you or remove you from the safe and secure place in God's love.

Imagine wrapping yourself up in God's love like a blanket, that warms and comfort, holds and protects. Allow the knowledge of this love to bring a peace and calm to your heart. Eternal life isn't just for when you die someday. It's here today and it's found securely in the arms of God's love for you. In Christ, he freely offers you life that is full, beautiful, and good. Fasten your heart to Jesus today.

Lord Jesus, I fasten my heart to your love and receive your mercy today. Strengthen me to walk in the fullness of the eternal life you have already given me.

Keep yourselves in God's love as you wait for the Lord Jesus Christ with his mercy to give you life forever.

JUDE 1:21 NCV

The world gives us conflicting messages about where real life is found. Some will say it's found in romance, others in money or achievement, or the party life. In reality, these earthly things eventually disappoint. The unending and real life is found securely in Jesus. Don't allow distraction to come in and steal your focus away.

Have you looked to other things as the source of life? Realign your heart around God's love today. Open your arms and heart to him. Run fully into his outstretched arms for an encounter with his love. Stay put, right at the center of God's love, and lay aside the other things you look to for satisfaction. True and lasting life is available this very moment in the presence of Jesus.

Lord Jesus. I open my arms to you, ready to receive real life found in you.

What distractions do you need to set aside today to more fully enter the love of God?

The Man

Then Jesus came out wearing the crown of thorns and the purple robe. And Pilate said, "Look, here is the man!"

JOHN 19:5 NLT

At this moment Jesus is made to look like a king. Everyone was mocking him and hurling insults at him. Jesus became the kid that everyone made fun of, the one who was bullied. Pressed into his head was a crown of thorns and draped over his open wounds was a purple robe.

Jesus took all of this for us. Imagine the amount of pain there must have been with a crown of thorns pressed down onto his head. This man who by no means had to do what he did. He never had to take the punishment that we deserve. He gave himself up so that we could look upon him and find salvation. Let that sink in for just a moment.

Lord, your body was broken for our sins and for our broken hearts. Lord, today may we remember the cost of our lives that you freely took upon yourself.

When Jesus came out wearing the crown of thorns and the purple robe, Pilate said to them, "Here is the man!"

JOHN 19:5 NIV

When it comes to Jesus and the suffering leading up to his death, he never once complained. He stood there being mocked as king. If everyone there would have known that he is the King of kings and Lord of lords, they probably wouldn't have had the attitude they did.

When we think of Jesus and the words "here is the man," covered in blood and flesh hanging off him, do you see a man? Scripture also says that people didn't recognize him as a man because he had been beaten so much. Sin came at great cost, and Jesus took it so that we could have life. Stop for just a minute and think about what Jesus did so that we could have life.

Jesus, we praise you not just as a man but as the King of kings. Lord your death gives us life and today Father we rejoice because of your death and resurrection.

When you think of Jesus, do you picture him as just a man or as a king?

Finished

When Jesus had received the wine, he said, "It is finished."
Then he bowed his head and gave up his spirit.

JOHN 19:30 NRSV

Standing off the distance, you watch another group of men on the cross. It's the worst way to die. Their gradual, slow, and painful death is a result of them no longer being able to push themselves up to breathe. The person on the cross struggles for air and eventually suffocates.

As you are watching, you hear a loud voice cry out, "It's done!" No one does that on the cross. No one has the strength to. Yet Jesus yelled out for all to hear. The price for our sin is done. The weight of sin is gone. The penalty for all is gone. All shame and guilt for those in Christ is finished. Jesus paid it all, so you can have life. He did not die fighting; he freely gave everything up, so you can have eternal life.

Lord, you gave it all for us. Thank you for giving us hope and defeating death so we can have life.

*When Jesus had received the sour wine, he said, "It is finished,"
and he bowed his head and gave up his spirit.*

JOHN 19:30 ESV

When building a house, every home owner wants to hear "it's finished." Every racecar driver loves to see a checkered flag—it means the race is finished. During the last week of school everyone waits for the final bell to ring because it means school is finished. Everyone is thrilled the day school is out because we know it's done!

When Jesus let out in a loud voice "it is finished," he meant all people now have access to the father. Every person, no matter what tribe, nation, color, background, previous crime, everyone now has the opportunity to approach the throne room of God. Jesus was the perfect sacrifice for everyone. In his death, we now can live for him. He gave it all so you could have it all, and because of that we can rejoice that we now have life.

Lord your death has given us life. Everything you went through was for us. Lord we praise you because you have defeated all things and we can live for you because of what you have done.

How can you give Jesus everything, just like he gave everything for you?

Fear to Joy

That Sunday evening the disciples were meeting behind locked doors because they were afraid of the Jewish leaders. Suddenly, Jesus was standing there among them! "Peace be with you," he said. As he spoke, he showed them the wounds in his hands and his side. They were filled with joy when they saw the Lord!

JOHN 20:19-20 NLT

In this passage, Jesus had already risen from the dead, but the disciples were not yet aware of this new kingdom reality. Instead, they hid in fear for their lives. You may be walking in fear and can't make sense of what God is doing. It may even seem as though all is lost.

But even your fear will not keep Jesus away. Even locked doors will not keep Jesus from walking smack into the middle of your situation. Jesus wants to take your fear and confusion and replace it with his peace and joy. God's will for your life is that you would not bend to fear, but instead stand firm. Jesus paid the ultimate price for you to be a recipient of that peace today.

Lord Jesus, I receive your peace today. Renew joy to my heart with the good news that you have triumphed over death and fear.

That evening, the disciples gathered together. And because they were afraid of reprisals from the Jewish leaders, they had locked the doors to the place where they met. But suddenly Jesus appeared among them and said, "Peace to you!" then he showed them the wounds of his hands and his side—they were overjoyed to see the Lord with their own eyes!

JOHN 20:19-20 TPT

When Jesus rose from the dead, everything changed. He triumphed over the power of death. He reversed the curse that came upon all creation in the garden. This marks the start of Jesus bringing about the restoration of all things, the coming together of heaven and earth. All things new. No wonder the disciples were overjoyed to see Jesus with their own eyes.

While the power of God triumphed, and death could not keep its grip on Jesus, he still carried the scars. These scars are an eternal reminder of the price that was paid for our liberation. Jesus is fiercely devoted to our restoration. Jesus declares his peace over you today.

Lord, thank you for paying the ultimate price that I may have peace and life in you.

What locked doors in your life does Jesus want to walk through?

Living Sent

"Peace be with you. As the Father has sent me, so I am sending you." Then he breathed on them and said, "Receive the Holy Spirit. If you forgive anyone's sins, they are forgiven. If you do not forgive them, they are not forgiven."

JOHN 20:21-23 NLT

Jesus lived as one who had been sent by Father, living in complete and total obedience. Jesus tells us that he only did what his Father said. He lived in full dependence on the Holy Spirit. At this point in the story, Jesus had risen from the dead and knew he would soon be leaving earth. This story would no longer just be about the miraculous works of Jesus, the Son of God, making wrong things right.

Instead, it would become an unstoppable movement driven by the multiplication of his kingdom through the disciples. They are now given the authority to bring this same restoration work to the world. He says the same to you today. You are to live as one sent by the Father, redeemed by Jesus Christ, filled and empowered by the Holy Spirit. Wherever you go today, live as though you have been sent by Jesus.

Lord Jesus, thank you for sending me to bring restoration to the world through your Holy Spirit. I say yes today.

Jesus repeated his greeting, "Peace to you!" And he told them, "Just as the Father has sent me, I'm now sending you." Then, taking a deep breath, he blew on them and said, "Receive the Holy Spirit. I send you to preach the forgiveness of sins—and people's sins will be forgiven. But if you don't proclaim the forgiveness of their sins, they will remain guilty."

JOHN 20:21-23 TPT

Your mission is to continue doing the work Jesus started when he was here. You are sent in the name of Jesus to bring heaven to earth. You are sent to declare God's love, power, and forgiveness to those walking in the shame of their sin.

Imagine Jesus breathing on you today with a fresh filling of the Holy Spirit. You're not alone on this mission God has given you. You have been given the same authority that Jesus carried when he was here on this earth. You are not called to just be a passive observer. No, you are called to partner with the Holy Spirit in this kingdom restoration project God is doing on earth.

Lord Jesus, I breathe in a fresh touch from the Holy Spirit today. Empower me to preach the forgiveness of sin.

What would change if you lived as if you were sent by Jesus?

Follow Me

Peter turned and saw that the disciple whom Jesus loved was following them… So when Peter saw him, he asked Jesus, "What's going to happen to him?" Jesus replied, "If I decide to let him live until I return, what concern is that of yours? You must still keep on following me!"

JOHN 21:20-22 TPT

We scroll through our social media pages looking at the good looks, beautiful clothes, social lives, and travel photographs of others and wonder why their lives are so much better than ours. How much of our time is spent comparing ourselves to others? Peter did the same thing, by concerning himself with the fate of another disciple.

Jesus' response cuts to the heart: Stop worrying about others. What concern is that of yours? Your job is to follow Jesus. Stop looking to what others have. God has uniquely created and sent you. Look to Jesus and what he says about you and who you are. Follow Jesus. Keep your eyes on him. Don't look to the right or the left. Don't get sucked into the comparison trap.

Jesus, help me live today with my eyes fixed on you rather than concerning myself with the blessings that others have.

Peter turned around and saw behind them the disciple Jesus loved... Peter asked Jesus, "What about him, Lord?" Jesus replied, "If I want him to remain alive until I return, what is that to you? As for you, follow me."

JOHN 21:20-22 NLT

Jesus has just spent time restoring his relationship with Peter and refining his calling and purpose: to shepherd the people. Even in light of this powerful moment, Peter was still distracted by the calling and purpose Jesus had for someone else. If you read further in this story, you see that even after Jesus' convicting words, there was a rumor going around that this disciple would live forever. Peter still missed Jesus' point.

What is Jesus calling you to do? His plans and purposes for others is not your concern. Every person's journey will be different, and that's okay. When we place our focus on following Jesus, our worries about other people become less important and his plans for us become clearer.

Jesus, I'm sorry for being distracted by people when my focus needs to be on you. Strengthen me to redirect my energy toward wholeheartedly following you.

What would change in your life if you turned your gaze away from others onto Jesus?

Spirit of Truth

"When the Spirit of truth comes, he will guide you into all truth. He will not speak on his own but will tell you what he has heard. He will tell you about the future. He will bring me glory by telling you whatever he receives from me."

JOHN 16:13-14 NLT

In this passage, Jesus makes a profound promise to his followers: the Holy Spirit, the presence of the living God, will live in us and show us the way forward. And he will speak to us what he has heard directly from the Father. The Spirit of truth will never lie to us or lead us in the wrong way. This means you don't have to worry where to find truth. Following the Holy Spirit means he will guide you into the right way ahead.

Thank God today that he has put a guide directly inside of you with the Holy Spirit. Connect with him in the stillness and listen to his guidance. He loves to give glory to the Father and accomplishes this by speaking to his children. Tune your heart to listen.

Holy Spirit, help me to listen and hear your voice. I will follow you wherever you lead me.

"When the truth-giving Spirit comes, he will unveil the reality of every truth within you. He won't speak his own message, but only what he hears from the Father, and he will reveal prophetically to you what is to come. He will glorify me on the earth, for he will receive from me what is mine and reveal it to you."

JOHN 16:13-14 TPT

Did you know the Holy Spirit wants to speak to you about your future? He wants to show you what is to come in your life, the plans he has for you, and the future he is preparing for you. This is a promise we can stand firm in that comes straight out of the mouth of Jesus.

If you're feeling like you might be missing out on the reality of this promise, begin asking the Holy Spirit to speak to you about what he is planning for you. You may not get a lot of specifics or crystal clarity right away. In his timing, he will reveal all that is to come. We can trust him in this.

Lord Jesus, thank you for the Holy Spirit who lives in me, who is committed to revealing truth to me.

What does the Spirit want to say to you about your future?

ask

> *"Here is eternal truth: When that time comes you won't need to ask me for anything, but instead you will go directly to the Father and ask him for anything you desire and he will give it to you, because of your relationship with me. Until now you've not been bold enough to ask the Father for a single thing in my name, but now you can ask, and keep on asking him! And you can be sure that you'll receive what you ask for, and your joy will have no limits!"*

JOHN 16:23-24 TPT

Does this mean we have carte blanche to get anything we could dream or imagine from God? Can we ask him for fancy cars, lavish vacation homes, and diamond rings? No, he's not a vending machine. But we can't deny the reality that there is a promise in this passage that our prayers will be answered.

The basis for this promise stems from the place of favor we have as beloved children of God. Because of the foundation of relationship that we have with Jesus, fullness of joy is available to us here and now.

Father God, I want a heart in alignment with your heart. Help me to ask for the things that you want to give me.

> *"At that time you won't need to ask me for anything. I tell you the truth, you will ask the Father directly, and he will grant your request because you use my name. You haven't done this before. Ask, using my name, and you will receive, and you will have abundant joy."*
>
> JOHN 16:23-24 NLT

As Jesus is preparing his disciples with the news that he will soon be leaving them, he wants them to fully understand that there is real and tangible power in his name. He's instructing them to pray in and through the name of Christ. Before Jesus, we didn't have full access to God. But when we pray through Jesus, we are guaranteed that God hears us.

This isn't just a magic spell that ensures we get the things we want. In fact, later in Acts we see the dire consequences of men using Jesus' name for their own personal gain (Acts 19:11-20). As Spirit-filled believers, we are given authority to use the name of Jesus. Ask and you will receive.

Lord Jesus, thank you for the power in your name.

What do you need to ask God for today in the name of Jesus?

Life and Glory

*After saying all these things, Jesus looked up to heaven and said,
"Father, the hour has come. Glorify your Son so he can give glory
back to you. For you have given him authority over everyone. He
gives eternal life to each one you have given him."*

JOHN 17:1-2 NLT

In the moments before Jesus was arrested, tried, and crucified, he lifted up a prayer from the depths of heart to the Father. He knew what he was about to endure, foreseeing the extreme suffering at hand. He had a perspective that was eternally farther reaching than what was about to happen to him. His gaze was fixed on God receiving the utmost glory through all this.

Glory is a churchy word we use a lot. It's about ensuring that God is the one who gets the honor, respect, surrender, and worship that he deserves. This was Jesus' heart cry. When you face times of struggle, suffering, trials, or challenges, remember that it gives you the opportunity to bring glory to God. When you choose to trust him in challenging times, he gets glory.

Lord Jesus, I choose to wholeheartedly trust you in my difficult times, knowing that you will be made more beautiful to those around me.

This is what Jesus prayed as he looked up into heaven, "Father, the time has come. Unveil the glorious splendor of your Son so that I will magnify your glory! You have already given me authority over all people so that I may give the gift of eternal life to all those that you have given to me."

JOHN 17:1-2 TPT

Jesus' heart was bursting with joy over the reality that enduring the cross would give him the ability to offer eternal life to anyone who would take it. Jesus has now been given the authority to seek out those wandering away from heart of God. He leaves the ninety-nine to go after the one. And he does this with love and compassion.

God's plan for you is that you would receive the gift of eternal life; fullness of life that starts here and now. And life that continues for all of eternity. Jesus paid the ultimate price that you may be made right with him. Thank him today for the gift of eternal life, knowing that you belong to Jesus.

Lord Jesus, I am overjoyed today with the truth that eternal life is available in you.

How is God getting glory with how you're living your life?

Knowing God

"This is eternal life, that they may know you, the only true God, and Jesus Christ whom you have sent."

JOHN 17:3 NRSV

In Jesus' prayer to the Father we see him define this idea of eternal life: eternal life is knowing God. And we have the awesome privilege of being able to know him now. This isn't just for when we die someday. The moment a person comes to know Jesus personally, their eternal life begins.

Do you know God? If you've been following Jesus for a while that may seem like a simple question. But how well do you know the heart of Jesus? How closely are you walking with him? Do you know what brings him joy and what makes him sad? The more we know him, and more he reveals his true nature to us, the more we become like him. There is an open invitation for you today to know him more and to step into your eternal life now.

Lord Jesus, I want to know you more. I open my heart today and take one step closer to you.

"Eternal life means to know and experience you as the only true God, and to know and experience Jesus Christ, as the Son whom you have sent."

JOHN 17:3 TPT

We build up a lot of concepts of what we think God must be like based on our own experiences. If we experience an angry father in this life, we may believe that God is angry with us. Friends abandon us or family neglect us, and we think God must do the same. But the truth is Jesus shows us what God is like.

An experience with the only true God has the power to change us forever. This was Jesus' prayer for us, the church, to know and experience God, in the fullness of all he is. Pray today that you may more fully know and experience the fullness of Jesus Christ. This is a dangerous prayer. The more we know Jesus, the more he begins to change us and make us more like him.

Lord Jesus, I want to more fully know and experience you. Open my heart to receive greater understanding of who you are.

Does your life look like Jesus?

Completing the Work

> *"I brought glory to you here on earth by completing the work you gave me to do. Now, Father, bring me into the glory we shared before the world began."*
>
> JOHN 17:4-5 NLT

Jesus' prayer to the Father in his final days points us to a greater reality. Jesus' mission was to live in complete and total obedience to the Father's plan for him, even if that meant a brutal death on the cross. As followers of Jesus, we are to pattern our lives after him. Our model is Jesus, and we are to live in the same way. The essence of Jesus' prayer for the church is that we may bring glory to the Father with our lives by completing the work he has given us to do.

And you have a unique calling and purpose. You may not know what that is yet, but be encouraged today that you were made with a purpose in mind. God's plan for you is that you would bring glory to the Father by the way you live your life, in surrender and obedience to him.

Lord Jesus, I desire to complete the work you have given me to do here on earth, that you might get the glory. Help me to live in obedience to you.

> *"I have glorified you on the earth by faithfully doing everything you've told me to do. So my Father, restore me back to the glory that we shared together when we were face-to-face before the universe was created."*
>
> JOHN 17:4-5 TPT

Imagine being one of the disciples overhearing Jesus' prayer. This man whom they had traveled with, eaten with, and done life with was saying something deeply profound about himself: he had been with the Father since the dawn of creation, in face-to-face perfect love and unity.

Jesus willingly left that level of deep intimacy and glory with the Father to come to earth, that you might be restored and welcomed into that same intimacy again with the Father. He gave up everything for you. And you get the privilege to live a life in faithful obedience to him too, just like Jesus. You're not alone in this. Jesus is with you.

Lord Jesus, thank you for leaving heaven to come down to earth to save me. I want to faithfully do everything you ask me to do.

What is Jesus calling you to do today?

Surrendered Lives

"All who belong to me now belong to you. And all who belong to you now belong to me as well, and my glory is revealed through their surrendered lives."

JOHN 17:10 TPT

Lives surrendered to Jesus is God's plan for us. The challenge for us is oftentimes giving up control of our lives over to Jesus. There are still areas that we cling to, that we think we can manage better on our own, or that we really don't want God to get his hands on because he might call us to live differently. We can be stubborn at times.

It seems counterintuitive to let go of control and hand it over to God. But if you have said yes to Jesus, you belong to him and you can trust that you are much better off surrendering everything over to him. When you let Jesus into all areas of your life, he gets more glory. He is made more famous and beautiful to those around you. Surrender everything to Jesus today, trusting that you truly belong to him.

Lord Jesus, I want you to receive glory through my surrendered life. I let you into all areas of my life today.

"All who are mine belong to you, and you have given them to me, so they bring me glory."

JOHN 17:10 NLT

In Jesus' prayer to the Father he reveals a key part of your identity. Jesus says to you today, "You are mine." There's a lot of perks that come with belonging to Jesus. You are wanted. You are known. You are secure. You are loved to the very core of your being, even in your weakness.

Rest in this reality today that you are found deeply and fully in the heart of God. The more you live as one who belongs to Jesus, the more and more glory that Jesus gets. Step fully into your identity today as one who known fully by Jesus. You have not been cast aside or forgotten. No, you are found smack dab in the middle of the love between Jesus and the Father.

Lord Jesus, I want to live as one who belongs to you. Help me find rest and security in the reality that I am yours.

What changes for you if you embrace the reality that you belong to Jesus?

United as One

"I ask that by the power of your name, protect each one that you have given me, and watch over them so that they will be united as one, even as we are one."

JOHN 17:11B TPT

The Father and the Son are the same God. Jesus is praying to the Father that we the church might have the same level of unity between us as the Father and Son have together. God's plan for us is to be unified. That seems like a high order in our divisive culture and political climate.

As the people of God, we need his help in this. Agree with Jesus today by praying this back to him. Ask this for the church and for the followers of Jesus you interact with every day and all over the globe that you will never meet this side of heaven. We are called to be one.

Father, Son, and Holy Spirit, thank you that you are one God. Watch over us, the church, and help us to be unified as one.

"Now protect them by the power of your name so that they will be united just as we are."

JOHN 17:11B NLT

Jesus' prayer for us is that we may be protected and watched over by a God who loves us. Jesus prayed it, so we know God has heard this prayer that rings out over us throughout the ages. This protection is meant to create unity among us. We are to diligently guard ourselves against disunity in the body of Christ.

In our humanness it's easy to get sucked into responding to conflict out of an "us versus them" mentality. We see ourselves as always right and others as wrong. But Jesus' heart is for a unified church. Do you need to lay aside being right for the sake of unity? We are under the loving protection of Jesus, who cries out for unity for us. Let's step into this more fully today.

Lord Jesus, thank you for your prayer of protection over the church. Help me to be one who strives for unity before rightness.

What would the church look like if we were as united as the Father and Son?

Joy Overflowing

"Now I am returning to you so Father, I pray that they will experience and enter into my joyous delight in you so that it is fulfilled in them and overflows."

JOHN 17:13 TPT

Moments before the crucifixion, Jesus' mind is set on our joy. That's a convicting thought. Knowing the suffering he would soon endure, he was concerned with ensuring we might be recipients of his joy. God's plan for you is to be full of his joy, even in the most challenging circumstances.

Joy is much deeper and richer than fleeting happiness, which is rooted in your circumstances. True joy can't be taken away. His plan for you is that you may have his joy is such fullness that it overflows into all your interactions, situations, and circumstances. And this joyous delight is found in the place of intimacy between the Father and Son that you have been invited into. Enter into Jesus' joyous delight today.

Lord Jesus, thank you that you desire me to be a recipient of your joy. I open my heart to receive it in full today.

"I am coming to you, and I speak these things in the world so that they may have my joy made complete in themselves."

JOHN 17:13 NRSV

People like to be around joyful people. There is something infectious about a genuinely happy person. This kind of joy is available to us in Jesus. It isn't just a fake slap-on-a-smile type happiness, but a well stirring up inside of us that comes only from the fountain of living water, Jesus himself.

Jesus longs for us to experience full, complete, and perfect joy that flows into every part of our lives. Having joy doesn't mean that you ignore difficult circumstances or pretend they're not happening. No, instead true joy that comes from Jesus is like a searchlight that guides you through the darkness. The joy itself is your strength. If you're walking through a confusing or difficult time, ask Jesus for more joy today.

Lord Jesus, I ask you today for the gift of joy in my life that would fill my heart with your delight.

How might your interactions change if you were overflowing with joy in Christ?

Keep Them Safe

"I'm not asking you to take them out of the world,
but to keep them safe from the evil one.
They do not belong to this world any more than I do."

JOHN 17:15-16 TPT

Jesus left the safety and perfection of heaven to come to the earth. This was done to rescue us from the power of sin and to reconcile us back to God. But in his coming, he became acquainted with the hardships and difficulties that we face every day. While Jesus disarmed satan on the cross, we still have a very real enemy who is at work in the world.

Jesus pleads with the Father to keep us safe from the evil one. There are times that we lose sight of who we belong to and live as though things here on earth are all that matters. Sometimes without even knowing it, our loyalties lie with the evil one. Lean into Jesus' prayer today that you no longer belong to the world. You belong to him.

Lord Jesus, I ask you to keep me safe from the work of the evil one today. Give me eyes to see clearly where he is working and to keep my focus on my heavenly home.

> *"I am not asking you to take them out of the world,*
> *but I ask you to protect them from the evil one.*
> *They do not belong to the world,*
> *just as I do not belong to the world."*

JOHN 17:15-16 NRSV

It may seem strange that Jesus doesn't want to instantly save us from the influence of the world. He clearly states in his prayer to the Father that he is not asking for us to be removed from world but that God would protect us from evil. Your circumstances may be swirling around you in such a way it seems nearly impossible to remember that there is hope on the other side.

Jesus' prayer for you is that you would know that this earth is not your home. You have an eternal home found in the loving arms of our Father, where wrongs are made right. But in the meantime, he is not calling you out of the world you're in. Lean into to God's protection, peace, and provision. He is with you in whatever challenges you face while you live in the world.

Lord Jesus, help me to live in this world while also knowing I don't belong here. Thank you for your protection today.

What changes if you focus on your heavenly home instead of your earthly challenges?

Make Them Holy

*"Make them holy by your truth; teach them your word,
which is truth. Just as you sent me into the world,
I am sending them into the world."*

John 17:17-18 NLT

You may feel the burden that it's on your shoulders to be more holy, to do the right thing, to live a perfect life like Jesus. But God's will for you is that this journey was never meant to be done alone. You need Jesus. And he pleads with the Father on your behalf. He is wholeheartedly committed to you becoming holy. He is set on you knowing his Word. He is devoted to you knowing truth. Jesus prays to the Father that he may be our teacher in his Word.

You have been set apart. He is doing the work in you to make you more like Jesus. Lean into this truth today. Rest in the reality that God is fiercely committed to you and the work he is doing in you. You don't have to do it alone.

Lord Jesus, I lean into the truth that you are committed to my holiness and teaching me truth. I want to know you, Lord.

> *"Your Word is truth! So make them holy by the truth.*
> *I have commissioned them to represent me*
> *just as you commissioned me to represent you."*

JOHN 17:17-18 TPT

On this journey with Jesus, he fills us with his Spirit and then sends us out into the world. Rarely do we ever feel completely ready for the work that Jesus calls us to. Oftentimes we're terrified that we'll mess it up or do it wrong.

But this is what you're made for. Jesus has commissioned you to represent him on this earth. That may seem like a very high calling and it is. But it is not meant to be a burden. Jesus believes in you. He is backing you. His Spirit lives in you and will empower you. Say yes to him today, knowing that this is his plan for you: to point people to him.

Lord Jesus, I know that you have called me to represent you on this earth. I say yes to this call, asking you to strengthen me by your Holy Spirit.

In what ways have you represented Jesus to the world?

Convincing the World

"You live fully in me and now I live fully in them so that they will experience perfect unity, and the world will be convinced that you have sent me, for they will see that you love each one of them with the same passionate love that you have for me."

JOHN 17:23 TPT

Jesus' prayer points to a powerful life-giving truth for us: that he lives fully in us. He doesn't hold back his presence or only give us a little bit of himself until we clean up our act. He has poured out the fullness of himself into his followers. He pulls us close to him and pours out his lavish love on us.

This was not just for our own benefit. He did this for the benefit of those who are still far away from him. When we walk in this extravagant love, it reveals the beauty of Jesus to those who don't yet know him. When we live as ones who are deeply loved, secure, and filled with his joy, people can't help but be drawn to Jesus in us. They will be convinced of who Jesus is when we walk in love.

Lord Jesus, help me to live as one is who deeply loved and in turn point people to you.

> *"I am in them and you are in me. May they experience such perfect unity that the world will know that you sent me and that you love them as much as you love me."*

JOHN 17:23 NLT

Think for a second how much the Father loves Jesus the Son. His very own flesh and blood, who was with him from the foundation of the world. This is Jesus, who never sinned, who lived in perfect surrender to the Father, living a selfless life poured out for the sake of the world.

When God looks at you, he sees you through the lens of Christ. Jesus is saying in this prayer that the Father loves you with the same passionate love that he has toward Jesus. Even in your failures, know that you are loved. Simply. Fully. Live today as one who is deeply loved.

Lord Jesus, thank you for seeing me through the lens of Christ and loving me. I want to live in such perfect unity that the world will know you, Jesus.

How would things change if you lived as one who is loved like the Father loves the Son?

Where I Am

"Father, I want these whom you have given me to be with me where I am. Then they can see all the glory you gave me because you loved me even before the world began!"

JOHN 17:24 NLT

It can be easy for us to wander off. It happens in subtle ways. Skipping church or small group here or there. Choosing to watch TV instead of connecting with God in prayer. Thinking one bad choice really won't matter in the long run. Jesus' prayer for you is that you would never be separated from him. That you would always walk close to him.

This prayer is meant to draw you near to him rather than cause you to turn your back in shame or guilt. Where is Jesus working in the people around you? Where is Jesus moving? His prayer is that you would always be sensitive to his presence and aware of whatever he is doing. When we are with Jesus where he is, God gets glory, and we enter more fully into the loving relationship between the Father and the Son.

Lord Jesus, I want to be where you are. Increase my sensitivity to your presence.

> *"Father, I ask that you allow everyone that you have given to me to be with me where I am! Then they will see my full glory—the very splendor you have placed upon me because you have loved me even before the beginning of time."*
>
> JOHN 17:24 TPT

Jesus is currently seated at the right hand of the Father, in perfect glory. Jesus' prayer that we be with him where he is means that he is praying for the eternal salvation for his followers. That we would never be separated from him, even for one moment.

You are found in Christ. You are seated in heavenly realms with Christ as we speak. This is your true identity and place with God. You are found in him. Few have seen the fullness of Jesus' glory on this side of heaven, but you can stand firm in the truth that this is Jesus' prayer for you: to fully know and see Jesus for who he is.

Lord Jesus, thank you for making a way for me to always be with you wherever you are. Reveal your glory to me.

Are you with Jesus where he is?

god Revealed

"I have revealed to them who you are and I will continue to make you even more real to them, so that they may experience the same endless love that you have for me, for your love will now live in them, even as I live in them!"

JOHN 17:26 TPT

Jesus came to show us what God is like. The religious leaders of Jesus' time perpetuated a lot of misconceptions about God. They falsely believed he was a god who demands we follow rules at the expense of loving people.

Jesus' prayer to the Father reveals a central part of his mission: to reveal what God is really like. Jesus promises in this prayer that he will continue to reveal to us what God is really like. He reveals God as a reckless lover and forgiver of sins. He reveals God as one who searches for the outsider. He reveals God as one who heals the sick and raises the dead. Pray today that Jesus would continue to reveal to you what God is really like. He loves to do this.

Lord Jesus, you have shown me what God is really like. Continue to make the Father even more real to me.

> *"I made your name known to them, and I will make it known,*
> *so that the love with which you have loved me may be in them,*
> *and I in them."*

JOHN 17:26 NRSV

Jesus loves to live inside you. Have you ever thought about that? Even with your dark corners, un-swept areas, and dirty laundry. He loves to love you. And he is committed to cleaning you up, making you more and more like him.

His overwhelming love dwells in your heart, the love that the Father has for Jesus. This is an ongoing journey into the deeper places of God's love. His plan for you is that you might see him for who he is. And the more you see him for who he really is, the more you will love him. He is so beautiful that love will overflow from your heart. You won't be able to help loving others with that same love.

Lord Jesus, thank you for loving me and living inside of me.
Continue to reveal yourself to me.

What misconceptions do you have of God that Jesus wants to correct?

Choose Life

"I call heaven and earth to witness against you today,
that I have set before you life and death,
blessing and curse.
Therefore choose life, that you and your offspring may live"

DEUTERONOMY 30:19 ESV

Life is all about choices. Will you choose eggs for breakfast or pancakes? Wear the blue shirt or the red one? What really matters when it comes to life decisions is whether you will live for your Savior. It's a choice between light or dark, blessing or curse, conviction or compromise.

The road ahead isn't always clear. Keep your spiritual eyes open. Choose today to live with the confidence that God will work through you and accomplish his will. He is for you and not against you. He will help you make the right choices.

Jesus, give me the boldness to stand up for what is right today, to choose the hard path of conviction and earnest devotion over the easy path of compromise.

"Today I have given you the choice between life and death,
between blessings and curses.
Now I call on heaven and earth to witness the choice you make.
Oh, that you would choose life,
so that you and your descendants might live!"

DEUTERONOMY 30:19 NLT

When you look back on your day, do you see how God led you
to make the right decisions? Did you choose a blessing or a
curse, the light or the dark? Choosing life means you choose
to follow the path God has set before you. Remember that
God is always with you in those moments when you make a
decision to glorify his name in your actions and thoughts—
and even when you don't. God will never leave your side.

We "choose life" on a daily basis. It's in the quiet moments as
you drift off to sleep, meditating on what the Savior has done
in your life. How did he work in your life today?

Lord, I will rest in the knowledge that you are always with me,
helping me to choose life every single day. I will prepare my mind
and spirit to make the right choices.

How did you choose life today?

Make It Good

God is not a man, that He should lie,
Nor a son of man, that He should repent;
Has He said, and will He not do it?
Or has He spoken, and will He not make it good?

NUMBERS 23:19 NASB

God is always making good in your life. Do you believe that?
Your friends, the family you're placed into, even the school
you attend or the job you have—God is working through those
around you to accomplish his will. Even in the midst of a dark
world, where it seems as though good is hard to find, God is
still there. He will always make good on his promises.

Today, listen to what God has to say to you. He will transform
your thoughts and actions, he will radically alter your outlook
on life. His desire is for you to recognize the good he is doing
in the world and to praise him. On this day, may you see that
he will do what he says.

God, help me to see the good you are doing, both in the world and
in my own heart. I choose today to become an avenue for your
will, even in a dark world.

God is not human, that he should lie,
not a human being, that he should change his mind.
Does he speak and then not act?
Does he promise and not fulfill?

NUMBERS 23:19 NIV

As you look back on the day, how did you see that God made good on his promises? He is constantly at work in your life and in the lives of those around you. The goal each day is always the same—it's about God's will, not your will. It's not the will of evil forces, not the will of any political party or any secular movement. Nothing can stand against the will of God.

You might say it's always the trending topic of the day—that God will speak and act, that he will promise and then fulfill. He won't leave you hanging. If you doubted that today, if the pressures of life were overwhelming, remember that he is still doing good.

Father, I want to be part of what you are doing in the world. I want to be part of the building process to make good and not dwell on what is broken and crumbling.

Where did you see God making good on his promises today?

With Us

He said, "Do not be afraid,
for those who are with us
are more than those who are with them."

2 KINGS 6:16 ESV

The prophet Elisha revealed to his servant in this passage that there were chariots of fire all around them. The angel armies, the host of heaven. They stood at the ready. Even when it seems like everyone is against you and you are surrounded on all sides, God is still in the middle of every battle. We might not realize it at the time, but he has already won every battle you face, no matter how dire. The forces of evil cannot overcome you.

What are you worried about today? Remember that God is with you. He will guide you. He is always aware of what you are facing. He is most interested in how you will glorify him today, because he has already conquered the darkness that seems so prevalent.

God, I know you are watching over me today. I know you have already won the spiritual battle in my life. Help me to see with spiritual eyes how you are with me.

*Don't be afraid," the prophet answered.
"Those who are with us are more than those who are with them."*
2 KINGS 6:16 NIV

After a long day, when you are tired and weary, rest in the utter conviction that God has already won the battle for your soul. The angel armies have already come to assist you. You are already victorious on the spiritual battlefield, whether that's at school, in your job, or with friends.

The forces of evil are always outnumbered. It's not even close to a fair fight. What has to change each day is your own spiritual perspective, that God will not let you slip away into darkness and despair. That each day, he will lift you into the light.

Jesus, help me to see that you have already come to my rescue. You rescued me from total destruction when I believed in your name. My daily skirmishes can never compare.

Which spiritual battle did God win today?

He Sees

You, my son Solomon,
acknowledge the God of your father,
and serve him with wholehearted devotion
and with a willing mind,
for the LORD searches every heart
and understands every desire and every thought.
If you seek him, he will be found by you;
but if you forsake him, he will reject you forever.

1 CHRONICLES 28:9 NIV

God is never confused by your thoughts or actions. He only sees a willing mind, one that is attuned to what he wants to accomplish through you. He searches your heart to find out if you are utterly devoted to him. That might seem scary. The God of the universe knows your true intentions in life. He knows your inner thoughts.

This is what makes the Christian life so exciting, because when we do turn our thoughts to him, we can find him. He will listen. He knows when you seek him.

Lord, I want to seek you today and every day. I know you will hear me when I pray, and I know you will listen when I cry out for your help.

You, Solomon my son, know the God of your father
and serve him with a whole heart and with a willing mind,
for the LORD searches all hearts
and understands every plan and thought.
If you seek him, he will be found by you,
but if you forsake him, he will cast you off forever.

1 CHRONICLES 28:9 ESV

God heard you today. Do you believe that? The assurance
from heaven is that when we seek him, we will find him.
When we speak, he will listen. And this is not a one-way
conversation. God doesn't just listen and then go silent. He
will act and speak through those around us. God will also
guide your life, because he knows your every thought and
every desire.

The question to ask yourself today is whether you really believe
he listens, and if you will choose each day to seek him. Do you
want to let God guide your life? Do you want to be known by
him, so that you can become part of his plan and direction?

Jesus, I know you hear me. When I cry out in the quiet moments of
life, you hear me. Please help me to seek you in every area of my life.

Do you believe that God heard you today?

Whole Heart

Then the people rejoiced because they had given willingly,
for with a whole heart they had offered freely to the Lord.

1 CHRONICLES 29:9 ESV

What does it mean to give from a whole heart? Most of us know all about half-hearted devotion. We follow a professional sports team when it's convenient. We buy from the same clothing store if we happen to be at the mall that day. Yet total devotion requires sacrifice. It takes time and money; it requires complete conviction in our thoughts and actions.

Today, when you head off to work or school, know that devotion is not something to take lightly. It means a willingness to give everything, not just the leftovers.

Jesus, I trust you. I want to serve you with my whole heart and give freely of my time and energy today because you are a wonderful Savior worthy of my devotion.

The people rejoiced at the willing response of their leaders,
for they had given freely and wholeheartedly to the LORD.

1 CHRONICLES 29:9 NIV

A "wholehearted" approach to living the Christian life means you are not giving Jesus the breadcrumbs, the bits and pieces that fall off the table after a meal. You are not just setting a place for Jesus at the table and spending a few minutes with him. Instead, your entire life is a banquet feast intended for your one true Savior. He's the reason you're even there.

Why do we departmentalize our faith? Because it's easier that way. Total devotion over the course of an entire day is much harder. How did your banquet feast go today? Did you think about Jesus once in a while or was he guiding you all day?

Lord, I want you to be at the center of every area of my life. I want to serve you and seek you with a whole heart, one that is utterly devoted, not partially devoted.

Was Jesus just a guest in your life today?

Strength

The eyes of the LORD move to and fro throughout the earth
that He may strongly support those whose heart is completely His.

2 CHRONICLES 16:9 NASB

Before you even roll out of bed, God is looking for you. He's
waiting for you. As you brush your teeth and comb your hair,
he's keenly aware of the choices you will make today. In fact,
he wants to "strongly support" you in every endeavor. The
choice to make is whether you will give your whole heart to
him, to offer your plans, your desires, and even your worries
to him.

What happens when you do? How will God work through you?
That's the exciting part. He promises to work through you in
a way that will be undeniable. Only God can accomplish so
many great things in your life, all for his glory. Are you ready?

God, I want to be a vessel for your will today. I know you will carry
me through the day, and my role is simply to stay devoted to what
you want to accomplish.

The eyes of the Lord run to and fro throughout the whole earth,
to shew himself strong in the behalf of them
whose heart is perfect toward him.

2 Chronicles 16:9 KJV

Did you see God work in your life today? He can make all
of the difference in the world, although you do have a role
to play. You don't have to be perfect, but you should always
work on your devotion to him, as the verse for today suggests.
What is perfect devotion? It means you won't just give Jesus a
portion of your life, to segment and divide your time. It means
you will set aside all earthly ambition for heavenly ambition.

At the end of each day, look back on your decisions and
reflect on how much you perfected this devotion and love
for your Savior. Was it all about you? Did you seek your own
will? Or did God work through you in a way that only his Holy
Spirit can?

Holy Spirit, take my entire life. Use me to your glory and your will.
Help me set aside my own success and earthly desires so that I
may see you work.

Who won the battle for control of your life today?

On the Path

I will instruct you and teach you the way you should go;
I will counsel you with my eye upon you.

PSALM 32:8 NRSV

Your devotional time in the morning is like using a spiritual GPS, a navigation system sent from above. You set your destination, you calibrate your life. God is the driving force all day long, so spending time with him means you will know which way he wants you to go.

It's an exciting adventure. Attuned to God's direction, knowing his plans for your life before you ever listen to any directions on your phone or the car, means you have a powerful guide. He will counsel you and keep his eye on you, instructing and teaching along the way.

Jesus, be the guide in my life today. Don't let me try to type out the directions for my own life or to follow my own way. Be the voice of guidance in my life.

I will instruct you and teach you in the way which you should go;
I will counsel you with My eye upon you.

PSALM 32:8 NASB

You have a choice every day to listen to God as the one true guide in your life. How did your navigation system work today? Did you listen with spiritual ears or were you half-listening?

The Bible is like a GPS in that you can find direction for your life, but you do have to read the instructions and listen to the voice. In the morning, you set your destination. At night, look back on the path you chose. If you went off course, stay on the path the next day.

God, help me to look back on the day and see where you guided my thoughts and actions. Help me to know how you directed me in every decision.

How is your spiritual navigation system?

Rules Are Good

May my tongue sing of your word,
for all your commands are righteous.

PSALM 119:172 NIV

Rules were not made to be broken, despite what you may have heard. As you get older, you realize rules are meant to protect us. The stop sign at the end of the street or the tax forms you have to fill out are intended to maintain order in society, not make you miserable.

That's why the Psalmist wrote about the joy of following the precepts of God, because God is good and so are his commands—every single one. Living a pure life, undefiled, is a better way to live. Of course, in Christ we find forgiveness, even when we break the rules. Grace waits for us just past the next stop sign. Yet it's worth considering today that God wants you to be holy and righteous, and it's perfectly fine to see rules as part of God's plan for your life.

Lord, help me to see your rules for a righteous life as a good way to live, and know they are not meant to cause constant guilt. In Christ, I'm forgiven and fully sanctified.

My tongue will sing of your word,
for all your commandments are right.

Did you follow the rules today? Know that there is great joy in
staying obedient to your calling in Christ, while at the same
time knowing that God wants us to reach even higher beyond
the rules and seek a relationship with him, one that leads to
fulfillment and joy.

So why bother with rules? For most of us, the idea of rule-
keeping and legalism can be depressing, but from Scripture
we know that rules come from God and are not intended to
frustrate us. Indeed, with the power from the Holy Spirit, you
can live pure and holy. If you do miss the mark, come back to
Jesus and seek forgiveness and restoration, one day at a time.

Jesus, I'm far from perfect. Help me to rest in the forgiveness and
grace you offer, and to see rules as good for me—a way to know you
more.

What did God teach you about grace today?

273

Lifting the Fallen

The LORD lifts the fallen
and those bent beneath their loads.

PSALM 145:14 TLB

That load you're carrying today—it is not too heavy for God. He is the lifter of loads. He can do more today than merely sustain you; he will lift you even higher than before. In fact, he is keenly aware of those who have fallen and need spiritual sustenance and restoration.

He knows your pain. On the cross, Jesus took the burden of sin and guilt—he took your place so that you can find restoration in him, a brand new life. God won't let you carry the worry and pain of life all by yourself, either. He has the power to lift fallen people.

Jesus, my burdens are too heavy today. Please restore me and lift my spirit.

The LORD sustains all who fall
And raises up all who are bowed down.

PSALM 145:14, NASB

We all have pain receptors, both physical and spiritual. When there's a pin-prick, we wince. When someone speaks a harsh word, we recoil. It's only human. Yet as you look back on the events of the day, think about how God was there even in the midst of your pain.

Here's the eternal promise. God sees you. No pain is too big. No anxiety or doubt will overcome you. Why is that? Because God is powerful and will restore you. Maybe it won't be right this moment (or maybe it will) but know that the promise of Scripture is clear. He will lift the fallen, he will restore the broken, he will wipe out the anxiety, and he will carry you.

God, the worries and pain in life are no match for you, the lifter of my soul. Thank you for seeing the pain and for keeping a close eye on me.

What was the exact moment when God noticed your pain today?

Mended

He heals the brokenhearted
and binds up their wounds.

PSALM 147:3-4 ESV

Most of us think of healing as physical restoration—the blind man sees, the lame walk. As you think of the events of the day, the conflicts that might arise, and the challenges you face, start seeing "healing" as more than a physical act. As the verse for today makes clear, God can heal a broken heart as well, and he cares for you and knows your pain.

Distractions will come, and the path won't always be perfectly clear. Picture God today as the person who leans down and mends your wounds.

God, you are my healer. Reach down and bind up these wounds—
emotional, spiritual, physical—and help me to stand in the face of
great challenges today.

He heals the brokenhearted
And binds up their wounds.

PSALM 147:3-4 NASB

When God heals you, it's like a fire in your soul. You want to let everyone know. You can't keep the secret for long, because you know only God can bring that type of restoration.

As you ponder the day, think back to how God worked in your life, how he brought about a change in plans or a change in viewpoint, how he restored a relationship and brought you one step closer to resolution. Spend some time thanking your Savior for that inner work and be sure to thank him for giving you salvation in the first place.

God, thank you for healing me. Thank you for binding up my wounds. Thank you for working in my life. I can only explain this wonderful work as a touch from your hand.

How did God restore you today?

Find Life

Those who find me find life
and receive favor from the LORD.

PROVERBS 8:35 NIV

Every new day is an opportunity to find life. This is the promise of the verse today: if you seek and find God, you will find life. But what does that really mean? You have one life to live. You can seek purpose and fulfillment, or you can seek riches and personal glory. There is a choice each day, and you won't find life by accident. The only way to find purpose and meaning is to seek the one who gave you your life in the first place.

Today and every day, set aside time to ponder the real purpose of life. Who are you really living for? What are your goals? What is driving you the most?

Jesus, I know you are the giver of life—physically and spiritually. Help me today to seek you with utter devotion so that you can reveal yourself and help me discover real peace.

Whoever finds me finds life
and obtains favor from the LORD.

PROVERBS 8:35 NASB

Have you ever gotten really lost driving late at night? If you take a wrong turn on a familiar road or enter an unknown area for the first time, it feels odd, and you want to get back on track. You want to figure out how to retrace your steps and return to a safe place.

For many of us, getting lost spiritually is even harder. You don't know what comes next. You are not sure of the best route. You feel a deep desire to find a new road. That's why it's so important to look back on your day and think about where you took a misstep, and where you can look for direction next time. Skip the guilt. Go right to renewal.

God, help me to seek you and find favor. Help me to calibrate my thoughts and actions to align with your will for my life.

How did God recalibrate your thoughts today?

Blessed to Bless

The people curse him who holds back grain,
but a blessing is on the head of him who sells it.

PROVERBS 11:26 ESV

Blessings come when you make good decisions on a daily basis. We're not talking about earthly blessings like a new car or a pile of cash. We hold back grain when we decide to compromise, or when we cheat on a test or speak badly about a friend.

Live today in such a way that shows you are more interested in the riches of heaven—the eternal rewards that come from living a pure life. That is: Pure thoughts. A kind heart. A righteous attitude. Live without compromising and you will see how God blesses you in spiritual ways, with peace of mind and a positive outlook on life. The good news? Once you experience these wonderful blessings, you can start blessing others in the same way.

Jesus, help me to understand what true spiritual blessings mean.

> *He who withholds grain, the people will curse him,*
> *But blessing will be on the head of him who sells it.*
>
> PROVERBS 11:26 NASB

Few of us wake up in the morning and decide to cheat on our taxes or steal an iPhone at the local gadget store. Well, some do—but most of us are aware of the consequences. Ironically, we don't think about spiritual consequences. Scripture paints a clear picture of receiving spiritual blessings as a way to bless others. What you do, what you think about, and what you say all have consequences—for you and others.

How did that play out for you today? Every small decision you made, even the ones about how you talk and how you treat others, have an impact on your spiritual demeanor. When you cheat, lie, or steal, you deprive yourself of spiritual blessings, and that means you're also depriving others when you focus on your own guilt and shame (and not on God's plan for you).

God, help me to avoid the distraction caused by sin, the guilt and shame that consumes me. Help me to see blessings as spiritual in nature and how I can pass them on to others.

How do you define blessing?

Darkness into Light

"I will lead the blind by ways they have not known,
along unfamiliar paths I will guide them;
I will turn the darkness into light before them
and make the rough places smooth.
These are the things I will do;
I will not forsake them."

ISAIAH 42:16 NIV

When God said in Genesis, "Let there be light," he wasn't only talking about the sun in the sky. God created the concept of light, the ability to shine, and even the absence of darkness. There's the light you see around you, and there's spiritual light. God wants to shine a light on your path today, to give you the help you need to avoid pitfalls and not trip over your own feet.

The question to ask today is whether you have found the light you need. God can help you see in the dark and he can overcome the darkness. The rough patches? They don't stand a chance because God can restore you even when you've taken a wrong path.

God, allow the light to fill me up and guide my every step today.

"I will bring the blind by a way that they knew not;
I will lead them in paths that they have not known:
I will make darkness light before them,
and crooked things straight.
These things will I do unto them,
and not forsake them."

ISAIAH 42:16 KJV

Did you stay on the straight and narrow today, or did things go a little askew? Not to worry—God has your back. He is all about correcting your path. He wants to straighten things out, and the only way to do that is to admit there's a little darkness going on inside of you. It's not eternal darkness; it's a hint of your former self, sin that has stuck around long past its expiration date.

Thankfully, you don't have to linger in the dark or stay bent and broken. The King James Version of this verse talks about making crooked things straight—we're all a little crooked, aren't we? Especially when we trust our own instincts instead of the Holy Spirit guiding us.

Holy Spirit, you are the light that guides me. You give me the hope to see in a dark world, even when it seems like the light has vanished.

How did you let God's light shine today?

Ancient Paths

Stand at the crossroads, and look,
and ask for the ancient paths,
where the good way lies; and walk in it,
and find rest for your souls.
But they said, "We will not walk in it."

JEREMIAH 6:16 NRSV

Do you know that you're not alone in your spiritual journey?
God is always with you, and many of the challenges you've
faced are not entirely unique (even though it might seem
that way). What we know from this passage is that many have
traversed the "ancient paths" and have battled with the same
challenges you face. You can overcome. In Christ there is
hope for any situation you are facing today. In fact, you have a
champion who is fighting for you.

God is not so remote today that he won't see what is troubling
you. He is always a prayer away. When you call out, know that
Jesus suffered as well, more than we can understand. God
raised him from the dead and restored him. That same power
is still available for you.

God, help me to see that I'm not alone. Help me to know that you
are with me and that this spiritual journey of life is not something
I have to walk alone.

> *"Stand by the roads, and look,*
> *and ask for the ancient paths,*
> *where the good way is; and walk in it,*
> *and find rest for your souls.*
> *But they said, 'We will not walk in it.'"*

JEREMIAH 6:16 ESV

God is always near. When you look back and think about the decisions you made, the path you took, and the plans you made, realize that you did not make those decisions alone. The Holy Spirit was speaking to you, often through Scripture and other Christians. What did they have to say?

How did you receive encouragement to keep focusing on Jesus today? The challenge for some of us is that we won't listen to that encouragement. We focus on negative feelings and attitudes. Research says it is easier to think a negative thought. It comes naturally to us. Choose the more rewarding path of joy, hope, blessing, and encouragement.

Jesus, help me to put aside any negative thoughts from the day that are playing in an endless loop in my head. Help me to focus on the joy of the Lord instead.

Did you listen to the voice of encouragement today?

Justice Roll

Let judgment run down as waters,
and righteousness as a mighty stream.

AMOS 5:2 KJV

Righteousness might not seem like the most exciting concept, mostly because it might remind you of rules. Guess what? God doesn't see it that way.

From this passage, we find out that God sees justice and righteousness as a mighty stream. The word picture here is intentional. Justice and righteousness can be a powerful force, rolling down a hillside in a way that is unstoppable because they are part of God's nature; they help you focus on what is right and just in your own life. It's not trivial at all. Choose to see righteousness as something powerful and good, a force to be reckoned with. Once you do, you're on a path to understand how God wants you to live.

God, help me to see justice as a powerful force—a raging river.

Let justice roll down like waters
And righteousness like an ever-flowing stream.

AMOS 5:2 NASB

Have you ever been in a roll call? You have to wait patiently until you hear your name. You can't focus on anything else or you'll miss raising your hand. In school, a roll call is not something you want to ignore. It can determine part of your grade (the teacher will think you're absent).

Funny thing is, there's a roll call when it comes to following Jesus as well. Justice rolls like a river and it's totally relentless. You have to pay attention to justice and righteousness in your life. Get distracted by other things and you might miss the opportunity God has for you.

God, help me today to see how you have called me out from my peers to live righteously and with an attitude of full devotion to your calling.

Did you call my name during roll call today?

How to Live

He has told you, O mortal, what is good;
and what does the Lord require of you
but to do justice, and to love kindness,
and to walk humbly with your God?

MICAH 6:8 NRSV

Do you want to know God's will for your life today? It's explained in this passage. Promote justice, be faithful, and live obediently. It's all spelled out clearly right there.

Some of us look for God's will in all of the wrong places and we think finding his will is an arduous task. We have to search for it every day, and we can get distracted and lost easily enough. Ironically, God has already revealed his will for your life in Scripture. The hard part is acting on his will and sticking to his plan.

God, I already know your will is for me to promote justice, be faithful, and live obediently. Help me to know that you have already given me this clear direction.

> *He has told you, O man, what is good;*
> *and what does the LORD require of you*
> *but to do justice, and to love kindness,*
> *and to walk humbly with your God?*
>
> MICAH 6:8 ESV

It's easy to get distracted in life. That shiny new gadget promises instant fulfillment. Our thought process usually goes like this: "If I can just buy that new phone, or those clothes, or that new car, then I will have more peace and fulfillment in life." That never works.

Think of God as someone who can give you a prescription for life that's not found at the drugstore. It's already available in this passage: a way to live that will bring lasting joy and peace, not a constant search for something new in life.

Jesus, you are the only fulfillment I'm seeking in life. Help me to set aside all aspirations for something new and to stay content with the promises you've already revealed.

How did God already reveal his promises to you today?

Sure Footed

The LORD God is my strength,
And He has made my feet like hinds' feet,
And makes me walk on my high places.

HABAKKUK 3:19 NASB

Have you ever bought a pair of shoes that seemed like they were too slippery? You walk up the street in the rain or snow, and you can't be sure you will make it more than a few steps. You decide right then and there to go and buy shoes with a better tread.

For anyone living the Christian life, it can be easy to slip and fall. Distractions come and go in life. Just when you think you are in a place where you are trusting God to guide you, along comes a temptation or a distraction that makes you slip up yet again. What's so wonderful about this passage from Habakkuk is that God promises to give us good spiritual tread. He will lead us to a place of sure footing and won't let us wander too far from him.

God, thank you for giving me the assurance of knowing your will for my life. Thank you that you are guiding me to the truth and the right way to live, one step at a time.

God, the Lord, is my strength;
he makes my feet like the deer's;
he makes me tread on my high places.

HABAKKUK 3:19 ESV

God does not want you to lose your footing. He's all about
guiding you into more spiritual maturity; he is not interested
in letting you stay spiritually stagnant. As you look back on
your day, you might see a pattern that suggests God is helping
you overcome things like habitual sin, a dark attitude about
life, or the allure of wealth and status.

Why is that? Because God wants you to find a better path in
life. He wants you to look up and move on, to make progress.
It's a step by step journey, one day at a time. To say God is
your strength is a way to express who has the power to help
you overcome.

Holy Spirit, you are my strength in life. I know you are there to
guide me and help me overcome any sin or distraction in my life,
and to find sure footing.

How did God give you a better path today?

No Worries

> *"Martha, dear friend, you are so upset over all these details!*
> *There is really only one thing worth being concerned about.*
> *Mary has discovered it—and I won't take it away from her!"*

LUKE 10:41-42 TLB

Worrying about a problem until it goes away is not a good strategy. In this passage, Jesus explains what actually works. Instead of fretting about the demands of life today—trying to force things to fit into a spiritual box or make sure all of your plans succeed on your terms—it's a much better plan to rest in the fact that devotion to God leads to fulfillment.

It wasn't that Jesus faulted Martha for hard work. It's that she was working hard for the wrong reasons instead of staying devoted. She wasn't placing all of her plans and goals into the hands of Jesus, she was merely working and serving. He is the reason we work. When you are properly oriented to his call, Jesus will turn your hard work into spiritual fulfillment.

God, I don't want to just work hard and never see any spiritual growth. Help me to start with devotion to you today, and then take my hard work and use it for your glory.

> *"Martha, Martha,*
> *you are anxious and troubled about many things,*
> *but one thing is necessary.*
> *Mary has chosen the good portion,*
> *which will not be taken away from her."*
>
> LUKE 10:41–42 ESV

After a long day, it's tempting to find the remote and just chill in front of the television. Instead of doing that, why not look back and see how God worked in your life? Spend a few minutes comparing what you tried to accomplish with the things God accomplished through you.

Really, there's no comparison. Work meant only for personal advancement and fulfillment can't compare to work that is for the Lord and meant for his kingdom causes. We always know which kingdom we're trying to advance, don't we? When we stay devoted to Jesus, we find that he is guiding every decision and yearns to work through us.

Jesus, I want you to work through me and not just work on my own. Please change my attitude about work to one that starts with devotion to you first and foremost.

How did you let God work through you today?

Prepared

"What no eye has seen, nor ear heard,
nor the human heart conceived,
what God has prepared for those who love him."

1 CORINTHIANS 2:9 NRSV

Did you notice something interesting about the passage for today? Read that last sentence again. All of the statements listed above depend on it. For those who love God. It means everything when it comes to knowing what God has planned for you today.

When you are in love, you make sacrifices. You start and end the day with utter devotion to your object of love. This passage makes a promise that God has a plan for you, one that will be great. You can't even fathom how amazing those fulfilled promises will be. It all starts with loving him first.

God, I love you. I want to live for you today—not just when it fits into my schedule but for the entire day and with everything in me.

> *"No one has ever seen this,*
> *and no one has ever heard about it.*
> *No one has ever imagined*
> *what God has prepared for those who love him."*

1 CORINTHIANS 2:9 NCV

Sometimes, a verse from a new translation of the Bible jumps out at you. One example is the passage for today. God has great things planned for you today. They were so new and unique that you have never even imagined them.

Now for the hard part. It's tough at times to pay attention to the little details, the areas where God directed you. It might have been something simple, like a kind word you offered to a gas station clerk. It might have more profound, like a new endeavor in life you didn't expect. Your blessings may be too many to count but think back on your day. How did God bring about something brand new? Remember to thank him for giving you that direction.

Jesus, thank you for moving and acting in my life in ways I never expected.

What simple blessings did God give you today?

Triumph

Thanks be to God, who in Christ always leads us in triumphal procession, and through us spreads the fragrance of the knowledge of him everywhere.

2 CORINTHIANS 2:14 ESV

We're all heading somewhere. It's the steps we make in life—one after the other—leading us to the next experience, the next adventure. In life, you have two choices. You can either follow that path of joy or despair.

The passage for today talks about a triumphal procession. Wow. That sounds like someone is happy and excited. It's a spiritual journey and a dance procession at the same time. Choose today to live with a sense of joy and purpose, to acknowledge that, as a Christian, God has a plan for you, and it is a plan filled with joy and meaning at every turn.

God, I'm excited. I get to follow the path you have for me. That's triumphant.

Thank God! He has made us his captives and continues to lead us along in Christ's triumphal procession. Now he uses us to spread the knowledge of Christ everywhere, like a sweet perfume.

2 CORINTHIANS 2:14 NLT

The dictionary defines "triumphal" as a celebration of great victory. It's a way to live your life, constantly aware that God has already pointed you in the right direction. He's in the "triumphal process" of revealing what he has planned for you.

It's going to be a wonderful journey. As you look back on your day, did you experience triumph and blessing? Did God reveal a bit more of what he has planned for you?

God, thank you for revealing (and reveling) in the plans you have for me.

How did God reveal his plans today?

Ambassador

We must all appear before the judgment seat of Christ, so that each of us may receive what is due us for the things done while in the body, whether good or bad.

2 CORINTHIANS 5:10 NIV

An ambassador is an official representative. This role is not to be taken lightly. To become an ambassador, you must show utter devotion to your country or cause.

The same is true as a Christian. As you think about your choices today and the activities that will present themselves, make sure you double-check your spiritual name tag. It says "ambassador" and you received that title the minute you accepted Christ into your life. This applies to everything you do and say, even on social media. As an ambassador, you will be judged according to how you let God work through your life each day.

Jesus, help me to represent your kingdom on earth in a way that is fitting for a king.

We must all appear before the judgment seat of Christ, so that each one may receive what is due for what he has done in the body, whether good or evil.

2 CORINTHIANS 5:10 ESV

Each day, you have a choice concerning the plans you make and the words you say. There's a choice between good and evil. Will you speak kindly to a friend or speaking harshly?

Of course as a Christian you can find grace at the end of the day for your actions, good or bad. What this passage is saying is that you will be accountable to God for how you lived, even in those quiet moments of solitude before your day starts or in the evening when you doze off to sleep. It all counts.

God, keep me perfectly oriented to your will.

How did you represent Jesus in your words and actions today?

Demolition Day

The weapons of our warfare are not of the flesh
but have divine power to destroy strongholds.

2 CORINTHIANS 10:4, ESV

A stronghold is a fortress meant to stand the test of time. Made of brick or stone, built on a mountain or in a valley—no one erects a stronghold that is intended to crumble. They rise above the landscape; it takes a lot to knock them down, a strong and powerful force.

In the spiritual realm, strongholds of sin seem immovable and impossible to destroy. We like being contrary, or abusive in our words, or intent on blaming others. These are deep-seated strongholds, built over many years. Fortunately, in Christ we can destroy any sin, no matter how firmly rooted in our lives. Do you believe that? Claim the verse today as a battle cry. It's demolition day and sin doesn't have a chance against the power of God in your life.

God, help me to obliterate my strongholds of sin today.

The weapons of our warfare are not of the flesh,
but divinely powerful for the destruction of fortresses.

2 CORINTHIANS 10:4 NASB

Did you win the battle against your strongholds of sin today? Habitual sins and long-developed patterns of self-destruction can tower over you, casting a dark shadow. Everyone around you knows these fortresses of sin are deeply embedded. Does everyone around you know that Jesus came to conquer those sins? If you use the right weapons—prayer, devotion, a community of believers—they cannot stand.

You will find victory not because you figure out an answer to every problem in your life. You will find victory when you lay your strongholds at the foot of the cross.

Jesus, you are victorious in my life. Sin cannot stand against you. It's finished.

Which stronghold did Jesus crush today?

Preach Peace

*He came and preached peace to you who were far off
and peace to those who were near.*

EPHESIANS 2:17 ESV

Even a quick reading of this passage in Ephesians reveals a wonderful truth. No matter where those around you stand in their relationship with Jesus—close or far away—there is a clear directive for all of us. We are supposed to keep preaching peace.

How does that play out in your daily routine? It might help to think of the alternative. If you speak poorly about others, create discord, or live in a selfish way, you cannot preach peace. The theme here is to keep preaching peace no matter what, and to keep placing your hope in the one who brings peace in the first place.

God, help me to preach peace to those around me today, no matter what.

He came and preached peace to you who were far away
and peace to those who were near.

EPHESIANS 2:17 NIV

Friends will let you down. That's a fact of life. Nobody's perfect. The one thing that seems to separate those who are more mature in their faith and those who let circumstance govern their behavior is that the more devoted among us listen closer to God's plans. God is on the throne, and no matter what happens in life, even if friends betray you, you can still talk about what Jesus is doing in your life; you can still preach peace and hope to those around you.

How did that go for you today? It's a challenge, because as you look back on the day, you might think you preached disunity, or discord, or despair. It's okay. Hope for tomorrow. As you mature in your relationship with Christ, peace will flow out of you.

Jesus, I'm not perfect. I don't always preach peace to those who are close to you and to those who are far away. Help me to testify about your power in my life.

Did you preach a message of peace to friends today?

Lean Forward

One thing I do: Forgetting what is behind and straining toward
what is ahead, I press on toward the goal to win the prize for
which God has called me heavenward in Christ Jesus.

PHILLIPIANS 3:13-14, NIV

At any track meet, runners always line up, crouch down,
and then lean forward, listening closely for the starting gun,
sprinting down their lane after the crack of the gun. They stay
focused on the ribbon at the end of the track, never looking to
the side and never slowing down.

As Christians, we can live this way as well. We don't need
to look behind us, but press on and lean toward the prize.
What is that prize? We already know that too. We're going in a
heavenly direction. Will you lean into it?

Holy Spirit, be my guide today. Help me to lean into you.

One thing I do: forgetting what lies behind and reaching forward to what lies ahead, I press on toward the goal for the prize of the upward call of God in Christ Jesus.

PHILIPPIANS 3:13-14 NASB

A wonderful truth about living for Jesus is that you have a clear goal: to push yourself toward the prize of knowing him more. You may have other goals, maybe to finish school or to land the perfect job. We don't always know the end result. The wonder of living the Christian life is that we do know where we are heading, we do know the ultimate goal.

Jesus wants you to lean forward. Don't look back. Press on so that when you finally lay down in bed for the night, you can think about what lays ahead of you the next day—another opportunity to serve him and to share your story about what he has done in your life.

Jesus, teach me about what it means to forget about the past. Help me to lean in the right direction. Guide me so that I'm always pressing forward, toward you.

How did you lean into Jesus today?

Start with Thanks

Give thanks in all circumstances;
for this is God's will for you in Christ Jesus.

1 THESSALONIANS 5:18 NIV

Giving thanks is not easy. Sometimes, you have to look harder for things to be thankful for. As you start your day, think about the most obvious gifts. The air you breathe, the sky above your head, the beautiful sun. Go one step deeper and think about friends and family who love you and who want the best for you. These are wonderful blessings.

On an even deeper level, Christ has given you life in him so that you can combat sin and live victoriously in him. There is no greater gift. Eternity starts now, because once you recognize that Jesus wants to invade every part of your soul, you can also recognize that this eternal mindset is one you can display for everyone to see on a regular basis—every day of the week.

Jesus, be the center of my life today.

Give thanks in all circumstances;
for this is the will of God in Christ Jesus for you.

1 THESSALONIANS 5:18 ESV

At the end of the day, it's easy to look back and see how God worked in your life. Even the tough circumstances, even the conflict—they are all helping to form you into the person God wants you to be. That formation process takes time. You can rest in the assurance that God is also taking one day at a time with you.

If you look hard enough, you can always find a reason to give thanks. Spend some time praising God in your prayer time today. Ask God to reveal how he worked to make you more like Jesus.

Lord, thank you for giving me eternal life in your Son.

What are you thankful for today?

Slow to Speak

Let every person be quick to hear,
slow to speak, slow to anger.

JAMES 1:19 ESV

For your devotions today, find a clock or a wristwatch that shows you the second ticking by. (If you use a smartphone, you can set a timer and see the digits moving.) When you watch a clock, especially one with a second-hand, time seems to move slower. Why is that?

For some of us, it's because we're always moving so fast. We rarely stop to think about time. In the same way, we rarely think about the words we're saying and if they will be a blessing or a curse to someone else. Try to be more intentional about what you say today, similar to how you watched the second-hand on a clock. Think about the impact you are making on others with your words, and if you are speaking in love and kindness.

Lord, help me to speak in a way that is uplifting to others.

Let every man be swift to hear,
slow to speak, slow to wrath.

JAMES 1:19 KJV

How do you listen quickly? That's a bit of a riddle. Our ears don't move, and we can't control how quickly someone else speaks. We can put a plunger on our words, though. To be quick to listen today means to refrain from speaking, and to engage in active listening—a way to cue another person into our interest level. Sometimes, it's a way of looking at someone, of turning your ear toward that person, of clueing in to the words they sat in an earnest way.

Being quick to listen also means being available. If you walk past someone, or start talking, or look at your phone, you are not listening with any purpose.

Holy Spirit, give me the insight I need to listen with purpose.

Did you listen intently today?

Planted Word

*Get rid of all moral filth and the evil that is so prevalent
and humbly accept the word planted in you,
which can save you.*

JAMES 1:21 NIV

Two actions take place when there is a gift involved. One part
involves the person giving the gift—Grandma at Christmas
putting a package under the tree. The second part is receiving
the gift. You have to crouch down under the tree and pick up
the gift. Without both parts, there is no actual gift-giving, and
the transaction breaks down. No new socks for you.

As described in this passage, we must also receive the planted
word with humility. It can save your soul. If you have never
stopped and received salvation from Jesus, acknowledge that
he is your Lord and Savior, and ask him to enter your life,
take away your sin, and become your purpose for living.

Jesus, you are the giver of life. Help me to receive that gift today.

*Lay apart all filthiness and superfluity of naughtiness,
and receive with meekness the engrafted word,
which is able to save your souls.*

JAMES 1:21 KJV

The word "engrafted" used in this passage (thank you, King James Version) means to become joined with something else. What does that mean in context? As a Christ follower, the Word you received can save your soul; it's the work of salvation, the grace that saves you from sin.

You are joined to salvation like a plant that has been grafted onto another plant. It's a miracle performed by the worker of all miracles. In Jesus, you are part of his purpose and plan. Each day, you are growing in your faith more and more, and you are becoming more like Jesus in your words and actions. It's a spectacular phenomenon.

Father, thank you for salvation. Thank you that you have given me life.

Have you thanked Jesus for the planted word today?

Righteous Prayers

Confess your faults one to another,
and pray one for another, that ye may be healed.
The effectual fervent prayer of a righteous man availeth much.

JAMES 5:16 KJV

It's easy to think your friends are there to hang out with you at Starbucks, and there's nothing wrong with a little social time. As you grow in your faith, you'll find that the best friends you have will be a sounding board. They will act like a reflection for your actions and words, and you'll know if you are maturing in your faith based on their response and feedback.

Then, as you mature even more, you will likely enter a phase when you can confide in friends and the other people God has placed in your life. It's so cathartic. To confess your faults means to admit where you screwed up, and to pursue righteousness not as a sideline activity but as a holy pursuit.

Lord, help me to find trustworthy friends who will challenge me. Help me to confess my weaknesses to them, and to be a sounding board for them as well.

Confess your sins to each other
and pray for each other so that you may be healed.
The prayer of a righteous person is powerful and effective.

JAMES 5:16 NIV

Supernatural power is available to all believers. It starts with your own confession of sin. That leads to a closer communion with God, who then reveals direction and plans as you devote your life wholly to him. In a community of believers, there is also power in confessing your sins and being honest and real about your shortcomings. We are all in this together.

What comes next? As you think about your day, know that God is working in your life through any circumstance, even the ones that seem the most difficult. Out of those trials will come renewal and an awakening about who has all of the power and who is in control of your life.

Father, help me to give up control and let you guide me. It's your power that sustains me, not my own power. It's your salvation that gives me hope.

How did God bring renewal in your life today?

The Source

Blessed be the God and Father of our Lord Jesus Christ! According to his great mercy, he has caused us to be born again to a living hope through the resurrection of Jesus Christ from the dead.

1 PETER 1:3 ESV

Modern culture likes to paint a bleak picture. We're hopelessly drifting as a society, people are isolating themselves, anger and resentment abound. The truth of Scripture stands in stark contrast. We have a living hope, which means it is relevant, active, vibrant, and real. You can place your hope in other things, but they are going to let you down.

That's why devoting yourself to Jesus as you start the day makes such a profound impact. You are not wallowing in misery or shame; you are living out the hope of the world in real-time. Will you let others see that you have this hope? Will you let Christ shine in such a way that friends and family won't be able to ignore the source?

Father, help me to live today with utter conviction to your cause and to see each day as an opportunity to share the living hope inside of me.

Blessed be the God and Father of our Lord Jesus Christ, who according to His great mercy has caused us to be born again to a living hope through the resurrection of Jesus Christ from the dead.

1 PETER 1:3 NASB

Our hope comes from a single source. Jesus Christ, raised from the dead, is the path of salvation, not only when you initially professed Christ but each day as you grow and mature. Do you believe that the resurrection power of salvation can change your entire outlook today?

It starts in the morning as you spend a few minutes praying, reading, and experiencing God in your devotional time. Will Jesus be the first person you think about when you wake up? Will you commit to leaning on your Savior for more than salvation?

Jesus, speak to me today and reveal yourself in my daily activities so that I can experience more of you. Touch my heart and heal me so that I may live only for you.

Will Jesus become your all in all today?

Power

Seeing that His divine power has granted to us everything pertaining to life and godliness, through the true knowledge of Him who called us by His own glory and excellence.

2 PETER 1:3 NASB

Everything in your life hinges on the power of the cross. As we see in this passage, the power you need to make good decisions, to live a holy life, to express kindness and love to others—it's all found in our devotion to him, not in worldly things.

Yet we drift away so easily. As you start the morning, think about where you could drift and give into temptation or distraction—which experiences and decisions might cause you to compromise. Jesus is right there in the middle of your decision process. He wants to help you and direct your path. Will you let the power of the cross be your guide?

Lord, you are the ultimate purpose for my life. Help me to stay true to that calling today.

By his divine power, God has given us everything we need for living
a godly life. We have received all of this by coming to know him,
the one who called us to himself by means of his marvelous
glory and excellence.

2 PETER 1:3 NLT

When the power of God guides your life, there's nothing quite
so enriching. It's a glorified way to live. With Christ, you have
the power to overcome sin, to speak words of encouragement
to others, to find meaning and purpose that goes beyond the
day-to-day routine.

The question to ask today, a serious question: Is that power
enough for you? Will you abide in Christ as a way to find
true fulfillment, or will you let the cares of the world and the
temptations around you encroach on that devotion? Let the
power of the Holy Spirit overwhelm you today in a way that
means you will not look to the left or the right. You'll stay on
the single path. You will only let the wonderful, supernatural
power of the cross guide you.

Holy Spirit give me the power to live only for you.

What is your power source?

In God's Image

Then God said, "Let Us make man in Our image, according to Our likeness; let them have dominion over the fish of the sea, over the birds of the air, and over the cattle, over all the earth and over every creeping thing that creeps on the earth."

GENESIS 1:26 NKJV

Your story begins long before you were born and before you did anything, good or bad. It begins before your parents were born and before they made any of the decisions that have shaped your life in positive ways or in painful ways. Your story begins with the God who created you in his very image. God, who made all things and made them good, created you to bear his image; he created you and called you "good" because he is good.

Hear the Word of God speaking to you of your great value today. Live today like a person who is unique, dignified, and valuable because you bear God's image. No one needs to add anything to your value and no one can take it away.

Creator God, I ask for the ability to see myself and my value as an image bearer today.

Then God said, "Let Us make man in Our image, according to Our
likeness; and let them rule over the fish of the sea and over the
birds of the sky and over the cattle and over all the earth,
and over every creeping thing that creeps on the earth."

GENESIS 1:26 NASB

How has taking your value from God's image set you free to
live for God and for others? You no longer need something
from them to make you feel worthy. He has already made you
worthy in Christ.

God gave you the infinite dignity of reflecting him to others.
You are God's image bearer in your home, created to reflect
God to them and for them. You are his image bearer in your
classroom, created to act like God would act if he were sitting
at your desk. You are his image bearer in your workplace,
created to work and rule in such a way that they see God's
glory. This is the great calling of image bearers.

Eternal God, allow the worthiness that you have given me in
Christ to become a blessing for the people I live with and love.

How does the new image of Christ that you bear set you free to
serve others?

A Place

*The Lord God planted a garden in Eden, in the east,
and there he put the man whom he had formed.*

GENESIS 2:8 ESV

God took that first image bearer and placed him in a garden.
The garden had a name. It was in the east and it had four
rivers that formed its boundaries. We are even told that there
was gold there and that the gold was good. The good place was
a good gift of the good God.

You have a place where God has put you. He formed you and
ordered the movement of your life to put you there. In fact,
he ordered the organization of nations and the migrations of
people in order to get you there. Where are you? What's the
name of your place? What are the names of its rivers? Is there
gold there or some other industry? As you go about your day,
pay attention to your place. Enjoy the good gift of the people
and the rivers and the industry. The Lord God has given you
a place.

*Almighty God, open my eyes to the creation that you have spoken
into being and that you maintain by your Spirit.*

The Lord God planted a garden in Eden, in the east;
and there he put the man whom he had formed.

GENESIS 2:8 NRSV

God gave the place to the man and the man to the place. God's people have always been placed: from Adam in the garden to Abraham in Canaan; to Jesus in the second garden; to you in your place with its rivers and gold and lots of people as well.

God is the owner of both the garden and the man. He never gives up the title to the place or to the person. God owns both you and the place where you live. God has plans for the place and he intends to use you to see it happen. You are there because God supernaturally put you there at this time. You are there as an image bearer, redeemed and restored, indwelt and empowered by the Spirit of God.

Eternal God, allow the stable identity that you have given me in Christ to become a blessing for the place that I live in and love.

Do you believe that God sent you to the place where you live?

Created to Work

The LORD God took the man
and put him in the garden of Eden
to work it and keep it.

GENESIS 2:15 ESV

The Lord God took that man and put him in that garden to work it and to keep it. God made Adam to be a worker. His job, before the fall, was to keep the garden, to plant seeds and raise flowers, and to prune vines to make them more fruitful. The word for work here is used elsewhere in the Bible for the act of worship and the word for keep is used for keeping God's commands. God created mankind in his image so that they would keep his commands in every place where he sent them. And his command is to be a worker.

God created you and put you in your place to work it. He created you in his image and gave you talents so that the place where you live and the people you live with will be more fruitful because of you.

Almighty God, give me great joy in the work you have given me to do and enable me to do it for your glory, by the power of your Spirit.

Then the LORD God took the man
and put him in the garden of Eden
to tend and keep it.

GENESIS 2:15 NKJV

There is an old-world custom when a restaurant opens of
gathering together with a pastor, coworkers, and friends
to bless the ovens. Ovens are the tools with which they will
tend and keep the place as image bearers. Blessing them is
recognizing that every part of that work is holy and every meal
served is an extension of the way that God serves us in Jesus
Christ.

Jesus lived the life you should have lived and he died the
death you should have died. He did the work that the Father
demanded and blessed all the nations of the earth as a result.
God has given you work to do in the place where he sent
you. And unless the work you do is explicitly immoral, it is
and can be a holy vocation. The work you did today was an
extension of the work God did for you in Christ.

Our Father, you sent your Son, Jesus Christ, to do the work that we
could not do on our own. Thank you.

What is the work that God has given for you to do?

Not Alone

The Lord God said,
"It is not good for the man to be alone.
I will make a helper suitable for him."

GENESIS 2:18 NIV

Everything that God made was good. Everything reflected his goodness beautifully. However, it was not good for the man to be alone. Alone did not reflect God's goodness properly. God made a helper for Adam, a partner in the task of image bearing and dominion keeping. God made a suitable helper, one that is in every way his equal and in every way another image bearer.

God created you to be in community, to be a worker and to be a helper. Who will you spend time with today? Name them. Who are the family members, friends, and coworkers that God has given to you? God is sending you to be the help that they will need today.

Our Father, you created me to live my life in relationship with other people who also bear your image. Help me to see how I can help them and to offer help with joy.

> *Then the LORD God said,*
> *"It is not good for the man to be alone.*
> *I will make a helper who is right for him."*
>
> GENESIS 2:18 NCV

God created you to be in community and he has placed people around you as a gift to you, as suitable helpers for the work to be done. You are not alone. God has given you his people. Who were the people that God gave to you today? How were they a help for the work that God gave you to do? How did you receive them? You are to receive them with the same joy with which Adam received Eve. You are to accept them in the same way God, in Christ, has accepted you.

The other person, beside Eve, who is described with this Hebrew term helper is God himself. You are not alone, not matter how lonely you may feel at times. God is your helper. As you look back on the day, where can you see God's help? Let that be a comfort to you tonight.

Our Father, you created me to live my life in relationship with other people who also bear your image. Help me to see you have given them to me for my benefit and theirs.

How have you seen God's help in your life and who has he used to bring it to you when you needed it most?

A Calling

Jesus came and spake unto them, saying, "All power is given unto me in heaven and in earth. Go ye therefore, and teach all nations, baptizing them in the name of the Father, and of the Son, and of the Holy Ghost: Teaching them to observe all things whatsoever I have commanded you: and, lo, I am with you always, even unto the end of the world."

MATTHEW 28:18-20 KJV

Most of us do not live in Galilee, the place where Jesus was standing when he gave this instruction to his disciples. We are the beneficiaries of men and women who obeyed the command to go. And some of them had to go a long way. The gospel took nearly 1,700 years to reach North America. It took another few centuries to reach us.

These are your people. This is your ancestry. You are the present front line of a people who go in response to Jesus' command. Now, wherever you go, go as a disciple of Jesus Christ.

Almighty God, thank you for those who brought the gospel to me. Now send me into my day as one of them.

Jesus came and told his disciples, "I have been given all authority in heaven and on earth. Therefore, go and make disciples of all the nations, baptizing them in the name of the Father and the Son and the Holy Spirit. Teach these new disciples to obey all the commands I have given you. And be sure of this: I am with you always, even to the end of the age."

MATTHEW 28:18-20 NLT

Where did you go today? Were you going as a disciple while you were there? God's plans are for you to be a disciple every place you go, all the time.

Here is the good news. All authority in heaven and on earth has been given to Jesus, not to you. Jesus came into the world to save sinners. That is, before you were given any command to go, Jesus had already gone. He came into a world full of sinners and he found you there. As you lay down to rest tonight, do not rest in your good work of going but rest in his good work of coming for you.

O God, you sent your Son into the world to save me. Now send me.

What places has God given you to go as his disciple?

A Purpose

*"All authority has been given to Me in heaven and on earth.
Go therefore and make disciples of all the nations, baptizing
them in the name of the Father and the Son and the Holy Spirit,
teaching them to observe all that I commanded you."*

MATTHEW 28:18–20 NASB

The will of God for you today is to make disciples. We can get
so confused and worried about doing the will of God that we
never actually get around to doing it. The will of God is not
some grand secret, and it is not necessarily the job that you
do to pay the bills.

The will of God can be done by butchers and bakers and
candlestick makers. The will of God for you is to make
disciples who will believe in Jesus, follow Jesus, and make
more disciples of Jesus.

*Almighty God, you have made me a disciple and have
commanded me to make disciples. Thank you for the grand life
purpose. Give me wisdom to live it today. Amen.*

"All power in heaven and on earth is given to me.
So go and make followers of all people in the world.
Baptize them in the name of the Father
and the Son and the Holy Spirit.
Teach them to obey everything that I have taught you."

MATTHEW 28:18-20 NCV

The great calling that God has placed on your life is to make disciples. Does your disciple have a clear faith in Jesus? Have they grown to be more like Jesus than they were a year ago? Are they more prepared to make disciples? Are these things true of you?

At the end of the day it is good to remember that you are a disciple and not the master, the student and not the teacher. Jesus is the teacher and he laid down his life for you. He has laid down his life for your sins and your failures—even your failure to make disciples.

Lord, you are the great disciple maker. Teach me to follow you and to bring others with me.

How has God grown you as a disciple?

Ever Present

"Remember, I am with you always,
to the end of the age."

MATTHEW 28:20 NRSV

You are not alone. You are never alone. You have a people and God is the first of your people. You will live with and work with many people today and you will encounter far more.

Some of them are your people and others are not, but God is yours every day. Some of them will contribute to your well-being and some of them will disappoint you, perhaps dramatically, but God will always be with you. Today, begin your day remembering that you belong to God in Christ.

In the name of the Father, and of the Son, and of the Holy Spirit, amen. I thank you, God, that you have made me your own and that you made that pledge public in my baptism.

"I will be with you always,
even until the end of this age."

MATTHEW 28:20 NCV

You have been baptized into Jesus Christ and the church. You have been baptized into a very real body of believers who have also been baptized into Christ. You were baptized into the church who heard your testimony and saw you standing in the water before God and the congregation; the ones who shed tears at your conversion and cheered at your new birth.

You are not alone. You have been welcomed into the body of Christ as seen in your baptism. And God has called you to welcome others as he has welcomed you.

Jesus Christ, head of the church both universally and locally, bind us together in holy love. Unite us together in baptism.

Who are your people? Who has God united you with through the waters of baptism?

Good News

How can anyone preach
unless they are sent?
As it is written:
"How beautiful are the feet of those
who bring good news!"

ROMANS 10:15 NIV

The world is a crazy place, but you have been given solid
ground through the teachings of Christ. You have truth in
his revelation. You know who you are, you know who God is,
and you know what God wants of you. You have good news for
the world and part of your purpose and the purpose of your
people is to teach that truth to the world by your words and by
your life.

As you go out into your day, act on the teachings of Jesus
Christ in all that you do. Obey the teachings of Jesus at home,
at work, and in your neighborhood.

Almighty God, give me wisdom today as I seek to obey you at home
and at work and in my neighborhood.

Before someone can go and tell them,
that person must be sent.
It is written,
"How beautiful is the person
who come to bring good news."

ROMANS 10:15 NIV

The good news for the world is also good news for you. Yes, Jesus commanded you to go, make disciples, baptize, and teach. There is no choice in the matter; you either obey or you disobey the one who has all authority in heaven and on earth.

Jesus took away your sin and conquered death for you before he uttered this command. He was undeterred by death and he is undeterred by your disobedience. At the end of the day, rest in the good news that Jesus has obeyed the Father fully for your salvation.

Gracious Father, give me confidence tonight that you are pleased with me because of the full obedience of Jesus.

How do the gracious commands of Jesus give you comfort today?

Weight of Glory

I consider that the sufferings of this present time are not worth comparing with the glory that is to be revealed to us.

ROMANS 8:18 ESV

When was the last time that you sinned against God? Does it seem far too recent and far too often. Be encouraged to live life in this real world as you struggle against present sin. When you put your suffering, whatever it is, on one side of the mental scale and you put the future glory that God has for believers on the other side, there is no comparison. The scales do not even tip. Your suffering has no "worth" in the financial system that measures glory.

What feels weighty and burdensome to you today will one day make absolutely no difference to you. This is not because God will treat it like it is worthless, but because you will come to recognize that what he has given you in Jesus Christ infinitely outweighs it.

Gracious God, allow me to see the value of Jesus Christ in my life today.

I consider that the sufferings of this present time are not worth comparing with the glory about to be revealed to us.

ROMANS 8:18 NRSV

Suffering makes us want to ask, "Where was God when…?" The gospel tells us that God created a good world, the suffering came in with sin. Jesus lived the life we should have lived and died the death we should have died, and one day God will make all things right. The answer that Paul wants us to carry away from this question is "God was on a cross."

If you have suffered as a consequence of your sin, know that Jesus died to forgive you. If it was caused by the sin of others against you, hear the good news that Jesus' death is a more radical justice than you could ever take in your vengeance. If you have suffered just because the world is broken, Jesus has made you a new creation and Jesus will make all things right one day. That is the glory that awaits and this glory outweighs your suffering.

Lord God and everlasting Father, as I lay down to sleep, let me know and be content with the full payment of Jesus for the sin of the world.

What sins or pains do you need Jesus to tip the scales for today?

Leaning In

The creation waits in eager expectation
for the children of God to be revealed.

ROMANS 8:19 NIV

Creation is eager to see the kind of people we will become when God brings us to glory. Creation is waiting for the weight of sin to be lifted. Paul depicts creation as a person longing, wishing things were different, wishing death was not real, wishing the graves were empty. Creation leans forward, like a person stretching her neck around the corner to see the parade. It's like a child on Christmas morning looking around the doorframe, hoping it is time to get up. Creation wants to be the first to see the sons of God made holy.

Creation, this present fallen creation, every bit of it, is preaching to us. Creation hopes for the completion of your redemption because glory is not just your future, but its future also. The redemption earned by Jesus will cover the created earth. He is now reconciling all things to himself. He is putting all the broken pieces back together, but we are still waiting for the completion.

Father, let the sun, moon, and stars encourage me toward holiness. Amen.

*The creation waits with eager longing
for the revealing of the children of God.*

ROMANS 8:19 NRSV

Creation teaches us to wait because sometimes we act too quickly. The wanting or longing is the important part of this passage because the desire to have glory cover the earth is worth waiting for. Creation teaches us to want that day, to want it for us and to want it for creation.

We are learning to desire, to ache, and to groan for being made like Christ. This is what we should be seeing in creation every day. We want all things to be made right, for all obstacles between God and us removed. We want to be out of this mortal body and into the eternal one. Creation is training us to want what God wants. We look forward to the day when we become holy, when we actually become like Christ.

Father, teach me to long for that day.

What do you long for to be made whole in your life?

Frustration

The creation was subjected to futility, not willingly,
but because of Him who subjected it in hope.

ROMANS 8:20 NKJV

The world is not right. The way things are is not the way
things should be. We know the world. We see the news, we
see social media—perhaps more than we should—and we
know that the effects of sin are seen far more readily than the
effects of righteousness. Paul's personification teaches us
that creation is subjected to futility and frustration.

Creation is frustrated with the effects of sin and it is
frustrated with us for how long it is taking for all things to
be made right. It is frustrated along with us over the present
brokenness of the world caused by sin. All present suffering
in our lives is caused by the effect of sin.

How long, O Lord? How long will the wicked prosper? How long
will sin and sinners get their way? How long will the effects of sin
seem to rule in your creation? Amen.

The creation was subjected to futility, not of its own will
but by the will of the one who subjected it, in hope.

ROMANS 8:20 NRSV

We are tempted to look at Adam's fall and to think, "All is lost." Yes, the world is subjected, but it is subjected to him with certainty. Creation waited eagerly for the revelation of the Son of God, just as it waits now for the revelation of the sons of God.

Jesus' life and death is the answer to creation's longing, just as it is to yours. The death of Jesus is necessary for creation's longing to be fulfilled, for the broken effects of sin to be made right. It was necessary for Jesus to die and it is necessary for you to lay down your life. When we talk about exercising a redemptive dominion, we mean a dominion of the redeemed. The Word of God teaches us to be frustrated with sin so that we take up the fight against it in our own hearts.

God, I believe you. I believe that the redemptive power of Jesus is stronger than the destructive power of sin.

Do you have certainty that God will make all things right?

Free from Bondage

The creation itself also will be set free from its slavery to corruption into the freedom of the glory of the children of God.

ROMANS 8:21 NASB

There is a future for us and for all things. Our future glory is of greater worth than all our present sufferings put together. We are learning to long for the future like creation does.

One day, God will make all things right. One day, God will set creation free from its present bondage. One day, the pains in childbirth will be no more and one day, the seeds we put in the ground will bear more fruit than they do weeds. One day, the lion will lay down with the lamb and one day, the child will play in the adder's den. Creation will be set free one day, but now there is slavery to corruption.

Lord, let me know with certainty that you are not out of control in the world. Let sin and brokenness lead me to long for your return.

*The creation itself will be set free from its bondage to decay
and will obtain the freedom of the glory of the children of God.*

ROMANS 8:21 NRSV

While creation still waits for the slavery to end, you have
already been set free in Jesus. You were dead in your
trespasses and sins, but now you have been made alive
together with Christ. You were by nature children of wrath,
but God has shown you great love and grace. You were slaves
to the kingdom of darkness, but God transferred you to the
kingdom of his beloved Son. You were slaves to sin, but God
has redeemed you from that slavery by purchasing your
freedom with the precious blood of Christ.

This is the freedom of the sons of God that will one day be
enjoyed by creation. No, it is not true of the whole world yet,
but it is true of you today.

*Eternal Father, you have set me free. I bring to you the places
where sin still keeps me bound up and in slavery. I believe you with
all my heart and ask that you give me that freedom every day.*

Do you live in freedom of the sons of God? How is creation
being set free because of you?

Free to Work

*We know that the whole creation has been groaning together
in the pains of childbirth until now.*

ROMANS 8:22 ESV

Creation, like a mother in childbirth, is moaning in pain and
anticipation. It is certain that the hard work we put in now
will bear fruit in glory later.

The created world we live in groans for us to be holy. This
morning, hear the Word of God through creation: the battle
against sin is worth it because it bears fruit in us and through
us.

*Almighty God, I can see the labor going on in creation and I want
what it wants. I want to be holy. Give me strength to continue
when life is difficult.*

We know that the whole creation has been groaning
in labor pains until now.

ROMANS 8:22 NRSV

The apostle is drawing us into the story of the garden in order to encourage us to live holy lives. In this verse, creation proclaims the work of Christ each day to all who will listen. Will you listen this evening?

In the garden, Eve followed creation in the form of a serpent and Adam followed Eve. One day all be made right. There will be a garden city in the new heaven and new earth where men and women from every tribe, tongue, and nation will live in the light of Christ. Between now and then, we labor and groan against sin, looking to God for victory.

Holy Father, I long to be set free from sin. Strengthen me for the battle. Let me produce good fruit for the world around me.

Where are you seeing good fruit from your work of fighting sin?

Get Dirty

Not only they, but ourselves also, which have the first fruits of the Spirit, even we ourselves groan within ourselves, waiting for the adoption, to wit, the redemption of our body. For we are saved by hope: but hope that is seen is not hope: for what a man seeth, why doth he yet hope for?

ROMANS 8:23-24 KJV

We are waiting just like the fallen creation. Your world is not as it should be this morning. Perhaps the morning news has brought with it the knowledge of some great tragedy. Perhaps it is much closer to home. Your world is not as it should be. That is okay for you to acknowledge this morning.

Even if the suffering is real in your life, pessimism is never the biblical solution. The groaning of creation calls us to groan as well. It calls us to lament from the heart to God about the sin that remains in each of us and in the world.

Almighty God, my world is a filthy place and I am dirty too. Give me a groaning heart for the sin that remains in me and in the world.

*Not only this, but also we ourselves, having the first fruits of the
Spirit, even we ourselves groan within ourselves, waiting eagerly
for our adoption as sons, the redemption of our body. For in hope
we have been saved, but hope that is seen is not hope;
for who hopes for what he already sees?*

ROMANS 8:23-24 NASB

What are you waiting for? Why are you still groaning? We are
groaning because the world is still wrong. The first thing that
is wrong with the world is you. The sin that has broken the
world still wages war against the members of your body. That
is why you are groaning. And that sin has a name. Name it. Be
specific with God and with yourself tonight and let the gospel
hope change your heart.

If you have put your trust in Christ then you are dead to sin
and alive to God. The hope of heaven is yours. Yes, you still
battle sin in your body because you are still in the fallen
world, but you wait eagerly, as creation has taught you, for the
day when even your body will be redeemed in full.

Gracious God, give me rest in the hope of my full redemption.

How has God broken the power of sin in your body?

Glorious

If we hope for what we do not see,
we wait for it with patience.

ROMANS 8:25 ESV

Bring to mind your present sin and sorrows. Remember those things that are causing you pain right now. Think about that person who has sinned against you and it has not been made right. Be mindful of your own very real sin. Give attention to the brokenness of creation that is sitting on your chest like a weight and making it hard to breathe. Now, be patient with yourself in hope.

To be patient with ourselves, we must start with the right hope. That is, it starts with knowing where you're going. You are going toward Christ-like holiness in both body and soul. You are not there, but that is where you are going. Be patient with yourself as a sinner but see yourself with hope—have a confident expectation about yourself that God will make you holy. Let go of the expectation of sinlessness, but never let go of the expectation of holiness.

God, let me give up the expectation of perfection but never give up the hope of holiness.

If we hope for what we do not yet have,
we wait for it patiently.

ROMANS 8:25 NIV

Can you not see signs of hope in your Christian brothers and sisters? Can you see it in your parents who are, obviously, less than perfect? Can you see it in school mates who worship Jesus in church but live like the devil in class?

Is there any believer at all in whom you cannot see signs of hope? Look again. That sinner is being conformed into the image of Christ. You are part of God's plan for doing that in them and he will even use the sin committed against you to help make it happen. Be patient with them. Because God is bringing you to glory, because that is your future, you do not have to react to the sin that you see in others. Instead, you can act in the hope that God will bring them to glory.

Holy Father, give me grace to give the grace that you have given me.

Who has God put in your life for you to give hope to?

God's Temple

Do you not know that you are God's temple
and that God's Spirit dwells in you?

1 CORINTHIANS 3:16 NRSV

You are the temple of the Holy Spirit. That is, you (plural) are the temple of the Spirit together with the other believers. The church is the temple of the Holy Spirit. Your church is the temple of the Holy Spirit in your neighborhood.

The Bible tells us that there is a temple in heaven where God dwells. He patterned a temple after it to be built by King Solomon where God would condescend to meet with sinful people when they brought a sacrifice. When the Spirit of God filled that temple, no one would dare to approach; and when the Spirit left the temple, everyone felt the judgment of God. You are the temple of the Holy Spirit. He dwells permanently in you because Jesus has offered himself as a sacrifice once and for all.

Almighty God, I thank you that you have made me your temple by the sacrifice of Jesus and the indwelling Holy Spirit.

Do you not know that you are God's temple
and that God's Spirit dwells in you?

1 CORINTHIANS 3:16 ESV

You are the temple of the Holy Spirit; you are God's building. It does not matter if you feel worthy—he is worthy. You are made worthy by the Spirit who lives in you. The house is made worthy by the occupant.

You are the temple of the Holy Spirit, so be careful how you build. The kind of life that you lived today said something to your people about what God is like. The way you loved them showed them something about the love of God. If you lived like the devil, then that is a problem. However, if you look back at the end of your day and wonder if what you have built will last. Remember that Jesus is the foundation and the cornerstone. He will last.

Almighty God, as I look back at the end of my day, may what I built on you live forever.

What are you building that will live forever?

Washed

Do you not know that the unrighteous will not inherit the kingdom of God? Do not be deceived: neither the sexually immoral, nor idolaters, nor adulterers, nor men who practice homosexuality, nor thieves, nor the greedy, nor drunkards, nor revilers, nor swindlers will inherit the kingdom of God. And such were some of you. But you were washed, you were sanctified, you were justified in the name of the Lord Jesus Christ and by the Spirit of our God.

1 CORINTHIANS 6:9-11 ESV

We all have a list of sins in our past. Some of us have long lists and the rest of us are better liars. Some of us have the kind of list that shames mothers and embarrasses sailors. Some of us have the kind of past that wakes us up at 2:00 a.m. wishing those things were never true.

God says that you were washed. He does not say that you were never filthy, but he promises that he cleans you in a way that you never believed would be true. Yes, such were some of you, but God washed you and now you are clean.

Praise the Lord. I am clean.

Do you not know that the unrighteous will not inherit the kingdom
of God? Do not be deceived. Neither fornicators, nor idolaters,
nor adulterers, nor homosexuals, nor sodomites, nor thieves, nor
covetous, nor drunkards, nor revilers, nor extortioners will inherit
the kingdom of God. And such were some of you. But you were
washed, but you were sanctified, but you were justified in the
name of the Lord Jesus and by the Spirit of our God.

1 CORINTHIANS 6:9-11 NKJV

Can you honestly say tonight that you have never committed
one of the sins on that list? Good. That is the grace of God.
But there are others that you have committed. Those who have
not committed the unspeakable sins have a list of "acceptable
sins." Those are the worst kind. They seem like little faux pas
but they wipe out generations. They seem like just forgetting
to wash your hands but then they spread like the plague.

Do not be deceived. Neither the arrogant, nor the self-
righteous, nor the judgmental, nor the liars, nor those with the
ability to lust without being noticed, will inherit the kingdom
of God. Such were some of you, but you were washed.

My God, please forgive the presumption that my sin was acceptable.

Where have you created an artificial line between acceptable
and unacceptable sins?

Bride of Christ

I am jealous for you with a godly jealousy;
for I betrothed you to one husband, so that to Christ
I might present you as a pure virgin.

2 CORINTHIANS 11:2 NASB

There is nothing more beautiful than a bride on her wedding day. She prepares herself to walk down the aisle—after she has already prepared the aisle she is to walk down. She dresses in white as a symbol of purity and gathers attendants and a room full of witnesses to solemnize and celebrate the joyous day.

You are the bride of Christ. You have been betrothed because Jesus has promised himself to you. He has offered his own body as a bride price. He has gone to prepare a place for you and will return to bring you to himself at a time determined by the Father. You are loved and you are safe because he is a faithful bridegroom.

Heavenly Father, you have called us your bride and you have given your Son as our faithful bridegroom. Give me great security today in his faithfulness.

I am jealous for you with a godly jealousy.
I promised you to one husband, to Christ,
so that I might present you as a pure virgin to him.

2 CORINTHIANS 11:2 NIV

There is nothing more pathetic than an indifferent bride. Have you noticed that sacred moment in a wedding when the groom first sees his bride all prepared for him and marching down the aisle for better or worse, for richer or poorer? His face comes alive with the joy of her devotion. Now suppose she didn't march or dress up but comes yawning down the aisle, in yoga pants, with her hair pulled back. How would he feel then?

Paul says that he is dedicated to present us to Christ a pure virgin, devoted to him in our pure doctrine. We are to devote ourselves to the doctrines of God because of who it is that we are marrying. Pick up your Bible and read it cover to cover. Then start again. Read an old book, visit an old sainted believer. Devote yourself to Christ by being devoted to true doctrine.

My Lord, I am yours. Make me wholly yours.

Are you devoted to Christ in your doctrine?

Measured by Righteousness

He made Him who knew no sin to be sin for us,
that we might become the righteousness of God in Him.

2 CORINTHIANS 5:21 NKJV

Give up whatever you are using to measure yourself this morning and measure the righteousness that has been given to you by grace through faith. If you measure yourself in any way, you will either despair because of your sin or become inordinately proud because of your self-righteousness. Either way, it will destroy you and others.

What are you measuring this morning? Stop it. Stop measuring your sin and stop measuring your success. Start measuring yourself by the gracious sacrifice of Jesus and by that alone. You are no longer counted as a sinner because Jesus took your sin on himself. He did not become a sinner, but he carried the due penalty for your sin so that you would not have to. He was treated as guilty so that you could be treated as righteous.

Almighty God, you have given your only Son to carry my sin away.
Give me faith today to confidently walk away from all self-
condemnation and self-righteousness.

For our sake he made him to be sin who knew no sin,
so that in him we might become the righteousness of God.

2 CORINTHIANS 5:21 NRSV

Now that your work of the day is done, return to the good news that the work of God for you is likewise done because Jesus has done it all. Jesus lived the life that you should have lived—a perfectly righteous life. God took your sin, the wrong that you did today, and he placed it on the cross of Jesus.

Take the wrong that you have done today, and leave it there with Christ. He has paid for your guilt. He has carried away your sin. He has purchased your redemption. He has reconciled you to the Father. As you prepare to rest, rest in the promise that God is measuring Christ's righteousness to your account.

Holy Father, thank you for taking my sin away and thank you for making me righteous in Christ. Give me a holy rest this evening because I know that I am right with you.

What sins or successes do you still measure rather than resting in the finished work of Jesus?

Adopted

He predestined us to adoption as sons through Jesus Christ
to Himself, according to the kind intention of His will.

EPHESIANS 1:5 NASB

You were born into the family of Adam and you belong to
Adam. He is your father, your covenant head, and you are like
your father. Adam abdicated godly dominion over the Garden
where God had put him in exchange for sinful independence
over a field of weeds and thistles that would only produce by
the sweat of his brow. Adam loved the pleasures of sin more
than he loved the joy of obedience. And Adam is your father
by birth.

But you have been adopted. Adam's past is no longer your
past. Adam's guilt is no longer your guilt. In the same way,
your own sinful and disobedient past is no longer your past.
You have been adopted into the family of God. God is now
your Father and Christ is now your brother.

Our God and Father, I was not born into your family and I do not
sufficiently resemble your family. I remember the past only long
enough to be grateful that I am no longer that person.

Having predestinated us unto the adoption of children by Jesus Christ to himself, according to the good pleasure of his will.

EPHESIANS 1:5 KJV

You have been adopted into the family of God by grace through faith in the life, death, and resurrection of Jesus Christ. You have been supernaturally re-born by the powerful work of the Holy Spirt who renews you from the inside out and lives within you even now. God has miraculously made you part of his own family and given you a new nature, one that is being remade in the image of Christ. God is, right now, remaking you to be like himself.

Once you were like your father Adam, guilty and corrupt. Now, because of your adoption, you are like your Savior Jesus and are becoming more like him every day. God will not stop remaking you until the work is done.

God of glory and of grace, you have given me new birth and have adopted me into your family. By the power of your Holy Spirit, please make me more like you.

In what ways is God making you more like himself?

An Inheritance

In him we have obtained an inheritance,
having been predestined according to the purpose of him
who works all things according to the counsel of his will.

EPHESIANS 1:11 ESV

This morning we remember with gratitude the debt that
we once owed because of sin. We owed a debt that was
insurmountable and unpayable because of our own sin, and
that was compounded by the debt we inherited as children of
Adam. Through our father Adam, we all inherited sin and sin
pays the dividends of death. Because of sin, both Adam's and
our own, we were under the sentence of death.

In Christ, that debt is paid in full. There is nothing left for
you to pay. There is no debt remaining for you to work off. A
withdrawal has been made against the inheritance of heaven
in order to set you free. As you set about your day, live as one
who has no debt, who has nothing left to pay.

Heavenly Father, the Bible tells us about your wealth by saying
that you own the cattle on a thousand hills. You have graciously
given what is yours to repay my debt. Let me never live like I am
poor again.

We have obtained an inheritance, having been predestined according to His purpose who works all things after the counsel of His will.

EPHESIANS 1:11 NASB

You have most likely done some sort of work today that is serving to provide for your own needs and the needs of others. Perhaps your work has gone toward paying off a debt or two. But none of your daily work has set aside an inheritance for you in eternity. That inheritance has been given to you free of charge by the grace of Jesus Christ. All the inheritance that Christ has earned as a good and faithful Son is yours both in this life and in the life to come.

What is the inheritance of Jesus? Heaven and earth are his inheritance. All the blessings of the Father are his inheritance. All of the promises of God belong to him. The inheritance that Jesus has earned has been given to you by faith.

Everlasting Father, you have given me riches beyond my wildest imaginations both in this life and in the life to come.

What kind of life would you live if you truly believed that you inherited the blessings that Jesus earned for you on the cross?

You Are Alive

God, being rich in mercy, because of the great love with which he loved us, even when we were dead in our trespasses, made us alive together with Christ—by grace you have been saved.

Ephesians 2:4–5 esv

You have been made alive together with Christ. The resurrection life Christ now lives, you also now live. The kind of life you have in Christ is the kind of life that he has in the resurrection. It's the real kind of life. The kind you had before you believed was a cheap imitation of the real thing.

When Adam and Eve were first created, they were fully alive. Then when their sin gave birth to death, they died. They died spiritually and were separated from God. That is the real death. Physical death is temporary, but you are alive in Christ.

Almighty God, grant me to live a new kind of life today.

God, who is rich in mercy, out of the great love with which he loved us even when we were dead through our trespasses, made us alive together with Christ—by grace you have been saved.

EPHESIANS 2:4-5 NRSV

The life that you now live is an in-Christ kind of life. The real kind of life cannot be found anywhere else. It is a gift to you according to the rich mercies of God and out of his great love for you. Life cannot be found anywhere else because no one else is rich in mercy and no one else loves you with an eternal love. It came to you while you were dead in your trespasses, and it was given to you by grace alone.

Life cannot be found anywhere else because there is no other true way to take away your trespasses. There is no other way to make a dead sinner alive than through faith in Jesus Christ, who loved us and gave himself up for us. You are alive because of Jesus, and he made you for a purpose.

Everlasting Father, you have made me alive. Lead me to live a life that matters.

Are you living a real, abundant, in-Christ kind of life?

God's Household

Consequently, you are no longer foreigners and strangers,
but fellow citizens with God's people
and also members of his household.

EPHESIANS 2:19 NIV

Belief in Jesus makes you a member of God's household. That is a beautiful picture, isn't it? The image refers to those who belong in the house. We can visualize a beautiful house with a front porch and a welcome mat. You knock on the door, tentatively, hoping to be let in from the cold. Instead, you are pulled in with love and affection.

You are a part of this family because of adoption. You share in the inheritance because of your relationship to the rich older brother. And now, you have a key to the house. Come in. Sit down. Grab something from the refrigerator and put your feet up on the couch. You are welcome here and all the rights of the family belong to you.

My God and Father, you have given me a home when I was homeless. You have welcomed me when I was a stranger. Give me the kind of confidence in your promises that I could be at home in them.

You are no longer strangers and aliens,
but you are citizens with the saints
and also members of the household of God.

EPHESIANS 2 :19 NRSV

God has made us one new household. The household of God is not a tenement or urban apartment complex in which one ethnic group lives there and another one lives over here, separated from each other. The household of God is not an aristocratic English mansion tucked away on a hundred acres of countryside in which the wealthy live upstairs and the poor live downstairs.

In the household of God there are no outsiders, no strangers; there are no classes and ethnicities do not divide us. He welcomes all through faith in Jesus Christ and his plan is to use you to welcome others. Tonight, consider who God would have welcomed into the family by your words, witness, and love. What strangers has God given to you as family?

Father, through the grace of Jesus, you have made us into one new family. Break down the walls that still keep us apart and help me to welcome others the way that you have welcomed me.

Do you feel at home in God's household, with God's family?

Member of Christ

Gentiles are fellow heirs and fellow members of the body, and fellow partakers of the promise in Christ Jesus through the gospel.

EPHESIANS 3:6 NASB

Paul uses the body illustration to show our mutual dependence. You are a member of the body, but you're only one member. It's a silly thought to say that the eye doesn't need the ear or that the mouth doesn't need the feet. It would be just as ludicrous to say that you aren't a necessary part of the body.

What is it that keeps you apart from the other members of the body of Christ? Do you doubt your own ability and think that you have nothing to offer? Are you sinfully independent and think that you are not in need of anyone else? Do you think you are the one eye in all the world who actually doesn't need an ear? God's plan is for you to be a fully functioning member of the body of Christ.

Almighty God, you have given me a local body of believers to be a part of and I am grateful for them. Teach me to love them, need them, and be of use to them.

This mystery is that the Gentiles are fellow heirs,
members of the same body, and partakers of the promise
in Christ Jesus through the gospel.

EPHESIANS 3:6 ESV

The body that you belong to is the body of Christ. That is, the local group of sinners that you gather with the week in and week out is the body of Christ. There is to be no jockeying for position like James and John, who wanted to sit at Jesus's right hand and left hand. We are all equal here because we share the dignity that is given to us by Jesus.

Jesus is the head of the body. He is the authority. He is the boss. There isn't a competition with him, nor should there ever be. In the same way, there is not to be a competition between believers. We are members of one body. When one part grows, the other parts grow. When one part weeps, the other parts weep. When one part of the body rejoices, we all rejoice with it.

Lord God, you are the head of the church. I humble myself before you and I pray that you would make me a healthy member of your body.

Are you a healthy member of the body of Christ?

Transferred

He rescued us from the domain of darkness,
and transferred us to the kingdom of His beloved Son.

COLOSSIANS 1:13 NASB

As you begin your day, stop to consider what kingdom you belong to. The Bible takes great pains to make it clear that Christians belong to the kingdom of God. It is the kingdom in which God rules and his people obey his commandments. It is the kingdom in which his will is done on earth as it is in heaven.

The Bible is just as clear that you have no rights to this kingdom by birth. You are naturally a member of the kingdom of darkness in which the devil-king manipulates poor souls to do his bidding and pay his tax. But the dark world is no longer your kingdom. You have been transferred into the kingdom of light, the kingdom of his beloved Son. That is who you are. That is your kingdom. He is your king. This is your life.

Almighty God, as I head out today, send me for the good of your kingdom.

*He has rescued us from the power of darkness
and transferred us into the kingdom of his beloved Son.*

COLOSSIANS 1:13 NRSV

What did you notice about the kingdom of God and the
kingdom of this world as you went about your life today?
Were there signs around you that pointed to one domain or
the other? Did you see the fruit of the devil or the fruit of the
beloved Son?

The kingdom that you live in is a kingdom of light and love
in Jesus Christ. It is a kingdom that is shaped by gratitude
because you have been rescued from the darkness. It is a
kingdom that is defined by the kind of love that God the
Father has for God the Son. You live in a kingdom that is
eternal. Regardless of what you saw in the world today, this is
your reality as a child of God. God has transferred you into his
kingdom and has plans for your life.

*Almighty God, you rule all things well. Give me eyes to see your
gracious hand in the midst of the things I do not understand.*

Where do you see God's kingdom at work in your life?

The Church

If I am delayed, you will know how people ought to conduct
themselves in God's household, which is the church
of the living God, the pillar and foundation of the truth.

1 TIMOTHY 3:15 NIV

The city of Ephesus was known for one of the wonders of the ancient world. The great Temple of Artemis was founded on the ground where a sacred stone fell from the sky, as we are told in Acts 19:35. That ground became the foundation of the great temple and men came from all over to worship the false goddess in her false ways based upon a falsehood.

Paul sets us up to visualize the church of Jesus Christ, built upon a different foundation. The church is built upon the truth of God in the gospel and the truth can be built upon in the church. The church is a better temple than the great Temple of Artemis because God actually dwells there. This is the truth upon which your life is built.

Lord God Almighty, grant me stability today based upon the local
church that you have built in this place.

If I am delayed, you may know how one ought to behave
in the household of God, which is the church of the living God,
the pillar and bulwark of the truth.

1 TIMOTHY 3:15 NRSV

The church that you worship with is only stable because the truth of God's word is stable. The church is built upon the foundation of truth and the church is the pillar or buttress that upholds the truth. We are to envision something like the flying buttresses of Notre Dame Cathedral, leaning in from the outside to keep the walls standing for over seven hundred years. The Temple of Artemis was known for a series of grand and impressive pillars that upheld the worship of an idol. The church of Jesus Christ has better pillars for worship of the true God.

We are to remember the two pillars of Solomon's temple that held up nothing in particular but that reminded us on entering the temple that strength and stability come into our lives from God as we worship him. Your weekly participation with the church where you live upholds the truth where you live.

Eternal God, make me a pillar in your house by weekly worship.

Does obedience to weekly worship bring stability to your life?

JULY 2

Sheep

*May the God of peace who brought up our Lord Jesus
from the dead, that great Shepherd of the sheep,
through the blood of the everlasting covenant.*

HEBREWS 13:20 NKJV

Believers are often called sheep in the Scriptures. Sometimes
we are obedient sheep that follow where we are supposed
to go. Other times we are rebellious sheep that bite the
hand that feeds us and wander away. Sometimes we are at
peace under the guidance of our Good Shepherd, our souls
restored, peacefully grazing along the riverside. Other times
we are like sheep without a shepherd, in danger from the cold
and the ravenous wolves that are hunting us from every side.

Remember that you are a sheep today. You are not the
shepherd. You are not a wolf. You are a sheep, and you have
heard the voice of the Good Shepherd who has called you into
an eternal covenant with himself.

*Gracious and compassionate God, you are the Good Shepherd
of the sheep and I am your sheep. Lead me into the peace of your
eternal covenant no matter what the day has in store for me.*

*May the God of peace who brought again from the dead
our Lord Jesus, the great shepherd of the sheep,
by the blood of the eternal covenant.*

HEBREWS 13:20 ESV

You are a sheep and God is the shepherd. You were one of a
hundred and you wondered off into the wilderness. Out of
his great love for you, he left the ninety-nine to go and find
you. And when he did, he healed your wounds, bound up your
broken limbs, and he carried you on his shoulders back to the
fold. He is a Good Shepherd.

He is a Good Shepherd and a good shepherd lays down his
life for his sheep. He bought you at the cost of his own blood.
He feeds you from his own table and he guides you with his
rod and his staff. The best news at the end of the day is not
the news that you are a sheep but that he is your shepherd. He
will not lose any who are his own.

*Father, you raised Jesus from the dead. You have given me new life
through his new life. Teach me to follow him closely.*

Are you following the Good Shepherd or are you wandering
like a lost sheep?

Gifted

As each has received a gift, use it to serve one another,
as good stewards of God's varied grace: whoever speaks,
as one who speaks oracles of God; whoever serves,
as one who serves by the strength that God supplies—
in order that in everything God may be glorified through Jesus
Christ. To him belong glory and dominion forever and ever.

1 PETER 4:10-11 ESV

God gives good gifts to his people. Life is a gift of God. Eternal life is also a gift of God that he gave you through faith. You have new birth through no more effort than what you contributed to your own birth. The gift that Peter refers to here is a supernaturally given ability for the purposes of God's work in the world.

The gift of birth comes to you through your parents, the gift of salvation through the will of God by the death and resurrection of Christ, and this spiritual gift comes from the ascended Christ who sent his Spirit to live within you. You are gifted.

Almighty God, give me eyes to see the gift that you have given me that is to be used for your glory.

Like good stewards of the manifold grace of God, serve one another with whatever gift each of you has received. Whoever speaks must do so as one speaking the very words of God; whoever serves must do so with the strength that God supplies, so that God may be glorified in all things through Jesus Christ. To him belong the glory and the power forever and ever. Amen.

1 PETER 4:10-11 NRSV

You are gifted in order to be a gift to someone else. That supernatural ability that the Spirit of God has given you is not for you. In fact, a self-edifying gift is a contradiction in terms. You have a gift in order to use that gift. You have that gift in the time and place where you are because the people around you need that gift. You are God's gift to them; the Spirit of God will care for them through you.

Use your gift to serve others. Use it with divine confidence and manage it well so that they can be happy and holy.

Gracious and giving God, use me so that others may be strengthened and give glory to you.

How has God gifted you to serve others?

One Day

There will no longer be any curse;
and the throne of God and of the Lamb will be in it,
and His bond-servants will serve Him.

Revelation 22:3 NASB

One day God will make all things right. That's how our story comes to an end. It may not feel that way this morning, but this is the truth of things. This is reality. Today you are experiencing the consequences of the curse, which is the fruit of sin, both Adam's and your own. Today there are tears and pain and sorrow and death. Today it is sometimes hard to believe that God is present among us.

Look at the state of the world we live in. Sometimes it feels as if God is not with his people. One day God will make all things right. One day there will no longer be any curse. One day the Lamb of God will be very present among his people. Today is not that day, but that day is coming.

O Lord God, let your promise of a new day be more powerful in my heart than the effects of sin in front of my eyes.

> *There shall be no more curse,*
> *but the throne of God and of the Lamb shall be in it,*
> *and His servants shall serve Him.*

REVELATION 22:3 NKJV

The promise of the new day, a day in which there will be no curse from sin, is intended to provoke a new kind of living from us today. The apostle Peter refers to it as a living hope and he teaches that the promise of that day should lead us to live holy and godly lives now. Our calling is to live as if that is truly the last scene of our story.

If the life that you are living will come to its final end in the presence of God, how might you live differently than you did today? Are you living for that day? Are you living by faith in God's promise to make all things right?

O Lord God, today is not that day. Today, I see the effects of sin in the world and it seems so big and impossible. Let me believe your promise and live with faith in this fallen world.

Is your life more shaped by the sin of today or the hope of tomorrow?

Naked

He said, "Who told you that you were naked?
Have you eaten of the tree of which
I commanded you not to eat?"

GENESIS 3:11 ESV

Genesis 2 closes with the picturesque scene of Adam and Eve together in innocence, without sin, naked and happy in a garden. Here we are, just a few verses later, and they have already attempted to cover themselves in a fashion that is almost laughable. At least, it would be laughable if it wasn't so terrible. "Who told you that you were naked?" God asks of Adam, knowing that the only way he would've come to that conclusion is if shame had come into their lives because they rebelled against God.

This is the world that we now live in. This is who you are now. You are no longer uncovered. You're no longer without shame. Like Adam and Eve, you and I need God to provide a covering so that we might live freely in the fallen world.

Holy Father, I am brokenhearted by sin in the world and by sin in me. Make sin and disobedience as ugly in my eyes as it is in yours.

> *He said, "Who told you that you were naked?*
> *Have you eaten from the tree of which*
> *I commanded you not to eat?"*

GENESIS 3:11 NRSV

There are two things that we know about every human that we meet. One, they are created in the image of God and therefore have infinite dignity and value. This is true regardless of any racial or social distinctions that our world might try to make. The other thing that we know is that they're sinful and broken, we just might not yet know what kind of sinner they are. Rightful expectations matter. People are sinful. People need Jesus. People need their nakedness to be covered.

God graciously provided a lamb sacrifice to cover Adam and Eve that they might continue to live instead of immediately die. He has provided a better covering for us in Christ, the Lamb of God. Jesus washes away the filth that clings to you because of your sin or the sin committed against you. Then he clothes you with his own white, righteousness garments.

Gracious God, you have covered my shame. Make me one who will also graciously cover the sins of others.

Where can you cover sin and shame rather than expose it?

Enticing

My son, if sinful men entice you,
do not give in to them.

PROVERBS 1:10 NIV

It's often easier to avoid being enticed if we are being enticed into something big. Usually none of us are going to say yes to robbing a bank if we haven't already started down a path of wrongdoing.

Enticement starts small. A lie here, an unpaid parking ticket there, and we are lead on a path we don't want to be walking down. Here the proverb encourages us not to give into the sinful people who entice us. That process starts by saying no to the little things that entice us and standing firm in the promises of God.

God, help me to say no to things that entice me away from your plans for me today.

My son, if sinners entice you,
do not consent.

PROVERBS 1:10 ESV

Consent is a big word in our society today. We have to give consent for everything. Doctors request consent to examine us, police officers ask consent before searching our vehicles, dating couples ask consent before kissing. Consent is a legal term that means agreeing to do something.

We must not agree to do what sinners do. First, if we agree with them then we are agreeing to sin. Second, when we consent we are indicating that what they are enticing us to do is something we agree with. As Christians, we cannot agree with sin. There are many ways we can disagree with sin; often the easiest and wisest option is to walk away from those enticing us. It removes us from the situation and avoids an unneeded confrontation.

Heavenly Father, forgive me if I have given consent to sin today. Help me to say no to sin in the future and give me strength to walk away each time.

How can you better walk away from enticement?

If Only

*Then you will understand righteousness and justice
and equity, every good path.*

PROVERBS 2:9 NRSV

If only it were that easy. If only we had this voice in our heads every moment of every day. If only we could pause, listen, and respond based on a voice telling us what is right, just, and fair.

God gave us his Word in Scriptures to help hear his voice, but to be able to hear his voice, we must know his Word. God gave us parents and teachers to help guide us, but we sometimes stopped listening to their voices because we disagreed with them. Often when we say God isn't speaking, it's not that he isn't speaking, it's that we don't like what he is saying. If only we would listen even when we don't agree with him.

God, I want to more clearly hear your voice. Help me today to listen closely and know what to do.

Then you will understand what is honest and fair
and what is the good and right thing to do.

PROVERBS 2:9 NCV

If only they had listened, they wouldn't be in this mess. If only humanity practiced equity, there wouldn't be poverty. If only, if only… there are a lot of if only moments in our lives. From the worldwide scale to our own personal path, if only can change everything. It expresses regret and an understanding that things could have been different if a prior decision was changed.

We can't change what has happened in our past, and we can't often make choices on a global scale, but what we can do is live so there are fewer if only moments. God's Word tells us we will understand every good path. If we follow his good path, righteousness, equity and justice will flourish and if only moments will diminish.

Lord, help me to live according to your path. I want to live with fewer if only moments and fully rely on your wisdom to help me follow you.

What is one thing you can do now to ensure fewer if only moments?

Leaky Wells

> *"My people have done two evils:*
> *They have turned away from me,*
> *the spring of living water.*
> *And they have dug their own wells,*
> *which are broken wells that cannot hold water."*
>
> JEREMIAH 2:13 NCV

There are few things better on a hot summer day than a cold drink of water straight from the source; cold, refreshing, and pure. The worst thing on a hot summer day, however, might be a drink of water from a puddle.

This is the image God gives us in Jeremiah. The people were given a choice, spring water or puddle water, and they chose puddle water. Gross. But how often have we done that in our lives when we have not gone directly to the source (God) and instead relied on others to teach us about him. He has given us his Word as the source and we often neglect it instead of drinking directly from it. His Word is the living water; we drink from it when we read it ourselves.

Help me to drink from your Word. I want to know you directly.
Thank you for being the source of life-giving words.

> *"My people have committed two evils:*
> *they have forsaken me,*
> *the fountain of living water,*
> *and dug out cisterns for themselves,*
> *cracked cisterns*
> *that can hold no water."*

JEREMIAH 2:13 NRSV

When water stops flowing it becomes stagnant. Stagnant implies not only still but also foul smelling. This is why many farmers use a pump to pump fresh water into drinking troughs for their animals. Hydration is vital to life and when water becomes stagnant, it is dangerous for the cattle to drink.

The people of God had given up on him and instead were storing stagnant water in leaking cisterns. Our relationship with God is not one that is to be stocked up so we have reserves. Our relationship with God is a daily, moment by moment relationship. He wants to fill us on a moment by moment basis, but we often think we were filled on Sunday and try to hold onto that filling until the next Sunday. We can be filled daily.

God, I want to be filled every moment. Help me to rely on you as the source every moment of every day. Thanks for being there to fill me each day.

In what ways have you been drinking from puddles in your relationship with God?

Face Down

Like the bow in a cloud on a rainy day,
such was the appearance of the splendor all around.
This was the appearance of the likeness of the glory of the LORD.
When I saw it, I fell on my face,
and I heard the voice of someone speaking.

EZEKIEL 1:28 NRSV

What proceeds this verse in Ezekiel is his vision of who God is and his glimpse into heavenly things. The descriptions in the previous verses boggle the mind. They are man's finite ways of describing the infinite. They aren't meant to be a photograph but more of a painting. They are a visual interpretation of something that is indescribable.

What we can gain from understanding this verse in its context is that having seen all the heavenly things he had seen before, Ezekiel, when confronted with the glory of God, fell on his face in the Lord's presence. When we see amazing paintings or photographs we want to get closer and stare at them with intense regard. We study the brush strokes, the shadows, and the texture. When ultimate beauty and perfection in God is near, we fall down, unable to look, overwhelmed by his glory.

God, may your glory overwhelm me today. May I see who you are and your beauty be revealed to me.

All around him was a glowing halo,
like a rainbow shining in the clouds on a rainy day.
This is what the glory of the Lord looked like to me.
When I saw it, I fell face down on the ground,
and I heard someone's voice speaking to me.

EZEKIEL 1:28 NLT

The ultimate act of surrender is to the fall face down on the ground in front of someone. There is nothing you can do from that position. You are blinded to any attack, you can't easily get up and you put yourself in a very vulnerable position.

In the presence of God, there is no better position to be in than face down in front of him. He has the best in mind for you. You don't have to worry about an attack, you don't have to worry about getting up. God is there for you. Surrender in the presence of God is your best option. From a face down position, he can lift you up and place you where he wants you. When you surrender to God, face down in his glory, you allow him to glorify himself and you. He wants the best for you.

God, I fall face down in your presence so that you may be glorified.
So that I may fully trust you.

Are you face down in surrender or are you trying your own thing?

Not My Fault

He was pierced for our rebellion, crushed for our sins.
He was beaten so we could be whole.
He was whipped so we could be healed.
All of us, like sheep, have strayed away.
We have left God's paths to follow our own.
Yet the LORD laid on him the sins of us all.

ISAIAH 53:5-6 NLT

"It wasn't my fault—it was an accident. I shouldn't have to pay when it was an accident." We have all probably uttered some variation of those phrases over the course of our lives in an attempt to avoid responsibility or consequences.

In this poem Isaiah gives us a beautiful account of what happens when someone does the exact opposite of avoiding the responsibility. It really wasn't Jesus' fault: he had no sin, no blame, no blemish, and yet he willingly took our sins to the cross, so we could have a relationship with God. His pain became our completion; his punishment brings us healing. This is the moment in history that has changed eternity for all who believe.

Thank you for taking my sins on the cross. Thank you for standing in the place of my punishment.

He was pierced for our transgressions,
he was crushed for our iniquities;
the punishment that brought us peace was on him,
and by his wounds we are healed.
We all, like sheep, have gone astray,
each of us has turned to our own way;
and the LORD has laid on him
the iniquity of us all.

ISAIAH 53:5-6 NIV

It's not my fault. Some of the first words spoken by mankind were a variation of this. Adam blamed the woman God placed in the garden with him, the woman blames the serpent, and on and on the cycle goes to this day. If we can place the blame on someone else, we are going to try our best to do it. But the willing sacrifice of Jesus Christ for our sins was different.

The resurrection changes everything. It was upon a sinless Christ that our sins and iniquity were placed so we could be spared the punishment we so deeply deserve. Praise be to Jesus for his sacrifice sets us free.

Thank you, Jesus, for your sacrifice.

Have you truly appreciated the sacrifice of Jesus for your sins?

Blocked Path

Paul and Silas traveled through the area of Phrygia and Galatia,
because the Holy Spirit had prevented them from preaching
the word in the province of Asia at that time.

ACTS 16:6 NLT

Sometimes things just don't go as planned. We miss the bus, the car has a flat tire, the bike chain is broken—any number of things can go wrong to make us miss our appointment, late for church, or miss the date with that special someone. Most of the time we brush it off, saying, "Shoot, what a waste." However, sometimes that missed appointment is part of God's plan.

In today's verse we see Paul and his travel companions were stopped from preaching the gospel in Asia. How is that even possible? Doesn't God want all people everywhere to hear the good news? Why was Paul prevented from preaching? We don't know for certain but what we can see from reading further in the book of Acts is that God had a plan to reach people in Macedonia. Perhaps the Holy Spirit has other plans for you today.

Holy Spirit, lead me today in plans. Help me to follow you and
your guidance and not my own plans.

They went through the region of Phrygia and Galatia,
having been forbidden by the Holy Spirit to speak the word in Asia.
ACTS 16:6 NRSV

"Road closed. Detour ahead." That sign can be one of the most frustrating signs for a traveler. But it can also be the most adventurous and open the door to new experiences. Taking a detour on the road of life can be adventurous also. Sometimes things just won't go as planned. Perhaps the class you wanted was full, or your college application was denied, or the dream job was offered to someone else. You could view obstacles and detours as disappointments, or you could see them as opportunities.

It's okay to be sad about the loss of your first choice. But then you should get back to what God has planned for you. If one college said no, notice that there are a few others out there. If you didn't get hired, there are other companies and businesses that are searching for workers. You were not meant to travel every closed road. Remember that a detour is not a dead end.

God, help me to see your road signs and follow your detours. Help me to know your path for me and not be overly frustrated when my plans have to change to follow your plans for me.

What current detour do you need to follow?

Run

Then the Spirit said to Philip, "Go over to this chariot and join it."
So Philip ran up to it and heard him reading the prophet Isaiah.
He asked, "Do you understand what you are reading?"
He replied, "How can I, unless someone guides me?"
And he invited Philip to get in and sit beside him.

ACTS 8:29-31 NRSV

Here are some reasons to run, in no particular order: being chased by a bear; chasing the ice cream truck; catching the last train; or when the Holy Spirit tells you to pursue a chariot.

The Holy Spirit had led Philip to a road that traversed the desert and then told him to run up to a chariot. Philip could have protested and said, "But I've already come this far. Isn't that enough?" But Philip didn't do that. Instead, he just took off running. Sometimes it takes work to follow the path of God for our lives.

God I want to run to where you need me. Help me hear your commands.

The Spirit said to Philip, "Go to that chariot and stay near it."
So when Philip ran toward the chariot,
he heard the man reading from Isaiah the prophet.
Philip asked, "Do you understand what you are reading?"
He answered, "How can I understand unless someone explains
it to me?" Then he invited Philip to climb in and sit with him.

ACTS 29-31 NCV

If Philip hadn't run when the Holy Spirit had said run, he would have missed out on this great opportunity to share the story of God with this man. Scripture tells us this man was a high-ranking official in Ethiopia, and that when he heard the gospel from Philip, he received Jesus into his life and was baptized.

Philip didn't let the opportunity pass by to share the gospel. He ran to follow God's command. He ran to share the good news.

God, is there someone you want me to run toward with the good news of the gospel? Show me where to run.

Who do you need to run toward?

Death of Hope

Jesus cried out again in a loud voice and died.

MATTHEW 27:50 NCV

With his last shout, it seemed to those still waiting for something big to happen, all hope died as Jesus died on the cross. Those close to him had left everything to follow this Jesus of Nazareth. He spoke with confidence; his teachings were so clear and held such authority. They were certain he was the Messiah. The miracles confirmed he was extraordinary. But then, on the cross, all hope had died. We know the rest of the story. We know three days later the true hope is resurrected. But his followers left that night with darkness in their souls.

Perhaps we are in that darkness also, thinking all hope has died in our lives. We might believe there is nothing that can happen that will change our circumstances. But the truth is that there is a hope that comes. There is hope that is beyond death. Hope that comes from the resurrected Christ.

God, it seems like there is no hope in my current situation. Help me to see beyond the situation to the hope that Christ can bring.

Jesus cried again with a loud voice and breathed his last.

MATTHEW 27:50 NRSV

It was not by chance that Christ died on the cross. We can read that Christ set out with confidence toward the cross. It would have been easy at any point for Jesus to have turned around or to have made a change of plans. However, his death was not the death of hope, but instead the birth of hope.

Earlier he had talked about a kernel of wheat needing to die and enter into the ground in order to bring new life. Here his life was given, he was laid into the ground, and even while those around him felt heavy with grief, hope had just been waiting to be raised to life. Hope springs forth from the death of Christ.

Thank you, Jesus, for your death. Thank you that your death brings me life.

Are you trusting fully in the hope that Christ's death offers you?

Get Up and Walk

Peter said, "I have no silver or gold, but what I have I give you;
in the name of Jesus Christ of Nazareth, [a] stand up and walk."
And he took him by the right hand and raised him up; and
immediately his feet and ankles were made strong.

ACTS 3:6-7 NRSV

Do you ever wish you had courage like Peter to say something like this to someone who you see asking for money? The funny thing is, Peter did not have so much confidence just a few weeks before this, when he lied to the servant girl about even knowing Jesus. Now, he speaks in boldness about the fact that God was going to heal this man.

There was no doubt or timid claim—it was an order. "Get up and walk." Where did that courage come from? Peter had seen Jesus both die and then be raised to life. Then the risen Christ had reinstated him and given Peter the keys to the kingdom. This Peter we see in Acts 6 is a Peter who had seen the risen Christ and wanted all he came in contact with to know about him.

God, give me courage like Peter today.

Peter said, "I don't have any silver or gold, but I do have something else I can give you. By the power of Jesus Christ from Nazareth, stand up and walk!" Then Peter took the man's right hand and lifted him up. Immediately the man's feet and ankles became strong.

ACTS 3:6-7 NCV

The power of God is real in both word and deed. It was one thing for Peter to boldly command that the man get up and walk; it was another thing for the man to get up and have his feet and ankles become strong.

When Jesus comes into a person's life, things change. That doesn't mean that all physical sickness is going to be healed, but there is power. Lives are changed with Jesus. Just as this man was able to walk, we too are able to walk free from the burden and guilt of sin when we encounter Christ.

Thank you, Jesus, for the healing in my life. Thank you for lifting the burden of sin and allowing me to get up and walk freely.

Are there sins that are still burdening you?

No Other Name

Salvation is found in no one else,
for there is no other name under heaven
given to mankind by which we must be saved.

ACTS 4:12 NIV

This is a tough pill to swallow for many today. How can Christians be so intolerant? What about all the other sincere believers of other religions? What about the commitment others have made to their beliefs? What about those who have never heard about Jesus?

But the reality is that God made the world and he makes the rules. That may seem harsh, but hold on. He has given Christ to die once for all the sins of the world, making a way for everyone who believes. This verse isn't a verse of condemnation for the world; it is instead the offer of salvation to the world. This salvation is found only in Jesus, but Jesus isn't hard to find.

Thank you, Jesus, for salvation. Thank you for providing a way for me to enter into eternity with you.

Jesus is the only One who can save people.
No one else in the world is able to save us.

ACTS 4:12 NCV

The great thing about God is he provides a way. We don't have to work for it. There is nothing we can do to save ourselves. The Bible is clear that the only way to be saved is through Jesus. Other people give you lists, rules, practices that they promise will grant you, maybe, a pathway to peace or hope.

Before people follow Christ, they sense something isn't right. Many have searched different ways and they all end up empty. The words of Peter ring as true today as they did when he first said them: "No one else in the world is able to save us." And the great thing is Jesus did everything that needs to be done so all we need to do is believe.

Thank you, Jesus, for providing the way. Thank you that the work has been done and I need only believe in you.

Do you believe that Jesus is the only one able to save?

The Gate

*"I am the gate. Whoever enters by me will be saved,
and will come in and go out and find pasture."*

JOHN 10:9 NRSV

To get on a train, you usually have to use a ticket. Scan it, the
gate opens, and you get in. In some cities, the gates open just
as you walk up to them. This helps tourists who have lost their
tickets and keeps others from being held up. Not accustomed
to swiping tickets, first timers frantically look for their ticket
and where to swipe it. In an effort to keep things moving, the
transportation company has posted gate agents to tell people, in
a variety of languages, "Walk through the gate; it's open for you."

If Jesus is the gate, it is our job to announce the gate is open
to those who want to walk through.

*God, I am thankful that you are the gate for me and others. Help
me to announce that the gate is open.*

"I am the door, and the person who enters through me will be saved and will be able to come in and go out and find pasture."

JOHN 10:9 NCV

The job of the announcer at the gate is fairly easy. Everyone getting off at this station knows what beauty awaits them as they pass through the gates and walk toward the beautiful seventeenth century castle and gardens. And while the train station isn't the ugliest building one has ever seen, great beauty and true creativity lie just beyond the gate.

While we may never be able to convince someone that following Christ is worth passing through the gate, it is our job to let people know the price of passage has been paid by the gate owner. We can also share the beauty that awaits in a relationship with Christ.

Help me to continue to point people to the open gate of Jesus and the relationship that brings a full life.

Are you announcing the good news that the gate is open and passage is free?

Upside Down

*"So those who are last now will someday be first,
and those who are first now will someday be last."*

MATTHEW 20:16 NCV

Jesus concludes his teaching about the kingdom with this proclamation. The concluding remark is that everything will be different in the kingdom. It's completely unfair, we might think. Our sense of justice gets thrown off. We worked harder, ran faster, and climbed higher and Jesus just throws it all out the window and says those who are last will be first and the first will be last. Not fair. We want to be first, to win the prize. But the reset is a complete reset.

The world's sense of fairness has never been God's sense of fairness. In kingdom matters, because of sin we all deserve death and we all have the option to receive life. That is how the kingdom works: we receive life when death is what we deserve. The sacrifice of Christ turned the world upside down.

Help me lay down my desire to be first and receive the kingdom understanding of Christ's sacrifice.

> *"The last will be first,*
> *and the first will be last."*
>
> MATTHEW 20:19 NRSV

"It's not fair." That phrase has echoed throughout creation since the fall of mankind. Imagine Adam telling God, "It's not fair. It was the woman you put here with me. She should be punished, not me." Cain cried, "It's not fair you accepted Abel's sacrifice and not mine." Moses could have stated, "It's not fair that I don't get to live in the Promised Land." The Israelites, "It's not fair we have to wander the desert and not enter the Promised Land."

Yet in the kingdom of God all these things were fair, right, and just. Until Jesus hung on the cross. The blameless, sinless Son of God, hung on a cross for sins he never committed. He did not cry out, "It's not fair," but instead he said, "not my will, but yours be done." It was not fair and yet it paid the price that we could not pay to enter again into the kingdom. It turned our world upside down.

God, help me to see things through the kingdom perspective. I want to see your version of fair.

What ways have you cried "it's not fair" when it was really God's kingdom at work?

About the Heart

"Blind Pharisee! First clean the inside of the cup and dish, and then the outside also will be clean."

MATTHEW 23:26 NIV

Some religious people find it easier to put parameters on behavior than to change motivations. Jesus' harsh words in this verse are meant to correct people of his time who had fallen into this trap. They had followed the rules found in Scripture and demanded everyone else to do the same. They had defined the rules and refined the rules and clarified the rules and made sure that everyone they taught also followed the rules.

Yet they followed the rules because they wanted to be seen as righteous by those around them, not to be in a right relationship with the Creator. They focused on outward appearances and outward right living without examining the motivations of their hearts. Jesus tells them to focus on the inside. Why are you doing what you are doing? If you change your motivation, your behavior will change.

Lord, I do want to do what is right, but more importantly, I want to be right with you on the inside. Help me to be in a right relationship with you.

*"Pharisees, you are blind! First make the inside of the cup clean,
and then the outside of the cup can be truly clean."*

MATTHEW 23:26 NCV

Jesus isn't telling the Pharisees to ignore right living. He
instead is making sure that right living comes from right
motivations. God does care about what we do and how we act.
After all, he wrote his law and standards on our hearts.

He didn't do this so that we could judge who is in a
relationship with Christ or not, but so we could be close
with God. The standards he set up are standards for right
community and right relationships with each other. But
we often take the standards as the litmus test for whether
someone is a Christ follower or not. As a result, those who
want to be noticed for their righteousness are tempted to
heap burdens upon burdens of pressure on themselves to
be seen right by others. Let Jesus be your motivation and the
changes of behavior will follow.

*Gracious God, thank you for caring more about me. I mess up
sometimes. Thank you for forgiving me and looking deeper to my
heart.*

How are you doing with cleaning the inside of your life?

Pointing to Light

He himself was not the light,
but he came to testify to the light.

JOHN 1:8 NRSV

When we give directions, we tend to use easily identifiable objects or places. We might tell someone, "When you get to Walmart, turn left. After the high school, take the second right. If you see a McDonald's you have gone too far." We never try to point people toward objects that are going to move. We would never say, "Turn left after the stray dog. Keep going straight when you see the mom pushing the stroller." It's important to point to things that are recognizable and not moving.

This was John's job. His purpose was to testify about Jesus. He wasn't Jesus, he didn't have to provide the way, he just gave people directions and pointed them toward the light of Christ. That's our role too. Point to Jesus. He isn't moving. We can show those around us toward the light of Christ

God, help me to point to your Son. May my life be an example of how to get to you.

John was not the Light,
but he came to tell people
the truth about the Light.

JOHN 1:8 NCV

On a dark night, spotting a light in the distance isn't that difficult. Deciding what that light is, however, is a different story. When we are somewhere new and see a light off in the distance, we can speculate about its source or what it is illuminating. But unless we get up close or see a sign or have it explained to us, we won't know what it is that we are seeing.

John knew the source of the light and it became his mission to tell about the light. Jesus was the light, and he was coming to take away the sins of the world. Look to the light. Run to the light. If we are Christ followers, it is also our mission to point out the light of Christ for those who don't know what it is.

Help me know you more so I may better talk about the light with those around me.

Who in your life needs you to point out the light of Christ?

Good Friends

Since they could not get to Jesus because of the crowd, they dug a hole in the roof right above where he was speaking. When they got through, they lowered the mat with the paralyzed man on it.

MARK 2:4 NCV

The man's friends had a problem. They wanted their friend to be healed by Jesus but the vast number of people prohibited them from getting there. So, they took some initiative and ripped off the roof and lowered their sick friend into the presence of Jesus. Those were some good friends. They had carried their buddy up the ladder onto the roof, and then with their hands made a hole in a roof big enough to lower their friend through.

It is important to have good friends who will help you get into the presence of Jesus. Find the friends that will get you closer to Jesus, even when you don't know how to get there.

God, help me to find friends that will help me move closer to you.

When they could not bring him to Jesus because of the crowd, they removed the roof above him; and after having dug through it, they let down the mat on which the paralytic lay.

MARK 2:4 NRSV

What would you do to help a friend see Jesus? There will probably be very few times where you literally need to remove the roof of a house to help a friend see Jesus, but there may be times that you have to push aside other things to help clear the path.

It won't always be crowds of people that get in the way of your friends seeing Jesus. It might just be "things." Sports, money, possessions can all come between your friends and Jesus. Maybe your role as a good friend is to help your friend clear out what is between them and Jesus. A good friend helps people be near Jesus.

Help me see how my friends can come nearer to you and how I can help them.

Are you being a good friend?

Equal Pay

Whatever you give is acceptable if you give it eagerly. And give according to what you have, not what you don't have. Of course, I don't mean your giving should make life easy for others and hard for yourselves. I only mean that there should be some equality.

2 CORINTHIANS 8:12-13 NLT

Most of us hold on to our hard-earned money because we live at the edge of our means. When you look at your spending, you may be able to identify a few things that could be given up for the sake of being able to save a little more for times when you and others are in need.

God doesn't ask you to give so you make yourself poor, but he does want you to be part of helping those who do not have as much as you do. Is there something that you can hold back from spending your money on today so you can give to a greater cause?

God, thank you for providing me with all that I need. Give me wisdom to know how to spend well so I can have a little extra to give when you show me someone in need. Help me to be a good steward of your money.

Right now you have plenty and can help those who are in need. Later, they will have plenty and can share with you when you need it. In this way, things will be equal.

2 Corinthians 8:14 nlt

God's system of equality is always the best system. When you have plenty, make sure to give, so when you are in need, others will be generous to you. It's a bit of a "pay it forward" situation and it makes sense that our generosity will someday come back to us.

God doesn't want us to have divisions because some are poor and others are rich. Instead, he longs for us all to have what we need.

God, help me to be generous even when I am the one in need. I know you want a heart that is motivated by love and equality for all people. I pray you would use me to be a part of this wonderful proficiency of giving and receiving.

Do you need to be more generous, or do you need to pray for some generosity to be extended your way?

Ask Away

*"Give your servant therefore an understanding mind
to govern your people, able to discern between good and evil;
for who can govern this your great people?"*

1 KINGS 3:9 NRSV

Solomon was a young man just starting his rule as the king of Israel. The God of the universe came to him and said, "Ask away. What do you want?"

Here God extends the offer to Solomon and instead of asking for money, an easy life, or a beautiful spouse, he asked to be given the ability to wisely lead the people God had entrusted to him. We often work very hard to get rich or live in comfort. Do we work as hard to gain wisdom and insight? Solomon put his desires for popularity below the needs of the people to be well led. Wisdom is better than money.

Lord, I ask that you would give me wisdom as you gave Solomon wisdom. I want to lead the people you have put in my life in the right way.

> *"I ask that you give me a heart that understands,*
> *so I can rule the people in the right way and will know*
> *the difference between right and wrong.*
> *Otherwise, it is impossible to rule this great people of yours."*

1 KINGS 3:9 NCV

Solomon asked for wisdom, but God said, "You want wisdom? I'll give you that and more." He encouraged Solomon to ask away. Then the Lord blessed him with so much more. God is generous. He richly rewarded Solomon with more than he could ask or imagine.

God has promised eternal life for those who believe in his Son Jesus. But he doesn't make us wait until heaven to receive it. He promises us a full and abundant life, here and now. Following Jesus is a great adventure.

God, thank you that you answer prayers and keep your promises.
Help me to ask you for your promises.

What promises does God have for you today?

As You Go

When an attempt was made by both Gentiles and Jews, with their rulers, to mistreat them and to stone them, the apostles learned of it and fled to Lystra and Derbe, cities of Lycaonia, and to the surrounding country; and there they continued proclaiming the good news.

ACTS 14:5-7 NRSV

The good news of Jesus has always been divisive. In the early days, a large number of people began to agree with the teaching of Christ. But there was also a large group that did not—and they were worked up into an angry frenzy. Eventually they decided to kill two of the church leaders, Paul and Barnabas, by stoning them.

Paul and Barnabas showed their bravery by continuing to another town and preaching the gospel there. Over and over again, Paul and those who traveled with him were mistreated for proclaiming the good news. And while they may have moved to the next town, they never stopped preaching that Jesus is the way to the Father.

God, help me to know when it is good to move on and share the gospel elsewhere, and when I should stay.

Some who were not Jews, some Jews, and some of their rulers wanted to mistreat Paul and Barnabas and to stone them to death. When Paul and Barnabas learned about this, they ran away to Lystra and Derbe, cities in Lycaonia, and to the areas around those cities. They announced the Good News there, too.

ACTS 14:5-7 NCV

Nobody would have blamed Paul and Barnabas if they had thrown in the towel and hid somewhere to avoid being persecuted. From town to town they were chased because people were upset that so many people were coming to Jesus.

Paul could have left that town and said, "My work is done. It's too hard. I am going to retire by the beach." But Paul knew the importance of preaching the eternity-changing gospel of Christ. Even under threat of death and knowing people were going to be upset, Paul still preached because he knew that people's eternal destiny was at stake. God leads those who follow him. So, if you preach "as you go," you can know that sharing the gospel will never be in vain.

Help me, Jesus, to share your good news with people all around me. I want to be like Paul and be known as someone who shares your story everywhere I go.

Have you shared the story of Christ with someone recently?

Child of God

You are all children of God
through faith in Christ Jesus.

GALATIANS 3:26 NLT

Paul argues that we can't do things that will make God love us more or less. The reason for this: we are children of God through Christ Jesus. In other words, because we are his children we are loved immensely.

It's like when we see a mom holding a child on her lap and another child comes to sit also. She doesn't say to the first, "You have to get down so your brother can come up," she moves the child over and makes rooms for the second child. This analogy falls short because the mom's lap is only so big, but God's lap is infinite; he has room for all his children and loves them individually with a deep and profound love. You are a child of God.

Abba Father, thank you for calling me your child.

You were all baptized into Christ,
and so you were all clothed with Christ.
This means that you are all children of God
through faith in Christ Jesus.

GALATIANS 3:26 NCV

Can it really be that simple? Yes, it can. You are a child of God because of your trust in Christ Jesus. It's not because of your church attendance, your generous giving, your good deeds, your beautiful singing voice in worship songs, your volunteering in the nursery, your servant-hearted dishwashing after the potluck, your helpfulness with the old lady across the street, or even babysitting the unruly neighborhood child.

You are a child of God because of trust in Christ Jesus. And with that relationship comes great benefits and family expectations. But following the expectations doesn't make you a child—trust and faith in Jesus does.

God, thank you for making me part of your family. I am so grateful that you want me as your child. Help me to know what it means to be your child.

Have you tried to earn your relationship with God?

Saving Sinners

What I say is true, and you should fully accept it: Christ Jesus
came into the world to save sinners, of whom I am the worst.
But I was given mercy so that in me, the worst of all sinners,
Christ Jesus could show that he has patience without limit.
His patience with me made me an example for those who would
believe in him and have life forever.

1 TIMOTHY 1:15-16 NCV

We can forget that God has been merciful to us. Many people
have been saved since they were young. They were blessed
to be raised in church and spend a lot of time with church
friends and people. But this might also mean they don't
always realize just how merciful God has been.

Paul came to know Christ later in his life. As a result, he was
someone who never forgot how sinful he was before knowing
Jesus. This helped him to communicate to other sinners their
need for salvation and the power of God through Christ to
offer that salvation. His knowledge of his past life kept him
ever pressing forward to share the gospel with those who had
not yet believed. Christ Jesus came to save sinners.

Help me to remember your love for sinners and share your love with
them.

I can testify that the Word is true and deserves to be received by all, for Jesus Christ came into the world to bring sinners back to life—even me, the worst sinner of all! Yet I was captured by grace, so that Jesus Christ could display through me the outpouring of his Spirit as a pattern to be seen for all those who would believe in him for eternal life.

1 TIMOTHY 1:15-16 TPT

Paul was saved to be an example. That's what he was saying here. To be clear, the first and foremost reason that you were saved is because God loves you. Secondly, God loves others like he loves you. He loves others with the same intense love that he loves you. He loves sinners and he wants to use you to reach them with his love.

Paul calls himself the worst of sinners, so there is no sinner incapable of being loved and transformed by the grace of Jesus. This is what is amazing about the love of God. There is no one around you that isn't loved by God. He wants to save sinners, using your grace-filled life as an example.

Thank you for loving me and those around me. Help me to share my story of your grace in my life with those around me.

Who around you needs to hear the story of grace at work in you?

Ugly Crying

"Not so, my lord," Hannah replied, "I am a woman who is deeply troubled. I have not been drinking wine or beer; I was pouring out my soul to the LORD. Do not take your servant for a wicked woman; I have been praying here out of my great anguish and grief."

1 SAMUEL 1:15-16 NIV

Hannah's prayer was so heartfelt that it seemed to the local religious leader that she was drunk. She was weeping so hard before the Lord that no words were coming out of her mouth. She did not pray with fancy words, because words couldn't even come out of her mouth. She sat ugly-crying before God, baring her heart's desire to him.

Prayer doesn't have to done with fancy words or clever sayings. Prayer is allowing your heart's desire to be heard by God. Sometimes that means when our heart is heavy, we will be ugly-crying before God. And the great thing is that he hears, and doesn't mind, our ugly-crying—even when the words won't come out.

Hear my heart, Lord.

*Hannah answered, "No, sir, I have not drunk any wine or beer.
I am a deeply troubled woman, and I was telling the Lord about
all my problems. Don't think I am an evil woman. I have been
praying because I have many troubles and am very sad."*

1 Samuel 1:15-16 ncv

Sometimes we judge others and ourselves when we pray in
a group. Jenny didn't pray out loud; she must not know how
to pray very well. Steve? That dude prays like a poet; I wish
I could pray like him. Tom says "just" every other word. But
Tina—Tina seems to have the best prayer life because she
knows all the names of God.

The ability to pray out loud is not an indication of a person's
mastery of prayer. God hears our heats and wants us to honest
with him. He wants us to pray what we feel and believe. Talk
with God like you talk with others. He will hear and enjoy the
conversation.

*Lord, help me to reveal to you my heart and thoughts through my
prayer. Thank you for hearing me and having a conversation with
me.*

Have you revealed your heart to God through prayer?

Restored to God

Restore us to yourself,
O LORD, that we may be restored!

LAMENTATIONS 5:21 ESV

After five chapters of beautifully painful crying out to the
Lord about their misery and hard times, the people of Israel
beg to be restored. But it is an interesting phrase they use:
"Restore us to yourself."

The author of Lamentations realized that no matter what
troubles had arrived and no matter what struggles the people
of Israel had endured, if they were going to be fully healed,
they must restore their relationship with God. The same is true
for us. In order to be fully restored and to be free from pain,
we must be restored to God through Christ. Only then will we
be able to receive eternal life and spend eternity in heaven,
fully restored to the relationship that was lost at the fall.

Lord, my heart hurts and my soul aches. Restore me to the
relationship with you. May my life be right with you and may you
restore the joy of salvation to me.

Bring us back to you, LORD, and we will return.
Make our days as they were before.

LAMENTATIONS 5:21 NCV

The author of Lamentations knew something that we often forget: it is God who brings us back to himself. We can never run far enough to be where God is. We can never run fast enough to catch up. We can never work hard enough to earn his presence. In God's amazing grace, we simply need to ask him for restored relationship.

The people of Israel had endured many hardships, many difficulties, and huge amounts of loss. When they came to the end of themselves, instead of trying to pick themselves up by their bootstraps, they cried out, "Bring us back to yourself, O Lord." They realized that they were far from him, yet he was still close. We can pray that same prayer. "Lord, restore us to you so our lives may be renewed as in days before."

Restore me Lord. Renew my life in you. Reveal your nearness to me.

What do you need to be restored from?

Sweet as Honey

"Son of man, feed your stomach and fill your body
with this scroll which I am giving you."
Then I ate it, and it was sweet as honey in my mouth.

EZEKIEL 3:3 NASB

The scroll presented to Ezekiel was filled on both sides of the paper with words of woe, cries of grief, and wails and groans. Even in dream logic the scroll would have been bitter, sour, and caused a stomachache. But in God's economy, every word he speaks is for the nourishment of our souls.

We are not given scrolls to eat, but we are given the written Word of God as collected in the Bible. We need to read it and find the nourishment for our souls. Even when we don't like what we read or find it difficult, it is good for our souls.

Lord, thank you for your Word that encourages and strengthens me. Help me to long for your Word as I long for food and drink.

> *"Human, eat this scroll which I am giving you,*
> *and fill your stomach with it."*
> *Then I ate it, and it was as sweet as honey in my mouth.*

When people are healthy, they normally don't need a reminder from someone else to eat. If people are growing, expending energy, and just living a normal life they are going to get hungry and eat.

In the normal scheme of things, people need to eat food. The same is true with our need for God's Word in our lives. If we are growing and alive in Christ, we need his Words to sustain us. Scripture is for the nourishment of our souls in relationship with Christ.

Heavenly Father, I want my relationship with you to be alive and growing. Help me to nourish my soul by giving me hunger pains for your Word.

Do you hunger for the lifegiving Word of God?

Thanking Others

I always thank my God as I remember you in my prayers,
because I hear about your love for all his holy people
and your faith in the Lord Jesus.

PHILEMON 1:4-5 NIV

This verse contains simple words, but words that convey so much. There are a few phrases that people who travel should learn in the language of their destination. They'll need to use those common everyday phrases like "hello" or "goodbye." They'll need to be able to ask where the bathrooms are and how much something costs. It would also really help travelers if they used polite phrases like please and thank you.

That last phrase especially goes a long way in making relationships. When we say thank you, we place value on others. When we forget this simple phrase, it may seem we expect people to serve us.

Help me, Lord Jesus, to be thankful.

*I always thank my God when I mention you in my prayers,
because I hear about the love you have for all God's holy people
and the faith you have in the Lord Jesus.*

PHILEMON 1:4-5 NCV

In spoken French there is a phrase that roughly translates
to "it should be me thanking you." It is used by people in
a service industry when a customer thanks them after a
purchase. Sometimes, in a funny exchange, the person
receiving their change again says, "Thank you," and then the
worker says, "Thank you," until finally the customer gives in
and says, "You're welcome."

Imagine if we did this in the local church. "Thanks for
watching my kid in the nursery." "Thanks for letting me
watch your kid." "Thank you for thanking me, but really
thanks." "It really was a blessing to watch your kid. Thank
you." "You're welcome." Perhaps people would like to help out
a bit more if we did a better job of thanking them.

Heavenly Father, help me to be thankful.

Who do you need to thank today?

Stay Bold

I know where you live. It is where Satan has his throne.
But you are true to me. You did not refuse to tell about your faith
in me even during the time of Antipas, my faithful witness who
was killed in your city, where Satan lives.

REVELATION 2:13 NCV

Would living where Satan has his throne give us more or
fewer reasons to go and preach the gospel of Christ? In this
passage in the book of Revelation, Jesus is encouraging
the faith and boldness of the Christians in a town called
Pergamum. He says that despite how difficult their situation
is, despite the fact that Satan had grabbed a foothold and
placed a throne in their town, they continued to be faithful
witnesses for Jesus.

It's easy to talk about Jesus with those around us who love
Jesus. It's harder to talk boldly about Jesus in a culture that
is opposed to him. The Christians of Pergamum were an
example to us in preaching Jesus even in difficult situations.
They were bold even in the enemy's throne room.

God, help me to stay bold in my witness for you, even when others
around me might be opposed to you.

"I know where you are living, where Satan's throne is. Yet you are holding fast to my name, and you did not deny your faith in me even in the days of Antipas my witness, my faithful one, who was killed among you, where Satan lives."

REVELATION 2:13 NRSV

It is important to remember that the "you" in this passage is plural. It is not a single person that Jesus is speaking to, but the church at Pergamum. The church gathered together in the name of Jesus. Together they proclaimed the name of Jesus to others around them. It can be assumed, because of the hardships they faced, that there were days when some people in the church wanted to scale back their outreach efforts. When their dear brother was killed for his faith, they could have easily decided to hide and keep quiet. But the boldness of their faith came from being together and encouraging each other.

When you are feeling disappointed, nervous, or not wanting to share Jesus with others, find other believers and ask them to pray for you—perhaps even to go with you. Stay bold even in the face of evil.

God, thank you for those around me that follow you. Help me to encourage them to be bold and let them encourage me to be bold also.

Are you being bold?

No One Else

Simon Peter answered him, "Lord, to whom can we go?
You have the words of eternal life. We have come to believe
and know that you are the Holy One of God."

JOHN 6:68-69 NRSV

Simon Peter wasn't often one to remain silent when Jesus
spoke or asked questions. In fact, he would often speak
before thinking, ending up with his foot in his mouth. In this
moment at least, Simon Peter makes a statement that has
never rung more true. Out of his mouth came a proclamation
of faith that we all must come to agree with: "There is no one
else to go to. Your words give eternal life."

Even after making this claim, Simon Peter denied Jesus three
times and then went back to fishing instead of proclaiming
the gospel. But when the resurrected Jesus restored him to a
right relationship, Peter understood the profound truth of his
statement—and he followed these words for the rest of his life.

Help me to remember there is nowhere else but to your lifegiving
words that I can go.

Simon Peter answered him, "Lord, who would we go to?
You have the words that give eternal life.
We believe and know that you are the Holy One from God."

JOHN 6:68-69 NCV

Jesus asked his closest disciples if they too were going to leave him. He had just taught that life wasn't going to be easy if they followed him. Others had decided to return home and follow a different path. But Peter declared, "No one else is the Holy One from God."

This was a huge revelation coming from his followers at that time. Jesus, by his actions, had revealed who he was. Simon Peter and the closest disciples figured it out and were forever changed. They had spent many days and hours with him, watching him do miracles. They couldn't help but realize that there is no one other than Jesus who can give eternal life.

Jesus, I believe the testimony of those closest to you that you are the giver of eternal life and the Holy One sent from God.

Who else have you trusted in to bring you life?

Love Is Action

*Dear children, let us not love with words or speech
but with actions and in truth.*

1 JOHN 3:18 NIV

Love requires action. It is hard for someone to believe you love them if you have not shown them that you love them. For instance, imagine walking by your grandparents' house and noticing that your grandma fell down and was struggling to get up. You have the ability to help her, but instead you yell "I love you." from across the street. How will she respond? It that really love?

The Bible says that the world will be able to know people are Christians by their love for one another. Love is action. Love compels people to act. It could be as important as helping someone in need or as simple as sitting down and listening when someone needs to talk. Love is action.

Lord, help me to show love to those I care about.

Little children, let us love, not in word or speech,
but in truth and action.

1 JOHN 3:18 NRSV

It is important to tell people we love them. It's not always easy to do it meaningfully, especially if we aren't used to saying it. Or, if we use the word love too freely, perhaps the phrase becomes watered down. Figuring out how to use the phrase "I love you" appropriately and authentically is one of the most important aspects of being human.

But even more than speaking a phrase, love is more profoundly expressed in actions. Loving others might mean leaving the last Kit-Kat bar for them. Loving others might mean giving up our plans so that we can help someone move. Loving actions keep us thinking and acting for the benefit of others, not only for ourselves. The action of love is more than words. It is how people know your words are true.

Lord, let me love in action as well as in my words. Help me to see how to better show love to others.

Who do you need to love today?

That Person

About this we have much to say that is hard to explain,
since you have become dull in understanding.

HEBREWS 5:11 NRSV

These were not the most encouraging words ever written in
the book of Hebrews. You can almost sense the exasperation
voiced here by the author. Everything he had written before
were the basics, the things that he had already taught them
about Jesus and the Christian life. He wants to take them
deeper, to see them come into the fullness of life that Jesus
offers and wants for them.

The Christian life is both simple and complicated. Jesus loves
us, and we can be in relationship with him, but the depth of
theology and his riches would take many lifetimes to explore.
Don't be that person who doesn't dive deep into the person of
Jesus and the riches he has for you.

Lord Jesus, help me to know you more. I want to dig deeper into the
depths of who you are.

We have much to say about this, but it is hard to explain
because you are so slow to understand.

HEBREWS 5:11 NCV

There is a reason that there are a variety of levels of books available to read. See Spot Run would not be a book you might pick up to sit and read by the fire on a cool winter's evening. It doesn't have the same depth as a novel or biography.

Yet for the Hebrew followers they had settled for a See-Spot-Run-relationship with Jesus. That can true for us sometimes too. We can settle for knowing just a little of Jesus because it seems easier and doesn't require us to move beyond our comfort zone. But just like learning to read we need to move beyond what we are comfortable with and perhaps have a Shakespearean level in our relationship with Jesus.

Jesus, help me to not be lazy in my relationship with you. I want to be deep in my love for you.

Have you become lazy in your relationship with Jesus?

Divided Tongue

*Praises and curses come from the same mouth!
My brothers and sisters, this should not happen.*

JAMES 3:10 NCV

It's really easy to get involved in talking badly about people.
It's so simple to slip into being critical of others and speaking
poorly about them. There's a story about a Christian who
encountered a homeless man in the church bathroom and
began calling him names and yelling at him to leave.

It's hard to see the love of Christ in someone when they are
verbally mistreating the very people that Christ came to save.
In his letter to Christians, James emphasizes the importance
of taming the tongue. It is important to the message of Jesus
that his followers have tight control on what they say.

*Jesus, help me not to have a divided tongue. I want to praise you
and encourage others.*

From the same mouth come blessing and cursing.
My brothers and sisters, this ought not to be so.

JAMES 3:10 NRSV

Think back over the day. How many times did you use your words to encourage, uplift, and bless? How many times did you use words to put down, demean, or curse?

Everyone has reasons that negative words and phrases come out of their mouth. But no matter what your reasons might be, the words you use have power and impact. When we claim to follow Jesus and then put others down, our tongue is divided. It naturally makes people doubt the reality of your Christian life. Controlling the tongue is an important part of the faith. Here's some good news, though: you don't have to do it on your own. Christ will help.

Help me to not have a divided tongue. Show me where my words have caused hurt and pain.

Is there someone you need to ask forgiveness from for the words you have spoken?

Beauty

When I consider your heavens,
the work of your fingers,
the moon and the stars,
which you have set in place,
what is mankind that you are mindful of them,
human beings that you care for them?

PSALM 8:3-4 NIV

There are some amazingly beautiful places in the world. A quick Google image search would reveal pictures beyond description of places beyond amazing. When we are given the opportunity to actually see some of those places in person, the feeling can be overwhelming.

Yet above all that beauty and majesty, God created humankind to be loved uniquely. We are flawed people who often go our own ways and do things that destroy the beauty of God's creation. Yet God still cares for us far more than we will ever understand. He cares for us because he created us uniquely in his image.

God, thank you for loving me and calling me your child. You created all things beautiful including me.

When I look at your heavens, the work of your fingers,
the moon and the stars that you have established;
what are human beings that you are mindful of them,
mortals that you care for them?

PSALM 8:3-4 NRSV

Have you ever stood in an empty field on a dark clear night when the stars are shining? If you think about it, in that moment you are but one person amongst seven billion people on the earth, spinning on a globe that is flying around the sun. All around the universe planets are spinning and orbiting and moving across the cosmos that God created for his glory.

In the middle of that field, staring up at the stars, you just might begin to realize that you are loved uniquely and individually by the God who created all this beauty. You are loved by the Creator of the universe. That is beautiful.

Thank you for loving me.

How can you ever thank God enough for loving you?

Count the Ways

I will give thanks to the LORD with my whole heart;
I will recount all of your wonderful deeds.

PSALM 9:1 ESV

It would be impossible to thank God for every gift he has given us and for all he has done for us. He is a God that is constantly giving and working on our behalf. Each step we take and every breath we breathe is a gift and blessing from God.

It takes so little effort to say thank you to God. But if we stopped to thank him for everything we would be unable to do anything else. We need to figure out how to be mindful of thankfulness while going about our lives. It is good to get in a practice of giving thanks with our whole heart and recounting daily, weekly, monthly, and yearly what God has done for us. We can learn to practice thankfulness in all occasions.

Thank you for all you have done and will do for me. Thank you for breath to breathe and life to live.

I will praise you, LORD, with all my heart.
I will tell all the miracles you have done.

PSALM 9:1 NCV

The writer of this Psalm declares, "I am writing a book on your wonders." What a poetic way to reflect upon the idea that God is constantly working and astounding us. Such a book would have a lot of pages. Throughout the Old Testament the Israelites set up remembrance stones to remind them, and those who would come after them, to be thankful for what God has done. Perhaps we can learn a lesson from the author of this Psalm and from the Israelites to take time to write down and remember the things we are thankful for.

Find a notebook and fill it simply with phrases of thanksgiving. It may take some time to get used to doing this. But as you do, you will find more and more things will fill that notebook as you develop your ability to count the ways that God has blessed you.

Thank you, God.

How many ways were you blessed by God today?

Choose Carefully

*The righteous choose their friends carefully,
but the way of the wicked leads them astray.*

PROVERBS 12:26 NIV

It was the sort of summer night you dream about: a smoky pink sunset, boat motors humming, friends laughing, picnic tables littered with snacks. But below the happy-go-lucky surface, life was moving. One friend was leaving for basic training in four days. A few more were heading off to college. Some friends were moving away, some were changing schools, and others were trying their best to ignore the fact that school was hiding around the corner.

No one talked about the fact that this was the last night they'd all be together. But all of them, conscious of it or not, were shaped by one another. They had tasted the sweetness of having like-minded friends. Friendship is one of the most important aspects of life. Friends have the power to bolster you with strength and sit with you in weakness. The people you spend time with impact both your mind and your spirit. Choose carefully.

Father, give me wisdom to search out friends who are after your heart the way I desire to be.

Good people take advice from their friends,
but an evil person is easily led to do wrong.

PROVERBS 12:26 NCV

Perhaps this morning's reading got you thinking about your own friendships. Take a minute and do an honest assessment. How does your spirit feel after you've talked with certain friends? How have they encouraged you in your walk with God? Conversely, what do you bring to your friendships? When was the last time you prayed out loud with a friend, or went out of your way to meet a need they had?

When you live right, you are a good guide to others in your life. Unfortunately, the same is also true to living wrong. The influence of your words, your actions, and your motivations has more power than you think. And in turn, your companions have the power to steer your thinking as well. The question then becomes this: Where do you want your friendships to lead?

Father God, orient my friendships toward you. Give me the ability to be a good guide for the people in my life and point my words and counsel toward your character and your heart.

Thank a close friend today for the way they've encouraged you recently.

Don't Be Troubled

*"The peace I give is a gift the world cannot give.
So don't be troubled or afraid."*

JOHN 14:27 NLT

The text notification read, "Your account balance has reached zero." Your heart rate rose slightly, and your shoulders started inching up your spine. You knew you were getting low on cash, but the fearsome truth of bottoming out your checking account left you with a raw, gnawing sense of worry in the pit of your stomach.

Daily stuff is not always easy to manage. Finances can be tight, and the space between paychecks can feel like a hot, wavering desert. No matter the stage of life, (buying books for college, budgeting for rent, needing new tires on the car) money or the lack of it wants to dictate our sense of wellbeing. Money, health, jobs, and major life decisions all promise the idea of peace: if you only have this, make this, feel this, do this, you'll be safe. But Jesus' promise is the only thing that will not let you down. His peace is beyond rational understanding. Even when circumstances threaten our perceived sense of security, Christ is there, offering what we really need.

Abba Father, I need your peace this morning. Throw it over my shoulders and wrap me in your truth. You give me what the world cannot. Help me trust that it is enough.

"I leave you peace; my peace I give you. I do not give it to you as the world does. So don't let your hearts be troubled or afraid."

JOHN 14:27 NCV

Jesus, in preparing his friends for his departure, gave them a truth that didn't make sense at the time. They had no context for the sort of peace he was talking about, the peace that stared down worldly hardship until it collapsed, deflating it of its power.

Even now, we have a hard time grasping and holding onto this type of peace—the peace Jesus gave us in place of his physical presence. The peace that surpasses all understanding. Maybe that's why he spelled it out for us. If something threatened your peace today, take the time tonight to push back against it with the truth of John 14:27. Claim its power, and thank God for his provision over and above the concerns of your life.

Jesus, I need your peace. I need it more than I need money in my bank account, food in my cupboard, or security in my job. Your gift stands above all those things, covering them with love. Fill me with trust.

Claim peace in anxiety by practicing deep breathing and moving your eyes around the room.

Reckless Love

"What do you think? If a man owns a hundred sheep, and one of them wanders away, will he not leave the ninety-nine on the hills and go to look for the one that wandered off? And if he finds it, truly I tell you, he is happier about that one sheep than about the ninety-nine that did not wander off. In the same way your Father in heaven is not willing that any of these little ones should perish."

MATTHEW 18:12-14 NIV

Last spring, a worship song called Reckless Love exploded on the Christian scene. In it, the writer focused in on a line in verse twelve reminding us that God's unexplainable love will go so far as to leave its post shepherding the whole flock to go after the one sheep that suddenly isn't there anymore. The one. Over the ninety-nine.

Is there someone in your life that's not showing up anymore? Someone who used to be a part of your friend group, your church, your flock? Or is it, perhaps, you? The God of the universe, who didn't think twice about comparing himself to a normal guy who looks after animals, loves that person, and he loves you. His desire is for anyone who has left his side to return. No questions asked. No harsh words spoken.

Father, thank you for your never ending, seemingly reckless love. Give me eyes to see who needs it today.

"If a man has a hundred sheep, and one wanders away and is lost, what will he do? Won't he leave the ninety-nine others and go out into the hills to search for the lost one? And if he finds it, he will rejoice over it more than over the ninety-nine others safe at home! Just so, it is not my Father's will that even one of these little ones should perish."

MATTHEW 18:12-14, TLB

Ask yourself an honest question tonight. What kind of shepherd would you be? Would you be content with the idea of keeping majority, or do you see yourself leaving the group that's safe and going after the one that's gotten away? Jesus made it clear, as he spoke with a child on his lap, that it's God's will that none of his children be separated from him. None. Your heavenly Father gives you the ability to help carry out his will and plan. You just need to listen to his teaching and apply it to your life.

Does it come naturally to risk the safety of most for the sake of one? No. Our culture tells us to cut our losses and do better next time. But Jesus sees it differently, and we need to as well.

Father, I need your insight. Even when it's countercultural, or against my norms and nature, help me keep my priority on restoring your sheep to the fold.

Who is the one you need to go after in your life?

Planting the Seed

*I solemnly urge you before God and before Christ Jesus—
who will someday judge the living and the dead when he appears
to set up his Kingdom— to preach the Word of God urgently at all
times, whenever you get the chance, in season and out,
when it is convenient and when it is not.*

2 TIMOTHY 4:1-2 TLB

Paul's advice here is so important: preach urgently, whenever you get the chance. When the time is right and when the timing seems off. When it's easy and when it's not. Why? Because of the parable of the seed and sower. The sower doesn't know which seeds are going to fall on rocky soil, or dry soil, or fertile soil. He just knows it's his job to take the seeds in that bag and get them into the ground. God will handle the rest.

It's not our job to see every single seed from fledgling stem to towering plant. But it is our role to be spreading seeds everywhere we go, waiting eagerly for the work of Jesus to take root and transform those who hear.

Father, give me the sense of urgency that Paul wanted to impart to Timothy, and show me the places where I should start throwing more seeds.

In the presence of God and of Christ Jesus, who will judge the living
and the dead, and in view of his appearing and his kingdom,
I give you this charge: Preach the word; be prepared in season
and out of season; correct, rebuke and encourage—
with great patience and careful instruction.

2 TIMOTHY 4:1-2 NIV

Alex had been trying to get her high school French teacher to come to church ever since she started taking his classes. She wasn't pushy, and she didn't make a big deal out of it; it was just something she wove into their easy-going conversations. Imagine her joy and surprise when finally, a few weeks before she left for college, her favorite teacher joined her and her family at church.

People may not always agree with the biblical truths we share, but they are generally willing to listen to a friend who is taking the time to talk and show interest in them. Alex's ability to make the most of her opportunity allowed her to plant a seed. What are you planting today?

Father God, give me wisdom and grace in my interactions with everyone I encounter today. Season my conversation with your truth. Make me ready to speak up on your behalf.

Do you have an unplanted field next to you? When can you get started?

Teach Well

The disciples came to him and asked, "Why do you speak to the people in parables?" He replied, "Because the knowledge of the secrets of the kingdom of heaven has been given to you, but not to them."

MATTHEW 13:10-11 NIV

Teachers, from day one, start studying their students. They figure out what lessons will work in a group and which ones might not. They identify learning styles. They get to know their students in order to understand how they think. Jesus did the same thing. He knew the limitations that his hearers had and how they would best be able to understand what he was saying.

Do you have younger siblings? Are there younger students on your team? Are you a parent? A book club leader? A manager? Everyone's audience might look different, but one thing needs to be constant. We need to understand how best to reach our students, whoever they may be.

God, if you have placed me in a capacity to teach others, allow me to pause and assess how I'm doing today. Am I understanding them? Am I sharing knowledge effectively? Where can I improve?

*The followers came to Jesus and asked,
"Why do you use stories to teach the people?"
Jesus answered, "You have been chosen to know the secrets about
the kingdom of heaven, but others cannot know these secrets."*

MATTHEW 13:10-11 NCV

Story, it seems, is a catchphrase of our society right now.
We are asked about our story, or challenged to rewrite our
stories, or told to own our stories in so many different
contexts that the idea of story has lost a little of its magical
luster. Jesus' use of story was different. He explained that
storytelling was a tool. It made difficult spiritual teaching
easier to understand. It gave context to new ideas. It gave
hearers a foothold as they climbed into what Jesus was saying
and tried to understand how it applied to their lives.

If you're running into difficulty explaining something to
someone, look to Christ's example. His stories were from
every day, commonly understood themes of his time like
farming, sheep herding, and water gathering. How can you
use things from your everyday life to better communicate the
truth you want to share?

*Lord, give me insight into how best to share your love and truth
with those around me.*

What part of your story can you tell today that shares a biblical
truth?

Solid Strength

Be to me a rock of refuge,
to which I may continually come;
you have given the command to save me,
for you are my rock and my fortress.

PSALM 71:3 ESV

In Taylors Falls, Minnesota, there's a place called Interstate State Park that features natural pot holes drilled into the rocks by swirling eddies of the St. Croix River. Some of the pot holes are small, smooth, bowl-shaped indentations, while others are caves deep enough to walk into. When you're standing inside the bigger potholes, it's easy to have a sense of what the psalmist meant when he said, "Be to me a rock of refuge." Nothing gets through a wall of rock. Not wind. Not heat. Not fire. Not ice. A fortress of rock is the ultimate protection.

The question then is this: Is God this kind of refuge to you? Or do you feel only the hard hopelessness of your current situation? Let God take whatever is in your path today and use it as the place where you continually redirect your worries, surrendering them to the solid strength of his power.

Father, let me see you as my rock of protection, the place I come to over and over to find shelter from whatever is going on today.

Be my rock of safety where I can always hide.
Give the order to save me,
for you are my rock and my fortress.

PSALM 71:3 NLT

In studying this verse, it feels important to trace a few of the words back to their original Hebrew. Did you know that anyone can do that? You don't have to be a Hebrew scholar (although you might have a far greater understanding if you were.). Just hop online, search the verse reference and add "Hebrew text" behind it. Options for reading the Hebrew characters and translations abound.

The phrase rock of safety where I can always hide finds its roots in the words abode and retreat. Now contrast that with the idea of you are my rock and my fortress, which translates evenly as crag (a steep mountain overhang or escarpment) and fortress. Those two ideas of rock feel very different—one a warm, sheltering home, the other a guarded stronghold. Understanding God as both a refuge and rampart gives us the ability to love him even more for the multi-faceted nature of his character.

Father, thank you for the nuances of language, and the different ways we have of seeing and understanding who you are.

Do your own Hebrew word study and learn more about the original text of the Bible.

True Purpose

You will say, "How I hated discipline!
How my heart spurned correction!
I would not obey my teachers or turn my ear to my instructors.
And I was soon in serious trouble in the assembly of God's people."

PROVERBS 5:12-14, NIV

No one likes discipline. We hate being told that we're doing something wrong, that our ideas are misguided, or that we have failed. Often, this is because we do not separate our true selves from our actions. Without making that necessary distinction, discipline can feel like an attack on who we are as people, rather than guidance on our actions.

Discipline is a necessary part of life. It comes at us from all angles: from our heavenly Father, from our parents, from teachers, even from ourselves. So how we receive it becomes incredibly important. Make it a point, today, to identify how you react when you are redirected in your actions. Do you want to raise your hackles like a hissing cat? Practice instead measuring your attitude and maintaining a posture of learning, which is the true purpose of discipline.

Father, find out my weaknesses in the areas of discipline
and give me opportunity to practice reacting with honor and
understanding.

Then you will say, "I hated being told what to do!
I would not listen to correction!
I would not listen to my teachers
or pay attention to my instructors.
I came close to being completely ruined
in front of a whole group of people."

PROVERBS 5:12-14 NCV

Enjoying the bright crunch of a Honeycrisp apple is a delight. But few understand what it takes to get a tree to produce the well-rounded profile of these delicious, softball sized apples. The saplings have to be planted, then watered frequently. They must be staked to keep from growing crooked, which can cause the trunk to split during times when the tree bears more weight. The lower trunk should be wrapped and mulched to prevent rot and disease. Finally, each year they should be pruned to promote even growth and proper balance, which allows the tree to hold the heaviness of next year's fruit.

Fruit is the goal of all that discipline, and in our lives, it should be the same.

God, tend me gently. Train me to take your discipline as a fruit tree benefits from the direction of an orchardist and develop in me a rich fruit that's evidence of your hand.

What are two areas of your life you'd like to see God develop better fruit in?

Needing God

God, you are my God.
I search for you.
I thirst for you
like someone in a dry, empty land
where there is no water.

PSALM 63:1 NCV

Some years, rain is just as prevalent in the fall as it is in the spring. However, spring rain is full of promise and life, and fall rain is just… wet. Cold. In northern climates, it's the precursor to snow. The thing is, the ground needs moisture in every season. It generates and sustains life, filling hungry roots with the water they need to survive.

Likewise, we as believers need the same sort of root-filling hydration. Without it, we start to brown around the edges, losing parts of ourselves that lack Jesus' living water. Perhaps that's why one hymn writer so plaintively repeated, "I need thee, oh I need thee." Our souls need reminding, tending, watering. Do not neglect the places your spirit is crying out today.

Father God, I come to you. Let me stop here, in your presence, and tell you how much I need you. Help me throw off all that's worrying me right now and claim you, your truth, and your promises in my life.

O God, you are my God, I seek you,
my soul thirsts for you;
my flesh faints for you,
as in a dry and weary land where there is no water.

PSALM 63:1 NRSV

Hymns have a lot of connotations for people. Some churches thrive on them, some avoid them at all costs. Whatever your feelings are on the subject, history has seen fit to preserve these songs of praise. There's nothing like them. Today's worship songs are beautiful and charged with emotion. They sound musically similar to a lot of secular songs found on the top of the charts, and that's okay. They are being born in today's current, just as hymns were in their time.

The most important part, as worshippers of Christ, is to worship. If that means using a hymnal and piano, great. If that means going to church and hearing a professional grade concert, great again. What matters most is the attitude of the worshipper's heart. Singing "I need thee, oh I need thee" or "God I need you, oh I need you" is all the same heart cry to Jesus. Worship comes in many forms, and the God we praise loves it all.

Lord God, you are worthy of every kind of praise.

Look up a hymn and try using the chorus as a prayer.

Fight

I have fought the good fight, I have finished the race, I have kept the faith. Finally, there is laid up for me the crown of righteousness, which the Lord, the righteous Judge, will give to me on that Day, and not to me only but also to all who have loved His appearing.

2 TIMOTHY 4:7-8 NKJV

If you've ever run a foot race, you know the pressures it entails. Other runners can hem you in or hold you back. Terrain can tangle your feet. Mishaps with clothing or bad shoes can spoil everything. For everything that can go right, so much can also go wrong.

When Paul recounted his own race to Timothy, imagine the relief he must have felt. Paul fought deeply for the cause of Christ and he finished his race, all the while keeping close his faith in Christ. Nothing tripped him up enough to make him stop running. Is there anything threatening your race this morning? Someone who is whispering doubt in your ear? An event you can't make sense of? Keep fighting for every step you take. Don't allow someone or something else to steal your race.

Father, guide my steps. Keep my feet free from entanglement while I fight for my faith in you.

*I have fought the good fight, I have finished the race, I have kept
the faith. Now, a crown is being held for me—a crown for being
right with God. The Lord, the judge who judges rightly, will give the
crown to me on that day—not only to me but to all those who have
waited with love for him to come again.*

2 TIMOTHY 4:7-8 NCV

Close your eyes. Take a moment to imagine what it will be like
to stand in front of the living God at the end of your life. Take
in the wonder of his throne. The strength of his arms. The
approval in his eyes.

In your hands you hold your life's work. It was your chief aim,
your purpose in living. Your offering to God. What is it? What
do you hope to present to God when you meet him face to
face? Will you, like Paul, be confident in the way that you've
lived? If you're not sure, tonight is the best time to start
redirecting your actions to meet with your goals.

*Father God, give me vision for your goals, and make them my goals
as well. Come alongside me in the everyday and show me the places
you've set apart for me to accomplish your work as part of my race.*

Write down three things you'd like to offer God at the end of
your life.

The Truth

You have an anointing from the Holy One, and all of you know the truth. I do not write to you because you do not know the truth, but because you do know it and because no lie comes from the truth.

1 JOHN 2:20-21 NIV

A recent Barna group study noted that millennials and generation Z are particularly reluctant to talk about their faith with people outside the Christian belief system. Why? Because unlike generations before, they are living and socializing alongside a greater number of people who believe very differently than they do.

No one wants to be seen as arrogant, pompous, or judgmental. We fear what that will do to the small witness we do have, the little influence we cling to as though it's the most important thing in the world. Do not fear offending someone for the sake of the gospel. You know the truth. The truth. And it's something that outsiders do not know—and will not know—unless someone talks to them about it.

Lord God, king of heaven and of earth, you are truth. Help me to put my weight on this, trusting it with every step I take as I walk into the places where people need to hear from you today.

You have the gift that the Holy One gave you, so you all know the truth. I do not write to you because you do not know the truth but because you do know the truth. And you know that no lie comes from the truth.

1 JOHN 2:20-21 NCV

Read the last line of verse 21 one more time. Settle back for a moment and apply that to your worldview. Jesus is not a lie. His teaching is not a lie. His will for your life is not a lie. As people who believe in God and are given the Holy Spirit, followers of Jesus can stand firmly on truth—which is something outsiders cannot do. So, while they have the leeway to explore other belief systems and try them on for size, Christians have no need. Why? Not because we are uneducated, shallow, or narrow minded, but because we know the truth.

Learn. Listen. Love. Pay attention to those who believe differently than you. It is an honor to converse with someone about the things they hold close to their hearts. But do not forget that you know the truth.

Father God, bolster me in your truth and allow me to speak your name freely in my life.

Think of one person who believes differently than you do and make efforts to begin a new friendship.

459

Invitation to Trust

"The LORD himself goes before you and will be with you;
he will never leave you nor forsake you.
Do not be afraid; do not be discouraged."

DEUTERONOMY 31:8 NIV

If you've ever hiked at high altitude, you may have seen sections of trail that are marked with bullseyes. Why? Because when you get high enough, the trail stops and your path becomes a series of boulders. Navigating rocks and boulders takes effort, and it's easy to lose your way in finding sure footing and veer off course. Following the bullseyes ensures that you stay on track and reach the summit (sore legs and tired feet notwithstanding.)

Now imagine that you're hiking along, and instead of some forest worker with a spray paint can, you know that God has been the one to clear your path and mark your trail. What does that do to your ability to trust where he's leading you today? If the Lord himself goes before you and accompanies you and promises not to leave you, can you put down the weight of fear that you're carrying and confidently start making your way over the rocks of life?

Father God, let the comfort of your guidance bring me into
confidence today.

> *"The Lord himself will go before you.*
> *He will be with you; he will not leave you or forget you.*
> *Don't be afraid and don't worry."*

DEUTERONOMY 31:8 NCV

It's one thing to read a Bible verse that says, "Don't be intimidated. Don't worry." It's entirely another to turn around and look whatever you're afraid of in the face and let that verse guide your very physical and emotional responses to the situations you face in everyday life.

Sometimes it seems that God asks a lot from us. Doesn't he realize we've just lost someone we loved, or gotten a terrible diagnosis from the doctor? The answer is yes. His omnipotence allows him to know everything. Which means he also knows the depth of our terror, sadness, and fear. Difficult as it may be tonight, hold space in your circumstance for God and ask him to keep his word tonight. He will not let you down.

Lord God, meet me tonight. I invite you into my pain, my worry, my anxiety. Push through my doubts and surround me with the warm presence of your love.

Practice managing anxious thoughts by identifying and redirecting them to something that's concrete and true.

Faithful Servant

"The servant to whom he had entrusted the five bags of silver came forward with five more and said, 'Master, you gave me five bags of silver to invest, and I have earned five more.' The master was full of praise. 'Well done, my good and faithful servant. You have been faithful in handling this small amount, so now I will give you many more responsibilities. Let's celebrate together!'"

MATTHEW 25:20-21 NLT

By committing our lives to serving Jesus Christ, we commit to investing the treasure he has given us and growing it to an even greater value for his kingdom. When our Master returns, we should have something to show for our years of serving him and proclaiming his name on earth. By faith, we make good on our commitment to Jesus by sharing the gospel, and serving widows, orphans, and refugees in our land. We love as Jesus loved.

Yes, we will make mistakes, and of course God's grace is sufficient for us. Do what you say you will do; after all, God has kept his promises to you. Look forward to the day when you will hear the fulfilment of your commitment: "Well done, my good and faithful servant. Let's celebrate together!"

Oh God, how I desire to hear those words, "Well done." I want to be a good and faithful servant. Give me strength to do that, please.

"Then the one who had received the five talents came forward, bringing five more talents, saying, 'Master, you handed over to me five talents; see, I have made five more talents.' His master said to him, 'Well done, good and trustworthy slave; you have been trustworthy in a few things, I will put you in charge of many things; enter into the joy of your master.'"

MATTHEW 25:20-21 NRSV

We commit to being faithful, honest, and diligent, just as God is. Our lives are a representation of Jesus, and our ability to make good on our commitments illustrates God's faithfulness. We are modeling godliness to a godless world. We demonstrate his truth, love, integrity, and mercy to a world lost in sin. Make good on your commitments to the world in order to shine the light of Jesus in the darkness.

Spend some time reflecting on the faithfulness and dependability of God, and let that be your motivation!

Help me, Father, to be a faithful servant. I want to use the talents you have given me wisely.

What do you find to be the hardest part of keeping your promises?

Press Pause

Careless words stab like a sword,
but wise words bring healing.

PROVERBS 12:18 NCV

It happened again. You got into an argument, flung off the guard of your temper, and watched your hurtful words hurtle toward their mark. Maybe you watched the face of the person you attacked, or maybe you kept your eyes focused elsewhere, already too ashamed to look them in the eye.

As believers, we know all too well the pin-pricking sting of shame when our words cross the boundaries of what is healthy for us and for others. We become like soldiers choosing to take off the armor of God's character and open ourselves to attacks from emotions like anger, lust, depression, fear—both from the outside and the inside. Friend, do your utmost to guard your words for the sake of others, but also for the sake of yourself. Shame is a fearsome beast, one that is difficult to shake once it's latched onto you.

Father God, you know my struggles with guarding my tongue.
I pray for protection over my words this morning, that what I say
and do will be measured and wise.

Rash words are like sword thrusts,
but the tongue of the wise brings healing.

PROVERBS 12:18 NRSV

Do you consider yourself a wise person? Let's test that theory. Pretend you are attending a lecture on something you are knowledgeable in. When the speaker calls for discussion, are you the first to jump in, eager to show off your abilities? Or perhaps you're sitting with a friend who just lost their job. Do you feel the need to fill the space of their distress, talking strongly about the incompetence of their boss and the crummy economy?

Proverbs 12:18 cautions against quickly-spoken words that have not been weighed and measured, and praises words that are spoken with wisdom. Tonight, replay your interactions with others. Is there anywhere you could have paused in order to truly speak words from your heart, instead of letting emotions take control of your tongue?

Lord God, give me the wherewithal to pause when I'm not sure what to say, and allow your wisdom to come out of my mouth instead of my own reckless responses.

Challenge yourself to hold your tongue in a situation where you'd normally want to speak loudly.

Prudence

The clever do all things intelligently,
but the fool displays folly.

PROVERBS 13:16 NRSV

Perhaps you've seen the street-cam videos of people running into things because they are engrossed in their smartphones. If you haven't, look it up later. The sheer volume of people who do not see what's right in front of them because they simply weren't paying attention is staggering (literally.).

The writer of Proverbs speaks plainly in his admonition here. Why? Because it's the simple truth. Ignorance is like the step we miss when we make poor choices. It shows up when we divide our attention, argue without knowing all the information on a topic, or put ourselves in questionable circumstances and then wonder how we got tangled up in trouble. Are there places today that might pose a stumbling hazard to you? What can you do to pay attention more deeply and walk in a way that advertises God's grace?

Lord, keep me from stumbling into ignorance when I could be
walking upright, directed by your truth.

> *Every prudent man acts with knowledge,*
> *but a fool flaunts his folly.*
>
> PROVERBS 13:16 ESV

There are times in life when you find yourself stopped at a crossroads, deciding which direction to go next. The question is this: How can you be sure you're making the right choice? At a crossroads, one sign points one direction, and another points the opposite. How will you decide where to go? Well, what do you know about those two locations? Where will they take you? What is God doing in those places? What sort of community will you find there? Is the work that's available fulfilling? Does it offer ample places to rest and restore, or will it likely drain and tire you?

Using the knowledge God has given you about yourself and your circumstances can help you take your next steps with confidence. Ignoring knowledge and simply doing what you want in the moment may lead to serious consequences. Seek God's counsel, read his teachings, and trust yourself to know where he's leading you.

Father God, calm my beating heart. Allow me to assess my choices with clarity and wisdom, and to rest secure in the knowledge that no matter where I go, I will not step out of your grasp.

List the pros and cons of your next big decision, but don't forget to prioritize your spiritual growth and development.

In a Name

His name—by faith in his name—has made this man strong whom you see and know, and the faith that is through Jesus has given the man this perfect health in the presence of you all.

ACTS 3:16 ESV

People are often cautious with the name of Jesus in our culture. But to the lame man sitting at the temple gate in Acts 3, Peter's use of Jesus' name meant the difference between someone living a crippled, dependent life and a sure-footed independent one.

That morning, the lame man was laid at the beautiful gate as he always was, and he set to work collecting alms as he always did. But when he plied Peter and John with his cup, he received far more than he bargained for. In verse six, Peter said, "I have no silver and gold, but what I do have I give to you. In the name of Jesus Christ of Nazareth, rise up and walk." Jesus' name needs no caution sign, no warning signal. Faith in his name, his deity, his provision, and his love can change the world for someone. Will you be the one to speak it?

Jesus, the power that lives in your name is no fairy tale, and it carries just as much meaning and strength today as it did then. Give me grace to use your name freely in all circumstances.

It was faith in Jesus that made this crippled man well.
You can see this man, and you know him. He was made completely
well because of trust in Jesus, and you all saw it happen!

ACTS 3:16 NCV

Imagine Peter trying to explain the unexplainable—how did the lame man, the one everyone walked by every time they entered the temple, suddenly come to walk? The simplicity of his answer is staggering. "We have faith in the name of Jesus." It must have been terrifying the first time Peter performed a miracle. As a human, he had to have been thinking, What if this doesn't work?

Nevertheless, it didn't stop him from listening to God and calling down the power of Jesus' name on the life of the lame man. Likewise, we have no business being afraid of saying that the name of Jesus is the one thing that could change everything for someone else.

Jesus, let me live in the power of your name. Let me speak it with boldness and faith and expectancy.

Study more on the idea of expectant faith and its place in your life.

Practice of Presence

Whether you eat or drink or whatever you do,
do it all for the glory of God.

1 CORINTHIANS 10:31 NIV

In the mid-1600s, a man named Nicolas Herman was wounded in the Thirty Years War. Nicolas then decided to enter the Discalced Carmelite monastery in France, where he came Brother Lawrence. Brother Lawrence's primary assignment in the monastery was working in the kitchen. It wasn't a particularly stimulating job. He peeled potatoes. He flipped omelets. He washed dishes. He washed a lot of dishes.

But do you know what Brother Lawrence is most known for? Practicing the presence of God in the daily acts of life. He is the one who said, "We ought not to be weary of doing little things for the love of God, who regards not the greatness of the work, but the love with which it is performed." Paul and Brother Lawrence discovered an amazing recipe for contentedness: loving God in the mundane, minute-to-minute activities of life. Try it today and see what effect it has on you.

Father God, today I want to practice loving you in the middle of doing the dishes, working on homework, during practice—the list goes on. Help me to see your presence and reflection in the ordinary parts of every day.

Whether therefore ye eat, or drink, or whatsoever ye do,
do all to the glory of God.

1 CORINTHIANS 10:31 KJV

So, how did it go? Were you able to perform the everyday, boring stuff of life to God's glory? Or are you still scratching your head about what that really means? It might look like smiling when you made that basket in practice, loving God's design for our minds and bodies to connect and perform amazing physical acts. It could be helping out with the dishes, and praising God for running water and the food filling your stomach. Maybe it might look like realigning your attitude about something you don't really like doing, knowing that the way you do that thing can either detract from the love of God or build upon it.

This is no simple task. It takes training and direction from Scripture to check off your daily to-do list with the desire to glorify God as your chief intent. But with God's help and your continued effort, it's entirely, wonderfully possible.

Father God, glorifying you with even the smallest of daily acts seems like a lot to attempt. Build this ability in me as a second nature, that I may find, appreciate, and love you in everything I do.

Pick one boring thing you have to do every day and practice loving God while you do that thing.

Put It on Ice

*Brothers and sisters, each person, as responsible to God, should
remain in the situation they were in when God called them.*

1 CORINTHIANS 7:24 NIV

Young adulthood can be full of aches for change. Maybe you
believe you're ready for change right now, and staying where
you are for another year, or two, or three seems unbearable.
After all, God has pointed your heart in a certain direction;
shouldn't it be reasonable to go now?

Do not waste the time you have in the place you are by
wishing you were somewhere else. Remaining in your
current situation until the door opens for your next step is a
crucial part of maturity, obedience, and wisdom. God wants
you to live in his fullness, but one of the best ways to ruin that
is by constantly straining your eyes over the horizon, missing
what's in front of you by looking for what comes next.

*Father God, bring my eyes back to you, and back to the here and
now. Show me how to find contentedness in where you've placed
me today.*

Brothers and sisters, each of you should stay as you were when you were called, and stay there with God.

1 CORINTHIANS 7:24, NCV

In 1 Corinthians chapter 7, Paul emphasizes the importance of these words by repeating the concept not one, not two, but three times. Read verses 17, 20, and 24.

If you are distracted today by the call of something you are longing for, something that may be in the future, but isn't in your grasp tonight, put it in the freezer. Seriously. Write it on a strip of paper, throw it in a sandwich bag, and put it in your freezer. Freezing your desires doesn't mean giving up on them. It simply helps you acknowledge that now may not be the time, but the future is as close as God's feet next to yours, holding high ground and waiting for direction.

Lord, direct me in your time and give me patience in the waiting.

Write down your biggest worry, bag it, throw it in the freezer, and leave it there.

Firsthand Experience

We have not been telling you fairy tales when we explained to you
the power of our Lord Jesus Christ and his coming again.
My own eyes have seen his splendor and his glory.

2 PETER 1:16 TLB

Years ago, C.S. Lewis brought up the idea that Jesus was either a liar, a lunatic, or Lord. Since then, many great thinkers and writers have fleshed out the idea that people must look at the evidence and decide what to do with the person of Jesus. Peter's foresight speaks to our very human nature. If we didn't see it happen, it's easy to question the truth. Maybe that's why our culture thrives so much on taking pictures. It's easy proof.

But go back to Peter scratching out his second letter to the church, most likely from prison. He knew the power of God's grace and its ability to transform lives; he felt it, saw it, lived it. He spoke in earnest, reminding those who hadn't met Jesus that his deity was real, and that listening and applying his teaching—and enjoying the resulting fruit in our lives—proves to ourselves and to others that God is indeed faithful.

Lord Jesus, though we may not have the social media post to prove
it, we can trust your teaching as recorded by your servants because
of the inerrancy of your Word. Build in us faith to listen and obey.

For we did not follow cleverly devised tales when we made known to you the power and coming of our Lord Jesus Christ, but we were eyewitnesses of His majesty.

2 PETER 1:16 NASB

Peter had the privilege of knowing Jesus. He fished with him. Sat side-by-side and learned from him. Witnessed his miracles. Peter saw Jesus in his fully human/fully God duality and had the remarkable opportunity of being able to speak of the experience firsthand. When you've been an on-the-ground witness to something amazing, you tell stories of that event in incredible excitement and detail. Why? Because you were there.

Think back to a time when you saw Jesus at work in your life, or in the life of someone close to you. Fill in all the details: the smells, the location, the emotions running through your body. Your story about your encounter with the living God can change someone's life. Seeing Jesus move in your life is no fairytale. It is truth. It is power on display. Have the strength to stand witness to those moments and see them as they are: evidence of God's love and might in your life.

Jesus, open my eyes to see the places you are working, and open my mouth to stand witness to your power in this world.

Write down the most vivid experience you've had where God has done something real in your life.

Beyond Reproach

Urge the young men to be sensible; in all things show yourself to be an example of good deeds, with purity in doctrine, dignified, sound in speech which is beyond reproach, so that the opponent will be put to shame, having nothing bad to say about us.

TITUS 2:6-8 NASB

People joke about the concept of adulting, but on the days you accomplish those big-ticket grownup responsibilities like buying a microwave, washing your sheets, remembering to change your oil, or convincing yourself to eat at home instead of going to the latest hotspot everyone's been 'gramming at, it feels like a huge deal.

So yes, adulting may be hard, but sensible living isn't just something parents make up to torture their kids. Sensible, responsible living speaks for itself. If your life is to reflect Christ, then having your affairs in order, your possessions well-cared for, your finances clean, and your interactions with others well-intended will speak volumes about you before you even open your mouth. Does the way you live your life reflect your faith in Jesus and the teaching of his word? If not, straighten out the wrinkles, check an extra box or two off your to-do list, and make an extra effort today to live beyond reproach.

Lord Jesus, thank you for loving me as I am, while still encouraging me in clear-headed living for the sake of your name.

In the same way, urge the young men to behave carefully, taking life seriously. And here you yourself must be an example to them of good deeds of every kind. Let everything you do reflect your love of the truth and the fact that you are in dead earnest about it. Your conversation should be so sensible and logical that anyone who wants to argue will be ashamed of himself because there won't be anything to criticize in anything you say!

TITUS 2:6-8 TLB

Let's be honest. Taking life seriously doesn't sound like very much… fun. But don't be mistaken. God is not calling you to a life of drudgery and frown lines. In fact, one of the very best ways of witnessing on Jesus's behalf is by living out the joy he's lovingly, lavishly given us. So what does that mean here in Titus? Fight back the urge to see this pattern for living as boring and straight-laced. Love widely. Look after the needs of others. Practice everyday kindness as though your life depended on it.

Set your standards for behavior and living high; the benefits you will reap will far outweigh any annoyance at following the rules.

Father God, thank you for giving me a blueprint for living a clean and clear-conscience life. Give me the wherewithal to follow it and push back any worries about feeling lame or uncool.

Look up the phrase "dead earnest" and study more on what it means.

Power of Yeast

You were running well; who hindered you from obeying the truth?
This persuasion did not come from Him who calls you.
A little leaven leavens the whole lump of dough.

GALATIANS 5:7-9 NASB

Baking bread is one of those things that doesn't seem to make sense. After all, you can buy a loaf of cheap bread at the store for a dollar. Why spend the hours it takes to make a proper loaf of homemade bread? Aside from the fact that anyone in nose-distance will be inviting themselves into your kitchen, Galatians 5 will start to make even more sense. So often, biblical teaching is drawn from real life examples. But in an age where we are increasingly digitalized and less hands-on, those examples sit further and further away from our daily reality.

Go buy a few simple ingredients today. Flour, water, salt, and yeast are the only things you need for a basic loaf. Pinchofyum.com/no-knead-bread has a great recipe. Then watch what happens when the tiny packet of yeast you add at the beginning transforms the entirety of the dough from a flat, heavy mass to an airy loaf of goodness. You'll be better able to understand the first half of the passage tonight when you see the results up close. P.S. Don't forget to buy butter.

Lord Jesus, thank you for real-life examples that make it easier to understand and solidify your teachings.

You were running a good race. Who cut in on you to keep you from obeying the truth? That kind of persuasion does not come from the one who calls you. A little yeast works through the whole batch of dough.

GALATIANS 5:7-9 NIV

Let's say you have loaf of bread rising in your kitchen right now. Crazy, right? Something so small as yeast can have so much power; enough, in fact, to take over the whole chemical makeup of an object and change its outcome.

Now think of your own life. Do you have any yeast lurking around your relationship with truth? Is there an outside idea that has you questioning your beliefs? Has something happened to make you question God's role of authority and goodness in this world? The world wants to cut in on your race and challenge your commitment to biblical truth. They want to tell you there are no absolutes and tolerance is the key to peace. And the second you start believing them, you start changing as sure as yeast will interact with flour and water.

Lord God, guard my mind and my feet. If this Christian life is a race, preserve me from being cut in on, or held back, or stopped completely by the enemy who wants nothing more than to change my commitment to you.

Don't just think about it. Do it. If you haven't already started, pick a day this week to try making bread. Don't forget to share.

Unashamed

*I am not ashamed of the gospel, for it is the power of God
for salvation to everyone who believes,
to the Jew first and also to the Greek.*

ROMANS 1:16 NASB

If you have had the pleasure of being engaged to be married,
think for a moment about how proud you are of your beloved.
You tell everyone how wonderful they are. You talk about the
things they are known for, the things they are skilled at, the
ways they've made you grow as a person and as a couple.

Now consider that Jesus calls the church his bride. This might
seem like an odd example at times, but when you push through
the white tulle layers, you see at the root God's longing and
desire for a lasting relationship with his chosen and created
people. Earthly relationships are a beautiful example of the
unashamed love that we ought to have for the gospel of Christ,
the story that is so much bigger than a story. Do you feel that
kind of love and pride for the gospel of Jesus, or are you wary of
being misunderstood if you mark yourself as a believer?

*Lord Jesus, let me think long and hard about this question today.
I want to be unashamed of your gospel and your truth, but
sometimes it's so difficult when I fear being misunderstood or
judged. Give me boldness. Give me pride. Remind me of the shout-
it-to-the-rooftops joy of my first love for you.*

I am not ashamed of the Good News,
because it is the power God uses to save everyone who believes—
to save the Jews first, and then to save non-Jews.

ROMANS 1:16 NCV

This morning you dug into a deep question about your pride in the name and message of Jesus. Have you had time to think more about it tonight?

Don't be afraid to admit that you are afraid of what the outcome might be if you stand boldly for Christ. All of us are at the beginning, but do not be mistaken. God's word doesn't come back void. You tell the story. You share the method. Then wait and see the unfolding of God's work in someone else's life. Perhaps it'll be in your time together, or perhaps it won't. Either way, you will have stood true to God and lived not in fear and shame of talking about the gospel, but with pride and joy.

Lord God, give me boldness, strength, and trust that you will hold up your end of the bargain. Your story is worth telling. Your method works. I believe in you God. Unleash me with your love.

Write out answers to the questions above. What can you learn about yourself?

The Bank

*Keep your lives free from the love of money and be content with
what you have, because God has said, "Never will I leave you;
never will I forsake you." So we say with confidence, "The LORD is
my helper; I will not be afraid. What can mere mortals do to me?"*

HEBREWS 13:5-6 NIV

When do you find the most confidence during the month? If
you're anything like most people, it's right after the two-week
marker on which you got paid. Money has a way of calming
people down. It's a steadying influence; with it, you feel like
you can do anything. Without it, it's easy to lose your ability
to find contentment. Hebrews turns that paradigm upside
down. Here we learn that money should be of no consequence
to our state of mind, because God himself promises never to
leave or forsake us.

But what does that mean? We need money to live, don't we?
Of course. But the real question is this: Do we need it in order
to be content? God says no. God asks us to look to him for our
needs and to rewire our brains to understand what security
looks like. Spoiler alert: it won't be in our bank account, and it
may not be as easy as pulling out our shiny red debit card. No
matter. God's promises never run out at the end of the month.

*Father, the way you provide for me is so much deeper than dollars
and cents. Give me faith to recognize where my true security lies.*

Don't love money; be satisfied with what you have. For God has said, "I will never fail you. I will never abandon you." So we can say with confidence, "The Lord is my helper, so I will have no fear. What can mere people do to me?"

HEBREWS 13:5-6 NLT

You've seen it in movies; the rich man has all the power. He wears designer suits and gold-framed sunglasses and walks nonchalantly down the stairs of his private jet. People listen to whatever he says, and when he turns away, he always wears a self-assured little smile. It's an achingly common theme. If money is power and power is happiness, then happiness must be money?

It depends on who you're listening to. And if the world has bent your ear that direction, perhaps now is a good time to be reminded that Christians have something far stronger to cling to than cash. We have Christ himself as our helper. Friend, do not give in to the temptation that money will satisfy your deepest needs. Look confidently to God, bear his witness, prove his promises, and wait as he showers you with the richness of joy and trust in him.

Jesus, be my secure and confident hope, my strong defender, my great provider. Thank you.

Think of three times God has come through for you in ways that didn't involve money.

Actual Need

"Don't be concerned about what to eat and what to drink. Don't worry about such things. These things dominate the thoughts of unbelievers all over the world, but your Father already knows your needs. Seek the Kingdom of God above all else, and he will give you everything you need."

LUKE 12:29-31 TLB

Paleo. Plant-based. Intermittent Fasting. Whole30. Counting Macros. Carb Cycling. Vegan. Dairy Free. Gluten Free. The options for how to eat today are astounding, and each one is different from the next. What doesn't change, however, are the underlying promises each diet makes. And while each diet may have its benefits, you may not realize how much of your time, money, and energy are spent on only eating certain things.

Food and drink can quickly become an obsession because it fuels not only our health and wellness, but also our security and emotions. By contrast, the kingdom of God can seem far away and abstract; that is until we start focusing our energy and passion in that direction, and consequently see God provide for our needs far above and beyond the promises from the latest diet trend.

Father God, do not let me be distracted by the promises of what a diet can do when it is you alone who can meet all my needs. Please keep my eyes from wandering elsewhere and fix them instead on your kingdom and your work.

"Do not seek what you will eat and what you will drink, and do not keep worrying. For all these things the nations of the world eagerly seek; but your Father knows that you need these things. But seek His kingdom, and these things will be added to you."

LUKE 12:29-31 NASB

It's amazing, the things you see differently when you read them again a second time. In this passage, there's a contrast in verse 30 that's easy to miss. The world eagerly seeks after great food and drink. Magazines, travel agencies, and discount warehouses are constantly in a boom because of it. But your heavenly Father already knows that you need these things. And if God knows what you need, but directs you in the next verse to seek his kingdom instead which do you think is more important?

The world will tell you that driving across the country to find new foods and drink old wine is one of the surest ways to happiness. Jesus tells you to direct your energy toward the work of the kingdom so that he can give you the food and drink you need.

Lord God, I want to be after your heart and your kingdom. Put my priorities in the right place and allow me to see your blessing as a result of my obedience to your Word.

If you are struggling with weight, size, or muscle mass, try taking a media fast from any apps, people, or sites that make you feel bad about yourself.

Role of Salt

"Salt is good; but if even salt has become tasteless, with what will it be seasoned? It is useless either for the soil or for the manure pile; it is thrown out. He who has ears to hear, let him hear."

LUKE 14:34-35 NASB

If you spend any time in the kitchen, you'll soon learn that salt is one of the main staples in creating flavor in food. With it, you can transform plain cucumbers into crisp, briny pickles. You can shake up the profile of an avocado. You can brine, cure, and preserve any manner of meats. Salt is a sort of magic that's been around since the dawn of time. In some countries, salt lies locked within the earth in veins or layers and must be mined out. But here's the rub. If the open earth is exposed to rain, sun, and air, the salt loses its saltiness entirely. However, the salt that stays closed within the rocks, away from the elements, will hold on to its flavor indefinitely.

If we are supposed to be salt and light, as Jesus preached in the Sermon on the Mount, then we have to understand two things. One, as salt we have an important, day-in-day-out sort of role in our world. We need to be everywhere, in everything, enhancing those around us with the gospel of Jesus. And two, we have to be careful—incredibly careful—not to leave ourselves exposed and risk the salt of our influence fading.

Jesus, help me see the places I provide the salt to—my classes, my teams, my study groups, my work, my creative circles, my friends. Keep me strong and effective for your name's sake.

"Salt is good, but if it loses its saltiness, how can it be made salty again? It is fit neither for the soil nor for the manure pile; it is thrown out. "Whoever has ears to hear, let them hear."

LUKE 14:34-35 NIV

According to a recent study conducted in 2018, Americans waste 150,000 tons of food per day. That breaks down to around a pound of food per person per day. Take a quick stock check of your fridge and pantry. You'll probably find something lurking that needs to be thrown out. And if you were to weigh that Tupperware of leftovers you forgot from last week, or the orange in the drawer that's a little too bruised? You guessed it. It's probably at least a pound.

God wants us to steward our resources well; this includes the resource of our lives. We don't want to waste our purpose. The parables at the end of Matthew 14 all detail some aspect of our readiness to follow God. Take some time to study them and identify the different aspects of waste Jesus is talking about.

Holy Spirit, please show me any places where I am subjecting my resources to waste. I want to follow you wholeheartedly, and to live fully as a result.

Write down the themes from the four parables at the end of Matthew 14.

Get Ready

*We keep on praying for you, asking our God to enable you to live a
life worthy of his call. May he give you the power to accomplish all
the good things your faith prompts you to do. Then the name of our
Lord Jesus will be honored because of the way you live, and you
will be honored along with him. This is all made possible because
of the grace of our God and Lord, Jesus Christ.*

2 THESSALONIANS 1:11-12 NLT

When you go for a hike in a national park, you can expect
a few things when you pull into the parking lot. You'll find
a trailhead and a map outlining the path. You may find
restrooms and a source of running water. Once you start
hiking, you see a cleared trail. This doesn't change the fact that
if you want to get from the parking lot to the mountain top, or
the waterfall, or wherever the trail promises to take you, you'll
have to start walking and keep walking the entire distance.

What it does mean is that you've been enabled to go the
distance. And in the same way, you can pray for yourself and
for others that God will empower you to go where he calls you.
This requires you to understand something, though. God's
power is not abstract. God's power is active, and if you ask for
it to be present in your life, you better be ready to lace up your
boots and get moving. The way is set. Are you prepared?

*Father God, give me faith in your power. Prove it to me over and
over so that my trust in you and your ability to work in my life is
like a reflex reaction in times of question.*

To this end we always pray for you, that our God may make you worthy of his calling and may fulfill every resolve for good and every work of faith by his power, so that the name of our Lord Jesus may be glorified in you, and you in him, according to the grace of our God and the Lord Jesus Christ.

2 THESSALONIANS 1:11–12 ESV

There's a huge sense of relief in this verse. Do you see it? We can ask God to make us worthy of our calling. That means that when we feel a certain "resolve for good," or want to do something that helps others or makes a difference, we can expect help in accomplishing it by his power. Why? So the name of Jesus can be glorified in our lives.

We should feel absolutely over the moon about what this Scripture means in our lives. First off, God again reveals how much he works through prayer. Second, he gives us the ability to turn the things we want to do for him into reality. And third, when those things are finished and credit is given where credit is due, God's name can be recognized even more than it was before.

Holy Father, open my eyes to the places you have given me desires to work and influence and make a difference. Let me be faithful in praying for them and asking for your purpose and power to be present.

Ask God for clear direction in where he's leading you next in your life.

Let Wisdom Pour

"To those who listen to my teaching, more understanding will be given. But for those who are not listening, even what little understanding they have will be taken away from them."

MARK 4:25 NLT

Imagine a runner who trains for a marathon, completes it, then stops running. After a year has gone by, she remembers how much fun she had on race day—how satisfying it felt to cross the finish line feeling strong and accomplished. She shows up to run the marathon the next year but, several miles in, she realizes she won't make it. She's lost her base. To go the distance, you can't just want to run; you need to train.

Following Christ is similar. You need to build—and maintain—your base. If you want to follow Christ, you have to be a Christ-follower. Read your Bible. Pray for understanding. Put what you learn into practice every day.

God, thank you for your Word. Every time I read it, I understand more of who you are. From this solid base, more and more of the world makes sense. I am strong. I can go the distance. Give me a hunger to keep listening, God, because I want to grow as strong and go as far as I can.

*"Those who listen with open hearts will receive more revelation.
But those who don't listen with open hearts
will lose what little they think they have!"*

MARK 4:25 TPT

You have two water bottles. One has a lid on, the other does not. Both are half full. Held under the faucet, which bottle will be filled?

To be filled to the top with Jesus' wisdom, we must remain open. Closing our hearts to teaching that feels inconvenient, or makes us uncomfortable, leaves them closed to teaching that would help us grow.

Jesus, I give you permission to take the lid off my heart. Let your wisdom pour, let your knowledge fill me to the brim, and let your love overflow. I want to know you so well that everything you say becomes music to my ears.

Is there a teaching of Jesus' you struggle to embrace? Pray for an open mind, so you can understand the heart behind his words.

Listen and Watch

We are God's handiwork, created in Christ Jesus to do good works,
which God prepared in advance for us to do.

EPHESIANS 2:10 NIV

Do you remember the first time you were chosen for
something? Maybe it was a part in school play. Maybe it was
getting a job and working for someone you really admired.
Maybe it was getting into the college you wanted. Whatever it
was, when you were chosen, you probably felt the beginnings
of a few new emotions: responsibility, a desire to do well, a
wish to really accomplish something.

But did you know that those emotions don't need to stress you
out? You don't have to chase and worry and grasp blindly at
the things God has put in your heart to do. You don't have to
wonder what your purpose is, or if you even have a purpose
in this life. You are God's handiwork. He made you with the
inherent ability to the do things that he has prepared for you
to do. If you don't know what those things are today, be still.
Trust your Father and ask him to reveal his plans for your life
to you. Then wait expectantly, ears up, eyes open, ready to see
where God leads.

Lord God, I know you have a purpose for my life. Even if I can't see
what the end goal is, help me pick out the next step in the path, the
next light on the runway before takeoff.

God has made us what we are. In Christ Jesus,
God made us to do good works,
which God planned in advance for us to live our lives doing.

Ephesians 2:10 NCV

Are you an ideas person? No matter where you go, being a person who's able to generate thoughtful, purposeful ideas will always be needed. But did you know that your ideas don't just materialize out of nowhere? They don't just magically pop into your brain.

God has been at work in us since he created us, and he knows the things he wants us to accomplish in our lives for his glory. We may not know exactly what those things are (as much as we wish we did.) but we can rest assured in the fact that they are there. We don't often know when and how God will reveal them to us, but it's important to be dressed and ready for whatever comes. Those simple ideas you have had might turn into unique opportunities for fellowship and discipleship. Share your ideas, hop on a team, volunteer your time. God is at work—don't miss his leading to fulfill your unique and important purpose.

Spirit, nudge me in the direction you have for me today and give me the ability to trust where it is you're leading me.

Brainstorm five ministry ideas, then share them with a leader in your church.

The Quiet Life

Do all you can to live a peaceful life. Take care of your own business, and do your own work as we have already told you. If you do, then people who are not believers will respect you, and you will not have to depend on others for what you need.

1 THESSALONIANS 4:11-12 NCV

Nobody talks about the quiet life. It doesn't look glamourous on Snapchat, or inspiring on Instagram, and it doesn't get as many likes and comments from your family and friends on Facebook. Living a quiet life means you're not constantly putting yourself out there. You are content using your gifts and your talents in the capacity that's in front of you, without bringing fame and recognition to yourself.

Minding your own business means staying out of petty arguments, not making snarky comments, and saying exactly what you mean so there's no room for misunderstanding. Earning your own living means work. Work hard. Support yourself. Don't expect to get rich quick or wish for the rich and famous lifestyle. Think about how living this way could change the way you live and portray your life today.

Jesus, show me the allure of a quiet life, a life that creates space and margin for you to speak and be at work.

Aspire to live quietly, and to mind your own affairs, and to work with your hands, as we instructed you, so that you may walk properly before outsiders and be dependent on no one.

1 THESSALONIANS 4:11–12 ESV

Paul's advice here wasn't to advocate the boring life. He had missional living in mind—doing life in a way that brought glory and happiness to God and peace to those who followed him. Living quietly, minding their own affairs, and working with their hands was a way to witness without words to those living around Thessalonica.

Sometimes we forget that the simple way we conduct ourselves can have an impact for the kingdom of God. This way of life demands respect, because as easy as it may sound on paper, living and going about the day in this manner takes an incredible amount of willpower and strength. Are there places in your life today that need quieting down?

Spirit, as counter-cultural as it may be, show me how to live quietly, and calm the places in me that want to seek my own fame and popularity.

Journal about three ways that you could practice quiet living.

Raw Reality

You, Sovereign LORD, help me for your name's sake;
out of the goodness of your love, deliver me.

PSALMS 109:21 NIV

David was dealing with some pretty heavy stuff when he wrote Psalm 109. Imagine seeing him in a courtroom, approaching the bench as though he was talking with the judge, asking him to be fair, to deal well, to have mercy. David wasn't just allowing himself to be bowled over by his circumstances. He was standing up straight, asking God to fulfill his promise and preserve his name.

Are you in a place today that's threatening to knock you over? Have you expectantly asked God to deliver you, to pull you out of your worry and fear and calm the anxiety racing through your heart? If not, take this morning to be frank with God about your feelings and ask for his help in resolving whatever situation is bothering you today. Notice how freeing it feels to give God, as David did, the raw reality of your petitions.

Heavenly Father, you are so capable of holding everything I bring to you. Hear my boldness, take my fear, handle me with care.

You, O God the LORD,
Deal with me for Your name's sake;
Because Your mercy is good, deliver me.

PSALMS 109:21 NKJV

Have you ever held God to his promises to you? Sometimes it feels like we keep God at a holy distance; he is God after all, and even though he declares his love for us, well, there's just a lot of roughness going on in the world. David's boldness here and throughout the Psalms is an important reminder that God can take it when we have questions about a situation or doubts about his intent for good in our lives. "Deal with me for your name's sake," he cries. "Because your mercy is good, deliver me."

Friend, do not for a moment think God only wants to hear your praise. He loves you. He knows you. He wants to prove himself to you for his name's sake because it gives you the all the more reason to glorify him when his mercy comes through as he promises it will.

Father God, hear me when I cry to you tonight. Deal with me out of the goodness of your mercy, that I can praise you all the more.

Do a topical study on the idea of boldness before God's throne.

Outfit of the Day

As God's chosen people, holy and dearly loved, clothe yourselves with compassion, kindness, humility, gentleness and patience.

COLOSSIANS 3:12 NIV

Do you have a favorite outfit? Maybe it's a giant hoodie that wraps you up and immediately makes you feel comfortable. Maybe it's your favorite pair of jeans, the ones that slide on perfectly and can take you anywhere. Maybe it's a certain shirt that flatters your build and gives you confidence.

As you're thinking about your day and choosing an outfit that matches those activities, what if you prayed to also be covered in compassion, kindness, humility, gentleness, and patience? Maybe you could throw a few sticky notes in your closet or on your bathroom mirror with this verse written on it. That way with each wardrobe change you make, you can be reminded that it's not just about creating the perfect outfit of the day, but empowering the person underneath with the ability to live out the qualities in Colossians 3:12.

Jesus, as I'm getting dressed this morning, let me be concerned not only with what's going on the outside of my body, but the inside as well. Let compassion, kindness, humility, gentleness, and patience be what people notice most about me in my interactions with them.

God has chosen you and made you his holy people. He loves you.
So you should always clothe yourselves with mercy, kindness,
humility, gentleness, and patience.

COLOSSIANS 3:12 NCV

Studying the Bible in a variety of different translations can
be incredibly helpful as we can see multiple options for
understanding what the original Hebrew and Greek words
are communicating, since those words themselves often
had layers of meaning. So when gentleness becomes quiet
strength, we gain a broader understanding of what the word
gentleness actually means; in this case, it takes on a certain
force because it denotes power and restraint.

In the same way, when patience becomes discipline, we start
to understand that there's an endurance aspect to the way
we're expected to live. The original Greek word is hupomone:
a remaining behind, a patient enduring. Think about this
tonight and see if adding a new layer of understanding to
these familiar words might change the way you put them on
and live them out today.

*Father God, thank you for the doors that knowledge can open, and
for my widened understanding of your Word.*

Write Colossians 3:12 on something and stick it somewhere
you'll see it when you're getting dressed.

Becoming

Do everything without grumbling or arguing, so that you may become blameless and pure, "children of God without fault in a warped and crooked generation." Then you will shine among them like stars in the sky as you hold firmly to the word of life. And then I will be able to boast on the day of Christ that I did not run or labor in vain.

PHILIPPIANS 2:14-16 NIV

It's no joke, this Christian life. Sometimes it feels like the Bible asks a lot of us, doesn't it? But remember everything we've read about Christ empowering us to live out his calling. Don't look at verses like this as just another rule to follow, or another place to fail in over and over. Instead, see it as an opportunity to become.

Becoming anything is a life-long process. We don't decide to do something and automatically do it. If we want to be skilled at something, it takes practice. It takes failing over and over and resolving to do better next time. Today, resolve to take another stab at going about your day without grumbling or arguing. If you mess up, take a deep breath and try again. Remember, becoming is a process.

Heavenly Father, help me to push past my nature. Thank you for grace in my moments of becoming.

Do everything without complaining or arguing. Then you will be innocent and without any wrong. You will be God's children without fault. But you are living with crooked and mean people all around you, among whom you shine like stars in the dark world. You offer the teaching that gives life. So when Christ comes again, I can be happy because my work was not wasted. I ran the race and won.

PHILIPPIANS 2:14–16 NCV

Have you ever spent time star-gazing? It doesn't have to be this ultra-romantic or picture-perfect event. Sometimes it's just lying on the trampoline when the sky has gone black and the world above becomes a network of light. Sometimes it's pausing for a few seconds after you get home late from work to look up and be reminded of the hugeness of the universe.

When Paul asks us to shine like stars, remember this: people are drawn to stars. They always have been. Stars hold a sense of wonder and amazement. Be a star. Understand the power and light you hold when you hold Jesus. Take responsibility for the way you draw people in and use it to share the message of life that has changed yours.

Lord Jesus, creator of the stars, make me shine as strong and bright as they do against the darkness.

Go star-gazing this week and praise God for his imagery in the Bible.

Good Days

I trust in your unfailing love.
I will rejoice because you have rescued me.
I will sing to the Lord
because he is good to me.

PSALM 13:5-6 NLT

What makes a good day? Is it everything going our way? Is it achieving our goals? Is it a bit of good luck or good news? Very often we let what happens each day dictate how we feel. We trust that good days include good things and we often see bad days as punishment.

Every day is a day that can include singing and rejoicing. Whether everything goes your way today, or it feels like everything is going wrong, the truth is you are still a rescued soul and God is still good to you. Not because of what you've done or how your day is going, but because you are truly loved by him.

God, please help me to sing and rejoice no matter what happens today. If things go great I will praise you, and if things are very hard I will praise you. Help me trust you today because you never fail me.

I have trusted in your steadfast love;
my heart shall rejoice in your salvation.
I will sing to the LORD,
because he has dealt bountifully with me.

PSALM 13:5-6 ESV

It isn't that God always gives us what we want. In fact, a lot of the time that would probably be a horrible idea because we don't see the whole picture. God doesn't give us what we want, he gives us what he wants.

The great news is he always gives us more than we deserve. He deals "bountifully" with us, providing more than we have any right to ask. Our response to that generosity is to praise him.

Father, thank you for being so generous to me. I am so glad you delight in giving your children more than we deserve. Help me see the many ways each day that you provide rescue and love for me.

What in your life is a gift from God that you are grateful for?

Nothing to Fear

The LORD is my light and my salvation—
whom shall I fear?
The LORD is the stronghold of my life—
of whom shall I be afraid?

PSALM 27:1 NIV

Fear comes in many shapes and sizes. There are big things that cause fear, like important relationships or work we need to do. There are little things that cause fear, like not being sure what to wear in the morning or running late.

The truth is both beautiful and confusing: we have nothing to fear. God has us. Fears, both big and small, cannot overpower his grip on us. We cannot be snatched from God's loving hand, so ultimately there is nothing we need to fear.

God, being unafraid is easy to say and hard to do. Please help me
today to see the ways you keep me safe. Help me to understand you
are with me and I don't need to be afraid, no matter what.

The LORD is my light and the one who saves me.
So why should I fear anyone?
The LORD protects my life.
So why should I be afraid?

PSALM 27:1 NCV

It is much easier to say we shouldn't be afraid than it is to stop fearing. It comes in waves, feeling confident in God one moment and then worrying about what might happen the next. We wish it was easier to just believe God was taking care of us.

God doesn't need to convince us, because he is the same no matter what we think or do. He is patient with us, because if we truly take time to look at our lives, it becomes evident that he has been with us. Even in hard times when we felt alone, even when life is unfair, a close examination of our lives will show evidence of God at work. We can rest in the truth that God is with us no matter what.

Thank you, God, for working on my behalf even when I don't see it. Thank you for fighting against the things in life that want to pull me away, and for holding tightly to me even when I am afraid and full of panic or worry. Please give me peace as I rest tonight and help me to focus on you.

What things feel big in your life but are small compared to God?

Small Steps

When people's steps follow the LORD,
God is pleased with their ways.

PSALM 37:23 NCV

God knows the best path for you, but he doesn't force you down it. He offers direction through his Spirit and through Scripture. When we turn to those things for direction, we can be confident in the direction we are going. It is not about where we are, it's about where God is.

God doesn't want us to flounder about, unsure what to do. He also doesn't want us acting without thinking. The space in between those two approaches is the beautiful tension we live in each day. God encourages us to think through what we know about him and let it guide us. It is a constant exercise of both trust and critical thinking. Where is God leading you today?

Heavenly Father, thank you for leading me even when I'm not following. Thank you for guiding me, even when I don't notice that's what you are doing. I pray that you will help me to see your leading today and take steps toward you.

The LORD directs the steps of the godly.
He delights in every detail of their lives.

PSALM 37:23 NLT

God loves the little things in our lives. We can have the tendency to turn to God only when big things happen, or only when we've exhausted all the "non-God" options we can think of. But God loves being a part of the little day-to-day things, like a good friend who just enjoys spending time together.

We often have a tendency to not invite God into the simpler and smaller things in our lives. He wants to be present in our mundane tasks as much as he is present in our biggest challenges. Allowing God to be a part of everything, big or small, is one of the best ways to let him guide us through each day of our lives.

Thank you for loving the small stuff in my life, Lord. Please help me, nudge me, even when what I'm doing doesn't seem important, to realize that you are in it and with me. I pray I will be able to invite you into anything I'm doing, no matter how small.

What is a little thing in your life where you can pay closer attention to God's leading?

Broken Spirit

The sacrifice you desire is a broken spirit.
You will not reject a broken and repentant heart, O God.

PSALM 51:17 NLT

When we get on the wrong path we often feel like we need to work our way "back" to God. This kind of thinking comes from the belief that we must make up for our mistakes or God won't be with us. We can be fooled into thinking God wants us to give him things to prove our devotion.

Ultimately, though, God simply wants us to recognize we need him. We are unable to earn our way "back" to God, partly because he is still with us. No matter how far we've wandered from his plan for us, he is still with us. He doesn't need us to get back to him, he needs us to rest in him.

God, please protect me from thinking I need to prove myself to you.
I am grateful that you don't ask anything more than for me to
surrender. Help me to see how much I need you.

The sacrifices of God are a broken spirit;
A broken and a contrite heart, O God, You will not despise.

PSALM 51:17 NASB

When we become aware of a way we've messed up or strayed from God's plan, the response is often panic. We want to fix it, make it right, and, if possible, cover our tracks leading in the wrong direction. Sometimes we only half come back to God, saying, "God, I can fix this. Just point me in the right direction."

The gift of Jesus is that he does not send us away from himself. When we've messed up, he does not send us on a difficult journey alone saying, "To find me you must go there." Instead, he opens his arms and says, "You must come here." When we are broken we are also accepted.

God, please help me to see any way I have strayed from the plan you have for me. Thank you for welcoming me back into your safe presence, and for loving me instead of despising me, even when I fail

Where might you be heading that is away from where God wants you to be?

Every Day

Each morning let me learn more about your love
because I trust you.
I come to you in prayer,
asking for your guidance.

PSALM 143:8 NLT

We rarely know exactly where God is leading us. It is uncommon for God to lay out specific day-by-day plans for us to follow. Instead God provides general guidelines for how to live life and then invites us to come to him daily for specific guidance.

We have two choices in how to respond. We can be frustrated that God won't give us the big picture (foolishly thinking we could understand it), or we can be grateful that every day is a new opportunity to learn more about God than we knew yesterday. God invites us to learn more about him every day.

Thank you, Lord, for giving me an opportunity every day to understand you a little bit more and to invite you to be a part of what is happening in my life right now.

Let the morning bring me word of your unfailing love,
for I have put my trust in you.
Show me the way I should go,
for to you I entrust my life.

PSALM 143:8 NIV

Many times we make the mistake of trying to anticipate where God is leading us so we can get there more quickly. We try to jump ahead to where we think he wants us tomorrow instead of paying attention to what he might want to teach us today.

Choosing to let God lead means having the patience to be concerned about today more than tomorrow. The only moment we are guaranteed with God is right now, we are not guaranteed tomorrow, yet we often miss what God is doing in us now because we are focused on later. Letting God lead us day-by-day, every day, is a key to experiencing his plans for you.

Heavenly Father, please help me to remain focused on today. When I begin to worry or concern myself about what is to come, please bring me back to what you are doing in my life right now so I can more fully experience your plans for me.

Where do you find yourself focusing on the future instead of the present?

Perspective

*A person may think their own ways are right,
but the LORD weighs the heart.*

PROVERBS 21:2 NIV

One of the main reasons we need God to lead us is because
we can't see the whole picture. It can become tempting
to go through the motions, believing we are making great
progress, but God sees in our heart that we've become lazy or
uncommitted.

The beautiful thing is that God knows what is in our heart,
even more than we do, and he wants to lead us to an even
better "heart place." We don't need to be scared of God
scolding us; instead we can embrace that he can see better
than anyone the best way for us to go forward.

*Lord, I am sorry for the times I think I know best and forget to ask
you about my life. Please remind me that you are working to make
my life better, and I should let you guide me by being honest with
you.*

You may believe you are doing right,
but the LORD judges your reasons.

PROVERBS 21:2 NCV

We might think it would be easier if everything was black and white and every decision was easy to make because there were specific rules about it. But that kind of system would take out some of the adventure of life. God created us, and the world, to be adaptable.

There are times where we do everything right and things still go wrong. Instead of feeling like we've been cheated, we must be open to the idea that God had a different plan in this situation. This is why checking in with him every day is important, because he can see the things we can't about our current lives. Asking God for guidance will help us escape our limited perspective.

God, you see much more than I do. Please help me to make the choices that will be the best for what you are doing. I know I can't see it all, but I am grateful that you choose to use me as a part of your bigger picture.

What do you need to ask God for guidance about?

Never Tired

Have you not known? Have you not heard?
The LORD is the everlasting God,
the Creator of the ends of the earth.
He does not faint or grow weary;
his understanding is unsearchable.

ISAIAH 40:28 ESV

It is easy to feel like God would grow tired of us. Any time we get things wrong, or realize we've missed the point, or end up feeling stuck and needing God's help again, we can feel like he is exhausted with us. But God never tires. His effort is always toward what he wants for us, and he doesn't get exhausted guiding us.

Sometimes we give up because we assume God wants to give up on us too. Nothing could be further from the truth. Whenever we stumble God is there to lend a steadying hand and encourage us to keep going. God doesn't get tired of us or with us. He is a never ending source of strength and encouragement to keep going.

Heavenly Father, thank you for your endless energy. Thank you that you don't give up on me when I am tired, but instead you grab hold of me and keep me going. Please help me to turn to you for my encouragement.

> *Have you never heard?*
> *Have you never understood?*
> *The LORD is the everlasting God,*
> *the Creator of all the earth.*
> *He never grows weak or weary.*
> *No one can measure the depths of his understanding.*
>
> ISAIAH 40:28 NLT

God will keep working in us no matter what. We can make that work harder through disobedience or laziness. We can make that work more confusing by making our own plans or neglecting to pray. We can make the work slower by being stubborn or fearful.

But God will never get tired of trying to work out his plan in our life. No matter the obstacle, hesitation, or challenge, God understands the goodness he has planned for us more deeply than we ever could, and he works toward it tirelessly. That is what his endless love looks like.

Thank you for working so hard for me, Lord. Thank you for working through the things that slow me down. And thank you for loving me so much that you never give up, even when I might want to. I love you.

Is there a way you could help "unblock" God's plan for you?

Proven Strength

> "Do not fear, for I am with you;
> Do not anxiously look about you, for I am your God.
> I will strengthen you, surely I will help you,
> Surely I will uphold you with My righteous right hand."

ISAIAH 41:10 NASB

You are not alone. As often as we might hear it, it is still hard to believe. Often, when it comes to God, if we feel alone it is because we assume we went the wrong direction. We equate that loneliness with missing God's plan for our life. Surely if we are where God wants us, we would feel amazing.

The Bible is full of people whom God was with, but they were going through difficult times. The disciples were regularly jailed or chased out of town precisely because they were doing what God wanted. Following God's plan does not mean life will be easy. Instead, it means that when things are difficult we can trust God is with us and we do not need to worry. He will be the strength we need to get through.

Lord, thank you for being the strength I don't have. Thank you for promising to be with me. And thank you that your plan leads me to difficult places, but I do not need to be afraid. You will never send me somewhere you are not also preparing me to go.

"Do not fear, for I am with you;
do not be dismayed, for I am your God.
I will strengthen you and help you;
I will uphold you with my righteous right hand."

ISAIAH 41:10 NIV

It is a great relief to realize we are not responsible to "pull ourselves up by our bootstraps" and get ourselves through tough times. That feeling of being alone in our struggles or responsible for our recovery goes against what God says about how we interact with him.

God does not say we can come to him once we prove that we are strong. That message would be cause for anxiety and worry. Instead, he says he will be our strength he will help us. Our responsibility is not to hold ourselves together but to come to the one who promises to hold us up.

God, thank you for being my strength. I am sorry for the times
I think I need to do it on my own and push you out of what is
happening in my life. Please help me to recognize and enjoy the
many ways you can take away my worry by trusting your plan.

What is an area in life where you are trying to fix things on your own?

Water and Fire

"When you go through deep waters,
I will be with you.
When you go through rivers of difficulty,
you will not drown.
When you walk through the fire of oppression,
you will not be burned up;
the flames will not consume you."

ISAIAH 43:2 NLT

The promise is not that we will avoid difficult times. That is not how God's plan works. God often calls us into very difficult times. Jesus' life is the perfect example of this. He went through horrible times, but he was always exactly where God wanted him to be.

The promise is that God will be with us through the hard times and prevent them from overcoming us. We will get wet, but will not drown. It may get hot, but we will not be reduced to ashes. God promises to protect us in hard times, not from hard times.

Lord, I know there may be places you ask me to go that are scary or hard. Please give me the strength to trust you as I head toward them and believe you while I am in them. Please protect me as I walk

When you pass through the waters, I will be with you;
and through the rivers, they shall not overwhelm you;
when you walk through fire you shall not be burned,
and the flame shall not consume you.

ISAIAH 43:2 NRSV

What keeps us from following God's plan? Sometimes it
is confusing, and we aren't sure where he is leading us.
Sometimes it is fear, and we aren't sure we want to go where
he says. God can already see the other side of anything he
asks us to go through, so he already knows it is worth it.

Are we willing to trust God to get us there safely? Are we
confident that God will guard us and get us to where he wants
us? Facing a difficult time or task doesn't always mean we've
gone the wrong way. Sometimes God calls us through the
hardest path because it brings us to the best destination.

God, please help me to grow the faith I need to follow you no
matter where you lead.

What difficult thing are you facing? Can you see that God
might have planned it for you to grow in your relationship
with him?

Soft Stone

I will give you a new heart, and I will put a new spirit in you.
I will take out your stony, stubborn heart
and give you a tender, responsive heart.

EZEKIEL 36:26 NLT

The best we can do on our own is soft stone. Even when we want our heart to be more open to God, if we try to do it by ourselves we will always have a heart of stone. What we need is thankfully also what God promises for us: that he will remove our stony, hard heart and replace it with a soft and responsive one.

Rather than struggle to get our hearts right so we can go to God, we are asked to come to him with whatever condition our heart is in and let him repair and replace it. God's plan isn't to wait until we figure things out—it is to get involved and transform the things we can't transform on our own.

God, I am certain that I try to fix my own heart instead of letting you work on me. I want to do it on my own, but I can't. Please replace my hard heart with your responsive heart and help me to see the areas in my life that I need to release to you.

I will give you a new heart and put a new spirit within you;
and I will remove the heart of stone from your flesh
and give you a heart of flesh.

EZEKIEL 36:26 NASB

God brings newness into our lives. He enjoys making
something better out of anything we give him. When we
embrace this, he is able to really get to work. He can put a
whole new spirit, with a new perspective and new desires,
into our heart.

We often get the order wrong. We try to change ourselves so
we can be close to God. Meanwhile God is always inviting us
closer to himself so he can change us. God's plan is for us to
walk side-by-side with him through life, and he transforms
us as we do.

Thank you for changing me whenever I am close to you. Thank you
that your presence is enough to make a difference in my life. Please
help me focus on simply being connected to you.

How can you spend time connecting with God in a new way
this week?

Close the Door

*"When you pray, go into your room and shut the door
and pray to your Father who is in secret.
And your Father who sees in secret will reward you."*

MATTHEW 6:6 ESV

You've probably seen it on Instagram. An open Bible, a coffee mug, probably a little sunlight pouring in through a window. The temptation to broadcast our Bible time can be strong, and we like the feeling of letting others know we are connecting with God.

Jesus encourages the opposite. He says to shut the door behind you and pray in secret. Rather than spending time making sure our spiritual life "looks just right," he says to close the door to everything else and "just be right" with God. The reward for getting rid of distractions to spend time with God is much greater than any amount of likes or comments.

Heavenly Father, help me to get rid of distractions when I am spending time with you. I want to find time where we are uninterrupted. Please remind me to focus on you when I start to take time away from you by being distracted.

*"When you pray, you should go into your room and close the door
and pray to your Father who cannot be seen. Your Father can see
what is done in secret, and he will reward you."*

MATTHEW 6:6 NCV

Jesus invites us to "close the door" to everything else but God
when we are connecting with him. This means being alone,
but it also means shutting out the distractions we carry with
us. It is easy to be distracted by to-do lists or daily schedules
when we are trying to connect with God. Learning to "close
the door" on these things is important.

It takes practice to stay focused during prayer time. There
is a battle for our attention, so we must practice being
intentionally focused on God. When we feel our attention has
drifted we must grab it and point it back in the direction we
are trying to go, toward Jesus.

*God, please help me to see the distractions that are taking away
from my attention to you. Help me to find a time and a place
where I can shut those things out to better connect with you.*

Where can you go to close the door on distractions?

Withdrawn

Jesus often slipped away to be alone so he could pray.

LUKE 5:16 NCV

There is something special about calmly spending time in creation. We are told that Jesus often withdrew to the wilderness to spend time in prayer. Sometimes he left at sunrise, other times in the middle of the day, still other times in the dark of night. It seems getting away from manmade things and to a quiet place of nature was a priority.

It makes sense. When God created us he placed us in nature, not a city. The world was created for us to enjoy. There is something deep down in us that comes alive when we are in creation. We don't need to hike to a mountain top; it could be as simple as a park bench. Anywhere where we can enjoy the world God made and pray to him there. Take a moment today to pray outside.

God, please help me to find some time today to enjoy your creation. Even if it is just for a brief moment, help me.

He would withdraw to deserted places and pray.

LUKE 5:16 NRSV

Do you have someone that you love to spend time with, just the two of you? Many of our friendships work as a group, but you know you've become close with someone when you enjoy one-on-one time together. This is one of the main reasons Jesus would go somewhere alone to pray.

It's not that he didn't want to pray when people were around, but that became a distraction. A lot of our spiritual life is a battle for attention and focus, and it's only become harder in recent years. The fact that you are taking time to do this devotional is a big deal, and you should feel encouraged by it. You are practicing a bit of what Jesus practiced whenever you make time to be alone with just him.

God, thank you for always being willing to meet me wherever I am. I confess that I don't always take the time to get away with you, and I pray that you will help me create quiet places where I can be alone for prayer.

Where is your favorite place to connect with God?

Same God

*God works in different ways,
but it is the same God who does the work in all of us.*

1 CORINTHIANS 12:6 NLT

Sometimes we look at other people's spiritual lives and think they must be doing it so much better. We wish we could have that kind of faith, or devotion, or boldness. We wonder why God doesn't work like that in us.

God works differently in each person. Our decisions and dedication matter, but even if we are equally as devoted, God will probably work differently in us. We are called to follow Jesus, not other Christians. God's plan for you is different than God's plan for anyone else. It is not a problem to follow Jesus differently than others. It is a problem to compare ourselves to others. We should be focused on Jesus and what he wants for us, and nothing else. If we do that we will live out the plan he has for us.

Jesus, please give me blinders so I don't compare my spiritual life to others. Help me to focus just on how you are inviting me to live. Thank you for designing a plan just for me that fits who you made me to be.

There are varieties of activities,
but it is the same God who empowers them all in everyone.

1 CORINTHIANS 12:6 ESV

Whenever someone is showing the gifts that God has given them, it's a chance to celebrate. It can be tempting to compare or wish we had the gifts someone else does. But comparing doesn't bring out the best, and if we all had the same gifts, it would be very dull.

Think of a painter who only used one shade of gray to paint. She could create some cool things, but nothing as spectacular as she could with a bunch of colors. The differences God has created in us is how he injects color into his masterpiece. It is the same artist (God) creating, but now there are many colors to choose from, and it makes something more beautiful. God needs you to be the exact shade and hue he's made you to be, because he has a plan for where to use you.

Father, thank you for your creativity and how you want to use me to create something beautiful. Help me to embrace how you've created me and see how I fit into the beautiful work you are creating.

What gifts or abilities has God given you?

Together

You are the body of Christ
and individually members of it.

1 CORINTHIANS 12:27 NRSV

Everyone has a part to play and we all need each other. This is one of the most encouraging things Jesus came to teach us. We are each invited to play our part in God's plan. The plan is for all of us to work together.

That is a relief. It can be easy to feel like we are on our own or have to do everything by ourselves. Jesus does ask a lot of us, and it isn't easy, but we also aren't alone. God's plans are designed in a way that work best when we work together. We need each other, which means we need you specifically. You have a part to play in the big things God is doing.

Please help me, Lord, to understand the part I am supposed to play. Please guide me so I can best fit with other followers of Jesus to best accomplish your plans.

You are the body of Christ,
and each one of you is a part of it.

1 CORINTHIANS 12:27 NIV

It is good to be reminded we are part of something bigger.
There is a comfort in realizing we don't need to figure
everything out. We simply need to focus on our part. We were
not designed to be the whole—we were designed to be a part
of something.

When we focus on everything there is to do or change, it
is overwhelming. God does not require us to fix or solve
everything before we can connect with him. Instead he
connects with us immediately and puts us to work doing our
part of his plan. When each of us focuses on the part God has
given us, then the whole body works together the way it should.

Thank you for letting me be a part of what you are doing. Help me
learn the best way to accomplish your plans for me so I can be a
part of accomplishing your plan overall. Thank you for inviting me
to be a part of what you are doing.

What is one area that God is inviting you to work on right now?

Start and Finish

Are you so foolish? Having started with the Spirit,
are you now ending with the flesh?

GALATIANS 3:3 NRSV

Who we are is a combination of what we've decided before and we're deciding for our future. There is not one moment in time that defines everything about us; instead, it is an ever-growing list of choices and decisions. It is possible to go a good direction for a while and then drift in a bad one. This is true for all of life.

In the same way that we shouldn't let bad decisions in the past keep us from making good decisions in the future, we can't let good decisions from the past blind us to potential bad decisions in the future. We can start well and finish poorly. This is why following God is a day-by-day journey, not a once in a lifetime experience.

Heavenly Father, please protect me from the decisions that would pull me away from you. Help me to catch places in my life where small choices could have big consequences. Please light up every corner of my heart and mind and help me continue to choose you.

*How foolish can you be? After starting your new lives in the Spirit,
why are you now trying to become perfect
by your own human effort?*

GALATIANS 3:3 NLT

A Christian's faith begins when they realize that Jesus has done the work to save us and there is nothing they can do to earn it on their own. Sadly, after that moment we sometimes start to try to earn God's favor again by being good or sacrificing. Any time we believe we are earning points with God we should be afraid, because we are probably doing the opposite.

God wants a relationship with us, not a report card. He is less concerned about getting every little thing right and more interested in whether or not we understand his heart. It is sad when we trade a loving connection with God for a set of "dos and don'ts" instead. If we work to know God, our choices will naturally turn toward the plan he has for us.

God, I am sorry for the times I start trying to control my faith or get you to like me more by obeying you. I know you aren't just trying to make sure I perform well, you want us to be connected and working together. Please help me give up trying to impress you and try to involve you in every area of my life instead.

What is a way you are trying to impress God even though you don't need to?

Dead Old Self

*Those who belong to Christ Jesus have nailed the passions and
desires of their sinful nature to his cross and crucified them there.*

GALATIANS 5:24 NLT

We aren't invited to just the outcome of Jesus' crucifixion,
but the process as well. Thankfully Jesus endured a physical
death so we don't need to. But we are still asked to go through
a spiritual death where we take our old passions and desires
and nail them to the cross.

It might seem like a gruesome image: taking apart our old
nature and executing it is meant to be a strong example.
Those things cause a lot of death and hurt in our lives; they
must be taken out. It is a practice that happens throughout
the life of a Christ follower. We must regularly kill things that
are growing in our life which get in the way of God's plan.
Thankfully, Jesus has given us a way to do that by making it
possible for the Holy Spirit to work in us.

*God, please give me the eyes to see the passions and desires I have
that aren't of you. Please give me the strength to nail them to the
cross by choosing to not let them have a place in my life. Give me
the joy of a life free of my old self.*

They that are Christ's have crucified the flesh
with the affections and lusts.

GALATIANS 5:24 KJV

Jesus invites us to kill or our old desires. Not because he
is testing us, but because he knows what is best for us. He
knows more than we do how dangerous those things can be.
They slowly pull us further and further away from his plan.

A sign of a true Christian is that they regularly give up things
they desire because they desire Jesus more. It is easy to
sacrifice things we don't want anyway. The real work comes
from choosing to give up things we want because we've chosen
something else we want more: a healthy relationship with
God. The great news is that God helps us in this process by
highlighting threats and giving us strength to overcome them.

Thank you for fighting for me and for what is best. I know there are
things I want that don't fit your plan for me. Thank you for giving
me the strength to resist them and choose you instead.

What in your life do you need to "nail to the cross" and give up?

Spiritually United

Make every effort to keep yourselves united in the Spirit,
binding yourselves together with peace.
For there is one body and one Spirit,
just as you have been called to one glorious hope for the future.

EPHESIANS 4:3-4 NLT

God's plan isn't just for us, it is for everyone. God never makes a plan for us that doesn't involve what he's doing with others. This is why spiritual community is so important. Community can be difficult and messy, but it is still better than trying to go it alone.

We get into danger whenever we start to think we must accomplish God's plan by ourselves. We can cut out God by seeing him as a director and not a partner. We also risk cutting out others by seeing them as competitors instead of cohorts. When God invites us to connect with him he also invites us to connect with others.

Lord, please help me to be a part of your great spiritual community. Help me know how to best support others, because that is a big part of your plan for me.

Making every effort to maintain the unity of the Spirit in the bond of peace. There is one body and one Spirit, just as you were called to the one hope of your calling.

<small>EPHESIANS 4:3-4 NRSV</small>

When we focus on just ourselves, we only have one person supporting us. Instead, when we work to support other Christians around us, and they do the same, we end up with many supporters. God's design is for us to focus on others more than ourselves. When we do that, everybody comes out better.

It's also often easier to see what God is up to in someone else's life than our own. When we invite others to be a part of our spiritual life, and when we do the same for them, it helps us gain important perspectives—perspectives we wouldn't have if we were just focused on ourselves. We are designed to be connected with other Christ followers.

God, please give me wisdom so I can see what you are trying to do in the lives of the people around me. Help me encourage them toward your plan for their life. And please bless me with people who can do the same in my life. Thank you.

Who do you have in your life that can encourage you in your relationship with God?

Not as Dark

In the past you were full of darkness, but now you are full of light in the Lord. So live like children who belong to the light Light brings every kind of goodness, right living, and truth.

EPHESIANS 5:8-9 NCV

Choosing to follow Jesus is like switching on the lights to our lives. Suddenly we can see things that were hidden and we are able to navigate life more clearly because it is easier to see opportunities and obstacles. It is a literal night and day difference.

If you sit in a dark room for a long time and then someone flips on the lights, it takes a while for your eyes to adjust. Similarly, we don't always adjust well to our new life of light through Jesus. We need to retrain our brain to function in a world where we can see things more clearly. We must remember that we have the light of Christ in us, so when dark or difficult situations come up, we don't need to stumble through them anymore. We can see more clearly because of Christ.

God, help me to remember that I have a better ability to see now because you are in my life. Thank you for giving me new vision and perspective.

Once you were darkness, but now in the Lord you are light.
Live as children of light—for the fruit of the light
is found in all that is good and right and true.

EPHESIANS 5:8-9 NRSV

Following Jesus makes us different than we were. Sometimes it is easy for us to tell that difference; other times it might be harder to see (especially if you grew up in the church). While God usually encourages us to look forward and not back, it is sometimes good to remember the darkness we came from.

Remembering the darkness we've experienced is important for perspective. Sometimes by looking back we can see how God's plan for us has taken us to much better places. Other times, looking back can encourage us that even if we are facing difficult times, they are still not as dark as they were before Jesus. Remembering that we were once in darkness helps us celebrate and embrace the life of light Jesus invites us to live.

Thank you for rescuing me from darkness. Thank you for guiding me somewhere better than I would have gone on my own. Thank you for opening my life to a beautiful light instead of darkness.

What is a darkness in your life that God has removed?

Practice

Keep putting into practice all you learned and received from me—
everything you heard from me and saw me doing.
Then the God of peace will be with you.

PHILIPPIANS 4:9 NLT

God brings peace into our life. Peace is a sense of being okay because we know God is with us. Peace in stressful situations, painful experiences, or confusing times are all possible because God is at work in our lives. He never wastes anything, good or bad.

But we can waste it, especially when we don't put our faith into practice. The path to peace is practice. It is one thing to say we believe; it is another to actually practice what we believe. When a hard time comes, do we trust God? When a temptation arises, do we ask God for help? When an opportunity shows up, do we trust God? The only way to experience God's peace is by practicing the things he asks us to do; that's why he asks us to do them.

God, help me to remember that I have a better ability to see now because you are in my life. Thank you for giving me new vision and perspective.

Do what you learned and received from me,
what I told you, and what you saw me do.
And the God who gives peace will be with you.

PHILIPPIANS 4:9 NCV

When we think about God's plan for us we probably think about big or ambitious goals, things that would take a lifetime to accomplish. It is true that God plans big things for us, but achieving those big things almost always comes through small steps day by day. The big things God has for us are broken into little things God asks of us.

God's plan may be for you to run a giant organization that helps others, but it might start with small opportunities to be generous and kind. Holding the door open for someone else might be the first step in opening doors to something bigger. While God is aware of the future, he asks us to focus on just today. The daily practice of doing what we've learned from God is the key to living his plan for our life.

Lord, I know I sometimes get distracted trying to focus on the bigger plan you have for me instead of the daily journey you've prepared for me. Help me to focus on what you are doing in my life today, so I can best practice living how you ask me to live.

What is something you feel God is encouraging you to do this week?

Content

*I know how to live on almost nothing or with everything.
I have learned the secret of living in every situation,
whether it is with a full stomach or empty, with plenty or little.*

PHILIPPIANS 4:12 NLT

When we think of being content we usually think of
having everything we want. To most of us, content would
be a comfortable place or great group of friends or an
accomplishment of some kind. But contentment is not found
in having everything we want—it is found in not wanting
anything more than we have.

The secret of being content in every situation is to believe
God is enough. God has promised he is with us. If we believe
that, what more could we need? Whether we have a lot or a
little, all we really need is God. Because of Jesus, we can have
him, because he has us.

*God, thank you that you are enough. Thank you that I never need
more than you. Help me to believe that is enough and to be content
in any situation.*

I know how to live when I am poor, and I know how to live when I have plenty. I have learned the secret of being happy at any time in everything that happens, when I have enough to eat and when I go hungry, when I have more than I need and when I do not have enough.

PHILIPPIANS 4:12 NCV

We can tell where our faith or trust is by what affects our joy. If our joy goes up and down with our friendships, or our bank accounts, or our achievements, then those things are where we are putting our trust. If little money means little joy, or a great achievement means great joy, we are not putting our faith in God.

God offers himself fully to his children. He ushers us in and invites us to take part in everything that is his. When our faith is in God, our joy is complete because God does not increase or decrease. God is the same and he is always enough. If we truly understand what we have in him there is nothing else left for us to want. We are content.

You are generous with everything you have. You offer more than I need and you take joy in doing so. I am sorry for the times I look somewhere else because all I really want is found in you. Thank you.

What causes your joy to go up and down? Is that where you're putting your faith?

Forgiven Forgiving

Bear with each other, and forgive each other. If someone does wrong to you, forgive that person because the Lord forgave you.

COLOSSIANS 3:13 NCV

What makes our relationship with God so beautiful is his forgiveness. Even though God had every right to be upset with humans, he chose instead to offer forgiveness. That forgiveness came through Jesus and was a very painful thing for him to offer—but he still did.

God tells us to forgive others for the same reason he chose to forgive us: because it is the best way to live. Forgiveness is good for those we are forgiving, but it is also important for us. When you forgive someone you aren't just doing them a favor, you're doing the harder thing because it is the better thing. God set the example for what is best and he invites us to follow him.

Please help me to forgive those I need to, even when they don't deserve it and even when the hurt they caused me was deep, because it is the best thing for me and it is how you want me to live.

Bearing with one another and,
if one has a complaint against another, forgiving each other;
as the Lord has forgiven you, so you also must forgive.

COLOSSIANS 3:13 ESV

Some say that true friendship can't exist until forgiveness has been extended. Think about your closest relationships. Chances are good that at some point there was a difficult situation and one or both of you needed to offer forgiveness to the other. Relationships that have been through this are always stronger than relationships that have not. Their strength has been tested.

God tells us to bear with one another, which means to help carry the weight. Life is difficult and sin makes parts of life too heavy to carry on by ourselves. Jesus carries the weight through his death on the cross and God instructs us to carry each other's weight through forgiveness.

God, please help me to ask for forgiveness. I know there are things I have done that have hurt others. Instead of ignoring it, help me to face it and trust that you will make something good come from my willingness to ask for forgiveness.

Who do you need to forgive? Who do you need to ask forgiveness from?

God's Work

The Lord is faithful; he will strengthen you and guard you from the evil one. And we are confident in the Lord that you are doing and will continue to do the things we commanded you. May the Lord lead your hearts into a full understanding and expression of the love of God and the patient endurance that comes from Christ.

1 THESSALONIANS 3:3–5 NLT

We often want to do the work of God ourselves. We think it's up to us to resist the devil or muster up our own courage. We think we must prove ourselves by trying to make our lives better, so that God will choose us. God has already chosen us so that he can make our lives better.

Learning to give up trying to do things on our own is one of the most difficult parts of following Jesus. It is also one of the most important. As long as we try to do things on our own, we are fighting for control of our lives. Following Jesus means surrender and letting God guide us instead. He helps us understand, but we must let him lead us there.

Lord, thank you for your patience when I fight for control of my life. I am sometimes stubborn and need you to guide me. Thank you for guarding me and protecting me in ways I don't see.

You yourselves know that we must face these troubles. Even when we were with you, we told you we all would have to suffer, and you know it has happened. Because of this, when I could wait no longer, I sent Timothy to you so I could learn about your faith. I was afraid the devil had tempted you, and perhaps our hard work would have been wasted.

1 THESSALONIANS 3:3-5 NCV

Following God is often described in the Bible with long, difficult terms. It is a journey that takes patient endurance because it is not over quickly. God's plan for us takes up our entire lives, and then some. It isn't just a season for us. Choosing to follow Jesus is the starting line to a lifelong race.

God is with us on the race. He knows the best path to take and guides us, he encourages us and gives us coaching on how to best run, and he even protects us and carries us when we don't have the strength to go on. It is important to realize we are running a long and difficult race by following God's plan, but we are never alone in it.

Thank you, God, for being beside me in difficult times. Thank you for guiding me when I am tired and not sure where to go. And thank you for cheering me on because you genuinely love being a part of my life.

What is something you need to patiently endure right now?

Prayer Plan

*I urge that supplications, prayers, intercessions,
and thanksgivings be made for everyone.*

1 TIMOTHY 2:1 NRSV

We are encouraged to pray for others. When our prayers
become inward focused it is harder to pray for God's plan
because God's plan involves much more than just us. Praying
for others is one way that we can discover what God wants
in our lives because it makes us look at how we might be
involved in what he is doing in other people's lives.

When we ask God to provide for someone, or we thank God
for something in their life, we are viewing other lives through
the perspective of God's plan. That kind of thinking can help
us start to see our own lives through that perspective as well.
Isn't it amazing how God can transform us by focusing us on
others? Take time today to pray for others.

*Thank you for including me in your work for others. Thank you for
listening to my prayers for others, and for using them to transform
me as well. Please help me see the way you see things.*

I tell you to pray for all people,
asking God for what they need
and being thankful to him.

1 TIMOTHY 2:1 NCV

Everyone needs prayer, from our closest friends to our enemies or people we don't get along with. Prayer opens up our heart to see others how God sees them. Are you unsure what to do in a relationship? Do you not know how to help someone? Do you wish you could take away someone's pain? Prayer is not a magic wand that instantly makes things better, but it is the key to understanding what others are going through.

Prayer is the act of coming to God with what we are experiencing. Rather than keep it to ourselves or trying to fix it on our own, prayer says "I need you" to God in difficult or confusing situations. And God never ignores our prayer. He may not answer how we wish he had, but he will never ignore us. He always works to help us see what is best.

God, please help me to not only pray to you about others but listen to you as well. I want to see things through your perspective, even if it isn't what I think I want right now.

Who can you pray for today?

Better Things

We have this as a sure and steadfast anchor of the soul,
a hope that enters into the inner place behind the curtain.

HEBREWS 6:19 ESV

The most important role of an anchor is to hold a ship in place during rough weather. That is what makes it such a powerful metaphor for God's love for us. No matter what we are going through, the hope that God gives can keep us in place and make sure we don't drift away.

God's plan often takes us to some difficult places, but it never abandons us there. Sometimes all that can be done is to "ride out the storm" and trust that God is holding our soul in place. His promises are trustworthy, they are strong, and they will not break. If we are connected to God, our souls are anchored safely.

Thank you for being strong and keeping me from drifting. Please
help me to cling to you, especially during the hard times of life.
I pray I will always hold on to you.

This hope is a strong and trustworthy anchor for our souls.
It leads us through the curtain into God's inner sanctuary.

HEBREWS 6:19 NLT

Before Jesus, people connected with God differently than we do today. There was a temple and in that temple was a very special room where God would meet with a priest. This was the holiest place in all of the world and was separated by a very heavy and large curtain. For everyone but the priest, God was hidden by this curtain.

The role of Jesus was to get rid of that barrier between God and his people. In a way, he went into the special room and tied us to God. Today's verse is reminding us that we are now directly connected with God, no longer separated. There is a great hope that comes from knowing we are anchored to God.

Jesus, thank you for doing what I could not do. Thank you for anchoring me so I am not dragged away by rough seasons. Thank you for reconnecting me to God so I can have hope.

Have you anchored yourself to God or to something else?

Joyful Testing

*Is your life full of difficulties and temptations? Then be happy,
for when the way is rough, your patience has a chance to grow.*

JAMES 1:2-3 TLB

When things are hard we might ask, "What am I doing
wrong?" We believe if we were doing everything right, then
things would be easier. Where we get this idea is unclear,
because life is full of examples of people doing everything
right and still struggling.

Jesus is the best example of this. He lived a perfect life.
Everything he did was right. Still, he was betrayed, arrested,
and executed. If that was the result of a perfect life, why do
we expect things to go great when we get things right? Our
goal shouldn't be a life without difficulty, but to endure any
difficulty because we know God can use it to grow us.

*God, please help me to lean on you when things are hard. Help me
to not be discouraged when things aren't easy, but instead see the
chances for me to grow more like you.*

Count it all joy, my brothers, when you meet trials of various kind, for you know that the testing of your faith produces steadfastness.

JAMES 1:2-3 ESV

Nothing worth doing is easy. We are designed to get better through hardship. Have you ever seen a baby learning to crawl or walk? It takes a lot of falls and bumps to learn the mechanics of motion. Of course, the easy thing would be to just lay on their back all day. But something in them is hard-wired for the challenge because it makes them better. They smile and giggle as they realize they can walk.

It is the same in our spiritual life. We might have a lot of bumps and bruises as we learn to walk, but it is so much better than just laying on our back our entire lives. God encourages us to move forward, to keep working on each step, because it will help us grow. We can take joy when we fall down because it means we are trying to walk.

God, I ask that you guide me as I try to grow and learn. Comfort me when I fall over and help me trust that you are leading me toward something better. Help me to see the rough times as chances to be grown by you.

What hardship in your life right now can God use to help you grow?

Lively Faith

Just as the body without the spirit is dead,
so faith without works is also dead.

JAMES 2:26 NRSV

Following requires action. Saying we follow Jesus but not acting on it is like saying we're a pro athlete because we watch them on TV. We are invited to be followers of Jesus, and following is an active experience. We must get up and move from where we are to where God wants us to go.

If we are unable to follow through, then our faith is dead and useless. What is the point in being a Christian if it doesn't change how we live? Faith is not measured in church attendance or the number of prayers recited, but in allowing God to direct our day-to-day life toward his plan. We are invited to follow. We are invited to move. We are invited to act. And through that, we are invited to live.

Lord, please give me the energy to keep moving in the direction you've given me. Give me the strength to act even when I'm tired or unsure. Give me the ability to move toward your plan for my life.

Just as a person's body that does not have a spirit is dead,
so faith that does nothing is dead!

JAMES 2:26 NCV

Real faith causes action in our lives. If we believe Jesus is who he says he is, and we agree with the things he teaches, then we have no choice but to act on it. That might mean reaching out to someone who makes us uncomfortable, or helping someone when it is inconvenient, or choosing to forgive someone who has hurt us. If we can't do these things it is like our faith is on life-support and at risk of dying.

When we follow through and act on our faith it breathes a new kind of life into us. Our faith becomes more vibrant and more exciting. It grows and becomes stronger with each bit of practice. The quickest way to grow our faith is to act on our faith and allow God to teach us and refine us in those times.

Show me where you want me to act. Help me see the moments each day that are an opportunity to live as someone who follows you, Jesus. Please guide me and grow me through these chances so my faith can grow more and more.

What is an action of faith you can take this week to grow?

Extended Grace

He gives more grace. Therefore He says
"God resists the proud,
But gives grace to the humble."

JAMES 4:6 KJV

When we come to God we can come as people who think they deserve his love, or as people who understand it is a gift. The story of the Bible is the story of humans losing what they had, having life itself taken away. And it is the story of Jesus offering life again as a gift of grace.

Imagine if you went to a birthday party and the guest of honor demanded a present. Even if you had brought one you would feel offended that they feel entitled to it, because you know you didn't have to give it to them. It's the same way with God, who isn't interested in people who think he owes them something. Instead, he takes great joy in those who know they don't deserve what he offers but are so grateful when he does.

God, I want to be a grateful person. Please help me to remember how little I deserve so I can be even more grateful that you give me more than I could ask for. If I am demanding or entitled with you, please correct me.

He gives grace generously. As the Scriptures say,
"God opposes the proud
but gives grace to the humble."

JAMES 4:6 NLT

Do you have someone who is genuinely excited to see you each time you meet? You probably look forward to seeing them again, don't you? Conversely, you maybe know somebody who is always impatient and makes comments about you being late. We probably try to avoid time with those people as much as possible.

Whenever we come to God it is like a parent who looks forward to seeing their kids. God doesn't just love us—he also likes us. God enjoys us and enjoys time with us. Knowing that God loves us and likes us helps us to come to him humbly, without needing to keep up appearances. We can let him have the real us, flaws and all, because that is the person he already knows, loves, and likes.

Thank you for liking me. It is a great gift to have the Creator of everything enjoy time with me and enjoy connecting with me. Thank you for always being glad when I come to you.

How have you expressed gratitude to Jesus this week?

Worries

Give all your worries and cares to God,
for he cares about you.

1 PETER 5:7 NLT

God cares about us. That helps us know what our first response should be when we are worried or anxious. God doesn't get frustrated or annoyed when we share our fears with him; in fact, that's exactly what he wants. Anxiety comes from trying to do it on our own. Peace comes from knowing that we can't, but we also don't need to. We aren't designed to do things on our own. God's plan for us includes turning to him when we aren't sure what to do.

What would our lives be like if we saw worry as a reminder to turn to God? In times of stress it is natural to think about what you are going to do. Sometimes that fear turns to worry. What if our response instead was, "Oh. Here is something I can give to God." Not only is that better for us, it is what God wants as well.

Thank you for wanting to help me. Please help me to be quick to leave my worries with you, and trust that you are going to take care of me. Help me to make worry a trigger for me to turn to you.

Casting all your anxieties on him,
because he cares for you.

1 PETER 5:7 ESV

The thought of giving our worries to God is much simpler than figuring out how to actually do it. It would be great if there was an easy process to gather everything we are anxious about up in a box and give it to God. Like most everything in our relationship with God, it is more a process than an event.

Casting our anxieties on him really means choosing to shift the weight to God. Think of every worry like a sack of stones. God wants us to let him carry that weight as we continue the journey. He can handle it, and he wants to. His goal is to keep us going, and he asks us to trust him to provide what we need.

There is no reason for me to worry with you by my side. Please help me to feel the comfort of trusting you with the things I am worried about. Thank you for helping carry my weight.

What anxieties have you been carrying that you need to hand to God?

Peaceful Knowledge

*Grace and peace be yours in abundance
through the knowledge of God and of Jesus our Lord.*

2 PETER 1:2 NIV

The way to peace is, surprisingly, not achieved by focusing on peace. Peace is a side effect of knowing God, so the way to grow in peace is by growing in our knowledge of God. Peace can't be the goal, because then we aren't focusing on the one thing that will bring us real peace.

Getting to know God is the primary calling of our existence. We were literally created to experience God, which is why getting to know more about him causes so many great things in our life. When we focus on who God is instead of what God can give us, then we start to experience his best qualities, especially his grace and peace.

I want to know you more, Lord. I want to understand more about what you desire and how you ask us to live. I know that getting to know you more is the best way to live.

*May grace and peace be yours in abundance
in the knowledge of God and of Jesus our Lord.*

2 PETER 1:2 NRSV

Perhaps the best way to get to know God is by getting to know Jesus. Jesus is God in human form and the perfect example of a perfect life. The more we pay attention to how he interacted with others, what his priorities were, and how he connected with his heavenly Father, the more we can learn about what we should do.

That is one of the most beautiful things about the Christian faith. God does not sit in heaven and tell us to show him how much we love him. Instead he comes to us and shows us how much he loves us. Grace and peace are shown in Jesus' life, and by learning more about it we can experience that deep peace also.

It is such a gift to have Jesus as an example of how to live. Thank you for choosing to be with us and show us what you desire, and how much peace is available when we get to know you.

What is something you wonder about Jesus? Can you grow in knowledge this week?

Knock Knock

"Look! I stand at the door and knock.
If you hear my voice and open the door, I will come in,
and we will share a meal together as friends."

REVELATION 3:20 NLT

Jesus is a gentleman—he only goes where he is invited. He knocks, he doesn't barge in. Jesus waits for us to open up our lives to him, but he always accepts the invitation. We should never believe that God has left us. He is always ready for an invitation into what we are doing.

If we don't listen for his voice, we may forget to invite him in. That's why spending time every day, like you are doing right now, to connect with God is so important. He wants to be right with you in everything you are going through. He is simply waiting for us to invite him in.

I want to welcome you into my life, Jesus. I want to gladly invite you to come in. Thank you for being willing to step into whatever is happening with me as a friend.

> *"Here I am! I stand at the door and knock.
> If you hear my voice and open the door, I will come in
> and eat with you, and you will eat with me."*
>
> REVELATION 3:20 NCV

You know someone is a friend if you don't feel like you need to clean the house when they come over. You are okay with them seeing the "real" you and don't need to pretend you have it all together.

Jesus wants that spot in our lives. He wants to come into our lives and he is okay if it isn't all neat and tidy. That doesn't bother him because he cares about us. Sometimes we keep him outside thinking we need a minute to get cleaned up. This comes from our confusion about how God sees us. Jesus isn't knocking to inspect our lives; he wants to come in and be a friend. He'll even help clean up—just ask him.

God, I probably try to tidy up my life for you instead of just letting you in. Thank you for loving me even when I'm a mess. Thank you for enjoying me so much that you just want to have a relationship with me.

Do you try to tidy up your life for Jesus?

Seek and Find

Where then is my hope—
who can see any hope for me?

JOB 17:15 NIV

When you wake up feeling depressed, hopeless, or full of despair, it can be easy to focus your thoughts and attentions to inward self-destruction and defeating self-talk. When you can't see any hope for your circumstances to change, you need to surround yourself with others who can see what is true and good hiding behind your emotional pain and circumstance. They can reveal to you what is beautiful in your life as you share with them the circumstances you are in.

Therefore, when you cannot see a hopeful outcome, the beauty of God's work in your life, or the blessings surrounding you, seek out friends who can find it for you. Which one of your friends is the most life-giving? Can you find time to share with them your heart's pain before evening comes? Together, find time to celebrate the good things Jesus is doing amid the trial.

Jesus, you are good and everything you do is good. Thank you for my friends. Allow them to see what I cannot see, and be a source of encouragement to me this day as they reveal your goodness in my life.

Where, then, is my hope?
Who can see any hope for me?

JOB 17:15 NCV

Is your glass half empty or half full? Or are you just thankful there is something in the glass? Everyone will find themselves spiritually and emotionally parched. There are seasons when experiencing joy, peace, hope, and love will feel impossible. Fortunately, Jesus is the living water. When your hope is in him, it is not about a glass half full or half empty. Your hope for spiritual and emotional renewal is found in Jesus, who will always be the right amount of "living water" you so desperately need for your parched soul.

So drink deeply. Jesus, who is the source of all life, knows exactly where your hope has been hiding and how to reveal it to you. You may find that as you have fully received the revealed goodness of Jesus in your circumstance, you will be given eyes to help see the goodness in someone else's darkest hours.

Heavenly Father, thank you for refreshing my soul. I choose to drink deeply from your love. As the source of all hope I trust you will assure me in my darkest hours that a bright future rest in the days ahead.

For whom can you be the seeker and finder of hope amid their troubling circumstances?

Unexpected Goodness

You are good, and you do what is good.
Teach me your demands.

PSALM 119:68 NCV

There is nothing quite like having an unexpectedly good experience. Like when a friend surprises you with a free latte, or you manage to make your late grandmother's peach pie recipe perfectly the first time and it floods you with cherished memories. In these small and unexpectedly good moments God is giving you a taste of his tangible goodness.

Pay attention to the events of today. What unexpectedly good things might Jesus want to bring into your life? From the kind encouraging words of a friend, or the joy and affection you receive from your pet first thing in the morning, to the gentle voice of Jesus ministering to your soul while you pray. Enjoy these moments of goodness and see how he might be asking you to show unexpected goodness to someone else.

God, you care about the big and the small things in my everyday life. Thank you for giving me things I can see as acts of your love in my life. As I see them, allow me to give you praise in that moment.

You are good and do only good;
teach me your decrees.

PSALM 119:68 NLT

What do you do when you experience something unexpectedly bad? Like when you are in a car accident that wasn't your fault or your parent is diagnosed with an unexpected life threatening illness? In these moments you may tempted to ask, "Is God still good even when I am not experiencing his tangible goodness?"

Sooner or later you cannot rely on your life's circumstances to dictate your understanding of the goodness of God in your life. You must choose to believe this promise, because its truth is what provides you with hope amid the troubles. We can rest assured that even in those unexpectedly bad moments of life that Jesus is good and working to do good in your life. When you lean into the promise, you will experience his tangible love more than just moments of unexpected goodness on your best days.

Lord, never let me believe the lie that my unexpectedly bad circumstances are a punishment from you because of my behavior. Instead, fill my eyes and heart with your tangible goodness.

How in the past week have you seen God show his tangible goodness to you?

Wholeheartedly

*"Love the LORD your God with all your heart
and with all your soul and with all your strength."*

DEUTERONOMY 6:5 NIV

Being in a loving, committed, and healthy relationship is
one of the greatest joys you can experience on earth. It takes
incredible strength to love someone with all of who you are
because you know there is so much risk involved in being that
vulnerable. If your love for someone is not fully reciprocated,
then there is a noticeable void, and it creates opportunities
for you to receive your deepest hurts.

With Jesus, you never have to worry that the fullness of your
love will be mishandled, abused, or unrequited. It's why the
Lord commands you to love fully, openly, and with everything
inside of you. As you go throughout your day, ask yourself if
you have been keeping anything back from Jesus because you
are afraid of how he will respond. Then release it to him and
experience another level of his love.

*Lord, I give you myself wholeheartedly today. Thank you for being
trustworthy and responsible with my emotions. Receive the deepest
parts of me as an act of worship and devotion.*

"You must love the LORD your God with all your heart, all your soul, and all your strength."

DEUTERONOMY 6:5 NLT

Growing up you were often told by people in your life what you must do. You must clean your room. You must complete your homework. You must go to practice. You must get an education. You must get a good job. The list goes on. Today, you can create your own list of must dos that produce a heavy internal burden. If you dwell too long on the or elses associated with not following through on the must dos, then fear and anxiety begin to rear their ugly heads.

Is there an or else associated with not loving God with all your heart, soul, and strength? It may not be a negative consequence, but there will be the absence of a positive one. When you choose a spiritual status quo, you deny yourself the depth of life you can have in Jesus. Reorient the entirety of your heart toward him. It will be difficult, and yet it is the only thing that will fully satisfy your soul.

Jesus, I want all of you, so I give you all of me. I know you are waiting to take me places I have not yet been. Give me the strength of faith I need to love you with all of my heart and soul.

Are you loving the Lord with a half heart or a whole heart?

Clear Expectations

"What does the LORD your God require of you? He requires only that you fear the LORD your God, and live in a way that pleases him, and love him and serve him with all your heart and soul."

DEUTERONOMY 10:12 NLT

Taking part in a group project can be a great experience. However, depending on others to complete their portion of the work is a risky proposition. If they fail to fulfill their requirement, it creates more work for everyone else. Yet, if that person meets the requirements, you would consider them to be trustworthy, faithful, and competent. Their qualities then produce in your heart a sense of confidence in that person. A confidence that would convince you to trust them with even greater tasks and responsibilities than before on the next project.

So it is with the Lord. He wants to entrust you with great responsibility in the kingdom of heaven. This only comes when we meet the requirements consistently. He knows we will never be perfect, which is why every day you have a new chance to meet the requirements. As you do, take inventory of the greater spiritual responsibilities entrusted to you. They are the attainments of one who fears, loves, and serves him.

Lord, I won't ever be perfect, and I will often fail. Thank you for still choosing to trust me to participate in your mission to bring light to a dark world. Show me how I can meet your requirements today.

Now, Israel, this is what the LORD your God wants you to do:
Respect the LORD your God, and do what he has told you to do.
Love him. Serve the LORD your God with your whole being,
and obey the LORD's commands and laws
that I am giving you today for your own good.

DEUTERONOMY 10:12–13 NCV

Having clear and consistent expectations prevents confusion,
frustration, and disappointment. Thankfully, your God is
a god of clear expectations. He wants you to know exactly
what steps you can take today as one of his children to be in
harmony with his plan for your life. Can we take every step
perfectly? No. But we can begin living, serving, and loving
in many ways that bring credibility to the relationship we
profess to have with him.

These are your steps to take. Evaluate your gifts, talents, and
passions and see if you are serving God in those areas with all
your heart and soul.

Heavenly Father, you know all of me because you created me.
Show me how I can serve you in unique and interesting ways in
accordance with how I am made.

How would your life be different if you took steps with Jesus
every day for the next year?

Never Before

There has never been a day like it before or since,
a day when the LORD listened to a human being.
Surely the LORD was fighting for Israel!

JOSHUA 10:14, NIV

What is today going to be like? It may be the best day of your life or the worst. One thing is certain, there will never be a day in your life like it, before or since. Too often people take their days for granted, allowing the routines of life to become unhealthy in their monotony. These people live the phrase: same thing, different day. You may have to do some of the same things, but it is a different day, and with it comes different possibilities.

What routines can you change in your day that would allow you to experience Jesus like you haven't before? Can you fast a meal and pray or learn the words to a new worship song? Could you drive a different route to work or visit a new coffee shop? It's a new day and Jesus wants to do different things in your life. Are you open to the possibilities?

Jesus, I give you today. I ask that you bring new possibilities and experiences into my life so that I might experience you today like I haven't before or since.

There has never been a day like this one before or since,
when the LORD answered such a prayer.
Surely the LORD fought for Israel that day!

JOSHUA 10:14 NLT

What prayers are you asking Jesus to answer? You have the right as a child of God to go to the Father and request the things that burden your heart. You will be listened to and you will receive an answer. It is his prerogative as a good Father to answer your prayers in a way that is best for the family and for you.

What prayers can you celebrate being answered? What prayers do you need to mourn over not getting the answer you wanted? What prayers do you need to revisit because you haven't yet received your answer? Tonight as you get ready for bed, spend time in prayer. You may just get an answer that makes your tomorrow a day like never before or since.

Lord, I approach you with thanksgiving because I know I can place before you the burdens, joys, and hopes of my heart. All your answers bring peace to my soul.

What have you always wanted to ask God and what response do you hope to receive?

My House

> *"If you don't want to serve the LORD, you must choose for yourselves today whom you will serve. You may serve the gods that your ancestors worshiped when they lived on the other side of the Euphrates River, or you may serve the gods of the Amorites who lived in this land. As for me and my family, we will serve the LORD."*

JOSHUA 24:15 NCV

Tug-of-war is a fun game to play, but not when it's spiritual. Often you will find yourself on both sides on that internal rope, with temptations pulling one direction and your spirit the opposite. The beauty is that, as the one on both sides, you get to choose who wins. You have to decide daily if your spirit and life or your flesh and its desires will win the loyalties of your heart.

It's time to put on your referee shirt and declare verbally who is going to be the winner. Today, you have the chance to the worship the Lord in all of your actions. So pull hard, and trust that the strength of God will come alongside you to declare a swift and easy victory over the temptations you face.

Jesus, thank you for being my strength when I am weak. I choose to worship you today. The struggle is real, but so is the victory.

"If you are unwilling to serve the LORD, choose this day whom you will serve, whether the gods your ancestors served in the region beyond the River or the gods of the Amorites in whose land you are living; but as for me and my household, we will serve the LORD."

JOSHUA 24:15 NRSV

Doing something alone is always more difficult than when we do it with others. Your family can be the greatest resource you have in helping you walk with Jesus. Unfortunately, the opposite is also true. Thankfully, you have a spiritual family of people who are all seeking to serve the Lord despite the temptation to serve their own broken desires.

Embrace this family. Invite them into your greatest battles and recruit them onto your team to find spiritual victory. In turn, join them in their battles and together declare your intent to worship the one true God.

Yahweh, give me the courage to invite my spiritual family to stand with me against my temptations. Likewise, allow me to see how I can stand with them in their struggles so that together we experience victory.

What is your heart wrestling with now, and who can you invite to stand with you?

Listening for Truth

> *"Do not listen to the words of the prophets*
> *who are prophesying to you.*
> *They are leading you into futility;*
> *They speak a vision of their own imagination,*
> *Not from the mouth of the Lord."*

JEREMIAH 23:16 NASB

When you hear something that seems too good to be true, it almost always is. If a spiritual leader seeks to entice you to action by appealing to the selfish desires of your human heart, you may as well be listening to a lying used car salesman. Promises of immediate wealth, instant health, and powerful spiritual blessings are red flags informing your soul that you are being sold a false bill of goods.

Your loyalty should only rest with the prophet Jesus. His recorded words in the gospels, and the rest of Scripture is the litmus test of all truth. When a spiritual leader's words, actions, and heart line up with the recorded words of God you will see God's real vision for the world and your role in it.

Lord, I ask that the spiritual leaders in my life would be seekers of truth. Reveal to them your vision for the world and show me my place in your plans.

> *"Do not listen to what the prophets are prophesying to you;*
> *they fill you with false hopes.*
> *They speak visions from their own minds*
> *not from the mouth of the LORD."*

JEREMIAH 23:16 NIV

Have you ever been to a cheap all-you-can-eat buffet? You will find a wide variety of low quality food tempting you to try small portions of everything until you have overeaten. Your world is a buffet of belief systems. Each religion's doctrine and worldview is competing to win your heart. Each espousing a preferred future if you adhere to their way of thinking, living, and doing. The temptation is to adopt a little good from each one until you have a full plate.

Your plate will quickly empty because your soul will never be satisfied by any truth accept that which is found in Jesus. Listen for the words that are directly from his mouth and be amazed as they fulfill the desires of your heart.

Lord, thank you for being fully satisfying to my soul. Reveal to me the things I believe that do not reflect you fully and replace them with truth directly from your own mouth.

Who is the most spiritually trustworthy person you know?

575

Problem Solver

I say to myself, "The LORD is my portion;
therefore I will wait for him."

LAMENTATIONS 3:24 NIV

People are problem solvers by nature. In the age of Google and do-it-yourself YouTube videos it can feel intolerable to not have an answer to a problem right away. Thankfully, the Lord is the ultimate problem solver. He knows the answer, but he is calculated in his implementation, because when he solves the problem, it's final. He solved the problem of sin through Jesus, but his plan to do so took thousands of years—it was the perfect and only solution.

How many of your problems have you set before the Lord? The waiting can be difficult, but are you willing to wait for the perfect and final solution? Imagine the day when you no longer have to churn the mental gears relying on yourself, but can rest in the hope and certainty that the final solution is on its way.

Lord, give me the ability to wait on you today, the next day, and as many days that are needed. Give me patience and build my perseverance as I wait on your final answers.

*"The Lord is my portion," says my soul,
"therefore I will hope in him."*

LAMENTATIONS 3:24 NRSV

There are many circumstances in your life that you do not
choose. Where you are born. Who your family is and will be.
The natural color of your eyes and hair. They are your "lot
in life." The phrase doesn't have to be used in a despairing
manner. For the things you choose are also your lot in life.
When you choose the Lord you have a reason to hope because
he is the one who is capable of changing what we feel may be
unchangeable.

It's a reason to have hope—knowing that even your own sin
nature, which causes you to choose some of the things you
feel are unchangeable, can be completely transformed by
Jesus. The burden you carry and lament over today can be
your psalm of hope tomorrow. What story of transformation
do you want next in your life? When you choose the Lord, you
can guarantee that in time it will be so.

*Jesus, write in my heart a new song. Give me a new story to share
that will bring you glory.*

What problem in your life do you want the Lord to solve?

Fresh Meaning

*"God so loved the world that he gave his one and only Son,
that whoever believes in him
shall not perish but have eternal life."*

JOHN 3:16 NIV

If you have memorized any verse in the Bible, it is probably this one. John 3:16 is the gospel in a nutshell. It's rich in truth, power, love, and inspiration, and like a number one chart topping hit, this verse can sound played out to our hearts. But like all good love ballads, it will be belted out again and again, finding new meaning for each generation of listeners.

Maybe it's time to find new meaning in this passage. Read it again, slowly. Meditate for a few extra moments on the richness of these twenty-six words and then smile, because you just counted the words. Allow it to sing to your heart a new meaning, and then bathe in the joy of newly awakened emotion.

Lord, always let me read your Scripture with an open heart, fresh eyes, and receptive mind. Allow the truth of the most well-known Scripture in the world fill my heart with the joy contained within.

"God loved the world so much that he gave his one and only Son
so that whoever believes in him may not be lost,
but have eternal life."

JOHN 3:16 NCV

Death is the most unnatural thing in the world. It was never meant to exist and is only part of your story because sin is present in the world. Praise God that in this verse, the secret to eternal life is found. Not in your works, good deeds, or acts of devotion. It is found in the life, death, and resurrection of Jesus. He perished once physically so that everyone could be made alive spiritually.

What better knowledge than to know that you are spiritually alive. This is the gospel, the good news, that no matter what, death, the most unnatural thing in the world, is not part of your eternal destiny. Take time to give thanks to Jesus for this gift given to you, and rest tonight in a deep spiritual peace that your forever is secure in the hands of the Lord. Tomorrow, be motivated to give this same good news to all of those you know who have yet to experience this renewed life.

Jesus, you died so that I didn't have to. Use the joy I feel from your love to reach those who still need to experience it themselves.

How does the good news present in John 3:16 make you feel?

Pursue Peace

*"I told you these things so that you can have peace in me.
In this world you will have trouble, but be brave!
I have defeated the world."*

JOHN 16:33 NCV

When you were a child the caretakers in your life should have cared for your hurts, pains, fears, and frustrations. When you scraped your knees they should have given you a band aid. When you had to go school the first time they should have spoken encouraging words. Each time adults care for children, these small acts deposit courage into the heart of the child. Courage to rise up and face what is ahead of them because they know that even if they fail, their caretaker will be there to help.

Jesus is always looking to take care of you. He understands the fullness of your fears. Fear of rejection, failure, pain, loneliness. He understands the depth of it all, because he faced it all. What joy then to know that his experience means we will be encouraged exactly in the manner appropriate to our situation.

Jesus, you know what fears linger in my heart because you have faced them all yourself. Today, instill in me a spirit of courage and peace as I claim your victory over the world.

*"I have told you these things, so that in me you may have peace.
In this world you will have trouble, but take heart!
I have overcome the world."*

JOHN 16:33 NIV

When is the last time you found yourself in serious trouble? Maybe your actions meant that your job was on the line or a relationship you cherish was about to receive a deep wound. Possibly, you were the victim of circumstances brought on by other people's actions. No one likes trouble of any kind. They seek peace at all costs, even if the peace is only temporary. What did you do to find peace in your time of trouble?

As you move throughout your day consider the many troubles that might befall you. Unfortunately, you are guaranteed that some kind of trouble will make its way into your life eventually. If your immediate solution to your troubles is your own works, then you may find yourself coming up short and running high on anxiety. Instead, be encouraged by this simple truth: Jesus has overcome the world and all of its trouble, including yours.

Lord, give me the wisdom to run to you in my time of trouble, and fill my heart with a daily peace that only comes from you.

What is your plan for dealing with your greatest fears in this world?

Words

They arrived at Ephesus, where Paul left Priscilla, and Aquila.
He himself went into the synagogue and reasoned with the Jews.

ACTS 18:19 NIV

You have no doubt heard people say actions speak louder than words. Many Christians have adopted this to mean that they should show the love of Christ in tangible ways, but they don't need to tell people about the motivating truth behind their actions. They allow their fear of vocalizing their faith to mute their mouths, which makes their actions less effective.

When you participate in acts of service, or show someone grace or forgiveness, or say words of encouragement, but don't reveal the faith behind your actions, then only you get the glory. Followers of Jesus are meant to always give him glory, which means it's time to speak up about the motives behind our behaviors. People will not know what they are not told. When they know you are showing them this love because Jesus has shown you great love, then they have the opportunity to experience the love of God, not just the love of man.

Lord, help me to verbalize my faith in you to those around me.
When they see my actions as different from this world, give me the
words to say that will bring your name glory.

Then they went to Ephesus, where Paul left Priscilla and Aquila.
While Paul was there, he went into the synagogue
and talked with the people.

ACTS 18:19 NCV

Do you recall your most recent conversation with someone about Jesus? It could have been at church, in a small group, with a Christian friend, or with people at work. People like to talk about Jesus whether it is good or bad. It is common to have hesitation and even fear of these conversations with those who do not believe in God. How did you do today? Were you able to show Christian love and tell people why you were doing it?

You have had multiple chances to engage people in conversation about God. Some of those conversations were one sided. You spoke, they listened. Others, hopefully, turned into engaging discussions about faith, humanity, and spirituality. Our words are the conduit in which the gospel is delivered. Without our words, the actions of the gospel will never fully take root. Part of God's plan for your life is that you would not just be a doer of gospel, but a speaker of it as well.

Jesus, help me not to be ashamed of my faith in a culture that tells
me to stay quiet about it. People want to hear and talk about you.
Instill in me the courage to be vocal.

Who are you thinking about verbalizing your faith to?

Take Inventory

"Blessed are the poor in Spirit,
for theirs is the kingdom of heaven."

MATTHEW 5:3 NIV

Have you ever met someone with a proud or haughty disposition? The root cause of pride is a sense of superiority that arises from personal judgements toward others. When Jesus spoke the beatitudes in Matthew 5:3-12 he was giving insight into the attitudes of the heart that produce the greatest positive change in your world and bring a taste of heaven to earth.

Pride was the sin of the evil one. He falsely believed that he was superior over the Lord, which was the beginning of his end. If you choose to believe the lies your heart speaks when it judges those around you, then you will certainly inherit a heart of superiority which can keep you from experiencing the goodness of God in your life and the lives of those around you. Today, allow your mind to dwell on your salvation and allow it to produce empathy toward those who come into your life today.

Lord, as I meet others today, help keep my heart in check. Allow me to see others as you see them, so I can love them for who they are.

*"They are blessed who realize their spiritual poverty,
for the kingdom of heaven belongs to them."*

MATTHEW 5:3 NCV

When you write the inverse statement of Jesus' teaching you
will often discover the values of the evil one. "The overtly
prideful are blessed, for the riches of this world are theirs."
When we allow our satisfaction and sense of worth to come
from the material possessions of the world, our hearts
take inventory of our accomplishment and accredit all our
successes to our own hands. These deposits of self-reliance
always produce pride and a sense of superiority in our hearts.

As you move into the evening take an account of your day.
Make a list of all the things Jesus has blessed you with, and
remember that it is because he loves you that you have it. Your
natural talents, your possessions, and your relationships that
yield value are a testimony to God's goodness in your life.
Giving God credit for all of it will keep your heart focused on
Jesus, not on yourself.

*Lord, I have taken an account of all of my good things and
recognize they come from you. Thank you. Help me to always value
your kingdom more than my own.*

What judgements do you often make about others?

Okay to Mourn

"Blessed are those who mourn,
for they will be comforted."

MATTHEW 5:4 NIV

When you think about those in your life who have passed away, it rekindles the hollow feeling of loss. It's a deep, cold, and empty ache in the center of your heart. It's the recognition of your soul that death is not natural, fair, or respectful of age. If you are dealing with the loss of someone, the loss of a dream, the loss of an opportunity, or the loss of a relationship, then you need to know that mourning is the appropriate response to loss of any kind, and it does not have a timeframe.

You live in a world that wants you to get over your loss as quickly as possible. This world is uncomfortable with loss, because loss is the direct result of sin. This world will seek to make you feel as if you should be silent. However, if you are silent, you cannot receive comfort because no one knows you are hurting. Today, if you are dealing with any kind of loss, share it with a trusted friend and be comforted; or be the person who listens and extend someone else the comfort they need.

Jesus, you are the ultimate comforter of my soul. Thank you for sending your people to be listeners and comforters in my times of need.

> *"They are blessed who grieve,*
> *for God will comfort them."*
>
> MATTHEW 5:4 NCV

Hollywood is notorious for creating dramatic characters around the strong silent type. They have exemplified them as people who are undaunted and just do what must be done, regardless of the consequences to their souls. It's important to recognize that silence is not strength. The failure to mourn loss as you need to creates a hard, uncaring, and emotionally-stunted heart.

When people remain silent, they allow the pain inside to grow stronger. They allow their pain to dictate their actions, thoughts, and relationships. What pain are you giving power to in your life, because you have refused to share your burdens and mourn your losses? The Lord wants you to experience his comfort, so tonight start by sharing with him your greatest sense of loss.

Lord, you know all my loss and the pain in my life as a result. Hear me as I recount them to you and bring to my heart a deep sense of comfort and peace.

Who has been the greatest source of comfort in your life?

Pursue Gentleness

> "Blessed are the meek
> for they will inherit the Earth."
>
> MATTHEW 5:5 NIV

The beatitudes create a lifestyle for the believer. The attitudes, actions, behaviors, and values expressed within cultivate Christlikeness in the heart and life of the disciple. Meekness is not an attitude that many people find desirable. Overbearing, dominating personalities are given prominence. In opposition, the gentle, kind, caring, thoughtful, patient, emotionally strong and dependent on Jesus are promised to inherit the earth.

You may have heard it said, "Love your neighbor as yourself." Only a person who is meek in spirit, placing others' needs and importance above their own are able to live out this attitude. They have good will, good standing, and are known as dependable, reliable, and desirable among their friends.

Jesus, help me to value the attitudes the world neglects so that people might see your love for the world through my actions.

> *"They are blessed who are humble,*
> *for the whole earth will be theirs."*

MATTHEW 5:5 NCV

Have you ever seen a mother holding her newborn? The gentleness with which they hold, speak, and handle their baby is displayed with great intentionality. You see in them that gentleness is an attitude and action that comes naturally when you prioritize intentionality. How are you being intentionally caring, kind, and loving to those around you? When you are intentional with your desires to express these emotions, the byproduct will display the gentle steadiness of God's love for people.

In your dealings with people you will assign degrees of importance to your relationship with them. The more important the relationship, the more intentionality you will show. The gentle person is intentional in giving each person value simply because they are people on this earth. This is how you inherit the earth, by showing respect, honor, and dignity to others.

Thank you, Lord for being a gentle Father. Help me to never over- or underreact to the people in my life, but to be a person of intentional love with them.

Which relationships do you give the least attention?

Be Thirsty

"Blessed are those who hunger and thirst for righteousness,
for they will be filled."

MATTHEW 5:6 NIV

Remember that feeling of dissatisfaction after a meal you thought was going to be amazing? The food was adequate, but something was missing. In your brokenness, it feels like revenge, immediate action, or swift punishment for those who have caused you unjust pain will bring satisfaction. In the end your soul will find that something is missing, and it didn't satisfy like you had hoped.

Righteousness means to be in right standing. Your right standing with God comes only through Jesus and his love for you. God never responds to your wrongdoing with swift and immediate action. Instead, he seeks first your benefit because he knows your right stranding with him through Jesus is more fulfilling for you and him than immediate justice. What would it look like for you to be in right standing with those who have wronged you or you have wronged? How could God make that more satisfying to you than the alternative?

God, you are patient with me. Help me to be patient with others. Grow in me a strong desire to seek right standing with all of those in my life as I am in right standing with you.

"They are blessed who hunger and thirst after justice,
For they will be satisfied."
MATTHEW 5:6 HCSB

Nothing compares to the feeling of being one hundred percent right. Right with your answers, your decision, or in an argument with someone else, or even knowing you are in right standing with God. There is a victory, peace, and happiness that comes from being right or acting rightly. Conversely, nothing is worse than someone else flaunting their victory and increasing your sense of loss.

A thirst to be right in your thinking, believing, and acting is a good thing when you are actually pursuing what is right and righteous. It is damaging to those in your life when you are seeking to isolate and denigrate, increasing your personal sense of justice and exacting your rightness as a form of emotional revenge. The ministry of Jesus was always restorative and reconciliatory. How can you, in pursuit of living and acting rightly, ensure to make your righteousness also restorative for those around you?

Jesus, you are the only who lived one hundred percent rightly. As I pursue right thinking, believing, and acting, may I also be filled with grace and gentleness for those who have wronged me.

How can your relationships benefit from your pursuit of righteousness?

Show Mercy

*"Blessed are the merciful
for they will be shown mercy."*

MATTHEW 5:7 NIV

When you were a kid the code of Hammurabi was a simple system of a justice. An eye for an eye and tooth for a tooth seems fair. As you age, there seems to be more room for grace in your daily interactions. Justice takes on new meaning when you are the one about to suffer the consequences of your actions.

Mercy is your ability to show compassion and forgiveness to those within your ability to punish or harm. It's the same thing that Jesus displays to each of us every single day. As a recipient of this mercy, you understand what it means to grant mercy to others. Today, you may find yourself in the position to receive justice, but stop and ask Jesus if he may want you to consider offering mercy.

Jesus, it is difficult to show mercy to those who have wronged me. Please grow in me the desire to be merciful to others since you are merciful with me

> *"They are blessed who show mercy to others,*
> *for God will show mercy to them."*
>
> MATTHEW 5:7 NCV

Some nights, the thought of having to go through tomorrow feels overwhelming. You have found yourself at the end of your emotional and physical rope, and your pillow and a deep sleep are calling your name with the false promise that it will all be better in the morning. It may not be better in the morning, but with Jesus, his mercies are new. He gives you strength when you need it, on the day you need it, to deal with the troubles of that day.

Even if you are not dreading tomorrow, there will still be unforeseen difficulties ahead. Jesus shows you mercy when he spares you, often times unknowingly, from the effects of brokenness in the world. Can you recall a time when what you thought was going to be a horrible mess ended up being not so bad? That's the mercy of Jesus in your life. Take a moment and give him thanks for the mercy you received today, knowingly or unknowingly.

Lord, I am so thankful I experience your mercy every single day, and I ask to be able to see your mercy in my life tomorrow.

Why is mercy so hard to offer to others even though you receive it every day from Jesus?

Seeing God

"God blesses those whose hearts are pure,
for they will see God."

MATTHEW 5:8 NLT

Remember the phrase, "What goes in is what comes out"?
If you allow impure thoughts, images, desires, language,
violence, and self-centered behaviors to dominate your
thinking, then the lenses through which you view the world
will focus on things that only benefit you and your desires.
Your external speech, actions, attitudes, and behaviors will
be in your self-interest, not the interest of the kingdom.

These behaviors only produce self-focused lenses; and if
you can only see yourself, then it is impossible to see God.
God desires to be the king of your life. As king, his desires
are to become your desires. You are to take on his heart and
mind for the world in which you live, and then behaviors will
reflect Jesus himself. As you move throughout your day, keep
your eyes on the King in all your engagements and you will
see him at work in things.

Jesus, today give me a mind focused on you, and living for you so
that I will have perfect vision to see you in all things.

*"They are blessed whose thoughts are pure,
for they will see God."*

MATTHEW 5:8 NCV

It is difficult to remove a stain from light clothing. Try as you
might, sometimes there doesn't seem to be anything that will
wash it out. Your heart is stained by sin, and you can't remove
it on your own. All people who take their hearts to God for
a good cleaning are amazed when they feel emotionally,
physically, and spiritually renewed after their time with him.

Jesus is in the heart-cleaning business. When you experience
the restoration of your brokenness, you see God mightily
at work in your life. You will always feel farthest from and
blinded to God and his work in your life when your heart
is unclean. Thankfully, Jesus wants to clean all of the dirty
laundry in your life so that you see him clearly at work.
Tonight, show him the dirtiest parts of your heart and see his
cleaning power first hand.

*Heavenly Father, I want to see you and your mighty acts in my life.
As I give you access to the most broken parts of me, do your mighty
cleaning works.*

What are you putting into your life that is resulting in an
unclean heart?

Bringing Peace

*"God blesses those who work for peace,
for they will be called the children of God."*

MATTHEW 5:9 NLT

There is so much trouble in the world. Each act of evil adds to the turmoil. People who are for peace are actively stepping into the chaos, seeking to bring justice, mercy, and love in those spaces. They place God's values on display and bring goodness into an otherwise troubled place.

You are called to be an agent for peace in the world. The values of the kingdom of God are necessary to the soul when trouble arises. When you have the chance to step in and right a wrong, speak truth amid lies, or use your gifts and talents to minister to the hurting, you are actively working for peace. Today, you are blessed with endless opportunities to be called a child of God. So pursue the blessings waiting for you and those in your world.

Lord, your peace surpasses all understanding. It puts to sleep the turmoil and chaos in the world around me. As I seek you, allow your peace to flow from me into the world.

> *"Blessed are the peacemakers,*
> *for they shall be called sons of God."*

MATTHEW 5:9 NASB

One of Jesus's many titles was the Son of God. His life is characterized by acts of restoration. He restored those who were physically sick, hungry, spiritually hurting, and disenfranchised from their communities. He does the same thing for you today in the same way he did for those in his life two thousand years ago.

Today, you are invited to join him in doing the same works he was doing during his time on earth: helping those who are hurting and disenfranchised. You may feel inadequate to pursue the peacemaking work of Jesus in the world, but nothing is further from the truth. As you step into this ministry of emotional, physical, and spiritual restoration, Jesus will be with you to ensure its success. So get ready and enjoy the ministry of helping others.

Jesus, thank you for wanting me to partner with you in peacemaking ministry. Remove any feelings of inadequacy. Give me clarity that brings confidence and courage to your work among the hurting.

Who is Jesus asking you to help in their time of trouble?

Suffering

"God blesses those who are persecuted for doing right for the Kingdom of Heaven is theirs. God blesses you when people mock you and persecute you and lie about you and say all sorts of evil things against you because you are my followers."

MATTHEW 5:10-11 NLT

Doing what is right is rarely what is popular. When you are doing the right works of Jesus in the world, you can guarantee that it will place you in the crosshairs of the evil one.

This world wants you to take the easy, mass-accepted, broad roads of doing what is nice in their eyes. But doing the right thing, instead of the nice thing, is what following Jesus is all about. Today, do the right thing, even if it costs you something.

Lord, thank you for being with me when I am under attack for doing what is right. Sustain my heart for you amid the difficulties I may encounter as I follow you.

> *"Blessed are those who have been persecuted for the sake of*
> *righteousness, for theirs is the kingdom of heaven.*
> *"Blessed are you when people insult you and persecute you,*
> *and falsely say all kinds of evil against you because of Me."*
>
> MATTHEW 5:10-11 NASB

Few people are accustomed to genuine persecution. It isn't often you meet someone whose life or physical well-being is in jeopardy because of what they believe and the actions they took because of those beliefs. For Jesus and the early disciples this was a day-to-day reality. They were challenging the religious and societal status quo, calling people to a more intentional way of following God.

When you allow your desire for comfort to assuage you from living radically for Jesus in this world, you will find yourself accepted by everyone and ineffective for Jesus. Tonight, ask the Lord to reveal the step he wants to you to take. If you feel a little fear, that's a good sign you are on the right track.

Jesus, bring peace and comfort today to those in the world who are persecuted because of their faith in you. Give me the strength to handle the trials I will face as I follow you.

What kind of persecution are you most afraid to face because of your faith?

The Shepherd

*"My sheep listen to my voice;
I know them, and they follow me."*

JOHN 10:27 NLT

Did you know that shepherds live with their sheep? While the sheep are out to pasture, the shepherd spends day and night watching over them. The sheep become so familiar with the shepherd in their midst that they can actually distinguish between the voice of their shepherd and others if they were to come across another herd.

In order for the sheep to listen to the voice of the shepherd, they have to be in his proximity day and night for a long period of time. Have you ever wondered, Why isn't Jesus speaking to me? If you haven't been in his presence recently, his voice will be harder to distinguish. Thankfully, he speaks loudly through his written Word, the Holy Bible. Meditate on this passage for a few moments and ask Jesus how else he might want to speak with you.

Jesus, today I want to hear your voice. As I make the time to be in your presence this morning, speak to my heart and soul so I can experience a deep friendship with you.

> *"My sheep listen to my voice;*
> *I know them, and they follow me."*
>
> JOHN 10:27 NCV

There are so many people you can follow on social media. Friends, athletes, musicians, actresses, and actors. When you follow them, you are allowing them influence in your life. By watching their actions, you might be inspired to something similar. The point of following Jesus is to be exposed to his life. What did he do? What makes him smile? Who did he hang out with? What kind of food did he eat? What made him angry? When you know these answers you might be inspired to live similarly.

Every moment spent reading God's Word you are getting to know the Father, Son, and Holy Spirit. You are reading a first-hand account of their lives and desires through the eyes of their closest friends and appointed prophets. When you are struggling with why you are personally following Jesus, start following some of his friends and prophets throughout the Bible and see why the do. You might find yourself encouraged to do the same.

Father, my heart's desire is to know you and be one of your closest friends.

How has your friendship with Jesus influenced you to be more like him?

Ipseity

Be doers of the word,
and not hearers only,
deceiving yourselves.

JAMES 1:22 ESV

Hypocrisy is when you say one thing and then do the opposite. The opposite of hypocrisy is ipseity, which means that you will not compromise your true self in any context. When someone talks the talk and then walks the walk, they are living a life of ipseity. Followers of Jesus are people who hear his words and, in all contexts, seek to put them in action.

When you do the words of Jesus and believe them, you are living in the fullness of your faith. Acting on the words of Jesus will produce more wisdom, love, kindness, gentleness, joy, peace, patience, kindness, and self-control that will permeate your whole life.

Heavenly Father, help me to be my true self—the self that does the very things you have commanded so that I might experience a life of genuine authenticity.

Do not merely listen to the word,
and so deceive yourselves.
Do what it says.

JAMES 1:22 NIV

The evil one is the father of lies. He wants you to believe any
manner of untrue things about yourself, until you believe the
ultimate lie that your sin makes you unworthy of God's love.
That lie will motivate you to try to earn his love by doing good
works. When we get stuck in a works-based relationship with
God, then whether or not you experience God's love is in your
hands, not his.

Followers of Jesus do good works because they are grateful
that even though they are sinners, he loves them anyway.
There is nothing that can keep you from his love, except
your own rejection of it. There are people who live a life of
genuine belief, but not genuine gratitude. They are deceived
into thinking that since God loves them, they don't have to do
good works. When in reality, those who are loved by God and
love him desire to show it by their good works.

Jesus, I ask that you overwhelm my soul with knowledge of your love
for me so that my life is characterized by loving works of gratitude.

Which opportunities excite you where can show your love for
Jesus through good works?

A Little Help

*"The Helper, the Holy Spirit, whom the Father will send
in my name, he will teach you all things and bring
to your remembrance all that I have said to you."*

JOHN 14:26 ESV

When following Jesus is too much for you to do in your
own strength, you are on the cusp of experiencing a whole
new level of faith. The recognition that living for Jesus is
impossible without supernatural help is the beginning of
victory over the battles in your soul.

Just as the midnight hour sets on your heart after your own
strength has faded and your will power has ebbed away—
that is the moment the Holy Spirit is able to deliver your
heart, soul, and mind from the heaviness of your burden by
speaking the truth of God's promises to you in a revitalizing
way. What help do you need from God this morning? Because
if you ask for it, you are promised to receive the help your
heart desires.

*Jesus, today and every day I need your help to live a life that brings
glory to your name. Thank you for giving me your very own Spirit
to do just that.*

*"The Advocate, the Holy Spirit, whom the Father will send
in my name, will teach you all things and will remind you
of everything I have said to you."*

JOHN 14:26 NIV

As you read the Bible, do ever find yourself confused by
the customs, cultures, and teachings of the Old and New
Testaments? When you are thousands of years removed the
recorded historical events, it can be difficult to interpret. It's
tempting to think those portions are irrelevant in your day-
to-day life. Nothing is further from the truth. The Holy Spirit
is here to be your guide. He will help your heart understand
the personal application of the truths within the Bible. He
will speak to you through pastors, teachers, commentaries, or
even this devotional.

In the New Testament, Jesus is often called a teacher. Today
his teaching ministry continues through the Holy Spirit, who
is called Counselor, Advocate, and the Spirit of Wisdom.
When you need his guidance, reach out and ask. The next
time you sit quietly with the Bible, invite him to come along
with you and be inspired at the richness of his teaching.

*Jesus, I don't want to neglect parts of the Bible because I have
trouble understanding them. So I ask that your Holy Spirit would
help me understand and know your heart as I study your words.*

What part of the Bible have you found to be most confusing?

Pay Attention

"Today, if you hear his voice,
do not harden your hearts as in the rebellion."

HEBREWS 3:15 ESV

When your soul hears the voice of the Lord, there will always be two responses. You will harden your heart to it because you won't want to submit to a greater authority in your life, or you will be drawn to the idea of adhering to a truth that has the power to bring deep and eternal transformation. When you hear the words of the Lord in Scripture, prayer, or through a friend, pay attention to your response and seek to understand why you feel as you do.

Whether you find yourself hardening your heart or softening to the Lord, know that he has loved you enough to give you what you need to determine what he is asking you to do. He wants you to have a rich and full life that is found only by following him.

Lord, you have created my heart to be the testing ground of your position in my life. Thank you for continually pursuing me even when I am hard-hearted.

"If only today, you would listen to his voice. Don't make him angry by hardening your hearts, as you did in the wilderness rebellion."

HEBREWS 3:15 TPT

Children can be stubborn and often disobedient toward their parents. You can tell a child time and again not to touch a hot stovetop, but until they get burned they don't actually understand the sensation of burning. Inevitably, because they have knowledge but don't understand the pain of the consequence, they will touch the hot stovetop.

In the book of Exodus, Israel was warned of the consequences for rebelling and hardening their hearts against God during their time in the wilderness. Yet they didn't possess a genuine understanding of what a hard heart looked like in thought, action, and lifestyle until the consequences of their rebellion against God became real. It is time to embrace the wisdom in learning from others who have made the same mistakes we are prone to make. God never wastes anything. He wants previous mistakes to become tomorrow's wisdom.

Father, give me wisdom by helping me understand the consequences of a hard heart without having to make the mistakes that lead to that understanding.

Why does your heart respond the way it does when the Lord speaks?

Sound of Stillness

*"Be still, and know that I am God.
I will be exalted among the nations;
I will be exalted in the earth!"*

PSALM 46:10 ESV

You live in a fast-paced world that is getting faster. You have grown accustomed to getting the information, food, and communication you want from others instantaneously. This instant-access world can condition your mind to have no patience for anything other than the immediate. The concept of being still in your heart, mind, and actions is foreign. For most, being still also include looking at your phone.

When God asks you to be still, what do you think he is asking? Put the phone, tablet, laptop, TV, and other access to the world around you away. There is already so much clamoring for your attention internally, never mind the external world around you. Enjoy a moment of still quietness of heart and mind and be drawn into the worship your soul longs to give the Lord.

Lord, as I quiet myself to be still in your presence, allow my heart to exalt your name.

> *"Be still, and know that I am God;*
> *I will be exalted among the nations, I will be exalted in the earth."*
>
> PSALM 46:10 NIV

Did you have a busy day? Business creates internal noise. Your heart and mind are filled with noise that will keep you from hearing and experiencing the goodness of God. There is the emotional noise of our relationships with friends, family, teams, or work place; the noise of stress and anxiety brought on by obligations; noise from your stomach if you are hungry, or from your body if you are sick. Internal noise occupies great space in your mind.

It makes finding pockets of stillness in your mind as hard as finding a needle in a haystack. God has given you a natural time to be still. It's the time you are lying in bed before you go to sleep. This might be when the noise threatens to become the loudest, because you are no longer drowning it out with some kind external stimulus. The stillness you are asked to find is not stillness within yourself, but the stillness that comes into your soul from the noise of exaltation and praise that you give to the Lord.

Lord, as I lay down, may the noise of my life be silenced by the stillness of peace as my heart sings your praises.

What good things happened in your life today that you can exalt God for as you lie in bed tonight?

Fountain of Wisdom

If any of you lacks wisdom, let him ask God,
who gives generously to all without reproach,
and it will be given him.

JAMES 1:5 ESV

When was the last time you asked God for something and received more than you asked for? God will always give us what we need when we need it, and occasionally he overwhelms our hearts with his love and generosity. When it comes to wisdom, he knows we can never have enough. This is the one thing he promises to give you in generous amounts.

When you struggle to know what the right decision is, in any circumstance, spend more time praying for wisdom than worrying, stressing, and trying to find a solution. In all circumstances, God promises to give you the wisdom necessary in your time of need. It will give you peace and bring him glory when you choose wisely.

Lord, please give me your Spirit of wisdom. This world is complex and I am going to get more wrong than right if you don't guide my every move.

*If any of you lacks wisdom, you should ask God,
who gives generously to all without finding fault,
and it will be given to you.*

JAMES 1:5 NIV

You should never feel sheepish about asking God for anything you need. He isn't a cosmic vending machine dispensing your every want and desire, but he promises he will not say no when you ask for wisdom. He is a fountain of wisdom, and he fully wants you to succeed in living the life he originally intended for us before sin entered the world.

Wisdom is God's good gift this side of eternity to help you do just that. Even if the situation you are currently in was brought about by your own foolish decisions, the Lord promises he will not hold that against you. He wants to give you every resource necessary to get you out of that blunder and do it in a way where you experience freedom. If you are in a bind of your own doing, then reach out tonight and ask your generous Father to give you wisdom.

Heavenly Father, I know I make mistakes, but I will keep compounding those mistakes without your wisdom. In your love for me, allow your grace to show me the next step to take.

What are the circumstances in which you need God to give you a generous amount of wisdom?

Fear or Freedom

*There is no fear in love. But perfect love drives out fear,
because fear has to do with punishment.
The one who fears is not made perfect in love.*

1 JOHN 4:18 NIV

Creepy crawlies, ghosts, aliens, witches, things that go bump in the night. What kind of things freak you out? What are you most afraid of? Halloween night caters to our biggest fears. It makes us second guess our security and safety. Even when it is fun, Halloween can leave us chilled to the bone, shivering with fear. And some of us experience Halloween level fear on other days of the year as well.

Guess what? There is no fear in perfect love. The love that Jesus brought when he went to the cross casts out fear. Fear expects bad things. It expects punishment and discomfort. But Jesus brings life, freedom, and love. He brings forgiveness and acceptance. Perfect love from God can drive your fears away. Ask him to keep fear at bay today.

Dear God, today is a day that can be fun or fearful. Help me to remember that your love casts out fear. Help me to focus on your light rather than the darkness that can come with the night.

*Where God's love is, there is no fear, because God's perfect love
drives out fear. It is punishment that makes a person fear,
so love is not made perfect in the person who fears.*

1 JOHN 4:18 NCV

So, did you trick or treat? Did you hand out candy or bob for
apples at a party? Or was it a night like any other? Whatever
you did this Halloween night, hopefully you kept the fear
factor at bay. Maybe you remembered the promise that
perfect love drives out fear.

If you did find yourself in more fear than freedom or more
scared than safe, talk to God about it. Let him know what
fears crept in—real life fears that you are dealing with or
fantastical fears wrapped up in holiday folklore. He wants to
know all of them. And then, God wants you to trust him and
know that he loves you perfectly. You can call on him in any
moment of doubt or fear and know that he is there for you.

*God, it is easy to be afraid of things that are real or fake. Help me
to trust you and call on you whenever I face fear. Then, in your
perfect love, please drive my fear away.*

What fear are you facing that you need to trust God with?

Accepting Instruction

Listen to advice and accept instruction,
that you may gain wisdom in the future.

PROVERBS 19:20 ESV

Wisdom is knowing the difference between what is right and wrong and then choosing to do what is right. What is right is anything that brings glory to God and honor to others. To attain this knowledge in a multitude of categories is the result of years lived. While everyone is in the process of growing in wisdom, some people have acquired more. They are the "been there, done that" sort. These people have exceptional wisdom to offer in your time of need.

As you are moving through your day and encountering new challenges, ask yourself the question, "Who do I know who has experienced something similar?" It might be your parents, a teacher in your life, or trusted older friend. Very rarely is it a peer. Whether they navigated it successfully or failed miserably, wisdom is there to be gleaned. These people have been placed in your life to be instructors. When you listen to their guidance and see the fruit of their wisdom in your life, you make their wisdom your own.

Lord, thank you for the wiser people in my life who have already given me so much guidance. May I always have the ears to hear and the heart to listen to their words.

Listen to advice and accept discipline,
and at the end you will be counted among the wise.

PROVERBS 19:20 NIV

If you know any children, then you have seen how some actions of a child need to be corrected. While no one likes to undergo discipline, without correction they would remain unaware that their attitudes, actions, and assumptions were hurtful to others or harmful to themselves.

There are many things in this life that have the potential to hurt you emotionally and spiritually and leave you permanently scarred. The discipline of those in positions of authority over you in the small things is meant to give you the wisdom you need to avoid bigger mistakes with greater consequences in the future. When you experience appropriate discipline, it is an act of love, because it builds and reinforces the guardrails of wisdom in your life. The Lord promises that if you accept the discipline and learn from it, you will grow in wisdom.

Heavenly Father, I ask that you grow my wisdom as you see fit, and that if discipline is required that I would accept with humility.

Why are you tempted to reject the discipline and correction for authority figures in your life?

Run Run Run

Be not wise in your own eyes;
fear the LORD, and turn away from evil.

PROVERBS 3:7 ESV

It's not always hard to know the difference between right and wrong, but it can be very difficult to choose to do what is right. Often you will find yourself wanting to do the very thing that will cause you more difficulty in the future because you know it will feel good in the moment. The longer you wait to run into the arms of wisdom, the stronger the pull of evil.

Gossiping, lying, sexual immorality, drunkenness, laziness, and the like have been known to cause lifelong pain and suffering for you and for those around you. No one decision is isolated to one person. Others will pay a cost for your foolishness, but the same is true for your wisdom. Years of blessing, joy, and restoration can come from turning away from the evil you desire to do in the moment.

Jesus, give me the strength to choose what is right and allow me to see the blessings that come over the years by choosing wisdom and running from evil.

Don't depend on your own wisdom.
Respect the LORD and refuse to do wrong.

PROVERBS 3:7 NCV

Your will power is not as strong as you may think. There is a reason people who are recovering alcoholics avoid spaces where they are more likely to fail. You may not be a recovering alcoholic, but there are specific struggles you have that are unique to you. Just as you start to feel like you have achieved victory over that struggle is when you need to be even more cautious.

You may have heard the saying "a failure to plan is a plan to fail." What plan do you need to make today to ensure you don't fall back into your struggles? Putting up these types of fences in your life is a powerful tool in helping you refuse to do wrong when the opportunity presents itself.

Jesus, I want to obey you. I ask that you fill my heart and mind with a plan to be wise today so tomorrow I can successfully run from foolishness and evil.

Who in your life will directly benefit from you making wise decisions?

Spent Well

Look carefully then how you walk, not as unwise but as wise, making the best use of the time, because the days are evil.

EPHESIANS 5:15-16 ESV

There are few finite resources in the world, but your time on this earth is one of them. Every second, minute, hour, day you spend engaging in some kind of activity is time you will never get back. Additionally, you don't actually know how much time you have to spend. Which means playing around with evil is a dangerous game of chicken that you can't win.

Today, your life will be filled with opportunities to spend time doing good or pursuing evil: to spend yourself gaining wisdom or being involved in foolishness. When you spend any kind of currency, you always get something in return. You will either get the many blessings of Jesus or the many troubles of this world. If are faithful to spend yourself pursuing Jesus, he will help you make best of the one life you have to live.

Jesus, I ask that you are faithful with my investment of time pursuing you. Allow this morning's moments with you to yield a significant return of blessing.

Be very careful how you live. Do not live like those who are not wise, but live wisely. Use every chance you have for doing good, because these are evil times.

EPHESIANS 5:15-16 NCV

The word ignorant means that you are unaware of the consequences of your actions. The apostle Paul is affirming that, as a follower of Jesus, you don't have to live ignorantly. As you become more familiar with the Word of God, you will be filled with a knowledge that many people don't possess. Others are ignorant of the negative consequences they will reap by spending their time immersed in evil, foolishness, or even complacency.

Followers of Jesus know what brings glory to God and peace, blessing, and stability in their life. You can know and be enlightened, or as the Scripture says, be made wise when you read the Bible. When you are wise and know the heart of the Father, it allows you to make the most of every opportunity you have. Today, take some additional time to know the heart of the Father by spending time in his Word.

Lord, may I be enlightened to your desires for my life as I read your Word, so I can make the most of every opportunity for you.

How much time have you spent immersed in the Word of God this week?

Secret Sauce

*God gave us a spirit not of fear but of power
and love and self-control.*

2 TIMOTHY 1:7 ESV

By his Spirit you have the ability to be a light in a dark place.
The power of light is seen when it pushes back the darkness.
Today, allow God's love in your life to show empathy and
compassion that serves and meets the needs of others. You
can be a bright burning light of love for the world, and watch
the power of God manifest into spiritual restoration for those
you serve.

The evil one desires to quench the power and love of God in
your life; he will tempt you to indulge in yourself and your
own desires instead of the needs of others. If he succeeds,
he has limited your purpose in the world. Self-control is the
secret sauce that provides the means to avoid temptation and
amplify the power and love of God in your life.

*Jesus, I ask that my life be one that doesn't limit the power of your
love working through me in this world. Help me not to fall into the
traps of the evil one.*

*God did not give us a spirit that makes us afraid
but a spirit of power and love and self-control.*

2 TIMOTHY 1:7 NCV

There is nothing quite as emotionally defeating than failure.
Whether you have failed at something big or small, the
haunting memory of that emotion can keep you from ever
trying to succeed again. As you follow Jesus, the evil one
wants nothing more than to make you believe that your moral
failures limit your ability to be used by God to change the
world. When you allow your fear of failure to rule your life,
you are actively denying the powerful spirit that God has
given you.

Tonight, as you recall any failures of your day, share them
with Jesus in expectation that tomorrow you get a new chance
to embrace the Spirit of power, love, and self-control and
declare victory where once there was failure. This victory is
your story of God's love and power in your life to be shared
with others.

*Jesus, I ask that you give me victory over my temptation through
your power and love in my life.*

In what area of your life do you most desire to have victory
through the power, love, and self-control of the Holy Spirit?

621

Shine Bright

Those who are wise shall shine like the brightness of the sky above;
and those who turn many to righteousness,
like the stars forever and ever.

DANIEL 12:3 ESV

Before GPS and trustworthy maritime maps, sailors of the ancient world used the stars of the night sky to guide them across the oceans. The North Star was so bright and constant in its position that it became a sailor's primary compassing tool. Each night a sailor would find the North Star and chart his course. Who in your life has been your North Star? This person has always been a constant and bright light, guiding you across the difficult oceans toward the safe shores of God's grace.

As a follower of Jesus, you need to seek to become a bright star, pointing people to what is right, good, true, lovely, redemptive, and encouraging. When we step into a situation and help those who are emotionally and spiritually lost get back on course, we shine in their life as bright as the nighttime stars. Whose life is God asking you to shine in today?

Lord, I ask that you would fill my life with people who are
constantly bright stars pointing me to you.

The wise people will shine like the brightness of the sky.
Those who teach others to live right
will shine like stars forever and ever.

DANIEL 12:3 NCV

You will often meet people who have external qualities that make them appear unique, cool, or popular. Rest assured that the external things of the world all fade in time, and those who rely solely on material things to proclaim status or assert their influence will fade.

Wisdom is an internal quality. The more you attain, the brighter you will shine. It can be slow to earn, but it is worth more than gold. When you meet a wise leader they stick out among the crowd. Not because of their material qualities, but the quality of their character. Powerful leaders of people often seek out the wisest counselors. When you find yourself entrusted with the confidence of a powerful leader, you will see your wisdom influence many people toward what is right. Tonight, decide in your heart to be a person who will lead multitudes of people into what is right, because you dedicated your life to pursuing it yourself.

Jesus, I desire the material things in this world, but never let me desire them more than the internal quality of wisdom.

If someone asked for your counsel, how much wisdom could you offer?

Deep Waters

He reached down from heaven and rescued me;
he drew me out of deep waters.

PSALM 18:16 NLT

Every day is filled with up and downs—sometimes more downs than ups. Jesus does some pretty amazing things, one of which is reaching out and rescuing us when we are down. He is involved in every aspect of our lives. When we are out in the deep waters of life, we need to be rescued, just like the apostle Peter was rescued from the waves. The good news about Jesus is that he is always watching over us, ready when we call his name.

How often do you call on Jesus to be your rescuer? Just like doctors in our daily life come rushing in to bring healing, Jesus wants to do the same for our broken, sick bodies. Today is a great day to take time and ask the Lord to rescue you from the deep waters that you are encountering.

Lord, today will you guide me through my day? Lead me to your heart. And Father, rescue me from deep waters. Help me to keep my eyes fixed on you as you reach down.

He sent from on high, he took me;
he drew me out of many waters.

PSALM 18:16 ESV

When we are hurting and broken, we find comfort knowing that the Lord does not delay. He is sent from on high and takes action over and over again. As we live for Jesus, we are constantly reminded that we need to be rescued from many things, all the waters in our lives that are murky, swampy, and roaring with waves. There is immense comfort in knowing Jesus gives us peace.

It brings joy to our hearts to realize we are desired by a loving Savior who sees us. In the midst of our bad days and struggles with sin, we can rest in the hope that he continually seeks us out to redeem us and make us new. Jesus reaches down and rescues us when we call on his name.

Heavenly Father, thank you for seeing me and watching over me. Thank you for your forgiveness which is new every day. I praise you for your unfailing love and grace.

Does your heart fill with joy when you think about all the dirty water Jesus has rescued you from?

a gift

By grace you have been saved through faith.
And this is not your own doing; it is the gift of God,
not by works, so that no one can boast.

EPHESIANS 2:8-9 ESV

There is freedom in knowing that there is nothing we can do to make us more loved by God. We are made complete through Jesus, who gives us an abundance of grace. He freely offers salvation to anyone who believes and puts their faith in him daily—no strings attached.

There is no list that we have to complete for God's approval. He offers us grace and eternal life; all we have to do is receive it. Every day is like opening a birthday present from Jesus—a gift called grace.

Lord, thank you for the gift of salvation. Without it we would be lost, hopeless, and without a purpose. Thank you for extending your love, mercy, and grace to me.

I mean that you have been saved by grace through believing.
You did not save yourselves; it was a gift from God. It was not the
result of your own efforts, so you cannot brag about it.

EPHESIANS 2:8-9 NCV

In every activity we all want to be the star; from the lead role, to the quarterback, to the valedictorian. When it comes to our walk with Jesus, our hope in Christ is not about us. It is all about what Jesus has done for us.

We get to brag and tell others about all the amazing things Jesus offers us. Telling your friends about Christ and how much he loves them is the gift you get to share with others. As they open the present of salvation, you have the privilege of seeing the joy that overwhelms their face as they respond to the free gift found in Jesus. How amazing is that? We get to boast about Jesus and let him be the star every day.

Lord, help me to be a person that gives you all the glory. Help me to see that it's not about me but it's all about you. Help me to remember that you are the one that saves, not me. Help me to show this gift to others.

How often do I think about Jesus being the one who gets the attention?

Peaceful People

Work at living in peace with everyone, and work at living a holy life, for those who are not holy will not see the Lord.

HEBREWS 12:14 NLT

Drama, drama, drama is how one could describe some friendships and relationships. Scripture tells us that we are supposed to live in peace with others. That can be extremely difficult. Maybe that's why Scripture says to work at it. We are to put effort into living at peace. We are called by Jesus to be people of peace.

Among your friends, how many are known as a person who brings peace? If you were given the opportunity to be that type of person, would you take it? The good news is that Jesus asks it of us. What an opportunity today to be someone who is known as a person of peace. Everywhere you go, bring peace. It is such an honor that Jesus says to us, "Be people that bring peace to each other." Instead of choosing drama, could you encourage or lift someone up?

Father, today remind me to be a person who brings peace to every situation. Help me choose peace over drama today.

Try to live in peace with all people, and try to live free from sin.
Anyone whose life is not holy will never see the Lord.

HEBREWS 12:14, NCV

In this life we often give up. We stop trying to do what
we know is right and try to make our own path. We are
encouraged to try to live at peace and lead a holy life. When
we mess up, we know that Jesus gives us an abundance of
grace and strength to get back up and try again. As a follower
of Jesus, throwing in the towel is not an option. Scripture
encourages us to always strive to be more like him.

Trying to live a peaceful and holy life means we put effort into
and pursue this type of lifestyle. This type of life is going to be
very different from the worldly expectations we are used to.
Jesus calls us to live in a way that is in direct contrast to the
social norms of this world.

Jesus, thank you for always helping and guiding me to be more like
you. Lord, fill me with your Spirit which gives peace that surpasses
all understanding and guides my feet with the gospel of peace.

How would the world look different if you lived at peace with
the people around you?

Last

"Indeed there are those who are last who will be first,
and first who will be last."

LUKE 13:30 NIV

Being picked last for anything is the worst. Whether it's for a spelling bee or just backyard baseball, no one wants to be picked last. Everyone wants to be first. With the kingdom of God, everything is backwards. The last will be made first and the first will be made last. The broken, hungry child in the heart of Africa or even in your town will be made first. We love to be the first ones chosen, but as Jesus followers we are called to practice humility and take the back seat so others can have center stage.

Today, maybe you can help others be the star instead of focusing on yourself. Remembering that Jesus became nothing so we could have enteral life. You can choose to be last so someone else can be first.

Lord, today give me eyes to see areas in my life that I desire to be first in. Help me take a step back and help others have the center stage.

"Some who seem least important now will be the greatest then, and some who are the greatest now will be least important then."

LUKE 13:30 NLT

All around us there are people who are mocked and put down; they don't seem important or significant at all. Jesus has a practice of making outcasts critical to his mission. He had lepers and broken people go out and become world changers. Do we ever look at others and ask them to join us in the mission Jesus has for us? Or are we like the world and we look for the greatest people?

Jesus loves to find people who are the least important in the eyes of the world and use them to do significant kingdom-sized tasks.

Jesus, you are the Lord of my life. Thank you for leaving heaven and coming down to earth. You humbled yourself to save me. Lord, help me to become less so people can see you more.

In what ways could you reach out to the least important, telling them about Jesus?

Better Than Gold

A good name is more desirable than great riches;
to be esteemed is better than silver or gold.

PROVERBS 22:1 NIV

It seems like everyone is always pursuing a new car, fancy shoes, the latest trends, or a new phone. We fall into this category, even if we try not to. We often strive to be known for what "riches" we have, rather than who we are. Being admired and looked up to because of our actions and the way we live is something we often forget about.

As a person who says yes to Jesus, when someone hears our name they should respond with excitement. Everyone probably has a teacher they loved. The way they taught and acted is what made us appreciate and remember them. When people hear your name, do they think the same thing?

Jesus, your name is like sweet honey. People run to you and live for you. Father, today may my name be one that gives you praise and honor by the way I live.

Choose a good reputation over great riches;
being held in high esteem is better than silver or gold.

PROVERBS 22:1 NLT

There are many professional athletes who are known for their gold medals, how fast they can run, how many points they score, or having the perfect dance routine. There are also professional athletes known for bad behavior. How are you known in your job, school, and among your friends and family? Having a good reputation is better than gold or silver, which means we should put more thought into the words we say and things we do every single day.

In difficult times, making the choice to encourage and build up instead of tear down is when people truly see Jesus at work in your life. During your difficult times how do you want to be remembered?

Praise the Lord that silver and gold are not things we seek. Instead I seek your heart and your love, Lord. I praise you that I am called to be someone who loves others.

How do you choose to encourage people?

A Sacrifice

"Greater love has no one than this, that someone lay down his life for his friends. You are my friends if you do what I command you."

JOHN 15:13-14 ESV

There is no greater love than someone who lays their life down for another. When it comes to Veterans Day, have you thought about all the men and women who were willing to lay their lives down for you, a stranger?

Veterans are an example of what it looks like to be a living sacrifice. Jesus also asks us to be a living sacrifice for him. We should live our lives in such a way that when Jesus calls us, we give him everything. Loving others is what he did best. We should model our lives after Jesus by living a life of sacrifice and loving one another with no strings attached.

Lord, thank you for being with all the men and women in the military. Lord, help me to live a life of sacrifice for your kingdom.

The greatest love a person can show is to die for his friends.
You are my friends if you do what I command you.

JOHN 15: 13—14 NCV

Loving someone can be extremely difficult. Loving someone like Jesus does seems impossible. To love people like Jesus means we have to live like he lived: radically pursuing others and putting ourselves last.

Jesus calls us to live in such a way that we are willing to give up our own life. Obviously, loving our friends is one thing, but to put your life on the line for a stranger is completely different. This is what veterans do, but more importantly, what Jesus did for us on the cross. He died for you. Not just some people a long time ago. He died knowing you would hopefully someday know him. Once we know him, he asks us to enlist in his army, loving people with the gospel of Christ.

Jesus, you ask me to do some really tough things. Guide me tonight as I reflect on those I need to love unconditionally.

What does it look like to have sacrificial love and love people to the point of laying your life down for them?

Celebrate Life

"We had to celebrate this happy day. For your brother was dead and has come back to life! He was lost, but now he is found!"

LUKE 15:32 NLT

College sports have a tendency to be filled with celebrations, from beating a rival school to winning a bowl game. As a disciple of Jesus, we get to celebrate every day. We were once dead because of our sins and transgressions, without hope. Now, as we live for Jesus, we celebrate in the new life found in Christ. Every day we have the opportunity to cheer as we see what Jesus has done and is doing in our lives.

We no longer live in darkness but rejoice because we have life and are made new. Our lives get to be a celebration instead of a funeral. We celebrate because he has conquered death and given us life. Did you hear that? Jesus gives us new life.

Abba Father, you deserve all the praise in the world. Today, at the forefront of my mind, may I rejoice and celebrate because of the life you offer to everyone.

"We had to celebrate and rejoice, for this brother of yours was dead and has begun to live, and was lost and has been found."

LUKE 15:32 NASB

Playing in the woods can be fun until you realize you are lost and have nowhere to go. Oftentimes when people are lost they end up walking in circles. In our own lives we tend to do the exact same thing. Have you ever noticed that? We struggle with the same sins and same problems over and over again. Part of the good news of Jesus Christ is that we no longer have to wander around trying to find a path or way back.

Jesus finds us in the wilderness of life and guides us like a lighthouse. He shows us the way home. Jesus shows us where life and joy are found. For this reason, we can celebrate and rejoice.

Jesus, you are worthy of praise. You go into the wild and find us. You rescue us from the grip of death and give us new life. You are an amazing God who loves us.

When you feel lost, do you ever sense Jesus calling your name as he pursues after you?

Send Me

> *"I Am who I Am.*
> *When you go to the people of Israel,*
> *tell them, 'I Am sent me to you.'"*
>
> EXODUS 3:14 NCV

Has the Lord ever spoken to you and you wrestled with the question, "Is this really the Lord?" Moses had this same doubt, struggling with a speech problem and doubting if the Lord really told him to go and tell everyone that it was indeed the Lord that sent him. Sometimes when we hear from the Lord, it can be difficult.

Moses went into Egypt knowing that he was sent by God. When the Lord speaks to us and asks us to be part of his master plan, he not only tells us to go, but he goes with us. Realizing this gives us the complete, full confidence that God has sent us.

Lord, today will you reveal to me the places and people you have already prepared for me to encounter and help me to speak truth and grace into their life?

> *"I Am Who I Am.*
> *Say this to the people of Israel:*
> *I Am has sent me to you."*
>
> EXODUS 3:14 NLT

How cool is it that we get to be bold for Jesus? When the Lord speaks to us we have his full authority with us. Jesus has called for us to go and say to friends and family, "Jesus sent me to you." We can confidently share with others what Jesus has done for us. Just like Moses went to Pharaoh and said, "Let my people go."

We have such an awesome opportunity to say to others, "Jesus has sent me to you and this is his message." Everywhere we go we can take each step in confidence that our savior Jesus Christ has spoken to us and goes with us. The great I Am speaks to us every day and asks us to join with him.

Lord, you give us opportunities every day. Open my eyes to see your hands at work. Help me to speak to people that have hearts ready to hear and ears ready to listen to the gospel.

What opportunities are there for you to go, in full confidence, and be the hands and feet of Jesus, knowing that he is right there with you?

Rescued

Rescue others by snatching them from the flames of judgment. Show mercy to still others, but do so with great caution, hating the sins that contaminate their lives.

Jude 1:23 NLT

Firefighters are simply amazing. Every day they get called to take on fires in homes, businesses, schools, and woods. They always have the right gear when they run in: helmet, boots, pants, coat, air tanks, and mask, along with many other tools. They are equipped to rescue and fight the fire. They know what they are supposed to do. They also know where not go and how to protect themselves.

The same is true as followers of Jesus. We go out and share with people the hope found in Christ. The tools we use are the Word of God, prayer, and mercy. We are cautious as we share the gospel in a loving, respectful way. Yet, we speak truth about what sin does to us.

Lord, today reveal to me how sin has contaminated my life and show me how to live out grace and truth like you did.

Take others out of the fire, and save them.
Show mercy mixed with fear to others,
hating even their clothes which are dirty from sin.

JUDE 1:23 NCV

When an avalanche happens, rescue dogs go out and help look for people who are trapped under the snow. They are a great example of how we should be. We look for people who are headed for destruction and we show them the grace of God, while at the same time we hold firm to the Word of God.

Our sin is like a rotten bag of potatoes. Not only does it stink but it also spreads to all areas of our lives, just like one rotten vegetable spreads to the others. This is why sin is such a big deal. It infects everything. We must show sinners the tender love of Jesus while not compromising the Word of God. This is a difficult road to walk and call people to walk with us, but as we keep our eyes fixed on Jesus, he lights the way.

Jesus, your Word is the lamp to my feet. Father, lead me to the streams of life so my life would be a sweet aroma of your love.

Have you ever gone the wrong way down a one-way street? How did it make you feel?

Speak Out

We speak the Good News because God tested us and trusted us to do it. When we speak, we are not trying to please people, but God, who tests our hearts.

1 THESSALONIANS 2:4 NCV

Professional athletes get paid millions of dollars to play for a team. In the business world, some people get paid a lot of money to work for a company. We tend to do a lot of deeds and activities for the approval of others. We work hard so we can bring home more money and make others proud of us.

Jesus tells us to work for his approval, not others. It's much easier to strive for things when we know who we are working for and the eternal prize awaiting us. We should be living for Christ and have a heart that seeks his approval. Many times, other people have hidden agendas. Christ already loves us, and there is no greater joy than living for him.

Lord, today may my goal be to live for you and you alone. Create in me a heart that beats only for you.

On the contrary, we speak as those approved by God to be entrusted with the gospel. We are not trying to please people but God, who tests our hearts.

1 THESSALONIANS 2:4 NIV

What an honor for the Lord to entrust us with telling others about him. Sometimes it seems like he trusts us too much; we fear we might screw things up. Yet when we know we are living for the Lord and no one else, we have nothing to lose.

Living for an audience of one is something we have to constantly remind ourselves to do. We live to bring Jesus glory every day. He knows our hearts and thank goodness he does. We struggle as we check our hearts to make sure we are putting him first. Our goal should be to live like Jesus is the only one that matters, because he is.

Jesus, may my life be one that gives you all the glory. Help me to live with a mindset of being renewed daily. Lord, help me live a life pleasing to you.

What does an audience of one mean to you?

Hear Ye

Moses called all the people of Israel together and said:
Listen, Israel, to the commands and laws I am giving you today.
Learn them and obey them carefully.

DEUTERONOMY 5:1 NCV

Parents tell us what to do. It's part of growing up, and the younger we are, the more they have to instruct us. Moses is doing the same thing with Israel. He is pleading with them to listen and constantly trying to get their attention. After all, he has some pretty significant words to tell them.

As people we tend to take a long time to learn. Whether it is learning how to spell, ride a bike, or drive, it all takes practice and repetition. When it comes to following Jesus, we never get it perfect. This means that every day we need to be in his Word: memorizing it, learning it, living it out.

Father, today may I have ears to hear and a heart that is ready to listen to all your commands. May I walk in obedience as I live for you.

Moses convened all Israel, and said to them:
Hear, O Israel, the statutes and ordinances that I am addressing
to you today; you shall learn them and observe them diligently.

DEUTERONOMY 5:1 NRSV

Learning is not a strong suit for some of us. Most of the time
we run around the same tree of failures and screw-ups until
we finally learn. Our walk with Jesus probably resembles
a child learning to ride a bike. The training wheels are
off, so they fall down, scrape their knees, and walk away
disappointed only to come back an hour later determined to
try again.

Next thing you know, the child is riding down the street
flawlessly, only to suddenly hit the dirt again. Parents come
rushing to the scene, just like Jesus comes rushing to us when
we fall and are broken. In the midst of our brokenness, we
still have to listen and learn.

Lord, may I hide in my heart your Word. May I meditate on it day
and night and begin to put into practice your truth.

How would you describe what it looks like to listen, learn,
and live out the commands of Christ?

Show-and-Tell

"To you it was shown so that you would acknowledge that the LORD is God; there is no other besides him."

DEUTERONOMY 4:35 NRSV

Learning and being taught are two very different, yet similar things. Take changing a tire for instance. Ideally, it would be nice to understand it from the moment we look at it. But sometimes we don't understand. We change the tire and start driving, only to hear a clunk and see the tire rolling down the road. Not a great lesson to learn the hard way.

Instead of learning, maybe we should be taught. Being taught happens when someone takes you under their wing of knowledge and shows you how it is done. Knowing who Jesus is and what he has done for us is huge. Hopefully we were all taught of his love and are teaching others the same.

Lord, you truly are amazing. Thank you for sending people before me to teach of who you are, what you have done, and what you are doing still.

> *"He showed you these things so you would know*
> *that the LORD is God and there is no other.*

DEUTERONOMY 4:35 NLT

Everybody loved show-and-tell in elementary school. It was always a blast until Johnny brought his six-foot snake that could have eaten someone. To this day no one has forgotten that.

The Lord has revealed to us his amazing love, power, and grace. When you look at the stars in the sky, he breathed them into being. When you see the ocean, he held the waters in the palm of his hand to measure them. He even sent his Son to die on the cross for us. He has made it known to us that he is the Lord. What a mighty God we serve, and what an incredible and majestic show-and-tell he has given us.

Father, you are the world's greatest artist and teacher. Lord, I ask that you might reveal more of yourself to me tonight as I seek your face and know that you are God.

How has God revealed himself to you?

Be Strong

"I hereby command you: Be strong and courageous;
do not be frightened or dismayed,
for the LORD your God is with you wherever you go."

JOSHUA 1:9 NRSV

Being alone can be a horrifying experience. Waking up to no one home or being alone late at night isn't usually something we get excited about. We hear and see things we never noticed before, and in that moment, fear and panic settle in.

Joshua was heading into a place he did not know. He no doubt was starting to ask the question of what if… What if the people are huge? What if we run out of food? Yet the Lord reminds him not to fear or panic. The reason Joshua does not have to worry or second guess is because he isn't alone. The Lord is with him everywhere he goes. The same is true for you. Jesus is right there with you everywhere you go, every step of the way.

Jesus, sometimes fear, worry, and doubt cripple me. Father, rescue me and remind me that you are right beside me all the time.

> *"Remember that I commanded you to be strong and brave.*
> *Don't be afraid, because the LORD your God*
> *will be with you everywhere you go."*

JOSHUA 1:9 NCV

We allow ourselves to continually get beat up by sin and shame, giving in to the fear of failing to the point where we want to surrender. And sometimes, giving up and giving in seems to be the easiest way to go. We think that we don't have the strength or courage to get out.

Joshua is going through this same fear, and the Lord says, "Hey, don't become lazy. Stay strong. Don't fear. Don't let your failures and screw ups get in the way of what I have called you to." He tells us to have courage and strength, to keep on fighting. He always sees something in us that we don't. He puts the calling on our life to be who he has called us to be.

Lord, it is so awesome knowing that wherever I go, you go with me. You have not left me. Tonight, remind me that you never leave me and show me throughout the day that you are there.

Who does the Lord say you are?

Unbothered

I replied by sending this message to them:
"I am engaged in a great work, so I can't come.
Why should I stop working to come and meet with you?"

NEHEMIAH 6:3 NLT

It's 8:00 p.m. and a friend sends a snap asking you a question in the middle of studying for a very important exam. Next thing you know it's 11:00 p.m. and you haven't studied at all. This is when panic sets in and we begin to stress out because we wasted so much time talking to friends or keeping our streaks going.

It is so easy to become distracted by things that aren't even bad. In fact, a lot of the time they are good people and good things. Nehemiah is different than most; he has his eyes fixed on what the Lord has told him to do. He has a determination to do the will of his heavenly Father. He keeps working to make sure he reaches the prize at the end.

Lord, I don't want to waiver back and forth from what I know you have called me to do. Give me a heart like Nehemiah, one that chooses to stay firm to the end of the race.

I sent messengers to them with this answer:
"I am doing a great work, and I can't come down.
I don't want the work to stop while I leave to meet you."

NEHEMIAH 6:3 NCV

When we answer the call of Christ, we cannot afford to slow down the kingdom of God. We tend to get caught up in other opportunities. Many tasks and little things need to be done. No one bakes a cake without first having every ingredient, or builds a house without first knowing how much it will cost and making sure there is a way to pay for everything.

As Jesus-followers there is this thing called faith. We often don't see the end or how to carry out what we feel the Lord has called us to. This is where faith comes in, knowing that if he calls us to it, he will call us through it. Don't be worried about the "how to." Just answer the call and keep your eyes fixed on the author of it all. He will give you the answers.

Lord, today I need faith. Lord, I also ask for eyes to see through the red tape in life that can slow me down. I desire to answer the call you have on my life. I want to give you everything.

What is Jesus calling you to do and what will it cost you?

Reminisce

*Remember your Creator
while you are young,
before the days of trouble come
and the years when you say,
"I find no pleasure in them."*

ECCLESIASTES 12:1 NCV

When we are young we often don't think about the future. We spend a lot of time focused on sports, plays, choir, and fun activities. As we get old, we look back and think about the things we wish we could have done. We often don't think about things that can change the world.

What if we lived our lives all out for Jesus? He calls us to be kingdom-minded and kingdom-driven. Jesus wants all of our lives. We often give him some parts, but still hold onto little pieces. He desires our hearts always. From the time we are young, until the day we meet the Lord. He desires it all.

Lord, today would you mold my heart to be more like yours. Help me to pursue your heart and not my desires.

Remember also your Creator in the days of your youth, before the evil days come and the years draw near of which you will say, "I have no pleasure in them."

ECCLESIASTES 12:1 ESV

When people are older and lying on their death bed, they often think about all the things they wish they could have done. Living a life looking back on what you could have done is no life at all. Yet we all have things we wish we could go back and change.

Remembering who the Lord is today means you can live for him now, rather than later. Living for Jesus means you can have the joy of the Lord today, instead of waiting until you are older and wishing you had walked with the Lord longer.

Father, help me to live for you and may my life be one that pleases you. Guide me as I give everything to you, joining in all creation as one song singing praises to you the King of kings and Lord of lords.

How could you join in with all of creation, praising the Lord in everything you do?

Triumph

I will praise you, Lord,
because you rescued me.
You did not let my enemies laugh at me.

PSALM 30:1 NCV

Kids love to be lifted and tossed in the air by an adult. It is especially fun when Dad comes home and throws his kids in the air. They love it, Dad loves it and Mom tends to think the height is too high. At the end of the day, everyone loves to be lifted up by their Father.

Isn't it awesome to know that our heavenly Father lifts us up high over our enemies? We don't actually do anything—it's all him. He does not allow us to be beaten up or torn down by the things or people in this world. He lifts us up to a place of triumph and victory. The Lord does not allow our enemy to defeat us. Just like King David, the Lord delivers us from the grip of the evil one and lifts us up to a place of triumph.

Jesus, you are a mighty warrior that fights for me and protects me.
Today, Lord, lift me up over my trials and struggles in this world.

I will extol you, O Lord, for you have drawn me up,
and did not let my foes rejoice over me.

Imagine being saved from people who are pursuing you. In the midst of that fear and running, the Lord gives us victory. We triumph over our enemies.

Even on the days we struggle with sin and loving others, the Lord has saved us. He has brought us victory and hope. We do not have to live in fear of death. The enemy tries to shame us into feeling doubts; yet the work of the Lord causes us to shout with a voice of triumph.

Father, thank you for fighting for me and giving me victory over sin and death. Lord, you are so good. Thank you for all you have done for me.

What does a shout of triumph sound like?

Rejoice Court

Enter his gates with thanksgiving,
and his courts with praise.
Give thanks to him, bless him name.

PSALM 100:4 NRSV

No one really enters through gates nowadays. We enter through doors. Some swing open all by themselves and others pull open. When we walk through the doors of school or work, we are either filled with joy or we wish we weren't there. We often make the choice to complain instead of rejoice.

As a Jesus follower, our lips should be filled with thanksgiving and praise. We should be constantly rejoicing in what Christ has done for us, thanking him for all that he has done, as well as blessing others throughout our day.

Lord, you are so good. When I enter into your presence, you give me ten thousand reasons to be thankful.

*Come into his city with songs of thanksgiving
and into his courtyards with songs of praise.
Thank him and praise his name.*

PSALM 100:4 NCV

We all know the person who steals the spotlight when they enter a room. Everyone wants to be with them, lingering in their presence. For some reason, people are continually drawn to this person.

On Sunday mornings, we should enter the room with thanksgiving and praise. Often we have a complaining spirit or a list of everything that is wrong. Instead of dwelling on the negatives, what if we started thinking about all that the Lord has blessed us with? And what if we started recognizing that it's Jesus who is the star of the show?

Father, I am so thankful for all you have done. Lord, help me remember all you have done for me and have in store for me. Help me remember that you are the star of the show.

If you made a list of all the things the Lord has done, how long would it be?

Give Thanks

Thank the LORD because he is good.
His love continues forever.

1 CHRONICLES 16:34 NCV

Good morning, dear one. Aren't you glad for a good God who loves you? Start your day by giving thanks to him and praising him. Tell him why you love him and how you know he is good. You could even think through the last week and recall moments when God's goodness was obvious to you. Praise him for each of those instances.

God's love toward you will not end. He will just keep pouring out his love on you forever and ever. No matter what you do, his love will continue. Praise him for that as well.

Thank you, Lord, for being such a loving God. You are good and I praise you for all that you do for me every day. Help me remember to praise you all day long.

Oh, give thanks to the LORD, for He is good!
For His mercy endures forever.

1 CHRONICLES 16:34 NKJV

Take a look back over your day and see if you can find places where God poured his enduring love and mercy out on you. If you can, thank God out loud for those moments. Name each of them. Better yet, find someone to share this good stuff with. It is good to boldly give thanks directly to God. It is even better to share the good news of his love and mercy with others.

If you had a hard time thinking of something, ask God to remind you of how he loved you today. And as you head to bed tonight, find comfort in the Lord's love for you. Trust that his love and mercy for you endures forever.

Heavenly Father, thank you for loving me well today. I don't always take the time to notice what you do for me. Would you remind me to look for your goodness in every day? I love you.

Name at least one way in which God was good to you today.

Sing It

I will sacrifice unto thee with the voice of thanksgiving;
I will pay that that I have vowed. Salvation is of the Lord.

JONAH 2:9 KJV

During this time of year everyone becomes more aware of
others' needs. People are willing to give more money, donate
clothing and food, and basically give away anything to those
in need. They think of others more during this time of year
than at any other time.

Giving is one thing but sacrificing is another. A sacrifice is
something you choose to go without, even if you need it. The
Lord could be asking us to give up what we think we need
in order to hear him clearer or spend more time with him.
Either way, the Lord desires us to be living our lives from a
place of thanksgiving and sacrifice.

Lord, help me to have a heart of thanksgiving. Reveal to me the
things in my life I need to sacrifice so I hear you clearer.

> *I will praise and thank you*
> *while I give sacrifices to you,*
> *and I will keep my promises to you.*
> *Salvation comes from the LORD!"*

JONAH 2:9 NCV

Musicians are praised for their creativity and talent. We sing their songs all day long, and they're usually stuck in our heads too. When it comes to worshipping the Lord, we are praising his name.

Jesus is the Creator of the universe. Have you ever sung a praise of thanksgiving to him? Writing out lists is not something we all enjoy, but when we write things down we remember them better. Have you ever thought about making a list of everything the Lord has provided? Once you do, it's something you will always be able to add to. Thanking the Lord for salvation and living a life of sacrifice to him is what he desires most from us.

Father, thank you for saving me. You are the God who is above all others. Lord, remind me of everything you have created. May I join all of creation praising your name and being thankful for all you have done.

What are things you can be thankful for today?

Chain Breaker

He brought them out of darkness,
the utter darkness,
and broke away their chains.

PSALM 107:14 NIV

On the news, people are falling into sin head first all the time. It seems like our own lives are broken and messy. We screw up and fail every day. But in the midst of the mess, Jesus redeems us and sets us free. We can rest in knowing that Jesus chases after us; he climbs down into the mud and pulls us out. He is the only person that runs into darkness and brings people out.

How awesome is it that we serve a Savior who runs into the burning building, with flames and smoke pouring out, to bring us out of the fire? He redeems us and makes us new. Jesus takes those chains binding us and breaks them, setting us free. Isn't it incredible that we serve such a wonderful, powerful Savior?

Heavenly Father, you are the ultimate rescuer. You invade my life to make me new and rescue me. Today, may I be mindful of how you have rescued others.

He led them from the darkness
and deepest gloom;
he snapped their chains.

PSALM 107:14 NLT

Have you ever watched a fireman pull someone out of a burning building? This, no doubt, is a terrifying and yet hopeful moment. Scripture says that Jesus not only goes into the darkness to redeem us, but he leads us out. He shows us where the exit it is and then stays with us. We serve a God who is always coming to our rescue.

Jesus, in the midst of the danger and tough times, comes running in and snaps the chains that hold us back. He is a warrior that frees his people from the grip of darkness and says, "Follow me." We can walk right behind Jesus as he leads us out of the darkness and into the marvelous light.

Lord, in the midst of my life, I seem to continually walk back into darkness. Thank you for leading me back into your presence and filling me with hope.

Do you think there is a chain too big for Jesus to break?

911 Help

In my alarm I said,
"I am cut off from your sight!"
Yet you heard my cry for mercy
when I called to you for help.

PSALM 31:22 NIV

Sometimes it seems like the Lord is far away from us. We think he's probably off helping and listening to someone else, so he couldn't possibly be bothered with us. Often when we are in need of help, it seems no one is around.

Even though it feels as if he is far off, we can rest in knowing that God is right here beside us. He hears our prayers and he is not slow to answer them. He is the all-knowing and all-present God, who desires a very personal relationship with you every day. He hears you in your troubles and he is always there with you.

Lord, today may I sense your presence and your hand at work in my life. Reveal yourself to me in a new way today.

In panic I cried out,
"I am cut off from the LORD!"
But you heard my cry for mercy
and answered my call for help.

PSALM 31:22 NLT

Fear is real and at times we begin to panic. Whether it is over an exam or something big someone asked us to do. When panic creeps into our lives it can be crippling and our life gets put on hold. It's like a revolving door that we go into, but instead of getting out, we are trapped inside.

The Lord is so good at providing in just the right moment. He is not slow to give us hope, and in the perfect timing he gives us peace. He reveals himself to us in ways that speak directly to our needs. He is faithful and good, especially when we call on him to rescue us.

Lord, when my life gets chaotic and I feel the panic of life crawling in, would you speak to me and show me more of who you are, and your peace that surpasses all things.

When you are afraid or all alone, what are some characteristics of the Lord that you could you write down and remember?

Investment

Remember this: The person who plants a little will have a small harvest, but the person who plants a lot will have a big harvest.

2 CORINTHIANS 9:6 NCV

It is obvious to say a few seeds makes a few flowers but having seeds and not planting them means no flowers. Being a blessing to others has nothing to do with how much we have. It has everything to do with how we use what we have to be a blessing.

For some, a dollar is a lot of money and it may be too much to ask of them to give it up. For others, giving up fifty dollars may not even be a challenge. Whatever we have or whatever we are given, we are asked by the Lord to be a blessing to others. Whether we invest our time, energy, or money we are to be wise. Giving to the Lord is a way to make sure our resources make an impact for the sake of the kingdom.

Heavenly Father, thank you for blessing me with all the resources I have. Help me see areas where I can be a blessing to others with what I am given.

The point is this: whoever sows sparingly will also reap sparingly,
and whoever sows bountifully will also reap bountifully.

2 CORINTHIANS 9:6 ESV

We often hold back blessing others for different reasons. Sometimes we have made conclusions that may or may not be true about them. Other times we want to keep what we have to ourselves. According to the Word, what we give out will come back; whether it is sparing or bountiful is up to you.

We are constantly surrounded by stuff. We always want more and there will always be more to get. Sometimes learning to be content with what we have can be the most difficult lesson to learn. But we need to remember that everything we have belongs to the Lord. He has blessed us immensely, and we are called to bless others with what we have been given. The more resources we've been handed, the more we should be giving it all out.

Father, help me today to learn what it means to live off what I need and not what I want.

If you look in your room, how much stuff is a want? And how much is a need?

Mighty Warrior

Put on your sword, O mighty warrior!
You are so glorious, so majestic!

PSALM 45:3 NLT

During the middle ages knights would go off to battle. They would earn their scars and stripes by defeating the enemy. Poems and songs would be written about them. Even King David was praised long before the Middle Ages for his fighting and victories at war.

Guess who else is a mighty warrior? The Lord. Actually, he is the mightiest of all. There never has been nor will there ever be one greater. His weapon of choice is not the most precious handcrafted sword, but his Word. We see in other places in Scripture that the Word of the Lord gave life; it cuts through bone. The Sword of the living God changes our lives every day if we would just sit down and read it.

Lord, help me to make your Word a priority in my life. May we carve out time to spend it with you, the mighty warrior.

Put on your sword, powerful warrior.
Show your glory and majesty.

PSALM 45:3 NCV

Preparing for battle is something that is so foreign to us. Most people have never known what it is like to prepare for war or a battle. Having a mighty king that is known for his victory all over the land is huge. He puts on his sword and he is ready at all times to fight for you. The Lord is a one-man army that fights day and night for his people.

Our God not only prepares for battle, but he goes out into the battle and fights. He fights for you so that you may have victory. In our lives we have many battles: feeling like a failure, depression, anxiety. Or maybe the battle you face is completely different. Whatever we face, we have a God who readies himself to fight for you every day. He stands prepared and on guard to be your king and mighty warrior.

Lord, calm my heart tonight. Father, would you buckle your sword and prepare for battle as I give you my struggles and sins. Lord, fight for me and lead me into victory.

If the Lord is a mighty warrior, what do you think he looks like?

Shout It Out

Shout for joy to God, all the earth!
Sing the glory of his name;
make his praise glorious.

PSALM 66:1-2 NIV

College sports tend to bring out pride in everyone. Fans dress themselves up and go all out for their college team. When their team scores you can hear the shouts of joy all over town. They become overwhelmed with excitement when their team is winning and run around proudly sporting their gear well after the game has ended.

When it comes to the Lord, why don't we act like this? Our Sunday church gatherings should be better than the sporting arenas or the garage on game days. When we shout and sing, we do not just rejoice over a couple of points or a winning season. We rejoice because our God's name is higher and greater than any other god or sports team will ever be. We should be the ones that make our Lord known across the world because we are exclaiming his name so proudly.

Lord, today I am going to lift your name higher and louder than any other name. Reveal to me, Lord, just how glorious your name is.

Shout joyful praises to God, all the earth!
Sing about the glory of his name!
Tell the world how glorious he is.

PSALM 66:1-2 NLT

All of the earth is singing to God. The stars speak every night about the glory of God. The birds of the air and the fish of the ocean are bringing worship to God. All of creation sings about who God is and what he has done.

If we are to show the world the glory of God, we must go out and actually talk to others about what he has done. We have such incredible things to share about how he has made himself known to us, how he has rescued us, how much he loves us, and how great he is. The greatest of all, though, is sharing about the way Jesus Christ has saved us. And that is the very reason we should exclaim his name throughout the world.

Lord, I ask for courage and strength. Sharing my faith with friends and family is tough. I want to be bold and loud for you Lord.

How can you show boldness in sharing God's truth?

Stressed Out

Don't worry about anything; instead, pray about everything.
Tell God what you need, and thank him for all he has done.

PHILIPPIANS 4:6 NLT

Anxiety and worry are terrible. It is all too common to have a panic attack or be filled with stress. Struggling to find peace throughout the day can be crippling and depressing.

Even though Scripture says not to worry about anything, it seems like an impossible task. When you're down in the depths and lost in the chaos, we need to ask ourselves who is bigger than it all. Instead of focusing on the anxiety or stress, focus on praying to the Lord. Share your worries and fears with him. Give it all over to him, and then thank him for all that he has done for you in every aspect of life.

Lord, this life is so stressful. Today, Lord, I want to give you all the things that cause me stress and anxiety, that cripple me with fear and panic. Lord, I also want to thank you for what you have done and are doing in my life. Without you I would be lost. Thank you, Jesus.

*Do not worry about anything, but pray and ask God
for everything you need, always giving thanks.*

PHILIPPIANS 4:6 NCV

In the middle of the night anxiety, fear, and worry can plague us. It causes us to lose sleep, sometimes for days on end, resulting in extreme exhaustion. Maybe you don't wrestle with anxiety, but other things flood your mind; maybe it's fear and worry about that situation or test you'll have to face the next day.

No matter the situation, we are told to pray. We give our requests to the Lord. We make it known to him what is going on, and we trust him. We continually give it over, which sometimes means we keep running back and giving all of it to him again and again. Now, this in no way means he doesn't hear us; instead, he desires that we are always trusting him. That we always go to him, the conqueror of all, with everything. He wants our thoughts, hopes, dreams, fear, anxiety, depression; he desires all of us.

Lord, today my thoughts are yours. I give them all to you and ask, Lord, that you would give me peace and rest, knowing you are in control of it all.

Do you give the Lord all your thoughts?

Too Heavy

I was very worried,
but you comforted me and made me happy.

PSALM 94:19 NCV

It is very difficult to run with someone on your back. It is
even more difficult to run when someone has tied your
legs together. And still even more difficult to run with legs
that are cuffed at the ankles. We were made to walk and run
without being tied down. We have been given freedom in
Christ to defeat all fear.

Sometimes we become burdened with worry. The weight of it
all begins to bear down on us to the point where we can't go
on. God is renowned for bringing us comfort and wrapping
his arms around us when we cannot go any further. He gives
peace and joy. He comforts us and helps us to keep running
the race.

Lord, in the midst of the weight and the darkness, I ask that you
would comfort me. Wrap your arms around me and bring me
security.

When doubts filled my mind,
your comfort gave me renewed hope and cheer.

PSALM 94:19 NLT

Driving through fog in the early morning is very difficult. Sometimes we even have to pull over because we cannot see twenty feet in front of the car. There are days we feel foggy and it seems like we cannot keep going.

When doubt fills our minds, the presence of the Lord gives us hope and joy. You know that moment when the sun finally breaks through the fog and you feel the warmth on your face? That is what he is like. His presence changes everything for us. He is our strong tower, our hope; and he brings light to our life. He renews our minds and alters our outlook. Jesus makes everything new and he is the one that causes us to cheer his name loud for all to hear.

Lord, thank you for bringing joy when it seems like there is no joy. You bring me hope in the darkest days and Lord, today I ask that you would fill me again with your presence.

In what way do you experience peace from Christ?

Hello Lord

I prayed to the LORD, and he answered me.
He freed me from all my fears.

PSALM 34:4 NLT

When someone gets arrested they get one phone call. Oftentimes people call their best friend or someone who will help them. It seems like the last person we want to call is Mom and Dad. When we are in trouble, that tends to be when we run to the Lord.

When we are in our own personal jail cell due to worry, anxiety, sin, failures, or screw-ups, do we call on the Lord? Or do we dwell in our fear and guilt, thinking that no one will hear? The Lord always answers when we call. He breaks the chains that bind us up. He sets us free so we can live for him with nothing holding us back.

Lord, thank you for setting me free. You are so good and you are a chain breaker.

I asked the LORD for help, and he answered me.
He saved me from all that I feared.

PSALM 34:4 NCV

There are millions of self-help books out there. You can read about how to make your life better in five steps or even have a better tomorrow today. We should be seeking out the Lord. Not that he is hard to find, but we should be in a pursuit of him, as he pursues us.

The book of Matthew tells us that if we keep seeking, keep asking, and keep knocking we will find our answer. The Lord is waiting for us to run to him, so that he can rescue us. In the moments of chaos, we should seek the Lord for deliverance. Jesus is faithful and good; he desires to rescue and redeem us. All it requires of us is to seek him out. All the answers are found in his Word and he is faithful to reveal himself to us.

Lord, thank you for always being there. May I pursue you in my darkest days. Deliver me from the darkness and bring me into the light.

If you could call Jesus on the phone, do you think he would answer or would he shoot you a text?

My Achilles

I delight in weaknesses, in insults, in hardships, in persecutions, in difficulties. For when I am weak, then I am strong.

2 CORINTHIANS 12:10 NIV

Somedays it feels like we are the only one following Jesus. People make fun of us and call us names. Persecution begins to become a real thing for us. When this happens, do we get upset or do we run to Jesus?

As followers of Jesus, we should expect that the world does not approve of our lifestyle. It should be known to others that we live differently than the rest of the world. And In these moments, Jesus is where we find our strength. Our strength is not found in what we do, but rather in what he does for us.

Lord, thank you for giving me strength. Thank you for being the one that never fails and for renewing me daily.

*I am well content with weaknesses, with insults, with distresses,
with persecutions, with difficulties, for Christ's sake;
for when I am weak, then I am strong.*

2 CORINTHIANS 12:10 NASB

Being weak is not something the world values. Fragility or vulnerability are usually viewed as a bad thing. People are always seeking out strength and power. As a Jesus follower, we are weak, but we know where our strength comes from.

When times are tough and we do not know what to do, we can rest in Christ. He is the one that gives us strength and fights for us. It is in our weakness that we look to Christ. It is by his mighty hand and power that we are given strength.

Jesus, I am weak. I cannot handle what others say, what others do, and how others feel about me. Lord, help me to see myself the way you see me.

What makes a Christian strong?

The Secret Life

No creature is hidden from his sight, but all are naked and exposed to the eyes of him to whom we must give account.

HEBREWS 4:13 ESV

The science community is finding new animals all the time. We have been unable to find most of the sea creatures that live in the darkest areas of the ocean. There are animals in the rainforest we can't see. There are animals we believed were extinct that have been found alive.

The Lord can see them all. He created them all and not one of them is lost or forgotten, just like we are not lost or forgotten from the Lord's sight. He knows where we are and what we are doing—he sees everything. You are not forgotten. You are loved and seen every day by our heavenly Father.

Jesus, you see me. Lord, even though it seems like I'm forgotten sometimes, show me all the ways you love me.

Nothing in all the world can be hidden from God.
Everything is clear and lies open before him,
and to him we must explain the way we have lived.

HEBREWS 4:13 NCV

When you play hide and seek, you go to all possible lengths to stay out of sight. Once you are discovered, the items that covered you up are now known, and you cannot hide in that place again. You have been found.

People spend a lot of money trying to hide their past, sins, and problems. They act as if it can all disappear. Jesus has seen it all and knows. There is no need to run from it; instead, just confess it and move ahead. We all will have to give an account for what we have done. As a Jesus follower, he steps in and says it is paid in full. There is no need to run from our sin and past. We can just run to the one who forgives.

Lord, thank you that you give me a new name and identity.
Nothing is hidden from you and today, Lord, I ask that you would
inspect my heart, and if I am hiding anything I confess it to you.

What do you try to hide from God?

Waiting

Our hope is in the LORD.
He is our help, our shield to protect us.
We rejoice in him,
because we trust his holy name.

PSALM 33:20-21 NCV

Good morning, dear one. Are you waiting for something to happen today? Are you looking forward to something promised or hoping for something new? Sometimes waiting can be very hard.

God has proven himself faithful in the past. The writer of this psalm and his people trusted and rejoiced in God. They knew that the Lord was their help and shield. He was for them and not against them. You can rejoice in that as well. The things that the Lord has in store for you are worth waiting for. As you learn to lean on him, rely on him, and be confident in him, the waiting will surely get easier.

Dear God, waiting can be hard. Help me to wait expectantly for what you have in store for me. Help me be patient as I wait.

Our soul waits for the LORD;
he is our help and shield.
Our heart is glad in him,
because we trust in his holy name.

PSALM 33:20-21 NRSV

If you are a Marvel movie fan, you know about waiting for the special post-credit scenes at the very end of the movie. The scene may give a sneak peek into a future storyline or provide a glimpse into something continued from the movie. Whatever the scene shows, you have to wait for it as the credits roll. Usually, these scenes are worth the wait and a fun addition to an already awesome movie.

Guess what? Waiting for the Lord is even more worth it. God has every intention of protecting you and delivering you from harm. Sometimes this looks different than we expect, but we can trust him. He has something good waiting for you at the end of each mini-scene of your life. You don't have to wait until the very end of your life to know that God loves and adores you. Rejoice in him and trust his intentions for you.

Dear Lord, you are worth waiting for. Help me to trust you and love you more every day.

Are you waiting for God to do something specific in your life? If so, what is it?

Momentary Trouble

*Our light and momentary troubles are achieving for us
an eternal glory that far outweighs them all.*

2 CORINTHIANS 4:17 NIV

As you wake up today, what is on your mind? What worries do you have brewing in that bed head of yours? Maybe you are waiting to hear about a job or have a big test to take at school today. Maybe it's something much, much bigger. Whatever your worry, talk to God about it right now. Tell him what's bothering you and why. And then, take great heart that our troubles are only temporary.

The crazy thing about momentary troubles is that they can pave the way for greatness to happen. According to God's Word, these things actually bring us glory that will outweigh all the troubles that we feel now. Hang in there. Talk to God and trust him with your troubles. Look and see how God is using your circumstance through all sorts of things today.

Dear God, my bed head has some worries in it today. Would you please take my worry and turn it into a glory that I can see throughout my day? Thank you for loving me and carrying my troubles.

This slight momentary affliction is preparing us
for an eternal weight of glory beyond all measure.

2 CORINTHIANS 4:17 NRSV

Well, your day is almost done. And you made it. The worries and troubles you started your day with may still be lingering, but you've made it through another day. Look back on your day and see where God helped you in your worries. Did he bring a special friend to walk and talk alongside you? Did he provide an answer to a burning question? Did he help you find a connection that made your situation more bearable? How did God work in your life today?

As you go to bed tonight, remember that God loves you through all your easy times and even more so through all of your troubles. Trust him. And as you fall asleep tonight, ask him to show you glimpses of what the eternal glory might be like, taking all your troubles and worries to him.

God, thank you for helping me through another day. Even though I may have some problems that crept in or still seem to hang around, I know I can trust that you will do something good through it. Would you show me a glimpse of what goodness might come through my troubles of the day?

What temporary problems should you entrust to God tonight?

Rejoice Always

Rejoice in the Lord always.
I will say it again:
Rejoice!

PHILIPPIANS 4:4, ESV

If you went to church when you were little, did you learn the song to memorize Philippians 4:4? The catchy little tune reminded us to rejoice in the Lord always. And it made Bible memorization easy. There really was not much to remember. Simply, rejoice. In what shall we rejoice? The Lord. How often should we rejoice? Always. Now, say it again. See? Easy.

As you go about your day today, keep that simple verse in mind. And then, find reasons to rejoice in the Lord. When you see something beautiful, rejoice. If you have fun with a friend, rejoice. If your favorite tune comes on the radio, rejoice. If you ace a test or job interview, rejoice. If God shows you something new about himself, rejoice. Rejoice in the Lord always, and then do it again.

Lord, I rejoice in you. Thank you for giving me so many things to rejoice about. Help me to see the things you are doing and the way you are working, so that I can rejoice.

Rejoice in the Lord always;
again I will say,
Rejoice.

PHILIPPIANS 4:4 NRSV

How did your rejoicing go today? Were you able to rejoice in the Lord again and again? Imagine if you really soaked in what God is doing in your life so that you could rejoice in him. What difference would that make in your life?

If you were celebrating God all day, every day, and reveling in him (through soaking him up), you would be overflowing with hope and joy. You would pay greater attention to the work that Jesus is doing in and through your life. You would notice what God is doing in the lives of others. And then, you would share that with everyone you run into—directly or indirectly—because you would not be able to contain it. And God's kingdom would surely grow. So do it. Celebrate and revel in the one who made you. And then, do it again.

Dear Jesus, I celebrate you today. Help me revel in you so that I can spill out joy in my life and in the lives of others.

What would look different in your life if you rejoiced in the Lord always?

Radical Advice

*"You have heard that it was said,
'You shall love your neighbor and hate your enemy.'
But I say to you, Love your enemies
and pray for those who persecute you."*

MATTHEW 5:43-44 NRSV

What is the craziest advice you have ever been given? When Jesus gave the strong suggestion to love enemies and bless, do good, and pray for those who treat you badly, there must have been many in the crowd wondering if he had gone mad. But that is Jesus. He often said things that made people stop and ponder. What he really meant was to love your enemies.

Radical, right? Love your enemies and do good to those who don't do good to you. What a concept. Give it a try today. Take a baby step to do good to someone who doesn't "deserve it." Is someone popping into your head yet? If not, ask God to show you who to love and how to love them in a radical way.

Jesus, sometimes you give some crazy sounding advice. Help me to understand what you mean by loving my enemies. Show me who I need to care for in this radically different way.

*"You have heard that it was said,
'Love your neighbor and hate your enemies.'
But I say to you, love your enemies.
Pray for those who hurt you."*

How did the assignment of loving someone who didn't deserve it go today? That was not an easy task. If you managed to do it, give yourself a high five. If you didn't quite make it, don't worry. Tomorrow brings another opportunity.

When we hate our enemies or mistreat another, even if they mistreated us, it brings out the ugly in us. Jesus knew that only radical love would bring out the beautiful best in us. Notice that Jesus advised that we should pray for those who hurt us. That is a great place to start. Pray for your enemy and pray for your response to them. Then, watch your best come out.

God, it is not easy to love those who have hurt me. Help me to treat them in a way that brings you glory and brings both of us closer to you.

Who has hurt you that you need to love in a radically different way?

Joy Filled

Weeping may last through the night,
but joy comes with the morning.

PSALM 30:5 NLT

Some days are just hard. They can be filled with frustration or pain that may lead you to feel alone or filled with sorrow. Hopefully today is not one of those days for you. But if we are realistic, we know it can happen. Weeping that lasts through the night can come because of a break in a relationship, the loss of a loved one, or everyday drama piling up and overwhelming our spirits.

So what is the good news for you today? The good news is that, because of the Lord, joy does come. It does return. God does not want to leave you in a state of sorrow. He wants to lift you up and bring joy again. If you are in a place of weeping, ask him to return the peace and joy that you long for. It will come. Trust him to bring it to you.

Dear Lord, thank you for your promise that when we are in a place of pain, joy will come again. Help me to remember that whenever I am weeping.

His anger lasts only a moment,
but his kindness lasts for a lifetime.
Crying may last for a night,
but joy comes in the morning.

PSALM 30:5 NCV

Hopefully your day was joy-filled rather than pain-filled. Unfortunately, there is a chance that it was a rough day. You may be feeling really discouraged or hurt by something that happened or something that has been ongoing. If that is the case, you are not alone. God is with you and wants you to rest in him tonight. He wants joy to greet your soul with a smile in the morning. What a great picture that is. Pray for that to happen.

If today was a great day for you, remember that it was not a great day for someone else. Pray for those who may be feeling deep pain tonight. Ask that God would comfort them and care for them. Pray that joy would come in the morning and that their hearts would be refreshed with the break of day.

God, you know how my day went and what I need from you.
Thank you that when sorrow comes, it will not stay for good.

What would bring you joy in the morning?

No Wrath

God did not appoint us to suffer wrath but to receive salvation through our Lord Jesus Christ.

1 THESSALONIANS 5:9 NIV

Have you ever seen an animated movie or TV show where ants are fighting for their survival? They live down in the grass and run for shelter whenever the giant drops of rain fall or a baby toddles clumsily across the yard. When snack crumbs land nearby, it is like they hit the jackpot. The worst, of course, is when a kid pulls out his magnifying glass and tries to start a grass fire or make ant ashes. It is like the people are doling out suffering to the ants without regard for their well-being and only occasionally, accidentally, throwing them a crumb.

Some people view God in a similar way—as a grumpy old guy who doesn't really care much about them and throws suffering their way. But God is not like a mean-spirited, magnifying-glass-carrying kid. He does not want people to suffer wrath. He wants people to be saved from it. God gives far more than accidental picnic leftovers. He gives life eternal through Jesus' sacrifice on a cross. He saves a place for us at his table and calls us his own.

Dear God, help me to always see you for who you really are. Show me how much you love me and all you have done for me.

God chose to save us through our Lord Jesus Christ,
not to pour out his anger on us.

1 THESSALONIANS 5:9 NLT

Did you keep an eye out to avoid anthills today? How many times did the image of a mean-spirited, magnifying-glass-carrying kid pop into your head? Hopefully it made you laugh and then move on to remembering just how different God is.

If God has chosen to save us and does not want to pour out anger on us, maybe he wants us to do the same for others as well. When you are tempted to become angry at someone, rather than dumping out your wrath on them (or reaching for the magnifying glass to burn them), maybe you can find a way to care for them. Perhaps your care for them will figuratively or literally save a part of their day or a piece of their life.

Dear God, thank you for saving me. Now, help me to be more like you. Help me to pour out love and salvation, rather than anger or wrath.

How do you view God? As one who pours out anger or one who pours out love?

Forever

He died for us so that,
whether we are awake or asleep,
we may live together with him.

1 THESSALONIANS 5:10 NIV

If you know any verses in the Bible, you probably know John 3:16. What incredibly good news it is. First Thessalonians 5:10 basically says the same thing: that Jesus died for us so that we can live forever with him. He must think we are pretty special to do that.

Did you notice that these verses don't say anything about needing to be amazing or gifted or talented or perfect? God's gift of eternal life has way more to do with him and his love for us than anything we have to offer. Jesus's sacrifice is just that. It is a sacrifice for us and on our behalf. Why would he do that? Because he loves us and wants to be with us, not separated from us. Keep that amazing love in mind today.

Dear Jesus, I praise you and thank you for loving me the way you do. You love me so much that you died on the cross to spend eternity with me. Thank you.

*Christ died for us so that,
whether we are dead or alive when he returns,
we can live with him forever.*

1 Thessalonians 5:10 nlt

Is there anyone in your life that you can imagine giving up everything for? That person would have to be pretty spectacular. They would have to mean more than everything else to you. It might be easy to imagine giving up everything for a family member or someone you are in love with. It is unlikely you can imagine doing the same for someone who you hardly know or who has not really done anything for you.

But Jesus Christ did that very thing. Of course, Jesus did die on behalf of his mom, earthly dad, brothers and closest friends. But he also died on behalf of everyone else—those who had already died and those who hadn't even been born yet, including you. He died so that anyone who would choose to say yes to him could be with him for eternity. That is amazing love.

Dear God, what a crazy plan you had in mind to die for me and everyone else, past, present, and future. Thank you for your amazing love and the chance to be with you always.

What do you imagine living forever with God will be like?

Encourage

Encourage one another and build each other up,
just as in fact you are doing.

1 THESSALONIANS 5:11 NIV

You are an amazing and unique person created to do great things. This day was made with you in mind. Get out there, soak it up, and do what you do best. Be you.

It feels good to be encouraged and built up, doesn't it? Being supported makes all the difference in the way we see ourselves and in the ways we interact with the world. God wants us to live an encouraging lifestyle. He wants us to cheer others on and make a difference in another's life. As you go throughout your day today, look for ways to spur on others to be their best selves and do great things. Ask God to show you who needs that kind of motivation today. You can do it.

Dear God, you call us to encourage others and build them up. Help me to know who needs words of encouragement today. And help me to cheer them on.

Encourage each other and give each other strength,
just as you are doing now.

1 THESSALONIANS 5:11 NCV

If you did your assignment from this morning, didn't it feel great? Wasn't it life giving? When we motivate and encourage others, we often feel motivated and encouraged as well. Imagine what a beautiful world it would be if everyone spent more time raising others up and less time competing or putting others down.

When we do this, we can also support one another to grow in faith. We can do this by praying for one another, speaking truth, and holding each other accountable to living out Godly (or God-led) lives. If you were able to give encouragement today, keep going. Don't stop. Do it again tomorrow and the next day and the day after that. And if it was an unmet challenge today, don't worry—you have tomorrow to try again.

Lord, thank you that when we build up others, we get encouraged too. Help me to grow stronger in my faith and support others to do the same. I love you.

Who did you encourage today and who will you build up tomorrow?

Praise Him

Praise him with trumpet blasts;
praise him with harps and lyres.
Praise him with tambourines and dancing;
praise him with stringed instruments and flutes.
Praise him with loud cymbals;
praise him with crashing cymbals.
Let everything that breathes praise the LORD.
Praise the LORD!

PSALM 150:3-6 NCV

What kind of music do you like to listen to? Are you into rock, country, classical, hip hop, jazz? Is there an instrument that you really enjoy or maybe even play? Maybe you like to sing?

Guess what? Whatever kind of music style you like and whatever kind of instrument you enjoy, you can use it to celebrate and praise God. The writer of Psalm 150 suggests a pretty big range of instruments, singing, and dancing to praise God. He did not tell anyone to stay behind in this celebration song. Even if our styles may differ from one another, we can all use what we love to worship God. Just praise him.

Dear heavenly Father, I praise you. Thank you for being a creative God who gives us different styles of music and a big variety of instruments and voices to make noise with. May we use them all to praise you.

Praise him with trumpet sound;
praise him with lute and harp!
Praise him with tambourineand dance;
praise him with strings and pipe!
Praise him with clanging cymbals;
praise him with loud clashing cymbals!
Let everything that breathes praise the Lord!
Praise the Lord!

PSALM 150:3-6 NRSV

If you were writing a one-hundred-and-fifty-chapter book on your favorite subject, how do you think it might end? What would you highlight or how would you resolve it? The Psalms were not actually written as a book by one author in order. They were a collection of songs and poems by a few different authors.

The people who put this group of writings together as the Psalms wanted to end it with a strong and loud statement. So, they chose a piece that had a repetitive and clear message. Praise the Lord. And don't just sort of praise him, really praise him.

Dear God, I praise you. I praise you with all that I have and all that I am. Thank you for all that you are and all that you do in my life. Praise you.

What is your favorite way to praise God? *Listening to songs about Him, music and watching artists songs on how much they demonstrate how they love Him. I feel the same 699 way. ♡ 12-13-2021*

Wisdom with Words

He who has knowledge spares his words,
And a man of understanding is of a calm spirit.

PROVERBS 17:27 NKJV

How many times have you spoken something out loud that you wish you hadn't said? An angry word, an insult hurled, or an attempt at sounding more knowledgeable than you really are? Like watching a movie scene in slow motion, you scramble to gather back words you may have said impulsively only to realize it is too late. The damage is already done.

Solomon recognized that a wise or knowledgeable person should speak less and have a calm spirit. That recognition likely came from God-inspired wisdom. Solomon had more reason than most to speak often and use lots of words. He was, after all, a king who was well loved. Yet he knew it was sometimes best to keep quiet to keep the peace. Today, watch yourself and wait to speak. Try to follow in Solomon's wisdom and see how it goes.

God, I need to practice the art of speaking less and carrying a calm spirit. Give me guidance today to be slower to speak.

> *A truly wise person uses few words;*
> *a person with understanding is even-tempered.*
>
> PROVERBS 17:27 NLT

Well? How did it go? Were you able to speak less and carry more calm with you? Not an easy task, was it? Maybe you know someone who could handle that challenge like a pro. There are some people who don't say much, but when they do speak, you know you should listen. The words of someone like that tend to carry more meaning and value. You know they are not talking just to hear their own voice. They are more likely to be one you will seek advice from because they won't try to make something up just to sound smart.

As you go to sleep, ask God to give you wisdom like that. Wisdom to know when to speak and when to stay quiet. Wisdom that allows you to be even-tempered and calm in any circumstance.

Heavenly Father, I want to be someone who is wise, who knows when to speak and when to stay quiet. Teach me how to do just that. And teach me to be even-tempered whatever comes my way.

How can you practice the art of keeping quiet when it is the wisest thing to do?

Perfect You

*By one sacrifice he has made perfect forever
those who are being made holy.*

HEBREWS 10:14 NIV

Because of what Jesus did on the cross, you are being made holy and perfect. That seems hard to believe, doesn't it? Especially in a world where we know that nobody is perfect. The thought of calling yourself perfect may feel totally awkward. Knowing that everyone sins and falls short of God's glory also makes it hard to believe that you are, in fact, perfect. But because of Jesus, his love for you, and God's holiness given out to you, you are made perfect.

Does that mean you won't mess up or make mistakes? No way. But it does mean that God's forgiveness and grace is enough to clean the slate and wash you up into perfection. Wow. If that doesn't blow your mind, what will? And because of his Holy Spirit working in you, it also means that you will, in fact, legitimately live a more perfect life, making choices and decisions that honor God. Now go on and be perfect.

Dear God, thank you for working in my life to make me perfect in you. I know it is not because of what I do, but only because of you.

*With one sacrifice he made perfect forever
those who are being made holy.*

HEBREWS 10:14 NCV

Hopefully the idea of you being perfect today didn't go to your head. Hopefully it went straight to your heart. Ideally, you thought about the verses and devotional this morning and let it soak into you that God is making you perfect. By what Jesus did—his single offering of his own life for yours—he took all of your shame, hurt, and sin and pinned it to the cross. That doesn't mean life will look or feel perfect all the time. In fact, life will be hard. But God continues to perfect you and others who are walking with him and seeking him out. God is with you in your messiness, turning messy into beautiful perfection.

God loves you and wants you to go to bed tonight knowing that he is forming you into the perfect person that he created. May you allow him and his Holy Spirit to live and move and breathe you into a perfect you. According to Scripture, he already has.

Father, it is hard to understand that you see me as perfect. But I know your Word is true, so I want to trust that today. Continue to shape your perfection in me.

Which parts of your life do you think God can help perfect?

Just Two

> *"'Love the LORD your God with all your heart*
> *and with all your soul and with all your mind.'*
> *This is the first and greatest commandment.*
> *And the second is like it: 'Love your neighbor as yourself.'*
> *All the Law and the Prophets hang on these two commandments."*
>
> MATTHEW 22:37-39 NIV

Some people think the Bible is just a bunch of rules that make life boring and hard. But when it comes down to it, there really are only two main rules to follow. Once you understand those two, the rest will fall into place.

The first rule? Love God like crazy. If you love God with your whole heart, you will want to do things that please him. Nothing will be more important. Your words and actions will reflect him, not because you're "following the rules," but because you want to be like him. You will love things that he loves and stay away from the stuff he says is not good for you. Ask God to show you how to love him more today and see if that is easier than following a bunch of rules.

God, you really gave us two main things to remember—love you and love others. Help me to love you more today.

> *"'Love the LORD your God with all your heart,*
> *all your soul, and all your mind.'*
> *This is the first and most important command.*
> *And the second command is like the first:*
> *'Love your neighbor as you love yourself.'"*
>
> MATTHEW 22:37-39 NCV

Are you ready for the second rule? Here it is. Love people. Love other people as much as you love yourself. When you do, you will want good to come to them. You will be generous and kind to them. You will protect them, encourage them, and respect them and their things. That doesn't sound so hard, does it?

Isn't it freeing to know that these two rules can guide pretty much all you do? Instead of needing to memorize all the dos and don'ts, just love God and love others. Let all you do reflect that love. So much easier. Now get out there, love God, and love your neighbors as yourself.

Dear Lord, help me to love you and love others more. Show me how this looks in my every day. I love you.

What does loving God and loving your neighbor look like?

Thankful Always

We ought always to give thanks to God for you, brothers, as is right,
because your faith is growing abundantly,
and the love of every one of you for one another is increasing.

2 THESSALONIANS 1:3 ESV

God wants us to celebrate each other. He loves it when one believer encourages another. He also wants us to give thanks for one another and to walk together as we seek him and grow in him.

Guess what? There are believers giving thanks for you right now. Some you know and some you have never met. Even as these words were written down, the author was praying for you and thanking God for you. Thanks be to God that you are reading this devotional, growing your faith and nurturing your relationship with him. Today, remember that others are with you and cheering you on in your journey with Jesus.

Dear God, thank you that you want us to encourage and give thanks for one another as they grow in faith. I love that people I know and even some I don't are giving thanks for me as I draw closer to you.

We must always thank God for you, brothers and sisters.
This is only right, because your faith is growing more and more,
and the love that every one of you has for each other is increasing.

2 THESSALONIANS 1:3 NCV

How does it feel to know that others thank God for you and are cheering you on as you grow in faith? Hopefully it feels fantastic.

Now, can you think of friends or family members who are growing in their faith? If so, thank God for them right now. Praise him for the growth you see in them. Then take the next step and reach out to them. Let them know that you praise God for them and love to see them growing in faith. If no one comes to mind immediately, ask God who you should be praying for and who you can encourage in their faith. Reach out to them as well today. Connecting with others will not only encourage them and you, but it will also increase your relationship together as brothers or sisters in Christ.

Heavenly Father, thank you for my friends and family. Remind me to reach out and encourage them today.

Who are you thankful for today and who needs to hear from you today?

Not Futile

Submit yourselves therefore to God.
Resist the devil, and he will flee from you.

JAMES 4:7 NRSV

In 1989, a classic saying was birthed on the show Star Trek: The Next Generation. The Borg, an alien race that captured and absorbed other races into themselves, proclaimed that "resistance is futile." And on the show, it was nearly impossible to escape the Borg.

The devil, like the Borg, also wants to capture people by tricking them into thinking God doesn't love them or that God doesn't really have a good plan for them. The devil likes to deceive people with shiny things that draw them away from God's goodness. But the Bible says resistance is not futile. James says we should submit ourselves to God and resist the devil. When we do, the devil will run away. The devil knows he is no match for God. Remember that today when you feel tempted or discouraged. Resistance is not futile.

God, thank you that the devil is no match for you. Help me to cling to you, so the devil knows that I am yours and he has no claim on me.

Give yourselves completely to God.
Stand against the devil, and the devil will run from you.

JAMES 4:7 NCV

Resisting the devil is no futile act. It will send him on his way. But we cannot resist him on our own. We have to first submit to God and let him work his will in us. What does that mean and what does it look like?

It means that we need to pay attention to Jesus in all areas of our lives. We need to ask him what he wants us to do at school, at work, at home, in our entertainment, and within our relationships. We need look for him to be present and active in all we do. It also means that we need to pray for God to lead us and keep us from temptation. We can see God more clearly when we read the Bible, worship regularly, and hang out with others who also want to submit to God's plan. When we actively submit to God, we can resist the devil, tell him no, and watch him scamper away.

Lord, I want to submit to you and your will in my life. Help me to look for you in everything I do and in every step I make. And help me resist the devil and send him on his way.

What part of your life do you need to submit more to God?

Get Close

Come near to God, and God will come near to you.
You sinners, clean sin out of your lives.
You who are trying to follow God
and the world at the same time,
make your thinking pure.

JAMES 4:8 NCV

Do you know how much God loves you today? His love for you is deep and wide and it never runs dry. The Bible repeatedly talks about God wanting to be close to his people. He wants you to be near to him.

Say yes to God and move closer to him today. Be in his Word and talk to him now. And be honest with yourself and God about what you have done to keep yourself from him. Confess your sins and make things right by telling him where you have gone wrong. He is ready and waiting for you to draw close to him.

Father, I want to be near to you today. Please come near to me. I am sorry for the things I have done to push you away or sin against you and others. Forgive me and be close.

Draw near to God, and he will draw near to you.
Cleanse your hands, you sinners,
and purify your hearts,
you double-minded.

JAMES 4:8 NRSV

Isn't it good to know that God wants a relationship with us?
He wants to be close to us and does not keep himself from us.
He is always ready. At the same time, he will not barge into
our lives if we have slammed the door shut in his face. He
wants us to say yes and move closer to him.

We do this when we seek him and admit where we have messed
up. When we confess our sins and ask him to help clean us up
from the inside out, then God knows we mean business. Tell
God where you made mistakes today. Ask him to forgive you
and to help you clean up your life so that you can grow closer to
him. No need to worry; he will happy to respond.

Thank you, God, for wanting to be near to me. Forgive me for my
sin. I want to be close to you too.

What sin will you say no to so that you can say a louder yes to
God?

A Break

*"Come to Me, all you who labor and are heavy laden,
and I will give you rest."*

Life can be tiring. Hopefully you are not waking up tired—but maybe you are. Between school, work, friends, and responsibilities at home, it can be hard to keep up. Sometimes, don't you just want to put your feet up and rest?

God must know how tiring life can be. He said that we can bring him our work and our worries and he will give us rest. Tell God what is on your mind and what feels heavy to you today. Tell him how you just need a break. Let him listen and ask him to give you much needed rest.

Dear God, it is morning and I am already feeling a little (or a lot) tired. Will you take some of my worries away from me and give me rest instead? That would be amazing.

*"Are you weary, carrying a heavy burden? Then come to me.
I will refresh your life, for I am your oasis."*

MATTHEW 11:28 TPT

The day is coming to an end and soon you will be able to sleep and get some needed physical rest. But God isn't thinking of only your physical need for rest. He wants to give you much more.

God wants to take your burden or heavy loads in life to him—physical, emotional, social, mental, and spiritual. He wants you to sit quietly with him, listen to him, and allow him to refresh you. God wants to be like an oasis in a desert for you—a place where you can fill up and fuel up for whatever you need. He wants to give you his peace and grace so you can live more freely. Ask him for that as you head to bed and find rest.

*I need your true rest, Lord. Help me to trust you and rest in you
tonight. Thanks that you love me, God.*

What burden are you carrying that you want to give to God?

Great Things

Then our mouth was filled with laughter,
and our tongue with shouts of joy;
then it was said among the nations,
"The LORD has done great things for them."
The LORD has done great things for us,
and we rejoiced.

PSALM 126:2-3 NRSV

This morning as you start your day, take some time to think about some of the great things the Lord has done for you. Don't rush through the usual thanksgiving topics (you know… "thank you for my family, friends and food") and leave it at that. Really think about what good stuff he is doing and the good stuff he has already done in your life. Soak it up and speak it out.

If recognizing the great stuff God has done leads to a twinkle in your eye, a smile across your lips, or laughter in your throat, let that goodness flow. In fact, let it stick to you all day. Others may even notice that there is a little extra lift in your step. If they ask, don't be afraid to tell them. The Lord has done great things for you.

Wow, God. You really have done some great things in my life. Thank you. I hope others notice so I can tell them about you.

Then we were filled with laughter,
and we sang happy songs.
Then the other nations said,
"The LORD has done great things for them."
The LORD has done great things for us,
and we are very glad.

PSALM 126:2-3 NCV

Celebrate the great things that God has done for you today. Look back over the day and notice where God was doing something good in you or for you. Maybe he did something good in or for someone close to you.

Find someone to share at least one of those things with. Send them a message through social media. Call them up and fill them in. Walk into another room and tell a family member or roommate. The point is, don't keep all of this great stuff to yourself. Let others know what good things God is doing too. It can be an encouragement to them and an encouragement to God.

Dear Lord, thanks for all the great things you are doing for me.
Help me to remember these things so that I can share them with
others and bring more glory to you. I want to share your goodness
with others.

Who do you hope notices the great stuff God is doing in your life?

In the Mix

I can do all things through Christ,
because he gives me strength.

PHILIPPIANS 4:13 NCV

Life can sometimes throw you a big party. Everything seems to line up and be going well. Life can also sometimes throw you a big curve ball. Nothing seems quite the way it should be, and hard circumstances are thrown right into the mix. One makes you feel on top of the world. The other makes you feel at the bottom of the heap.

The thing is, Jesus is in the mix with you either way. He can give you the power you need to get through the day and move onto the next. No matter what kind of day you are having today, tell him about it. Ask him for the strength to do all that you need to do. Trust that he can help you make it through anything that comes your way.

Lord, I believe you and trust you. You are able to give me what I need to do all things. Be with me today and strengthen me.

I can do all things
through him who strengthens me.

PHILIPPIANS 4:13 NRSV

You made it through another day. It may or may not have been the day you were hoping for, but you did it. God was with you throughout it all, providing you with what you needed to take another step and another breath.

As you end your day, thank God for walking with you and strengthening you. If you feel exhausted now, tell him about it. He will not be surprised by anything you tell him. Ask him to refresh you as you sleep and give you the strength for another day. You really can do all things when Jesus is in the mix with you. Never be hesitant to ask him for his strength to work in you. And now, rest in Jesus as you head to bed.

Dear Jesus, thank you for giving me what I needed to get through my day. I love you and need your strength in me, daily, so that I can do anything that comes my way.

In the coming days, where do you think you need God's strength most?

Yikes

*Anyone who answers without listening
is foolish and confused.*

PROVERBS 18:13 NCV

Yikes. Those are some strong words in Proverbs. They are
kind of right though, aren't they? We all have seen someone
answer a question or give their opinion about something
before really even knowing what the question or concern
was. It likely left them looking silly or even foolish. If we are
honest, we have all probably done this a time or two… or
more. Double yikes.

Take time and listen to people before you respond. Practice
the pause before speaking. Not only will you have a better
response, but you will probably save yourself embarrassment
and frustration. This advice will come in handy no matter
where you are or who you are with. So, ask God to remind you
to listen more, talk less, and wait to respond.

*God, sometimes it is tempting to jump in and respond to people
before I really even listen to what they are saying. Help me to be a
better listener in all the interactions I have today.*

If one gives answer before hearing,
it is folly and shame.

PROVERBS 18:13 NRSV

How did you do today? Did you listen before you answered
or responded to others? Was it harder or easier than
you expected? Hopefully you were able to pause before
responding and to listen more than you spoke. If not,
tomorrow is another day. Talk to God about how you did and
what you need to do differently.

On the flip side, did others offend you today by jumping
in before they should have? If so, were you able to forgive
them, realizing that it is something you have probably done
before too? Talk to God about how it felt and how you need to
respond. Seek God's input on what you might say or do the
next time this happens to you. Take time now to really listen
to what he has to say.

Dear Father, I want to be wise and listen before I speak. Help me to
listen to you now and not rush to a response. Allow me some time
to really hear what you have to say.

Why is it so important to listen before you speak?

Keeping Watch

There were shepherds living out in the fields nearby,
keeping watch over their flocks at night.
An angel of the Lord appeared to them,
and the glory of the Lord shone around them,
and they were terrified.

LUKE 2:8-9 NIV

Can you imagine what it would have been like to be a shepherd hanging out in the fields that first Christmas when the angel appeared? That would have been amazing. Terrifying, yes, but undoubtedly amazing. What makes it even more amazing is that the shepherds were just out doing their job. They were keeping watch over their flocks. Because they were doing the job they were given, and presumably doing it well, they were in the place and space to have front row seats to an angelic announcement. Had they walked away from their duty or left their mundane task, they may have missed it.

Do you know that God may have put you in your job or your school so that you could keep watch over the things he wants to show you? God has plans for you right where you are. Keep watch and be ready this Christmas and beyond.

Lord, thank you for putting me where I am for a reason. Help me to keep watch for you and for what you want to show me this Christmas and always.

*That night, in a field near Bethlehem, there were shepherds
watching over their flocks. Suddenly, an angel of the Lord
appeared in radiant splendor before them, lighting up the field
with the blazing glory of God, and the shepherds were terrified.*

LUKE 2:8-9 TPT

Christmas Eve is here. Are you excited for Christmas
morning? You know what is coming and who we are
celebrating. But the shepherds had no idea what
was happening. They could never have imagined the
announcement that they were about to hear. If they had,
surely they would have been keeping watch even more
carefully, expecting and longing to see the new King come.
And likely, they would have invited all of their friends and
family to join them while they kept watch.

Knowing the gift of Jesus came that very first Christmas, get
ready and keep watch. Look for Jesus as he works in your life.
Be ready for God to show up in new and unexpected ways.
Don't take the good news of Christmas for granted. Invite
your family and friends to share in the wonder of Jesus. Keep
watch and see what God can do.

*Jesus, your arrival came as a big surprise to the shepherds. Help me
to keep watch over all the ways your arrival impacts me and my
world. Allow me to share your good news with others this Christmas.*

What are you most excited about for Christmas?

good News gift

> The angel said to them, "Do not be afraid. I bring you good news
> that will cause great joy for all the people. Today in the town of
> David a Savior has been born to you; he is the Messiah, the Lord.
> This will be a sign to you: You will find a baby wrapped in cloths
> and lying in a manger."
>
> LUKE 2:10-12 NIV

Christmas morning is finally here. Will you tear into presents
quickly without hesitation? Or will you meticulously break
the tape seal and slowly peel back the paper, trying to save the
paper to reuse later?

The angel in the field wasted no time in sharing the good
news gift with the shepherds some two thousand years ago.
He didn't stop to carefully explain all the back story of Jesus'
unique birth. He wasn't trying to save the best part for last.
He told them to not be afraid and then dove right into the
good news. Today, for this Christmas, dive right into the good
news of Jesus' birth. Grab a hold of it without hesitation and
then share it with others.

*Dear Jesus, thank you for coming into the world. You truly are the
best present ever. Help me to dive right into your good news and
share it freely.*

The angel reassured them, saying, "Don't be afraid. For I have
come to bring you good news, the most joyous news the world
has ever heard! And it is for everyone everywhere! For today in
Bethlehem a rescuer was born for you. He is the Lord Yahweh, the
Messiah. You will recognize him by this miracle sign: You will find
a baby wrapped in strips of cloth and lying in a feeding trough!"

LUKE 2:10-12 TPT

Isn't it cool that Jesus, the best gift in all of history, was
described as being wrapped... like a present? Of all the
descriptions that could have been used—dressed, swaddled,
cushioned, covered—the word wrapped was chosen. God
really has a way with words, doesn't he?

As you finish this Christmas day, may you be more excited
about the gift of Jesus than you have ever been before. Accept
his gift yourself and share him with others. Be open to all that
he has to offer you.

Merry Christmas, God. Thank you for sending Jesus. You wrapped
him up as the perfect gift for us. I want to take this gift and share
him with others more than ever before.

What is the best gift that you have been given?

Live in Peace

Rejoice! Strive for full restoration,
encourage one another, be of one mind, live in peace.
And the God of love and peace will be with you.

2 CORINTHIANS 13:11 NIV

Whether you are an only child or one of many siblings, you know that life at home is best when there is a sense of peace between all your family members. Arguing or fighting among family really stinks. Similarly, peace between classmates and co-workers makes all the difference in how you feel about going to school or work. All of us long for peace. We want to live in peace with those around us.

God wants that for us as well. You can help bring peace by encouraging others, being agreeable, striving for positive relationships, thinking of others' needs as much as your own, and praying for those you are with. Ask God to help you be a peacemaker today. Peace can start with you.

Holy Spirit, I want to be a peacemaker. Help me to listen to you
as I choose peace with those around me.

Put things in order, listen to my appeal, agree with one another, live in peace; and the God of love and peace will be with you.

2 CORINTHIANS 13:11 NRSV

A traditional song or prayer for peace, often called the "Prayer of Saint Francis," fits perfectly with this verse in 2 Corinthians. Here is just a portion of that prayer:

Make me a channel of your peace

Where there is hatred let me bring your love

Where there is injury, your pardon Lord

And where there's doubt, true faith in you

Make me a channel of your peace

Where there's despair in life let me bring hope

Where there is darkness, only light

And where there's sadness ever joy

Whoever wrote those words really understood what living in peace could look like. As you end your day, choose to live in peace.

Dear Father, thank you that you long for peace among your people. Help me choose every day to live in peace with those around me. Make me a channel of your peace.

Which line or lines of the Prayer of Saint Francis mean the most to you?

Crazy Calling

Make yourself an ark of cypress wood....
Noah did everything just as God commanded him.

GENESIS 6:14, 22 NIV

Do you ever feel like God is calling you to something really big? Like he might want you to do something that seems a little bit crazy or maybe even impossible. It might feel overwhelming and you may second-guess whether or not the calling you feel is really legit. Yet, we know from stories in the Bible that God called people to do crazy, amazing things all the time.

Consider the story of Noah. Noah was told to build a ginormous boat in the middle of dry land. It is likely that Noah was uncertain at first. He may have occasionally felt foolish as he was out hammering away on boat, particularly on sunny hot days. No doubt there were people who made fun of him. But he did it. He finished the boat. And the flood did come. Noah listened to God's "crazy idea" and, as a result, saved his family and two of every animal. Because Noah did what God commanded, he was used to jump start a re-creation on earth. What crazy thing is God calling you to do today?

Dear God, it is hard to understand a story like Noah. I'm not sure I want to take on such a big challenge as he did. Yet I know that you won't give me anything that you can't handle.

Build a boat of cypress wood for yourself.
Make rooms in it and cover it inside and outside with tar.
Noah did everything that God commanded him.

GENESIS 6:14, 22 NCV

Have you thought more about it? What is the big thing that God is calling you to do? It might not be building a boat like Noah or knocking down a wall like Joshua in Jericho. It might not even be something that other will people notice you've done. But you would know and God would know.

Is God calling you to reach out to someone who is lonely at your school? Is he asking you to go on a trip someplace to care for people who need love and support? Maybe God wants you to take a leap of faith in a career or job choice that you never would've considered otherwise. Whatever giant calling you are feeling, talk to God about it and trust him with it. You won't be the first person or the last person that God does giant things in and through.

Dear God, will you help me find out what big thing you have in store for me? Allow me to trust you more and more every day in little and big things.

What big thing do you think God might be calling you to do?

Not Uncaring

*A great windstorm arose, and the waves beat into the boat, so that
the boat was already being swamped. But he was in the stern,
asleep on the cushion; and they woke him up and said to him,
"Teacher, do you not care that we are perishing?"*

MARK 4: 37-38 NRSV

There was a big storm brewing on the Sea of Galilee. Jesus
and his followers were out on the sea in a boat. The waves
were high, the boat was rocking, and water was coming in.
The disciples were scared and maybe feeling seasick. But
Jesus was asleep, seemingly oblivious and unconcerned to
what was going on around them. What a contrast between the
chaos of the storm and frantic worry of the disciples, and the
calm in Jesus.

Clearly, Jesus knew more than the disciples in that very
moment. He was not afraid or worried. He knew what was
going to happen. But the disciples mistook his calm for not
caring. Friend, know that Jesus cares for you deeply. He cares
for every single bit of your life. Although he may seem quiet at
times, he is for you and loves you like crazy.

*Jesus, when you seem quiet, help me to remember that you are
there and that you care. Quiet my chaos with your calm.*

A very strong wind came up on the lake. The waves came over the sides and into the boat so that it was already full of water. Jesus was at the back of the boat, sleeping with his head on a cushion. His followers woke him and said, "Teacher, don't you care that we are drowning!"

MARK 4: 37-38 NCV

Have you ever felt like something is a big deal to you, only to find out later on that you didn't need to be so worried about it? In the moment, it's absolutely understandable that the disciples were freaking out about the waves pouring into the boat. It makes perfect sense that they would be panicking as the boat was tossed about and threatening to sink. And it is certainly logical that they would be frustrated that Jesus was calmly asleep through it all, right?

When Jesus awakes, he seems almost disappointed in the little faith of the disciples. After all, he points out again and again to them, he is with them.

Dear God, when storms are big and my world feels unsteady, help me to trust in you and not to worry because you are with me.

What storms have you been through lately?

Calming Storms

He woke up and rebuked the wind, and said to the sea,
"Peace! Be still!" Then the wind ceased,
and there was a dead calm.

MARK 4: 39 NRSV

In this story in Mark, Jesus and his disciples were in a boat when a big storm came up and created chaos and fear for the disciples. They were tossed side to side and taking on water. Jesus' disciples panicked and thought Jesus didn't care. Imagine how that might have felt.

Yet, when Jesus woke up, he spoke just a handful of words that caused the storm to stop. Just like that. He did not have to beg or plead or problem solve what would happen next. He simply spoke. Jesus is so powerful that he can speak a word and cause storms to still. What a powerful God we serve.

Dear Jesus, thank you that you are so powerful that you can calm a raging storm with your words. Help me remember your awesome power today when anything scary comes my way.

*Jesus stood up and commanded the wind and said to the waves,
"Quiet! Be still!" Then the wind stopped,
and it became completely calm.*

MARK 4: 39 NCV

Storms can be literal, like pouring rain, crashing thunder, lightning, and hail. And storms can be figurative, like the emotional storms that we sometimes feel inside. Jesus was easily able to calm the literal storm in the story above with just his words. Do you know that God can do the same thing for the storms inside of you?

If you are experiencing an emotional storm, tell Jesus about it. Maybe there's a relationship that has been stressed or trouble at school. Maybe you or someone you love is experiencing depression, illness, or discouragement. Know that God is with you and can still the storms inside of you. It may not happen as quickly or dramatically as it did that day in the boat, but reach out to him and ask for his peace. Then listen for his words of life and rest in his care for you.

Dear Jesus, I have some storms in my life. Would you come quiet them and bring me peace? I trust you and know that you can.

Which storms in your life do you need Jesus to calm?

Wrestling

The Lord's servant must not be quarrelsome but kindly to everyone,
an apt teacher, patient, correcting opponents with gentleness.
God may perhaps grant that they will repent
and come to know the truth.

TIMOTHY 2:24-25 NRSV

One of the top lines from the movie Nacho Libre happens when Encarnaciòn and Ignacio break up a fight between two of the orphans that live in the monastery. Ignacio, a cook in the monastery, tells the children, "I know it is fun to wrestle. A nice pile-drive to the face, or a punch to the face. But you cannot do it, because it is in the Bible not to wrestle your neighbor." What funny, but great, advice.

Although Nacho was not exactly right with what he said, it was Biblically-based for sure. God wants us to be kind to others and respond with patience and gentleness. As you go about your day today, keep Nacho's advice and God's Word close to heart. If you are tempted to argue or "wrestle" with a neighbor, take a deep breath and step back. Ask God to give you patience and gentleness instead.

Dear Lord, I want to be someone who is gentle and not quarrelsome. Help me to keep my cool today if I am tempted to argue. Thanks in advance.

A servant of the Lord must not quarrel but must be kind to everyone, a good teacher, and patient. The Lord's servant must gently teach those who disagree. Then maybe God will let them change their minds so they can accept the truth.

2 TIMOTHY 2:24-25 NCV

Besides the obvious, why wouldn't God want you to fight, wrestle, or argue with your neighbors? Clearly God does not want you to hurt anyone physically or be hurt, but there is a bigger purpose behind this instruction.

When we quarrel with others, we are more likely to push them away from the things we want them to know. It is harder for them to see God working in us or through us when we are hot-headed and quarrelsome. But when we are patient and kind, people are more likely to listen to what we have to say. They will have more opportunity to hear the good news of Jesus and respond positively. Therefore, choose kindness over quarreling every day.

Dear God, I want to point others to you. Help me to choose patience and kindness over fighting or arguing. Let me rest in your kindness now.

When are you tempted to wrestle with someone, rather than show kindness?

Praise from Nature

Praise the LORD from the earth,
Sea monsters and all deeps;
Fire and hail, snow and clouds;
Stormy wind, fulfilling His word;
Mountains and all hills;
Fruit trees and all cedars.

PSALM 148:7-9 NASB

Some people really like to spend time in nature. Many people find it especially easy to worship God when they are in creation and enjoying all that God has made. That makes sense. God made a beautiful world for us to enjoy.

It makes even more sense when we understand that all sorts of things in creation actually praise God too. According to these verses (and others), even non-living elements of creation praise God and fulfill a purpose in pointing to the Creator. Think of ways that sea creatures, fire, hail, snow, clouds, winds, mountains, hills, and trees could praise the Lord. Kind of wild, isn't it? As you enter your day today, look for the ways that things in nature seem to be praising God. And then, join them in their praise.

Dear Lord, thank you that all the things you created can praise you in one way or another. They all point to you. Help me recognize that today and praise you along with them.

Praise the LORD from the earth,
you large sea animals and all the oceans,
lightning and hail, snow and mist,
and stormy winds that obey him,
mountains and all hills,
fruit trees and all cedars.

PSALM 148:7-9 NCV

What do you find most fascinating about nature? Are there things in the world that confirm your belief in God because they are so unique or awe-inspiring? God's creativity is all over the earth and in the sea, from the tiniest to the most massive of creatures and inanimate objects.

Spend some time before you go to bed praising God for all that he has made. Let him know what you like most about his creation. Be specific in telling him what you like and why you like it. Ask him to show you something new tomorrow that you have not noticed before. If he does, pay attention to how it points you back to praising God.

Dear God, you are so creative. Thanks for all that you made. Will you show me something new in creation tomorrow, and in the new year ahead?

Which of God's creations do you think is most creative?